GROOVY PROGRAMMING

GROOVY PROGRAMMING
AN INTRODUCTION FOR
JAVA DEVELOPERS

Kenneth Barclay

John Savage

ELSEVIER

AMSTERDAM • BOSTON • HEIDELBERG • LONDON
NEW YORK • OXFORD • PARIS • SAN DIEGO
SAN FRANCISCO • SINGAPORE • SYDNEY • TOKYO
Morgan Kaufmann Publishers is an imprint of Elsevier

MORGAN KAUFMANN PUBLISH

Publisher	Denise E. M. Penrose
Publishing Services Manager	George Morrison
Senior Editor	Tim Cox
Assistant Editor	Mary E. James
Project Manager	Marilyn E. Rash
Cover Design	Chen Design
Composition and Illustrations	SPi
Production Services	SPi
Interior printer	Maple-Vail Book Manufacturing Group
Cover printer	Phoenix Color Corp.

Morgan Kaufmann Publishers is an imprint of Elsevier.
500 Sansome Street, Suite 400, San Francisco, CA 94111

This book is printed on acid-free paper.

Library of Congress Cataloging-in-Publication Data
Barclay, Kenneth A., 1947-
  Groovy programming : an introduction for Java developers /
Kenneth Barclay, John Savage.
    p. cm.
  Includes bibliographical references and index.
  ISBN-13: 978-0-12-372507-3 (alk. paper)
  ISBN-10: 0-12-372507-0 (alk. paper)
1. Java (Computer program language) I. Savage, W. J. (W. John) II. Title.
  QA76.73.J38B358 2006
  005. 13'3–dc22   2006036352

For information on all Morgan Kaufmann publications,
visit our Web site at *www.mkp.com* or *www.books.elsevier.com*

Printed in the United States of America
07 08 09 10   5 4 3 2 1

To Irene
–K.B.

To Salwa
–J.S.

CONTENTS

FOREWORD

Scripting languages are not new. Primarily, they are used on Linux and UNIX machines for things such as shell scripting tasks that automate software installations, platform customizations, scientific application prototyping with Python, and one-shot command-line jobs with bash scripts. Languages such as PHP have also been widely used for developing high-volume websites and scripting languages have been found to be suitable for serious business applications.

Usually, scripting languages are platforms on their own and do not necessarily interact with others. Although bindings may exist for bridging with other systems, the integration is not always intuitive or natural. Groovy seeks to fill that gap, bringing a genuine innovative language that can interact natively with Java by living on the same virtual machine.

Groovy brings a concise and expressive Java-like syntax to ease the learning curve for Java developers. But beyond the syntax, Groovy also provides two key aspects to the landscape by providing wrapper APIs around common JDK Application Programming Interfaces. It simplifies the implementation of common tasks and integrates meta-programming capabilities to develop powerful new language constructs or to easily manipulate existing ones.

Groovy can be used in various situations: as a shell scripting language to do data crunching and file manipulation tasks or to experiment with new APIs. It can also be adapted for creating full-blown small- to mid-size applications to leverage the wealth of Java libraries and components. Moreover, another important use is to marry Java and Groovy by embedding Groovy inside Java or Java EE applications. This can help write and externalize often-changing business rules or bring programmatic configuration to an application infrastructure.

Although the first two uses are quite common, I believe the embedded-use case is the most appealing and promising. Currently, developers have been using template engines for customizing and factoring out views, or they have used business rules engines to externalize some logic. Beyond the limited functionality set, however, programmers are often given little support. Fortunately, platform-hosted scripting languages such as Groovy can help bridge this functionality gap. This is evident with the success of Groovy and its child—Grails—a versatile model-view-controller (MVC) Web framework. Sun, too, believes in this alternative way of adding dynamicity to applications, by including a new Java Specification Request in Java 6: the javax.script.* APIs allow seamless embedding of any scripting or dynamic language into Java applications with a coherent programming API.

Scripting languages have evolved to a point of maturity where they meet the limitations of the standardized mainstream platforms. When those languages and platforms come across, that's when magic happens, and we can celebrate a marriage made in Heaven.

Ken Barclay and John Savage are respected teachers and are well positioned to introduce Groovy to both experienced developers and novices. They demonstrate in a clear manner how Groovy augments the Java platform and how to exploit many of its innovative features. The book is easy to read and not intimidating for those less experienced with programming. It is a complete exposition of Groovy that addresses all aspects of the programming language.

The structure of the book fulfills this aim by presenting the basics of Groovy in the early chapters and more advanced concepts in the latter. In addition, extensive appendices consider more detailed aspects of the language.

Deliberately, each chapter is relatively small and easy to absorb, yet they contain a large number of complete code examples, extensive exercises, and solutions. To illustrate Groovy in application, the book features a rolling case study that grows in complexity and sophistication by drawing on the materials from each preceding chapter. In addition, incremental development and unit testing are central themes in the text and are necessary to support Groovy's dynamic nature. The authors also consider Groovy as a multiparadigm language.

The authors' own experience suggests that Groovy has a place in the academic curriculum as well as the experienced developer's toolbox.

Have a fun time learning Groovy by reading this great book! You won't regret it.

Guillaume Laforge
Groovy Project Manager
JSR-241 Specification Lead

PREFACE

This book is an introduction to the scripting language Groovy. For Java developers, Groovy makes writing scripts and applications for the Java platform both fast and easy. It includes many language features found in other scripting languages such as Python, Ruby, and Smalltalk. As Groovy is based on Java, applications written in Groovy can make full use of the Java Application Programming Interfaces (APIs). This means that Groovy integrates seamlessly with frameworks and components written in Java.

Groovy, the scripting language, and Java, the systems programming language, complement each other. Both contribute to the development of programming applications. For example, components and frameworks might be created with Java and "glued" together with Groovy. The ease with which Groovy can make use of them significantly enhances their usage. The increasing importance of component architectures, Graphical User Interfaces (GUIs), database access, and the internet all increase the applicability of scripting in Groovy.

Groovy developers can take advantage of rapid application development features, such as those found in scripting languages. Groovy is suitable for many data or file processing tasks, testing applications, or as a replacement for Java in small- and medium-sized projects.

The syntax of Groovy is similar to the syntax of the Java programming language. This makes for a relatively short learning curve for Java developers. Other scripting languages for the Java platform are usually based on earlier predecessors. This is a major problem as they bring extra unwanted "baggage." However, as Groovy *is* Java, it offers a much more natural and seamless integration into the Java platform.

ORGANIZATION

The text is designed to quickly introduce readers to the principal elements of the Groovy language. It assumes at least a reading knowledge of Java. For the later chapters, experience with Swing, Standard Query Language (SQL), Spring, XML, Ant, and building Web applications would also be useful. The authors have sought to keep each chapter relatively brief and closely focused. Some readers may wish to dip into an individual chapter to pick out particular Groovy features. In any event, the shortness of each chapter should make its contents relatively easy to absorb.

Many chapters are supported by an appendix to augment the topics covered. For example, Chapter 7 considers the basics of defining and using Groovy methods. Appendix G then considers more advanced aspects, such as overloading and recursion, which are not central to the main text. Again, this helps to keep chapters short and targeted.

Most chapters also include many small, self-contained examples to illustrate language concepts. They are complete, and the reader is encouraged to execute them as part of the learning process. There are also end-of-chapter exercises, and the reader is encouraged to attempt them. However, both the chapter examples and the solutions to the exercises are available on the book's website.

A feature of the book is a rolling case study concerned with managing and maintaining a library's loan stock. At various points in the text, new Groovy features are applied to augment the functionality of the case study. For example, the case study in Chapter 11 exploits methods, closures, and files introduced in the preceding chapters.

Chapters 1 to 16 cover the basic features of Groovy. For example, there are discussions of Groovy methods, closures, lists, and maps as well as support for classes and inheritance.

The important topic of automated unit testing is also addressed. Groovy's rapid build-and-run cycle makes it an ideal candidate for developing unit tests. Groovy exploits the industry standard JUnit framework to make unit testing both easy and fun. Unit testing used in conjunction with Groovy combines the flexibility of a dynamically typed language with the safety offered by statically typed languages. To highlight this point, unit testing is an integral part of most of the case studies.

The second part of the book is presented in Chapters 17 to 24, where Groovy is used for more advanced applications. For example, persistence is implemented with the Spring framework in conjunction with the Cloudscape/Derby relational database management system. Groovy also supports XML and GUI applications through its novel builder notation. We finish by considering templates and web applications.

CONVENTIONS

Throughout the book we use an `arial` typeface to identify Groovy code and the output from scripts. We also *italicize* text when introducing a technical term. The book includes references to websites and to the bibliography.

We do not distinguish between a program and a script. Both terms are used interchangeably. However, we invariably mean a Groovy script.

SOFTWARE DISTRIBUTION

The authors have prepared a supporting website—`http://www.dcs.napier.ac.uk/~kab/groovy/groovy.html`—that contains the working scripts for all of the examples and case studies presented in the book. Answers to the end-of-chapter exercises are also included.

Groovy is under constant review and is subject to revision. It is the aim of the authors to use this website to keep the reader informed of significant changes. Therefore, the reader is advised to consult it for up-to-date information.

ACKNOWLEDGMENTS

The authors are deeply grateful to those involved in Groovy's conception, the committers that maintain its development, and those instrumental in the Java Specification Request (JSR-241) initiative (`http://www.dcs.napier.ac.uk/~cs05/groovy/groovy.html`). This book is our contribution to publicizing the Groovy language. We are indebted to Guillaume Laforge (Groovy Project Manager) who keeps Groovy "on-track" and to Andrew Glover (CTO, Vanward Technologies) for his excellent articles on Groovy on the IBM Developers website. We are also grateful for the encouragement and stimulation given by Professor Jon Kerridge (School of Computing, Napier University, Edinburgh) who sent us Groovy challenges that we might not otherwise have taken up.

The authors also wish to thank Denise Penrose, Tim Cox, Mary James, Christine Brandt, and their colleagues at Morgan Kaufmann, Elsevier for their help in the production of this book. Finally, we are grateful for the many helpful suggestions from our reviewers Andrew Glover and Sean Burke. Any outstanding errors in the text are the responsibility of the authors.

ABOUT THE AUTHORS

Ken Barclay and **John Savage** are lecturers in computer science at Napier University in Edinburgh, Scotland. They both have more than 25 years of experience teaching software development to students and professionals in commerce and industry. They have been actively involved with the evolution and development of object-oriented practices in C++, Java, Ada, and the Unified Modeling Language (UML).

Since their first involvement with object orientation, they have led the development of the ROME project—an object modeling tool—that is distributed with their books on object orientation and the UML. They are the authors of several publications about software development, including *Object-Oriented Design with UML and Java* (Butterworth-Heinemann/ Elsevier, 2003).

CHAPTER 1

GROOVY

This first chapter introduces Groovy as a unique scripting language designed to augment the Java platform. It offers Javalike syntax, native support for `Maps` and `Lists`, methods, classes, closures, and builders. With its dynamic weak typing and seamless access to the Java Applications Programming Interface (API), it is well suited to the development of many small- to medium-sized applications.

1.1 WHY SCRIPTING?

Generally, scripting languages such as Groovy are more expressive and operate at higher levels of abstraction than systems programming languages such as Java. This often results in more rapid application development and higher programmer productivity. However, scripting languages serve a different purpose than their systems language counterparts. They are designed for "gluing" applications together rather than implementing complex data structures and algorithms. Therefore, to be useful, a scripting language must have access to a wide range of components.

In general, scripting languages do not replace systems programming languages. They complement them (Ousterhout, 1998). Typically, systems programming languages should be used in applications that

- require the development of complex algorithms or data structures
- are computationally intensive
- manipulate large datasets
- implement well-defined, slowly changing requirements
- are part of a large project.

However, scripting languages should be used for applications that

- connect preexisting components

- manipulate a variety of different entities that change rapidly

- have a graphical user interface

- have rapidly evolving functionality

- are part of a small- to medium-sized project.

A major strength of scripting languages is that the coding effort they require is relatively small as compared to code written in a systems programming language. Often, the latter appears to be overly complex and difficult to understand and maintain. This is because it requires extensive boilerplate or conversion code.

These systems languages are strongly typed to ensure the safety and robustness of the code. With strong typing, variables must been given a type and they can only be used in a particular way. Although strong typing makes large programs more manageable and allows a compiler to (statically) detect certain kinds of errors, it can be intrusive. For example, strong typing is not helpful when it is difficult or impossible to decide beforehand which type of a variable it is. This situation occurs frequently when connecting components together.

To simplify the task of connecting components, scripting languages are weakly typed. This means that variables can be used in different ways under different circumstances. However, illegal use of variables is only detected when the code is actually executing. For example, although Groovy (statically) checks program syntax at compile time, the (dynamic) check on the correctness of method calls happens at runtime. As a result, there is the danger that a Groovy script that compiles cleanly may throw an exception and terminate prematurely.

Weak typing does not necessarily mean that code is unsafe or that it is not robust. Advocates have promoted Extreme Programming (Beck, 2004) as a software development process. This approach is characterized by an emphasis on testing. The result is a comprehensive suite of unit tests (Link, 2003) that drive the development. As a consequence, they help ensure the safety and robustness of the code by executing it in a wide variety of different scenarios. This is the basis of the approach we take when developing Groovy scripts. In fact, experience has shown that the combination of weak typing and unit testing in a scripting language is often better than strong type checking in a traditional systems programming language (see http://www.mindview.net/WebLog/log-0025). We have both the flexibility of weak typing and the confidence of unit testing.

1.2 WHY GROOVY?

The Java compiler produces bytecodes that execute on the Java Virtual Machine (JVM). Groovy classes are binary compatible with Java. This means that the bytecodes produced by the Groovy compiler are the same as those produced by the Java compiler. Hence, Groovy is Java as far as the JVM is concerned. This means that Groovy is able to immediately exploit the various Java APIs such as JDBC for database development (Fisher et al., 2003) and Swing for developing GUI applications (Topley, 1998).

Groovy aims to shift much of the "heavy lifting" from the developer to the language itself. For example, when adding a button to a GUI, we simply specify the code to execute when the button is pressed. There is no need to add an event handler to the button as an instance of a class implementing a particular interface. Groovy does this for us.

Groovy is an object-oriented scripting language in which everything is an object. Unlike Java, there are no exceptions to this rule. This brings an important element of uniformity to the language. Groovy is also dynamically typed so that the notion of a type lies within the object, not the variable that references it. An immediate consequence is that Groovy does not require the declaration of the type of a variable, method parameter, or method return value. This gives it the beneficial effects of significantly shrinking the code size and giving the programmer the freedom to defer type decisions to runtime.

Groovy also seeks to unify instance fields and methods declared in classes by supporting the concept of a *property*. A property removes the distinction between an instance field (attribute) and a method. In effect, a client considers a property as the combination of the instance field and its getter/setter methods.

Important data structures, `Lists` and `Maps`, are native to the Groovy language. A `List` object or a `Map` object can be directly expressed in a Groovy script. For novice developers and professionals alike, the immediacy of `Lists` and `Maps` can make their programming tasks that much simpler. Complementing `Lists` and `Maps` are *iterator* methods, such as `each`, that simplify how the elements in these collections are to be processed. The processing itself is described by a *closure*—an object that represents a code block. This immensely useful construct can be referenced by variables, parameterized to generalize its applicability, passed as a parameter to methods and other closures, and can be an instance field of classes. It has a huge effect on programming in Groovy.

Hierarchical data structures like XML can also be directly represented in a Groovy script with Groovy builders. Using notations found in XPath (see `http://www.w3.org/TR/xpath20/`), Groovy readily expresses the traversal of these structures and how to reference their parts. Once again, an iterator and a closure provide the mechanism to process them.

Groovy builders are generally applicable to any nested tree-structure. For example, they can be used to describe a graphical application that is assembled from various component widgets. Here, too, closures play a part, this time operating as event handlers for components such as menu items and buttons. Standard Query Language (SQL) processing also has the same uniform approach. Again, an iterator method such as eachRow combines with a closure to express how to process the rows of a database table.

CHAPTER 2

NUMBERS AND EXPRESSIONS

In this chapter, we are concerned with how we manipulate basic numeric values in Groovy. When doing so, we must be especially conscious that Groovy has been constructed as an object-oriented language. This means that everything in Groovy is ultimately an object—an instance of some class. For example, we are all familiar with the integer value 123. In Groovy, this is actually an object instance of the class `Integer`. To make an object do something, we know that we must invoke one of the methods declared in its class. Hence, to obtain the absolute value of such an integer, the Groovy environment invokes the method abs with the expression `123.abs()`. Equally, to ask 123 for the value that follows it (124), the Groovy environment calls the successor method, `next`, as in `123.next()`.

Because of this, if we wish to find the arithmetic sum of the values 123 and 456, then we might expect the Groovy environment to invoke the + method on the `Integer` object 123 as in `123.+(456)`. The `Integer` object 456 is the method parameter. This, of course, is hopelessly counterintuitive to the arithmetic skills we developed at school. Fortunately, Groovy also supports *operator overloading* (see Appendix I). This way, the + method can be presented as a binary operator between its operands, resulting in the more natural expression `123 + 456`. However, we should always be prepared to recollect that this is ultimately a method call to one object with the other object as a method parameter. In truth, for this example, the actual method call used by Groovy is entitled `plus` as in `123.plus(456)`.

This chapter deals with the manipulation of arithmetic values in a relatively straightforward manner. However, it is an important field of study in its own right, and we present a more detailed discussion in Appendix C.

2.1 NUMBERS

Groovy supports *integer* and *floating point* numbers (literals). An integer is a value that does not include a fraction. A floating-point number is a decimal value that includes a decimal fraction.

An integer is a whole number that may be positive, negative, or zero. Some examples of *integer literals* are 12345, −44, and 0. As noted earlier, each is an instance of the class Integer.

Numbers with a fractional part are represented as an instance of the class BigDecimal. Some examples of *floating point literals* are 1.23, −3.1415926. Note that a floating point literal must start with a decimal point to avoid ambiguity. We must present the fraction as 0.25 and not as .25. Equally, the negative of this same value must be presented as −0.25.

The classes for these simple numeric types are further explored in Appendix C.

2.2 EXPRESSIONS

Groovy supports an extensive collection of operators applicable to the numeric types. This includes the normal arithmetic operators as well as comparison operators, bitwise operators, and other miscellaneous operators. An *expression* is used to describe some computation and is a mix of operators and operands. The *arithmetic operators* are addition (+), subtraction (−), multiplication (*), and division (/). Also supported is the modulus operator, denoted by the percent symbol (%), used to compute the remainder upon dividing two integers. Table 2.1 shows various arithmetic operations applied to integer literals.

Note that division of two integers always results in a floating point value even when an integer might be expected. For example, the expression 6/3 produces the floating point value 2.0 and not the integer value 2.

TABLE 2.1 Integer arithmetic

Expression	Method call	Result
5 + 3	5.plus(3)	8
5 − 3	5.minus(3)	2
5 * 3	5.multiply(3)	15
5 / 3	5.divide(3)	1.6666666667
5 % 3	5.mod(3)	2

These same arithmetic operators can be applied to two floating point values. The results are shown in Table 2.2. The modulus operator applied to floating point values is discussed separately following the table.

Again, with the exception of the modulus operator, Groovy's arithmetic operators can also be applied to combinations of integer and floating point values. Some examples are shown in Table 2.3.

As shown by the tables, the division operator behaves normally, regardless the combination of integers and floating point values. All the following combinations yield the floating point value 2.6:

```
13.0 / 5
13 / 5.0
13 / 5
```

To obtain the integer quotient of two integer values we must use the intdiv method,

```
13.intdiv(5)
```

which yields the integer value 2.

TABLE 2.2   Floating point arithmetic

Expression	Method call	Result
5.0 + 3.0	5.0.plus(3.0)	8.0
5.0 - 3.0	5.0.minus(3.0)	2.0
5.0 * 3.0	5.0.multiply(3.0)	15.0
5.0 / 3.0	5.0.divide(3.0)	1.6666666667

TABLE 2.3   Mixed arithmetic

Expression	Method call	Result
5 + 3.2	5.plus(3.2)	8.2
5.6 + 3	5.6.plus(3)	8.6
5 - 3.2	5.minus(3.2)	1.8
5.6 - 3	5.6.minus(3)	2.6
5 * 3.2	5.multiply(3.2)	16.0
5.6 * 3	5.6.multiply(3)	16.8
5 / 3.2	5.divide(3.2)	1.5625
5.6 / 3	5.6.divide(3)	1.8666666667

The modulus operator (%) yields the integer remainder from the division of two integer operands. Therefore,

13 % 5	evaluates to 3
15 % 5	evaluates to 0

Note that it is illegal to invoke the mod method on a floating point value or on an integer value with a floating point parameter. Hence, the expressions 13.0 % 5.0, 13.0 % 5, and 13 % 5.0 all report that the method mod may not be invoked.

2.3 OPERATOR PRECEDENCE

As with normal, everyday formulas, an expression in Groovy is evaluated according to the *precedence* of its operators. The precedence, or priority, of an operator dictates the order of evaluation in arithmetic expressions. Table 2.4 shows the precedence of the basic arithmetic operators. (For a full list and a discussion of the *associativity* of operators, see Appendix C.)

From Table 2.4, multiplication, division, and the modulus operators are shown to have the highest equal precedence, while addition and subtraction have the lowest equal precedence. An expression involving a mixture of these operators will first perform all multiplication, division, and modulus operations, and then any addition or subtraction. Thus,

```
2 + 3 * 4
```

yields 14, since 3 is first multiplied by 4, giving 12, and then 2 is added to that result, producing 14.

Appendix C explores how associativity is used in determining how an expression such as 2 + 3 * 4 + 5 is evaluated. For the present, should we wish to ensure that the additions are performed before the multiplication, then we can use parentheses as in the expression (2 + 3) * (4 + 5), which yields 45.

TABLE 2.4   Arithmetic operators

Category	Operators	Example	Associativity
Multiplicative	* / %	x * y	Left to right
Additive	+ / −	x + y	Left to right

2.4   ASSIGNMENT

The *assignment operator* allows the assignment of some value to a program variable. The simplest form of the assignment statement is:

```
variable = expression
```

The effect of the *assignment operator* (=) is to evaluate the expression to its right, and the resulting value is then assigned to the variable on its left. Examples of assignment are

```
interest = principal * rate * time / 100
speed = distance / time
totalMinutes = 60 * hours + minutes
count = count + 1
```

The first example computes the simple interest on a sum of money (the `principal`) invested at a given `rate` for a given period of `time`. The second example finds the speed of an object, given the distance traveled and the elapsed time. The third example converts a time expressed as hours and minutes into a total number of minutes. The final example adds one to the current value for count.

The Groovy keyword `def` is required when a variable is used in a script for the first time. Its purpose is to introduce the *variable definition*. However, it is not required when the variable is used in subsequent assignments. Appendix C discusses this and related points in more detail. An example is:

```
def count = 0          // define and initialize
count = count + 1      // increase current value by one
```

Variables have names by which they can be referenced. These names are known as *identifiers* and are created by the programmer. A Groovy identifier is governed by the following rule:

An identifier is a case-sensitive combination of letters and digits, the first of which must be a letter. The underscore symbol (_) is permitted in an identifier and is considered to be a letter. An identifier must not be a Groovy keyword (see Appendix C).

Notice that we say age = 25, assuming that we have previously defined (`def`) age as a variable. For the moment, it is enough to realize that the assignment of 25 to the identifier age happens correctly. Further assignments to the variable age simply change its value. Here, age would be understood to refer to an integer value (see Section 2.6).

2.5   INCREMENT AND DECREMENT OPERATORS

Groovy also supports two unary operators for adding or subtracting 1 from the value of a numeric variable. A unary operator is one that applies to a single operand. They are known as the *increment operator*, ++, and the *decrement operator*, – –, respectively. Rather than have:

```
value = value +
```

we can write:

```
value+ +
```

Similarly, we can have:

```
value– –
```

instead of:

```
value = value – 1
```

Strictly, an increment or decrement operator placed before a variable is referred to as the *preincrement* or *predecrement* operator. An increment or decrement operator placed after a variable is referred to as the *postincrement* or *postdecrement* operator. Preincrementing a variable causes the variable to be incremented by 1 and then the new value is used in the expression in which it appears. Postincrementing a variable causes the variable to be used in the expression in which it appears and then incremented by 1. Predecrementing and postdecrementing are similar.

So, for example, x++ gives the original value for x to be used in the rest of the expression, and then increments it. Equally, ++x increments x, then delivers this new value. Thus,

```
def x = 10
def y = x++        // x has value 11; y has value 10
```

and

```
def p = 20
def q = ++p        // p has value 21; q has value 21
```

The two increment operators are implemented with the next method call. Thus, x++ is realized as x.next(). Similarly, the decrement operators use the previous method call.

2.6 OBJECT REFERENCES

In the assignment age = 25, we are exploiting Groovy's *dynamic typing* ability. The type of the value referenced by the variable age is determined at runtime, not during compilation. Dynamic typing often makes programming easier, and it is also the reason why Groovy is both concise and flexible. Execution of this assignment creates an Integer object with the value 25, and then makes the variable age reference it as shown in Figure 2.1.

The linkage between the variable and the object is known as a *reference*. The variable is said to refer to that part of memory occupied by the object. Any use of the variable, such as in the expression age + 22, uses this reference to obtain the object value associated with the variable.

Now consider the assignments:

```
def age = 25
def number = age
```

In Groovy, variables are always linked to objects. Hence, the effect of the second assignment is to have the number variable reference the same object as the variable age. This is shown in Figure 2.2 and is an example of *sharing* (or *aliasing*), for example, two variables referencing the same object.

If later in our code we assign a new value to the variable age, then the effect is demonstrated in Figure 2.3. Here, we show that the age variable now refer-

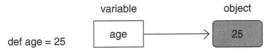

FIGURE 2.1 Variables and object referencing

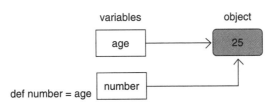

FIGURE 2.2 Sharing

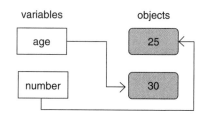

age = 30

FIGURE 2.3 New assignment

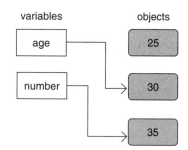

number = 35

FIGURE 2.4 Garbage

ences a different object while the number variable continues to reference the object first established by the assignment to age.

Finally, we consider the effect of assigning a new value to the number variable. Figure 2.4 reveals that the object representing the value 25 is now no longer referenced by any variable. Hence, we can never use it in any further code. It is an example of *garbage*, namely, an unreferenced object. In Groovy, a garbage collector will eventually sweep up the memory space occupied by the object and recycle its memory space for other uses.

These figures have demonstrated that we are free to assign new values to variables at any point in our code. Further, the new value may have a different type from the existing value. This is both a strength and a weakness of Groovy. For example, we are free to assign a String value to what was previously an Integer referenced by some variable. The danger is that we may fail to recognize this in our code and produce some unexpected behavior.

2.7   RELATIONAL AND EQUALITY OPERATORS

Some Groovy control statements, such as the if and the while statements (see Chapter 8), use a *condition*. A condition determines the *truth* or *falsehood* of some expression. These conditional expressions yield values that are either true or false. The *relational, equality,* and *logical* operators are used to form conditional expressions (see Appendix C for a discussion of the latter).

The *relational operators* are shown in Table 2.5. All four are binary operators. Each takes two arithmetic expressions as operands and yields the boolean value either true or false. Both are instances of the class Boolean. All of these operators are realized with the compareTo method call (Table 2.5). For example, a < b is implemented as a.compareTo(b) < 0. The method compareTo returns −1 if a is less than b, +1 if a is greater than b, or 0 if they are the same. This method is also used as the basis for sorting values.

Some examples of expressions using the relational operators are:

```
number < 0           // is number negative?
age >= 65            // is this a senior citizen?
index <= limit − 1   // has the limit been reached?
```

Since these relational operators have a lower precedence than the arithmetic operators (see Appendix C), the last illustration is interpreted as index <= (limit − 1).

The *equality operators* == and != are presented in Table 2.6. Again, they are binary operators and produce the boolean value true or the boolean value false. Both operators are implemented using the equals method. The compareTo operator is denoted by <=> and has the same precedence as the other two.

TABLE 2.5   Relational operators

Expression	Method call	Result
5 < 3	5.compareTo(3) < 0	false
5 <= 3	5.compareTo(3) <= 0	false
5 > 3	5.compareTo(3) > 0	true
5 >= 3	5.compareTo(3) >= 0	true

TABLE 2.6   Equality operators

Expression	Method call	Result
5 == 3	5.equals(3)	false
5 != 3	! 5.equals(3) // see Appendix C	true
5 <=> 3	5.compareTo(3)	+1

Some examples are:

```
def forename = "Ken"
def surname = "Barclay"

forename == "Ken"         // true
surname != "Barkley"      // true
```

Once again these equality operators ultimately become method calls. For example, the condition forename == "Ken" is actually implemented as forename.equals("Ken"). The method equals is programmed in the String class to determine whether the two values are the same. Similarly, if we have the two assignments:

```
def age = 25
def number = 25
```

then the condition:

```
age == number
```

produces the boolean value true. Here, the message age.equals(number) is evaluated using the method equals defined in the class Integer.

2.8   EXERCISES

1. Which of the following are valid Groovy literal values?
   (a) −123   (b) .123   (c) 0.123
   (d) 10.0e4   (e) 10E4
   For each that is valid, identify its class.

2. Use the rules of precedence and associativity to evaluate the following:
   (a) def m = 5
       12*m
   (b) m = 5
       def j = 2
       12*m/j
   (c) def f = 1.2
       (f+10)*20
   (d) def g = 3.4
       f = 1.2
       12*(g−f)

3. Give your reasons for deciding which of the following are valid Groovy identifiers.

   (a) `June` (b) `a$`   (c) `b`
   (d) `_Z`   (e) `name1` (f) `public`

4. Develop four diagrams in the style of Figure 2.1 to demonstrate the effect of the following:

   ```
   def value = 42
   def anotherValue = value
   value = 99
   anotherValue = 50
   ```

   What is the role of the garbage collector in this context?

5. Use the rules of precedence and associativity to evaluate the following:

   (a) ```
       def x = 12
       def y = 2
       x + 3 <= y*10
       ```

   (b) ```
       x = 20
       y = 2
       x + 3 <= y*10
       ```

   (c) ```
       x = 7
       y = 1
       x + 3! = y*10
       ```

   (d) ```
       x = 17
       y = 2
       x + 3 == y*10
       ```

   (e) ```
       x = 100
       y = 5
       x + 3 > y*10
       ```
       ```

STRINGS AND REGULAR EXPRESSIONS

The previous chapter was concerned with numeric values and the basic arithmetic operations associated with them. In this chapter, we consider Strings—an ordered sequence of characters used to represent textual information. This information might represent the name for an individual or file. Equally, it may represent a bank account number or the name of a programming language. We give further details on using Strings and regular expressions for Appendix D.

3.1 STRING LITERALS

A String literal is readily constructed by enclosing the string text in quotations. Groovy offers a variety of ways to denote a String literal. For example, Strings in Groovy can be enclosed in single quotes ('), double quotes ("), or triple quotes ("""). Further, a Groovy String enclosed by triple quotes may span multiple lines. Table 3.1 presents some String literals.

Note how the second example has double quotes nested within the outer single quotes. Equally, the third example has single quotes nested within the outer double quotes. In both, it is not necessary to escape these with the backslash escape character as, for example, in 'He said \"Hello\"!'. The final example shows text spanning multiple lines. This String literal includes the newline characters at the ends of each line.

A String enclosed in single quotes is taken literally. The other two forms of String are said to be *interpreted*. Any expression presented as ${expression}

TABLE 3.1   String literals

Literal	Description
`' '`	Empty string
`'He said "Hello"!'`	Single quotes (with nested double quotes)
`"He said 'Hello'!"`	Double quotes (with nested single quotes)
`"""one two three"""`	Triple quotes

`"""Spread`
`over`
`four`
`lines"""`
	Multi-line text using triple quotes

within an interpreted String is evaluated and the result is then part of the String. The following examples illustrate this effect.

```
def age = 25
'My age is ${age}'      // My age is ${age}
"My age is ${age}"      // My age is 25
"""My age is ${age}"""  // My age is 25
"My age is \${age}"     // My age is ${age}
```

Observe how in the first example interpretation does not apply to single-quoted Strings. Also, observe how, in the final example, escaping the dollar sign with the backslash escape character is required to turn off its use of interpretation. Our normal practice is to use double-quoted Strings only where interpretation is required. Otherwise, we use single-quoted Strings.

3.2   STRING INDEXING AND SLICING

Because Strings are ordered sequences of characters, we access an individual character by its position in the String. This is given by an *index* position. Note that positions can specify either a single character or a subset of characters. Either way, a String value is returned. String indices start at zero and end at one less than the String length. Groovy also permits negative indices to count back from the end of the String. String subsets can also be expressed using *slicing*. A slice allows us to extract a subsection of the String.

Consider the following String object referred to as greeting together with some sample indexing and slicing.

```
def greeting = 'Hello world'
greeting[4]       // o   index from start
greeting[-1]      // d   index from end
greeting[1..2]    // el  slice with inclusive range (see Chapter 4)
greeting[1..<3]   // el  slice with exclusive range (see Chapter 4)
```

```
greeting[4..2]     // oll backward slice
greeting[4, 1, 6]  // oew selective slicing
```

Note how slicing is denoted by 1..2 or 1..<3. This notation is known as a *range* and is discussed fully in Chapter 4. Suffice it to say that 1..2 is the index range 1 to 2 inclusive. The range denoted as 1..<3 is the exclusive range and includes all values starting from 1 and ending at the integer value less than 3.

3.3   BASIC OPERATIONS

The basic String operations include the concatenation of two Strings, duplicating Strings, and finding the length of a String. The minus method (or the overloaded – operator) removes the first occurrence of a substring. The method count determines the number of occurrences of a substring, while contains determines whether a String contains a given substring. Examples are:

```
def greeting='Hello world'
'Hello'+'world'        // Hello world       concatenate
'Hello'*3              // HelloHelloHello   repeat
greeting-'o world'     // Hell              remove first occurrence
greeting.size()        // 11                synonymous with length
greeting.length()      // 11                synonymous with size
greeting.count('o')    // 2
greeting.contains('ell') // true
```

Note how the first three examples illustrate operator overloading as introduced in the preceding chapter. For example, 'Hello'+'world' represents "Hello".plus("world"). The plus method is invoked on the String object "Hello" and is passed the String parameter "world".

Groovy Strings are *immutable*; they cannot be changed in place. We create a new String object by indexing, slicing, and concatenating other String objects. Hence, the illustration greeting-'o world' delivers the new String 'Hell'. The String object greeting is unchanged.

3.4   STRING METHODS

The String class includes many useful methods to manipulate String objects. Table 3.2 tabulates and describes some of the more common methods. The Signature/description column documents the name, number, type of parameters, and return type of the method. It also includes a short description of the effect of the method.

Appendix B describes how Groovy augments the classes of the Java Development Kit (JDK) by including additional methods. The Java String class includes methods such as concat, endsWith, and length (see http://java.sun.com/j2se/1.5.0/docs/api/index.html). The Groovy Development Kit (GDK) specifies the additional `String` class methods center, getAt, leftShift, and so on (see http://groovy.codehaus.org/groovy-jdk.html). These additional methods have been identified in Table 3.2 with an asterisk.

TABLE 3.2   String methods

Name	Signature/description
center *	`String center(Number numberOfChars)` Returns a new `String` of length numberOfChars consisting of the recipient padded on the left and right with space characters.
center *	`String center(Number numberOfChars, String padding)` Returns a new `String` of length numberOfChars consisting of the recipient padded on the left and right with `padding` characters.
compare-ToIgnoreCase	`int compareToIgnoreCase(String str)` Compares two strings lexicographically, ignoring case differences.
concat	`String concat(String str)` Concatenates the specified `String` to the end of this `String`.
eachMatch *	`void eachMatch(String regex, Closure clos)` Processes each `regex` group (see next section) matched substring of the given `String`. The object passed to the closure (see Chapter 9) is an array of strings, following a successful match.
endsWith	`Boolean endsWith(String suffix)` Tests whether this string ends with the specified suffix.
equalsIgnore-Case	`Boolean equalsIgnoreCase(String str)` Compares this `String` to another `String`, ignoring case considerations.

getAt *	`String getAt(int index)`
	`String getAt(IntRange range)`
	`String getAt(Range range)`
	The subscript operator for a `String`.

indexOf	`Int indexOf(String str)` Returns the index within this `String` of the first occurrence of the specified substring.
leftShift *	`StringBuffer leftShift(Object value)` Overloads the `leftShift` operator to provide an easy way to append multiple objects as `String` representations to a `String`.
length	`int length()` Returns the length of the `String`.
matches	`Boolean matches(String regex)` Tells whether a `String` matches the given regular expression.
minus *	`String minus(Object value)` Remove the `value` part of the `String`.
next *	`String next()` This method is called by the ++ operator for the class `String`. It increments the last character in the given `String`.

padLeft *	`String padLeft(Number numberOfCharacters)`
	Pad the String with the spaces appended to the left.
padLeft *	`String padLeft(Number numberOfCharacters, String padding)`
	Pad the String with the padding characters appended to the left.
padRight *	`String padRight(Number numberOfCharacters)`
	Pad the String with the spaces appended to the right.
padRight *	`String padRight (Number numberOfCharacters, String padding)`
	Pad the String with the padding characters appended to the right.
plus *	`String plus(Object value)`
	Appends a String.
previous *	`String previous()`
	This method is called by the − operator for the class String. It decrements the last character in the given String.
replaceAll	`void replaceAll(String regex, Closure clos)`
	Replaces all occurrences of a captured group by the result of a closure on that text.
reverse *	`String reverse()`
	Creates a new String which is the reverse of this String.
size *	`int size()`
	Returns the length of the String.
split *	`String[] split(String regex)`
	Splits this String around matches of the given regular expression.
substring	`String substring(int beginIndex)`
	Returns a new String that is a substring of this String.
substring	`String substring(int beginIndex, int endIndex)`
	Returns a new String that is a substring of this String.
toCharacter *	`Character toCharacter()`
toDouble *	`Double toDouble()`
toFloat *	`Float toFloat()`
toInteger *	`Integer toInteger()`
toLong *	`Long toLong()`
	String conversions.
toList *	`List toList()`
	Converts the given String into a List of strings of one character.
toLowerCase	`String toLowerCase()`
	Converts all of the characters in this String to lower case.
toUpperCase	`String toUpperCase()`
	Converts all of the characters in this String to upper case.
tokenize *	`List tokenize()`
	Tokenize a String with a space character as delimiter.
tokenize *	`List tokenize(String token)`
	Tokenize a String with token as delimiter.

A mix of examples follows (the space character is emphasized and shown as □):

```
'Hello'.compareToIgnoreCase('hello')      // 0
'Hello'.concat('world')                   // Hello world
'Hello'.endsWith('lo')                    // true
'Hello'.equalsIgnoreCase('hello')         // true
'Hello'.indexOf('lo')                     // 3
'Hello world'.indexOf('o', 6)             // 7
'Hello'.matches('Hello')                  // true
'Hello'.matches('He')                     // false
'Hello'.replaceAll('l', 'L')              // HeLLo
'Hello world'.split('l')                  // 'He', 'o wor', 'd'
'Hello'.substring(1)                      // ello
'Hello'.substring(1, 4)                   // ell
'Hello'.toUpperCase()                     // HELLO
def message = 'Hello'
message.center(11)                        //□□□Hello□□□
message.center(3)                         // Hello
message.center(11, '#')                   // ###Hello###
message.eachMatch('.') { ch ->            // print H e l l o
  println ch }                            //   on separate lines
message.getAt(0)                          // H
message.getAt(0..<3)                      // Hel
message.getAt([0, 2, 4])                  // Hlo
message.leftShift('world')                // Hello world
message << 'world'                        // Hello world
message.minus('ell')                      // Ho
message-'ell'                             // Ho
message.padLeft(4)                        // Hello
message.padLeft(11)                       // □□□□□□Hello
message.padLeft(11, '#')                  // ######Hello
message.padRight(4)                       // Hello
message.padRight(11)                      // Hello□□□□□□
message.padRight(11, '#')                 // Hello######
message.plus('world')                     // Hello world
message+'world'                           // Hello world
message.replaceAll('[a-z]') { ch ->       // HELLO
  ch.toUpperCase() }
message.reverse()                         // olleH
message.toList()                          // ['H', 'e', 'l', 'l', 'o']
def message = 'Hello world'
message.tokenize()                        // ['Hello', 'world']
message.tokenize('l')                     // ['He', 'o wor', 'd']
```

Note how the left shift operator << overloads the leftShift method. Operator overloading was introduced in Chapter 2 and is detailed in Appendix I.4.

Method `tokenize` splits a `String` into a `List` (see Chapter 4) of `Strings`. The first version of the method uses a whitespace character as separator. The second uses the `String` parameter to partition it. Method `split` splits a string around matches of the given regular expression (see Section 3.6 and Appendix D), delivering an array of `Strings`.

3.5   STRING COMPARISON

Groovy supports methods for comparing `Strings`. As mentioned in the previous chapter, the operators are overloaded versions of named methods. Thus, we compare two `String` objects using `str1==str2`, remembering that this is a convenience for `str1.equals(str2)`. Equally, the operator denoted as `str1<=>` `str2` represents `str1.compareTo(str2)`. This method returns −1 if `str1` is before `str2`, +1 if `str1` is after `str2`, and 0 if `str1` and `str2` are the same. This might be used to sort a series of `Strings`. `String` comparison examples are:

```
'ken'<=>'ken'            // 0    same
'ken'<=>'kenneth'        // −1   before
'ken'<=>'Ken'            // 1    after
'ken'.compareTo('Ken')   // > 0  after
```

`String` comparisons are lexicographic; therefore uppercase letters precede lowercase letters in the character set. Hence, as shown by the last two examples, `'ken'` follows `'Ken'` since `'K'` precedes `'k'`. Groovy adopts the Unicode (see http://www.unicode.org/) character set and this makes Groovy programs relatively easy to internationalize.

3.6   REGULAR EXPRESSIONS

A *regular expression* is a pattern that is used to find substrings in text. We have already seen in Table 3.2 that the `String` class has several methods that allow us to perform an operation using a regular expression on that `String`. The `matches` method returns `true` if the recipient `String` matches the given regular expression parameter. Then, for example, `"abc".matches("abc")` returns `true` while `"abc".matches("bc")` delivers `false`. The method `replaceAll` (see preceding text) replaces all regex matches inside the `String` with the replacement specified by the closure (see Chapter 9).

Groovy supports regular expressions natively using the `~"regex"` expression. The text enclosed within the quotations represents the regular expression. We might create a regular expression object with:

```
def regex = ~'cheese'
```

When the Groovy operator =~ appears as a predicate (expression returning a boolean) in if and while statements (see Chapter 8), the String operand on the left is matched against the regular expression operand on the right. Hence, each of the following delivers the value true:

```
'cheesecake' =~ 'cheese'
!('cheesecake' =~ 'fromage')
'cheesecake' =~ regex
```

The stricter operator ==~ requires an exact match. Hence, the following expression has the value false:

```
'cheesecake' ==~ 'cheese'
```

In a regular expression, two special *positional characters* are used to denote the beginning and end of a line: caret (^) and dollar sign ($):

```
def rhyme = 'Humpty Dumpty sat on a wall'
rhyme =~ '^Humpty'                              // true
rhyme =~ 'wall$'                                // true
```

Regular expressions can also include *quantifiers*. The plus sign (+) represents one or more times, applied to the preceding element of the expression. The asterisk (*) is used to represent zero or more occurrences. The question mark (?) denotes zero or once. The metacharacter { and } is used to match a specific number of instances of the preceding character. The following all yield true:

```
'aaaaab' =~ 'a*b'
'b' =~ 'a*b'
'aaacd' =~ 'a*c?d'
'aaad' =~ 'a*c?d'
'aaaaab' =~ 'a{5}b'
!('aab' =~ 'a{5}b')
```

In a regular expression, the period symbol (.) can represent any character. This is described as the *wildcard character*. Things get complicated, however, when we are required to match an actual period character. All of the following are true:

```
rhyme =~ '.all'
'3.14' =~ '3.14'           // pattern: 3 followed by any character followed by 14
'3X14' =~ '3.14'
'3.14' =~ '3\\.14'         // pattern: 3.14 literally!
!('3X14' =~ '3\\.14')
```

Great care is required when using the backslash character. In a normal String, it acts as the escape character and so "\\" represents the single backslash. A regular expression to denote a single backslash then becomes "\\\\". Confusingly, we need four occurrences to denote one backslash!

A regular expression may include *character classes*. A set of characters can be given as a simple sequence of characters enclosed in the *metacharacters* [and] as in [aeiou]. For letter or number ranges, you can use a dash separator as in [a–z] or [a–mA–M]. The complement of a character class is denoted by a leading caret within the square brackets as in [^a–z] and represents all characters other than those specified. The value true is delivered from:

```
rhyme =~ '[HD]umpty'
!(rhyme =~ '[hd]umpty')
!(rhyme =~ '[^HD]umpty')
```

Finally, we can group regular expressions to compose more complex expressions. Groups are formed using the (and) metacharacters. Hence, "(ab)*" is the regular expression for any number of occurrences of ab. You can also use alternation (denoted by |) to match a single regular expression from one of several possible regular expressions. Therefore, "(a|b)*" describes any number of mixed a or b. The following all yield true:

```
'ababab' ==~ '(ab)*'
!('ababa' ==~ '(ab)*')
'ababc' ==~ '(ab)*c'
'aaac' ==~ '(a|b)*c'
'bbbc' ==~ '(a|b)*c'
'ababc' ==~ '(a|b)*c'
```

Groovy also permits a pattern to use the / delimiter so that we do not have to double all the backslash symbols. Thus, the example:

```
def matcher = "\$abc." =~ \\\$(.*)\\.
```

can also be expressed as:

```
def matcher = "\$abc." =~ /\$(.*)\./
```

3.7   EXERCISES

1. Evaluate the following expressions:
   (a) "Hello" + "world"
   (b) "12" + "34"
   (c) "1" + "0"

2. Evaluate the following expressions:
    (a) `"Hello".length()`
    (b) `"".length()`

3. Suppose we have the `String` variable `str` defined as:

    ```
    def str="Hello world"
    ```

    Then, evaluate the following expressions:
    (a) `str.indexOf("or")`
    (b) `str.indexOf("Or")`
    (c) `str.lastIndexOf("o")`
    (d) `str.lastIndexOf("or")`

4. Suppose we have the following definition:

    ```
    def str="Groovy, Groovy, Groovy"
    ```

    Evaluate the following expressions:
    (a) `str.length()`
    (b) `str.indexOf("o")`
    (c) `str.lastIndexOf("o")`
    (d) `str.indexOf("o", 5)`
    (e) `str.lastIndexOf("o", 5)`
    (f) `str.indexOf("ov", str.length()-10)`
    (g) `str.lastIndexOf("ov", str.length()-4)`
    (h) `str.indexOf("o", str.indexOf("ro"))`

5. Suppose we have the following definition:

    ```
    def str="Groovy programming"
    ```

    Evaluate the following expressions:
    (a) `str.length()`
    (b) `str.substring(7, 14)`
    (c) `str.substring(1, str.length()-1)`
    (d) `str.endsWith("ming")`

6. Evaluate the following expressions:
    (a) `'Groovy' =~ 'Groovy'`
    (b) `'Groovy' =~ 'oo'`
    (c) `'Groovy' ==~ 'Groovy'`
    (d) `'Groovy' ==~ 'oo'`
    (e) `'Groovy' =~ '^G'`
    (f) `'Groovy' =~ 'G$'`
    (g) `'Groovy' =~ 'Gro*vy'`
    (h) `'Groovy' =~ 'Gro{2}vy'`

LISTS, MAPS, AND RANGES

In this chapter, we introduce the *list, map,* and *range.* All are *collections* of references to other objects. The List and Map can reference objects of differing types. The Range represents a collection of integer values. The List and Map also grow dynamically. Each object referenced in a List is identified by an integer *index.* In contrast, a Map collection is indexed by a value of any kind. Because the class of the objects maintained by these collections is arbitrary, the elements of a List might be a Map and the elements of a Map might be a List. In this way, we can create data structures of arbitrary complexity. This is examined in Chapter 6 and in subsequent chapters.

4.1 LISTS

The List is a structure used to store a collection of data items. In Groovy, the List holds a sequence of object references. Object references in a List occupy a position in the sequence and are distinguished by an integer index. A List literal is presented as a series of objects separated by commas and enclosed in square brackets. Table 4.1 illustrates sample List literals.

To process the data in a list, we must be able to access individual elements. Groovy Lists are indexed using the indexing operator []. List indices start at zero, which refers to the first element. Consider the following List object identified as numbers and some sample List accessing.

```
def numbers = [11, 12, 13, 14]    // list with four items
numbers [0]                       // 11
numbers [3]                       // 14
```

TABLE 4.1   List literals

Example	Description
[11, 12, 13, 14]	A list of integer values
['Ken', 'John', 'Andrew']	A list of Strings
[1, 2, [3, 4], 5]	A nested list
['Ken', 21, 1.69]	A heterogeneous list of object references
[ ]	An empty list

If the integer index is negative, then it refers to elements by counting from the end. Thus,

```
numbers [-1]   // 14
numbers [-2]   // 13
```

This indexing can also be applied to a List literal, as in:

```
[11, 12, 13, 14][2]   // 13
```

Once again, it is worth restating that the [] operator is the method getAt (see Section 4.2) defined in the List class. Hence, in addition to referring to a list element as numbers[3], we need to recognize that, in fact, we are invoking the getAt method on the List object numbers with the method parameter 3, as in numbers.getAt(3).

Additionally, we can index a List using ranges (examined later in this chapter). An *inclusive range* of the form start..end delivers a new List object comprising the references to the objects from the original List starting at index position start and ending at index position end. An *exclusive range* of the form start..<end includes all elements except the final end element. Examples of range indices are:

```
numbers [0..2]   // [11, 12, 13]
numbers [1..<3]  // [12, 13]
```

The List indexing operator can also be used to set new values into a List. Used on the left side of an assignment, the element at the given position is replaced by the value on the right of the assignment. The index can only be a single integer expression. If the replacement value on the right side of the assignment is itself a List, then it is used as the replacement.

```
numbers [1] = 22        // [11, 22, 13, 14]
numbers [1] = [33, 44]  // [11, [33, 44], 13, 14]
```

This assignment is provided by the method putAt (see Table 4.2).

A new item can be appended on to the right end of a List using the << operator (the leftShift method) as in:

```
numbers << 15       // [11, [33, 44], 13, 14, 15]
```

Equally, the + operator (the plus method) is used to concatenate Lists:

```
numbers = [11, 12, 13, 14]     // list with four items
numbers + [15, 16]             // [11, 12, 13, 14, 15, 16]
```

The – operator (the minus method) is used to remove items from a List:

```
numbers = [11, 12, 13, 14]     // list with four items
numbers - [13]                 // [11, 12, 14]
```

4.2   LIST METHODS

The Groovy List class supports a host of methods that make list processing pleasing and easy. The List class removes much of the work that would otherwise have to be programmed in an application. Table 4.2 tabulates and describes some of the more common List methods. Note that those methods with an asterisk are the augmented GDK methods.

TABLE 4.2   List methods

Name	Signature/description
add	boolean add(Object value) Append the new value to the end of this List.
add	void add(int index, Object value) Inserts a new value into this List at the given index position.
addAll	boolean addAll(Collection values) Append the new values on to the end of this List.
contains	boolean contains(Object value) Returns true if this List contains the specified value.
flatten *	List flatten() Flattens this List and returns a new List.
get	Object get(int index) Returns the element at the specified position in this List.

Continued

TABLE 4.2   List methods (*Continued*)

Name	Signature/description
getAt *	Object getAt(int index) Returns the element at the specified position in this List.
getAt *	List getAt(Range range) Return a new List that is a sublist of this List based on the given range.
getAt *	List getAt(Collection indices) Returns a new List of the values in this List at the given indices
intersect *	List intersect(Collection collection) Returns a new List of all the elements that are common to both the original List and the input List.
isEmpty	boolean isEmpty() Returns true if this List contains no elements.
leftShift *	Collection leftShift(Object value) Overloads the left shift operator to provide an easy way to append an item to a List.
minus *	List minus(Collection collection) Creates a new List composed of the elements of the original without those specified in the collection.
plus *	List plus(Object value) Creates a new List composed of the elements of the original together with the new value.
plus *	List plus(Collection collection) Creates a new List composed of the elements of the original together with those specified in the collection.
pop *	Object pop() Removes the last item from this List.
putAt *	void putAt(int index, Object value) Supports the subscript operator on the left of an assignment.
remove	Object remove(int index) Removes the element at the specified position in this List.
remove	boolean remove(Object value) Removes the first occurrence in this List of the specified element.
reverse *	List reverse() Create a new List that is the reverse the elements of the original List.
size	int size() Obtains the number of elements in this List.
sort *	List sort() Returns a sorted copy of the original List.

The following shows examples of these List methods and their effects.

```
[11, 12, 13, 14].add(15)              // [11, 12, 13, 14, 15]
[11, 12, 13, 14].add(2, 15)           // [11, 12, 15, 13, 14]
[11, 12, 13, 14].add([15, 16])        // [11, 12, 13, 14, 15, 16]
[11, 12, 13, 14].get(1)               // 12
[11, 12, 13, 14].isEmpty()            // false
[14, 13, 12, 11].size()               // 4
[11, 12, [13, 14]].flatten()          // [11, 12, 13, 14]
[11, 12, 13, 14].getAt(1)             // 12
[11, 12, 13, 14].getAt(1..2)          // [12, 13]
[11, 12, 13, 14].getAt([2, 3])        // [13, 14]
[11, 12, 13, 14].intersect([13, 14, 15])  // [13, 14]
[11, 12, 13, 14].pop()                // 14
[11, 12, 13, 14].reverse()            // [14, 13, 12, 11]
[14, 13, 12, 11].sort()               // [11, 12, 13, 14]
```

Be alert to the following code:

```
def numbers = [11, 12, 13, 14]
numbers.remove(3)
numbers.remove(13)
```

The first remove call seeks to remove the item at position 3 using the method remove(int index). The statement has the desired effect. However, in the second call, the programmer intends to remove the value 13 using the method remove(Object value). This fails, reporting an out-of-bounds exception, having attempted to call the first remove method. Had the List contained, say, String values, as in the following, then everything operates as expected. Groovy is able to correctly identify the required calls to remove.

```
def names = ['Ken', 'John', 'Sally', 'Jon']
names.remove(3)
names.remove('Ken')
```

4.3   MAPS

A Map (also known as an *associative array, dictionary, table,* and *hash*) is an unordered collection of object references. The elements in a Map collection are accessed by a *key* value. The keys used in a Map can be of any class. When we insert into a Map collection, two values are required: the key and the value. Indexing the Map with the same key can then retrieve that value. Table 4.3 shows some sample Map literals comprising a comma-separated list of key:value pairs enclosed in square brackets.

TABLE 4.3   Map literals

Example	Description
['Ken' : 'Barclay', 'John' : 'Savage'] [4 : [2], 6 : [3, 2], 12 : [6, 4, 3, 2]] [:]	Forename/surname collection Integer keys and their list of divisors Empty map

Observe that if the key in a Map literal is a variable name, then it is interpreted as a String value. In the example:

```
def x = 1
def y = 2
def m = [x : y, y : x]
```

then, m is the Map:

```
m = ['x' : 2, 'y' : 1]
```

Individual elements of a Map are accessed using the subscript operator (implemented by the method getAt; see Section 4.4). This time, the index value can be any class of object and represents a key. The value returned is the value paired with the key or the value null if no entry with that key exists. Consider the following Map objects referenced as names and divisors, and some simple indexing:

```
def names = ['Ken' : 'Barclay', 'John' : 'Savage']
def divisors = [4 : [2], 6 : [3, 2], 12 : [6, 4, 3, 2]]
names['Ken']                                          // 'Barclay'
names.Ken                                             // 'Barclay'
names['Jessie']                                       // null
divisors[6]                                           // [3, 2]
```

As with Lists, this indexing is provided by the getAt method (see next section). Equally, the putAt method supports indexing on the left of an assignment, as in:

```
divisors[6] = [6, 3, 2, 1]        // [4 : [2], 6 : [6, 3, 2, 1],
                                  // 12 : [6, 4, 3, 2]]
```

We must be especially careful to recognize that the keys for Maps are objects. In the names Map given previously, the keys are String objects. Similarly, the keys of the divisors map are Integer objects. Hence, it is perfectly possible to have the Map:

```
def careful =[ 1 : 'Ken', '1' : 'Barclay']
careful[1]                                    // Ken
careful['1']                                  // Barclay
```

The first entry has the `Integer` key assigned as 1, while the second entry has the `String` key assigned as `'1'`. We might have arrived at this by receiving input from the user, reading the first key as an `Integer` and the second key as a `String`. We must be especially diligent if this was not our intention.

4.4 MAP METHODS

The `Map` class supports a range of methods that make map processing very easy. The `Map` class removes much of the work that would otherwise have to be programmed in an application where a set of relationships need to be formed between pairs of objects. Table 4.4 tabulates and describes some of the more common `Map` methods. Again, those marked with an asterisk are courtesy of the GDK.

TABLE 4.4 Map methods

Name	Signature/description
containsKey	`boolean containsKey(Object key)` Does this Map contain this key?
get	`Object get(Object key)` Look up the key in this Map and return the corresponding value. If there is no entry in this Map for the key, then return `null`.
get *	`Object get(Object key, Object defaultValue)` Look up the key in this Map and return the corresponding value. If there is no entry in this Map for the key, then return the `defaultValue`.
getAt *	`Object getAt(Object key)` Support method for the subscript operator.
keySet	`Set keySet()` Obtain a Set of the keys in this Map.
put	`Object put(Object key, Object value)` Associates the specified `value` with the specified `key` in this Map. If this Map previously contained a mapping for this key, the old value is replaced by the specified `value`.
putAt *	`Object putAt(Object key, Object value)` Support method to allow Maps to operate with subscript assignment.
size	`int size()` Returns the number of key-value mappings in this Map.
values	`Collection values()` Returns a collection view of the values contained in this Map.

The following shows examples of these Map methods and their effects.

```
def mp = ['Ken' : 2745, 'John' : 2746, 'Sally' : 2742]
mp.put('Bob', 2713)        // [Bob:2713, Ken:2745, Sally:2742, John:2746]
mp.containsKey('Ken')      // true
mp.get('David', 9999)      // 9999
mp.get('Sally')            // 2742
mp.get('Billy')            // null
mp.keySet()                // [David, Bob, Ken, Sally, John]
mp.size()                  // 4
mp['Ken']                  // 2745
```

Notice how the values method returns a Collection of the values contained in a Map. Often, we find it useful to have these as a List. This is easily achieved with the code:

```
mp.values().asList()
```

4.5 RANGES

A *range* is shorthand for specifying a sequence of values. A Range is denoted by the first and last values in the sequence, and Range can be *inclusive* or *exclusive*. An inclusive Range includes all the values from the first to the last, while an exclusive Range includes all values except the last. Here are some examples of Range literals:

```
1900..1999     // twentieth century (inclusive Range)
2000..<2100    // twenty-first century (exclusive Range)
'A'..'D'       // A, B, C, and D
10..1          // 10, 9, ..., 1
'Z'..'X'       // Z, Y, and X
```

Observe how an inclusive Range is denoted by .., while an exclusive Range uses ..< between the lower and upper bounds. The range can be denoted by Strings or by Integers. As shown, the Range can be given either in ascending order or in descending order.

The first and last values for a Range can also be any numeric integer expression, as in:

```
def start = 10
def finish = 20
start..finish+1  // [10, 11, 12, 13, 14, 15, 16, 17, 18, 19, 20, 21]
```

TABLE 4.5   Range methods

Name	Signature/description
contains	`boolean contains(Object obj)` Returns `true` if this Range contains the specified element.
get	`Object get(int index)` Returns the element at the specified position in this Range.
getFrom	`Comparable getFrom()` Get the lower value of this Range.
getTo	`Comparable getTo()` Get the upper value of this Range.
isReverse	`boolean isReverse()` Is this a reversed Range, iterating backwards?
size	`int size()` Returns the number of elements in this Range.
subList	`List subList(int fromIndex, int toIndex)` Returns a view of the portion of this Range between the specified `fromIndex`, inclusive, and `toIndex`, exclusive.

A number of methods are defined to operate with Ranges. They are tabulated in Table 4.5.

The following show some examples of these Range methods and their effects:

```
def twentiethCentury = 1900..1999    // Range literal
def reversedTen = 10..1              // Reversed Range
twentiethCentury.size()              // 100
twentiethCentury.get(0)              // 1900
twentiethCentury.getFrom()           // 1900
twentiethCentury.getTo()             // 1999
twentiethCentury.contains(2000)      // false
twentiethCentury.subList(0, 5)       // 1900..1904
reversedTen[2]                       // 8
reversedTen.isReverse()              // true
```

Further details on Lists, Maps, and Ranges are given in Appendix E.

4.6 EXERCISES

1. Given the list [14, 12, 13, 11], express how we would obtain the List with these elements in descending order.

2. Determine the effect of the expression [1, [2, [3, 4]]].flatten(), and then state whether flatten recurses through nested Lists.

3. Given two Lists [11, 12, 13, 14] and [13, 14, 15], how would we obtain the list of items from the first that are not in the second, that is, [11, 12]?

4. A *stack* represents a last-in-first-out data structure, where all the operations occur at the stack top. The operations on a stack are (a) PUSH: place a new item on the stack top; (b) POP: removes the topmost item from the stack; and (c) TOP: deliver a copy of the topmost item.

   If a List is used to implement a stack with the stack top denoted by the final element of the List, then show how the stack operations can be realized as List operations.

5. Given a Groovy List object referenced as table, describe which elements are referenced by:
   (a) table[0]
   (b) table[table.size() – 1]
   (c) table[table.size().intdiv(2)] where there is (i) an odd number of items in the list and (ii) where there is an even number of items.

6. Distinguish between the effects of the following two List expressions:
   (a) table.sort().reverse()
   (b) table.reverse().sort()

7. Is the map names = ['Ken' : 'Barclay', 'John' : 'Savage', 'Ken' : 'Chisholm'] a valid construction in Groovy? What would the value of the expression names.Ken deliver?

8. Given the map divisors shown in Section 4.3, determine the effect of the following expressions:
   (a) divisors.containsKey(8)
   (b) divisors[6].sort()
   (c) divisors[6].intersect(divisors[12])

9. A software house is contracted to develop Groovy, Java, and C# projects. Each project has one or more programmers involved, perhaps with the same individual associated with more than one project. For example, the following shows Ken, John, and Jon involved with the Groovy project:

```
def softwareHouse = ['Groovy' : ['Ken', 'John', 'Jon'],
                     'Java' : ['Ken', 'John'],
                     'C#' : ['Andrew']
                    ]
```

Prepare expressions to answer the following:

(a) How many staff members involved with the Groovy project?

(b) Which staff members are involved with both the Groovy and Java projects?

(c) Which staff members are involved with the Groovy project but not the Java project?

10. A university has a number of departments, each of which is responsible for one or more programs of study. For example, the following shows that the Computing department has two programs, Computing and Information Systems. Respectively, they have 600 and 300 enrolled students.

```
def university = ['Computing' : ['Computing' : 600, 'Information Systems' : 300],
                  'Engineering' : ['Civil' : 200, 'Mechanical' : 100],
                  'Management' : ['Management' : 800]
                 ]
```

Prepare expressions to answer the following:

(a) How many university departments are there?

(b) How many programs are delivered by the Computing department?

(c) How many students are enrolled in the Civil Engineering program?

SIMPLE INPUT AND OUTPUT

Strictly, input and output facilities are not part of the Groovy language. Nonetheless, real programs do communicate with their environment. To produce simple text output in Groovy, we use statements of the form:

```
print xxx        print(xxx)
println xxx      println(xxx)
```

The methods `print` and `println` are used to display the value concerned (denoted by xxx). The value may represent a `String` literal, a variable or expression, or an interpreted `String`. Method `print` outputs its value, and any further output appears on the same output line. Method `println` advances to the next output line after displaying its value.

5.1 SIMPLE OUTPUT

Example 01 demonstrates how to print a simple `String` literal using the `print` and `println` methods.

```
print "My name is"
print("Ken")
println()

println "My first program"
println("This is fun")
```

When we execute this Groovy script, the output produced is:

```
My name is Ken
My first program
This is fun
```

The first two program statements are responsible for the first line of output. Method `print` displays its parameter on the console. Any further output continues on the same output line. The simple method call `println()` prints a line break. Note how the value parameter may optionally be enclosed in parentheses.

◆

From Chapter 3, we know that `Strings` enclosed in double quotes are interpreted, and any `${expression}` is evaluated and becomes part of the `String`. Example 02 shows this at work with some `print` statements.

EXAMPLE 02
Output of a value

```
def age = 25
print "My age is: "
println age
println "My age is: ${age}"
```

Running this script produces:

```
My age is: 25
My age is: 25
```

Note how the `println age` method call is used to print the value of the age variable.

◆

We can also print the contents of a `List` or `Map`. Example 03 shows how we use the same scheme as already cited.

EXAMPLE 03
Printing `Lists`
and `Maps`

```
def numbers = [11, 12, 13, 14]
def staffTel = ['Ken' : 2745, 'John' : 2746, 'Jessie' : 2772]

println "Numbers: ${numbers}"
println "Staff telephones: ${staffTel}"
```

The output is:

```
Numbers: [11, 12, 13, 14]
Staff telephones: ["Jessie":2772, "John":2746, "Ken":2745]
```

◆

5.2 FORMATTED OUTPUT

Formatted output is achieved with the printf method call. The formal description of printf is:

```
printf(String format, List values)
```

This method prints its values on the console. The values are any expressions representing what is to be printed. The presentation of these values is under control of the *formatting string*. This string contains two types of information: ordinary characters, which are simply copied to the output, and *conversion specifications*, which control conversion and printing of the values.

  Two simple illustrations of printf are shown in Example 04. In both examples, the List of values to be printed is empty. The format String comprises ordinary characters. The first printf method call displays its format String. Further output continues on the same output line. The second example includes the escape character \n, representing a newline. Any output after that will begin on the next line.

```
printf('My name is Ken', [])
printf('My name is Ken\n', [])
```

EXAMPLE 04
Simple formatted output

◆

In the next example, we include a List of values. The format String then includes conversion specifications for each of the values. The conversion specifications are introduced by the percent (%) character. In the first example, %d denotes printing an integer value. In the second, the %f conversion is used for printing floating point values.

```
def a = 10
def b = 15
printf('The sum of %d and %d is %d\n', [a, b, a+b])

def x = 1.234
def y = 56.78
printf('%f from %f gives %f\n', [y, x, x-y])
```

EXAMPLE 05
Conversion specifications

The output is:

```
The sum of 10 and 15 is 25
56.780000 from 1.234000 gives −55.546000
```

◆

A more detailed discussion of the conversion specifications is given in Appendix F. Example 06 illustrates using the %s conversion to print a string. In all three examples, the output string is enclosed in [and] to reveal the effect of the conversions. We see that %s simply outputs the string. The conversion %20s outputs the string right justified in a field of 20 characters. The conversion %−20s left justifies the output.

EXAMPLE 06
Field widths and
justification

```
printf('[%s]\n', ["Hello there"])
printf('[%20s]\n', ["Hello there"])
printf('[%−20s]\n', ["Hello there"])
```

The output is:

```
[Hello there]
[         Hello there]
[Hello there         ]
```

◆

5.3   SIMPLE INPUT

The object in defined in the Java class System represents the standard input, and is an object of the class InputStream. This class includes the method readLine, which reads a single line of input as a String. Hence, the method call System.in.readLine() can be used to obtain a line of input from the user. Example 07 shows this in a program to read a user's name.

EXAMPLE 07
Simple input

```
print "Please enter your name: "
def name = System.in.readLine()
println "My name is: ${name}"
```

◆

Method readLine returns a String value. We can use the method toInteger on that String to convert it into an integer value or toDouble to convert it to a floating point value. Example 08 shows three Groovy methods (see Chapter 7) that might be used to read various input values.

```groovy
def readString() {
  return System.in.readLine()
}


def readInteger() {
  return System.in.readLine().toInteger()
}


def readDouble() {
  return System.in.readLine().toDouble()
}

print 'Please enter your name: '
def name = readString()
println "My name is: ${name}"

print 'Please enter your age: '
def age = readInteger()
println "My age is: ${age}"
```

EXAMPLE 08
Miscellaneous inputs

Using `System.in.readLine()` implies that each input value is supplied as a single text line. The methods `toInteger` and `toDouble` expect that the input `String` be correctly formatted with no unexpected characters and no leading or trailing spaces.

The methods `readString`, `readInteger`, etc. will find uses in other scripts. We collect them as a set of static methods in the class `Console` that can then be imported into other applications. The class `Console` is found in the `console` package. Further information on this class is given in Appendix F.

```groovy
package console

class Console {
  def static readString() { ... }
  def static readLine() { ... }
  def static readInteger() { ... }
  def static readDouble() { ... }
  def static readBoolean() { ... }
}
```

◆

Importantly, the methods of class `Console` tokenize the input so that, for example, leading whitespace on an integer value is ignored by method `readInteger`. Example 09 shows how we use these methods.

EXAMPLE 09
Using the
Console class

```
import console.*

print 'Please enter your name: '
def name = Console.readString()
println "My name is: ${name}"

print 'Please enter your age: '
def age = Console.readInteger()
println "My age is: ${age}"
```

Executing this script might result in the following (user input is italicized and bold):

```
Please enter your name: Ken
My name is: Ken
Please enter your age: 25
My age is: 25
```

◆

Importantly, the Console class buffers and tokenizes its input so that more than one value may be given on one input line. Example 10 demonstrates how this is used.

EXAMPLE 10
Buffered and
tokenized input

```
import console.*

print 'Please enter your name and age: '
def name = Console.readString()
def age = Console.readInteger()
println "Name: ${name}, and age: ${age}"
```

Running this script, we could have:

```
Please enter your name and age: Ken 25
Name: Ken, and age: 25
```

◆

5.4   EXERCISES

1. Prepare a Groovy program to produce the following two lines of output:

   ```
   Programming in Groovy
   is fab
   ```

   using (a) two print statements and (b) one print statement.

2. Given the variable staffNumber declared and initialized as 123 and the variable staffSalary declared and initialized as 456.78 in a Groovy script, prepare output statements to produce the following output (note how the numerical values are directly aligned with the text):

   ```
   STAFF      PAY
   123      456.78
   ```

3. Write a Groovy script that reads the sum of money 123.45, increases it by 10%, and prints the new sum.

4. Develop a program that reads the total number of seconds since midnight, and then converts it to hours, minutes, and seconds, and presents it as hh:mm:ss.

5. Develop a program that reads a measure for the total number of inches and converts it to yards, feet, and inches (12 inches in 1 foot, 3 feet in 1 yard).

6. Develop a program to determine the perimeter and the area of a rectangle, given input values for its length and breadth.

CASE STUDY: A LIBRARY APPLICATION (MODELING)

This chapter illustrates how Groovy's Lists and Maps might be used in practice. For this first case study, we construct a simple model of the loan data maintained by a library. For a more realistic example, see those chapters in which we revisit the problem and construct a more elaborate implementation.

In keeping with modern practice, we develop the library application as a series of iterations. This lets us change the implementation of the case study in a controlled manner. The first iteration illustrates the use of a List and the second a Map.

6.1 ITERATION 1: SPECIFICATION AND LIST IMPLEMENTATION

A library maintains a record of books on loan to its borrowers. In this very simplistic solution, each book is known by its title and each borrower by his or her name. The library's database of books on loan can be represented in a number of ways. However, our choice is made easier by Groovy's support for two important data structures: List and Map.

One solution is to use a List to represent the loans database. Recall from Chapter 4 that the List holds a number of object references, each of which can be accessed by an integer index. The List can also grow and shrink dynamically. It is also important to realize that each element in the List can be any object.

This means that we are able to construct Lists of arbitrary complexity. In this first solution, each element in the List that represents the library database is itself a List of two elements, namely, the borrower's name and the title of the book on loan to that borrower.

Here is how we initialize the loans database:

```
def library = [ ['Ken', 'Groovy'],
                ['Ken', 'UML'],
                ['John', 'Java']
              ]
```

This gives us a List of three elements, each of which is a List of two elements. The first shows that the borrower Ken has the book titled Groovy out on loan, and the second shows that he also has the book entitled UML. The third records that John has Java out on loan.

From Chapter 4, we know that the List class supports a host of methods that make list processing very easy. For example, we can add new loans with the add method or the synonymous << operator:

```
library << ['John', 'OOD']
library.add(['Sally', 'Basic'])
```

We can print the List with:

```
println "Library: ${library}"
```

This gives us a visual check that the List contains the elements we expect (see following text for the actual output).

Putting all of this together, we might have the following Groovy script to establish the initial loan database, add two new elements, and then print the database:

EXAMPLE 01
A List
implementation

```
// initialize the loans database
def library = [ ['Ken', 'Groovy'],
                ['Ken', 'UML'],
                ['John', 'Java']
              ]

// add two new loans
library << ['John', 'OOD']
library.add(['Sally', 'Basic'])

// print the loan details
println "Library: ${library}"
```

It produces the output:

```
Library: [["Ken", "Groovy"], ["Ken", "UML"], ["John", "Java"], ["John", "OOD"], ["Sally", "Basic"]]
```

Although it is not well formatted, it will suffice for this first case study.

To illustrate further, we can determine whether Ken has borrowed the book titled UML with:

```
library.contains(['Ken', 'UML'])    // true
```

and determine the number of books on loan to all borrowers with:

```
library.size()
```

An updated script could be:

```
// as for the previous script
// ...

// determine if Ken has borrowed UML
println "Ken has borrowed UML? ${library.contains(['Ken', 'UML'])}"

// print the number of books on loan
println "Number of books on loan: ${library.size()}"
```

It produces the output:

```
Library: [["Ken", "Groovy"], ["Ken", "UML"], ["John", "Java"], ["John", "OOD"], ["Sally", "Basic"]]
Ken has borrowed UML? true
Number of books on loan: 5
```

◆

Notice that even in this simple example, we make effective use of the GDK methods such as leftShift (the << operator) available for the List class as well as JDK methods such as contains. This simplifies our task enormously and is a major strength of Groovy.

6.2 ITERATION 2: MAP IMPLEMENTATION

An alternative approach might be to use a Map to represent the loan database. Recall from Chapter 4 that the Map is an unordered collection of object references. It can grow and shrink dynamically. Each value in a Map is accessed by a key. When we insert items into a Map, we provide a key/value pair. These pairs are commonly known as map entries. Because the key and the value can be any class of object, we are able to construct Maps of arbitrary complexity, as we did with the List implementation.

For example, we can associate a List of borrowed book titles with a borrower. The key is the name of the borrower, and the value is a List of book titles on loan to that borrower. We can alternatively initialize the loan database with:

```
def library = ['Ken' : ['Groovy', 'UML'],
               'John' : ['Java']
              ]
```

resulting in a Map with two entries. The first has Ken as the key and an associated value that is a List containing two elements, Groovy and UML. They are the titles of the books on loan to Ken. Similarly, the second records that John has a single book on loan entitled Java.

We can add a new borrower and her associated books with:

```
library['Sally'] = ['Basic']
```

However, we must be careful when updating an existing borrower's List of book titles since the Map does not permit duplicate keys. Any attempt to add a duplicate key results in the original value being lost. Therefore, we implement making a new loan to John as:

```
library['John'] = library['John'] << 'OOD'
```

by creating an updated List then overwriting the original entry in the Map.

As with the List implementation, we can determine if Ken has borrowed a particular book with:

```
library['Ken'].contains('UML')
```

and count the number of borrowers with:

```
library.size()
```

As with the List implementation, we are making use of GDK and JDK methods that already exist for the Map class. To illustrate further, we might want the borrower names in alphabetical order and the number of books on loan to Ken. We can easily accomplish this with:

```
library.keySet().sort()
```

and:

```
library['Ken'].size()
```

Putting it all together, we have the following Groovy script:

```
// initialize the loans database
def library=['Ken' : ['Groovy', 'UML'],
             'John' : ['Java']
            ]

// add a new borrower
library['Sally']=['Basic']

// update an existing borrower
library['John']= library['John'] << 'OOD'

// display the data in various ways
println "Library: ${library}"

println "Ken has borrowed UML? ${library['Ken'].contains('UML')}"

println "Number of borrowers in the library: ${library.size()}"

println "Library: ${library.keySet().sort()}"

println "Number of books borrowed by Ken: ${library['Ken'].size()}"
```

EXAMPLE 02
A Map
implementation

The script produces the following output:

```
Library: ["Sally":["Basic"], "John":["Java", "OOD"], "Ken":["Groovy", "UML"]]
Ken has borrowed UML? true
Number of borrowers in the library: 3
Library: ["John", "Ken", "Sally"]
Number of books borrowed by Ken: 2
```

◆

As before, it is not well formatted, but it will suffice for our purposes. The main point is that because Groovy has native syntax for Lists and Maps, our programming task is made much easier. We will make extensive use of this feature in the chapters that follow.

6.3 EXERCISES

1. Using the List implementation of iteration 1, show how you might determine how many books a particular borrower has on loan.

2. Consider a situation in which it is possible that a borrower may belong to two different libraries. Using the List implementation of Iteration 1, show how you might determine which borrowers belong to both.

3. Repeat the case study using the Map implementation of Iteration 2 in which the key is the title of the book and the value is a List of the names of borrowers (assuming, this time, that the library has multiple copies of books).

4. Compare two Lists representing the names of staff involved in two separate project developments. A staff member may be involved in one or both projects. Find those staff involved in both projects. Find those involved in only one project.

5. Prepare a Map in which the keys are the names of individuals and the values are their ages. How might we find the age of John? How do we remove an entry from the Map? How might we determine the age of the youngest?

METHODS

A *method* is a name given to a segment of code that can be executed or *called* one or more times in a program. Methods may also be given *parameters* that act as input values to the method call. Each method call may use different actual parameters that determine the effect of the method when it is executed.

Methods in Groovy partition large programs into smaller manageable units, thus simplifying the programming task. Each method is responsible for a particular functionality required in the application. One method can call or execute any other method. Thus, a task represented by one method can be partitioned into subtasks realized by other submethods. Further, methods developed in one program may be incorporated into other programs, avoiding the need to reprogram them.

Groovy methods as described in this chapter are synonymous with *functions*, *procedures*, or *subroutines* found in other programming languages.

7.1 METHODS

A method is defined using the keyword def. The simplest form of a method definition is one with no parameters as shown here:

```
def methodName() {
    // Method code goes here
}
```

Method names are presented as program identifiers (see Chapter 2). If a method takes no parameters that is signaled by (), which cannot be omitted.

EXAMPLE 01
Simple method
definition

```
def greetings() {
    println 'Hello and welcome'
}

greetings()
```

Here, the method is named greetings. The method code involves printing a simple greeting to the user. The method is then invoked using the *method call* greetings(). The program output is:

```
Hello and welcome
```

◆

This method may also be written as in Example 02.

EXAMPLE 02
Method with three
statements

```
def greetings() {
    print 'Hello'
    print ' and '
    println 'welcome'
}

greetings()
```

◆

On this occasion, method greetings has three statements. Each is a separate invocation of the print statement. Here, each statement is given on a separate line. This generally improves the readability of the code and is the style used throughout this textbook. If we want two or more statements on a line, we must use a semicolon separator, as in:

EXAMPLE 03
Multiple
statements on a
single line

```
def greetings() {
    print 'Hello'; print ' and '
    println 'welcome'
}

greetings()
```

◆

Consider now a method that includes some variables. The program is required to read two integer values and print them in reverse order. To achieve this effect, the method must have two variables as repositories for the data values.

EXAMPLE 04
Method variables

```
import console.*

def reverse() {
  print 'Enter the two integer values: '
  def first = Console.readInteger()
  def second = Console.readInteger()
  println "Reversed values: ${second} and ${first}"
}

reverse()        // now call it
```

Running the script might produce the following (with the user input shown as bold and italic):

```
Enter the two integer values: 12
34
Reversed values: 34 and 12
```

◆

The next example is similar to the last. It reads some data, processes it, and displays the results of its computation. The processing involves some arithmetic operations. The program reads three integer values representing a 24-hour clock time expressed as hours, minutes, and seconds. This time is converted to its total number of seconds.

EXAMPLE 05
Converting a clock
time

```
import console.*

def processTime() {
  print 'Enter the time to be converted: '
  def hours = Console.readInteger()
  def minutes = Console.readInteger()
  def seconds = Console.readInteger()
  def totalSeconds = (60 * hours + minutes) * 60 + seconds
  println "The original time of: ${hours} hours, ${minutes} minutes
  and ${seconds} seconds"
  println "Converts to: ${totalSeconds} seconds"
}

processTime()    // now call it
```

Running this program might produce:

```
Enter the time to be converted: 1
2
3
The original time of: 1 hours, 2 minutes and 3 seconds
Converts to: 3723 seconds
```

7.2   METHOD PARAMETERS

A method is more generally useful if its behavior is determined by the value of one or more parameters. We can transfer values to the called method using *method parameters*. A method with three parameters appears as:

```
def methodName(para1, para2, para3) {
  // Method code goes here
}
```

The method parameters appear as a list of *formal parameter* names enclosed in parentheses following the method name. The parameter names must differ from each other.

To illustrate, let us revisit our method greetings. The first version simply printed a fixed message. We can personalize its behavior if we provide a parameter representing the name of the person we wish to welcome. Here is the new version.

EXAMPLE 06
Method parameters

```
def greetings(name) {
  println "Hello and welcome, ${name}"
}

greetings('John')
```

Running the program produces the output:

```
Hello and welcome, John
```

The actual parameter 'John' initializes the formal parameter name, which the method then prints.

7.3   DEFAULT PARAMETERS

The formal parameters in a method definition can specify *default values*. Where default values are given, these values are used if the caller does not pass them explicitly. Default parameter values are shown as assignments. Where default parameters are introduced in a method definition, then they may only occur after nondefault parameters. That is, default parameters may only be used for parameters at the end of the formal parameter list. Default and nondefault parameters may not be intermixed. For example, in the method:

```
def someMethod(para1, para2 = 0, para3 = 0) {
  // Method code goes here
}
```

the second and third parameters have been given default values.

The someMethod may then be called with one, two, or three actual parameters. If only one actual parameter is supplied, the other two default to zero. If two actual parameters are used, the final parameter is zero. The method call must include at least one actual parameter and at most three actual parameters. An illustration of default parameters is shown in Example 07.

```
def greetings(salutation, name = 'Ken') {
  println "${salutation} ${name}"
}
greetings('Hello', 'John')       // Hello John
greetings('Welcome')             // Welcome Ken
```

EXAMPLE 07
Default parameters

When we execute this script, we see that the second call to method greetings assumes that the name parameter has the default value 'Ken':

```
Hello John
Welcome Ken
```

◆

7.4   METHOD RETURN VALUES

A method can also return a value to its caller. This is achieved with the *return statement* of the form:

```
return expression
```

The statement indicates that control is to return immediately from the method to the caller, and that the value of the expression is to be made available to the caller. This value may be captured with an appropriate assignment.

The return statement is illustrated in Example 08. The method hmsToSeconds obtains a clock time through its parameters, and converts it into seconds. On this occasion, the method then returns the computed value to the caller. The calling code calls this method and prints the returned value.

EXAMPLE 08
Method return
values

```
import console.*

def hmsToSeconds(h, m, s) {
  return (60*h+m)*60+s
}
        // Get the input from the user.
print 'Enter hours to convert: '
def hours=Console.readInteger()
print 'Enter minutes to convert: '
def minutes=Console.readInteger()
print 'Enter seconds to convert: '
def seconds=Console.readInteger()

        // Now call the method.
def total=hmsToSeconds(hours, minutes, seconds)
println "Total number of seconds=${total}"
```

A session running this program could produce:

```
Enter hours to convert: 1
Enter minutes to convert: 2
Enter seconds to convert: 3
Total number of seconds=3723
```

◆

Finally, we note that the return keyword is optional. If it is omitted, then the value of the final statement is the value returned. Example 09 repeats the previous example, with method hmsToSeconds revised.

EXAMPLE 09
Implicit returns

```
import console.*

def hmsToSeconds(h, m, s) {
  def totalSeconds = (60*h+m)*60+s
  totalSeconds
}

        // Get the input from the user.
print 'Enter hours to convert: '
def hours=Console.readInteger()
print 'Enter minutes to convert: '
def minutes=Console.readInteger()
print 'Enter seconds to convert: '
def seconds=Console.readInteger()
```

```
    // Now call the method.
def total = hmsToSeconds(hours, minutes, seconds)
println "Total number of seconds = ${total}"
```

◆

7.5   PARAMETER PASSING

Method parameters in Groovy use a parameter passing strategy known as *pass by value*. This means that the value of the actual parameter is used to initialize the value of the formal parameter. For example, in the previous program the actual parameter hours is used to initialize the formal parameter h in the call to the method hmsToSeconds. A similar arrangement applies to the other two formal parameters.

In Chapter 2 (Section 2.6), we discussed how variables are object references. The variable refers to that part of memory occupied by the object. Figures 2.1 through 2.4 illustrated these concepts. This means that when a method formal parameter is initialized with its corresponding actual parameter, it is actually aliased with it. Figure 2.2 describes this effect. Hence, in Example 09, at the point of call of the hmsToSeconds method, the formal parameter h is an alias for the actual parameter hours.

An implication of this arrangement is that any assignment to a formal parameter within a method body establishes a new object for the formal parameter to refer. Consequently, the corresponding actual parameter is unaffected by this. We demonstrate this in Example 10.

```
def printName(name) {
  println "Name (at entry): ${name}"
  name = 'John'
  println "Name (after assignment): ${name}"
}

def tutor = 'Ken'
printName(tutor)

println "Tutor: ${tutor}"
```

EXAMPLE 10
Parameter aliasing

When we run this program, the output produced is:

```
Name (at entry): Ken
Name (after assignment): John
Tutor: Ken
```

◆

The method printName is defined in terms of a formal parameter name. First, the method prints this value at its point of entry into the method. It then assigns a new String object to this formal parameter variable. Following the consequence of Figure 2.2, the name parameter now references a new String object with the value 'John'. The final print statement in the method reveals that it does indeed have this new value. In the code, the printName method is called with the object ('Ken') referenced by the variable tutor as the actual value. Because this is also referenced by the name parameter at the point of entry to the method, then this is why Ken is the first line printed. After return from the printName method, the program finishes by printing the value of tutor. We see that this is unaffected by the change to the formal parameter.

A consequence of this aliasing of formal and actual parameters is that the swap method, as defined in Example 11, does not produce the effect that we might expect. The definition for method swap suggests that the parameters x and y have their values interchanged. This occurs during the execution of the method but, as has been explained, these changes are not reflected in the corresponding actual parameters. The execution of this program reveals what happens.

```
Enter the first value: 12
Enter the second value: 34
First: 12
Second: 34
```

EXAMPLE 11
Interchange method

```
import console.*

def swap(x, y) {
  def temp = x
  x = y
  y = temp
}

print 'Enter the first value: '
def first = Console.readInteger()
print 'Enter the second value: '
def second = Console.readInteger()

    // Now call the swap method
swap(first, second)
println "First: ${first}"
println "Second: ${second}"
```

◆

7.6   SCOPE

The method processTime in Example 05 has four variables: hours, minutes, seconds, and totalSeconds. These are referred to as *local variables* since they are introduced in this method. Local variables have the method body in which they are defined as their *scope*. This means that they can only be referenced in their scope and have no existence outside of this scope. Hence, elsewhere in the code, these variables have no meaning.

Earlier, we noted that method parameters appear as a list of formal parameter names enclosed in parentheses following the method name. The parameter names must differ from each other and they too represent names that are local to the method. When the method is called, these formal parameters are initialized with the values of the corresponding actual parameters. The formal parameters also behave as local variables with the method body as their scope.

This same mechanism is used for variables defined outside of a method, such as the variables first and second used in Example 11. Appendix B describes how a Groovy script is compiled into a Java class with a run method. Groovy variables defined outside a method using def are effectively local to the generated run method and cannot be referenced by any of our Groovy methods (see Example 12).

Example 12 includes the method printName and the defined variable tutor. From the preceding paragraph, we know that the variable tutor is local to the generated run method and cannot, therefore, be referenced in the method printName (see commented line in the method body).

```
def printName(name) {
  println "Name (at entry): ${name}"
  //name = tutor
  name = 'Ken'
  println "Name (after assignment): ${name}"
}

def tutor = 'Ken'

printName('John')

//println "Name: ${name}"        // ERROR: No such property
```

EXAMPLE 12
Variable scope

When we run this program, we have the output:

```
Name (at entry): John
Name (after assignment): Ken
```

◆

The two lines of output show that the formal parameter name is first initialized with the actual parameter value 'John'. Then it is changed by assignment to the String literal 'Ken'.

Note also the commented line at the end of the listing. The parameter name, like any variables defined within the body of the printName method, has the method body as its scope. Hence, these variables can only be referenced within the method. Any attempt to reference the name variable elsewhere in the code will produce an error as shown.

This scoping rule comes up again in Example 13. At the point at which a variable is defined is irrelevant, they still cannot be referenced in the body of a method.

EXAMPLE 13
Variables and
methods in same
scope

```
def tutor = 'Ken'

def printName(name) {
  println "Name: ${name}"
  //println "Tutor: ${tutor}"
}

printName('John')
```

The program output is, as we would expect, with the tutor variable inaccessible to the method printName (see commented line in the method body).

```
Name: John
```

◆

7.7   COLLECTIONS AS METHOD PARAMETERS AND RETURN VALUES

A Groovy method can accept a collection parameter, such as a List, and return a collection value. In Example 14, the method sort is used to order a List of values. If the second parameter is the Boolean value true, then the List is sorted into ascending order. If the Boolean value is false, then the List is ordered in descending order.

EXAMPLE 14
List parameter
and return

```
def sort(list, ascending = true) {
  list.sort()
  if(ascending == false)
    list = list.reverse()
  return list
}
```

```
def numbers = [10, 5, 3, 6]

assert(sort(numbers, false) == [10, 6, 5, 3])
```

◆

Here, rather than display the result, we have shown the assert keyword by which we make an assertion about the value returned from the sort method. Since the method does indeed produce the list [10, 6, 5, 3], the assertion is true and the program produces no output. Had the assertion been false, then an AssertionError would be raised and reported. A detailed discussion of assertions is given in Chapter 15.

Further aspects of methods, such as recursive methods and statically typed method parameters and return values, are examined in Appendix G.

7.8   EXERCISES

The reader should consult the supporting Appendix G before completing these exercises.

1. Prepare and test a method entitled square that returns the square of its single parameter.

2. Pre-decimal coinage in Great Britain had 12 pence in a shilling and 20 shillings in a pound. Write methods to add and subtract two of these monetary amounts. Both methods will require six parameters. The first three represent the first monetary amount and the remaining three the other amount. Each method should return the value expressed as pence.

3. Write and test a method to determine whether a given time of day is before another. Each time is represented by a triple of the form 11, 59, AM, or 1, 15, PM.

4. The values 1, 2, 4, 8, 16, ... are powers of the value 2. First, develop a method isEven that determines whether its single integer parameter is an even value. Then, using isEven, develop a recursive method isPowerOfTwo that determines if its single parameter is a power of 2.

5. Using (only) the methods head and tail (see Appendix G, Example 02), develop a method length that determines the number of elements in a list given as its parameter.

6. Using (only) the methods head, tail, and cons, develop a method reverse that reverses the elements of a List given as its parameter.

7. Prepare a recursive version of the length method given in Exercise 6.

8. Prepare a recursive method maxList that finds the greatest value in a List of integers.

9. Consider the lists [50, 20, 10, 5, 2, 1] and [25, 10, 5, 1] that represent, respectively, the coins in circulation in the United Kingdom and the United States. Develop methods changeUK and changeUS that, when given a monetary amount (of value 1 to 99 inclusive), deliver a List of the coins from the currency to equal this amount.

10. Develop a method (similar to the preceding exercise) entitled intToRoman that expresses an integer as Roman numerals. The integer value is given as the method parameter. The Roman value is returned as a List of Strings. As a simplification, the value 1984 can be expressed as MDCCC-CLXXXIIII.

11. A list of items, each comprising a list of pairs, can be used to represent a directed graph. The list graph = [['a', 'b'], ['a', 'c'], ['a', 'd'], ['b', 'e'], ['c', 'f'], ['d', 'e'], ['e', 'f'], ['e', 'g']] represents a graph in which node a connects to b, c, and d, node b connects to e, etc. Develop the method successors(node, graph), which returns a list of the successor nodes from node in graph.

12. Many graph algorithms work by following edges, keeping track of nodes visited so that one is not visited more than once. In a depth-first search, the subgraph reachable from the current node is fully explored before other nodes are visited. Develop the method depthFirst(node, graph) to return the list representing the depth-first search from node in graph.

13. Develop a method entitled explode that transforms a string into a List of Strings of size one. The method signature is:

```
def explode(str) { ... }
```

Now, develop the complementary method implode, which accepts a list of Strings and concatenates them into a single String:

```
def implode(strList) { ... }
```

Using these two methods, develop the method reverseString for reversing the characters of a String parameter:

```
def reverseString(str) { ... }
```

Finally, develop the method isPalindrome to return the boolean true if the single String parameter is palindromic, that is, reads the same forward and backward:

```
def isPalindrome(str) { .. }
```

14. Using the methods explode and implode from Exercise 13, develop a method remove that removes all occurrences of a given character from a string:

```
def remove(ch, str) { ... }
```

15. The greatest common divisor of two integers can be determined from Euclid's algorithm. It is defined recursively as:

```
gcd(n, m) = n                    if n == m
gcd(n, m) = gcd(n, m−n)   if n < m
gcd(n, m) = gcd(n−m, m)   otherwise
```

Implement a method to realize this and show that gcd(18, 27) is 9.

16. The Ackermann function is defined recursively as:

```
ackermann(n, m) = 1+m                                     if n == 0
ackermann(n, m) = ackermann(n−1, 1)                       if m == 0
ackermann(n, m) = ackermann(n−1, ackermann(n, m−1))       otherwise
```

Implement a method for this and show that ackermann(3, 3) is 61.

17. Implement the Quicksort algorithm to sort a List of values. Perform a Google search for its implementation.

FLOW OF CONTROL

The execution of a program statement causes an action to be performed. The programs we have developed execute one statement after another in a sequential manner. Because of this execution ordering of the statements, we describe the program logic as *sequential*. We can also create abstract actions with method definitions and then treat them as if they, likewise, were simple statements through their method calls. The statements we have explored include the assignment, input/output, and method calls.

Additionally, statements are provided in Groovy to alter the flow of control in a program's logic. They are then classified into one of three program *flow of control* structures:

- sequence

- selection

- iteration

8.1 WHILE STATEMENT

The fundamental iteration clause is the *while statement*. The syntax of the while statement is:

```
while(condition) {
    statement #1
    statement #2
    ...
}
```

The while statement is executed by first evaluating the *condition* expression (a Boolean value), and if the result is true, then the statements are executed. The entire process is repeated, starting once again with reevaluation of the condition. This loop continues until the condition evaluates to false. When the condition is false, the loop terminates. The program logic then continues with the statement immediately following the while statement. The group of statements is known as a *compound statement* or *block*.

Where only one statement is to be controlled by a while loop, the single statement may be presented as:

```
while(condition)
    statement
```

The program shown as Example 01 prints the values from 1 to 10 inclusive. Each iteration through the loop prints the current value of the variable count, and then increments it. The count is first set to the start value 1. The condition in the while statement specifies that the loop continues provided the count does not exceed the value of LIMIT.

EXAMPLE 01
while statement

```
               // Set limit and counter
def LIMIT = 10
def count = 1

println 'Start'

while(count <= LIMIT) {
  println "count: ${count}"
  count++
}

println 'Done'
```

The program's output is:

```
Start
count: 1
count: 2
count: 3
count: 4
count: 5
count: 6
count: 7
count: 8
count: 9
count: 10
Done
```

◆

Conventionally, we denote variables with fixed values by capitalization. They are generally known as *symbolic constants*. The value in defining such variables is that they document a given value with their name. Further, the definition occurs only once in the code, and only a single change is required to modify that value.

A typical use for a while statement is to loop over a series of statements an indeterminate number of times. A statement in the loop usually affects the condition that controls the looping. Example 02 demonstrates a program that reads an unknown number of positive integers, forming a running total for their values. The user enters any negative number to end the input loop.

```
import console.*

    // Running total
def sum = 0

print 'Enter first value: '
def data = Console.readInteger()
while(data >= 0) {
  sum += data
  print 'Enter next value: '
  data = Console.readInteger()
}

println "The sum is: ${sum}"
```

EXAMPLE 02
Sum of a series of positive integers

A sample session with this program is:

```
Enter first value: 1
Enter next value: 2
Enter next value: 3
Enter next value: 4
Enter next value: -1
The sum is: 10
```

◆

Note that in this example, if the first input value is negative, then the loop will never be obeyed and the program will finish with a zero sum. Because of this, a while statement is often described as causing the statement(s) under its control to be obeyed *zero or more times*.

8.2 FOR STATEMENT

The *for statement* in Groovy can be used to iterate over a Range, a collection (List, Map, or array; see Chapter 4 and Appendix E) or a String.

```
for(variable in range) {    for(variable in collection) {    for(variable in string) {
    statement #1                statement #1                    statement #1
    statement #2                statement #2                    statement #2
    ...                         ...                             ...
}                           }                               }
```

Example 03 repeats the first example in this chapter. Using a for statement is a more appropriate looping construct to use when the number of times to repeat the logic is known.

EXAMPLE 03
for statement

```
def LIMIT = 10

println 'Start'

for(count in 1..LIMIT)
    println "count: ${count}"

println 'Done'
```

◆

The next example demonstrates a for statement applied to a List.

EXAMPLE 04
Looping through a
List

```
// List
println 'Start'

for(count in [11, 12, 13, 14])
    println "count: ${count}"

println 'Done'
```

The output from this program is:

```
Start
count: 11
count: 12
count: 13
count: 14
Done#
```

◆

We can also iterate through the elements of a Map. In Example 05, the total age of the employees is recorded in a Map. It is worth noting that the loop variable staffEntry. Since we are looping through all the entries in a `Map`, then every item is a `Map.Entry` (see JDK documentation) object that references both the key and value. Hence, in the loop, we refer to the staff member's age with `staffEntry.value`.

```
        // Staff name and age
    def staff = ['Ken' : 21, 'John' : 25, 'Sally' : 22]

    def totalAge = 0
    for(staffEntry in staff)
        totalAge += staffEntry.value

    println "Total staff age: ${totalAge}"
```

EXAMPLE 05
Looping through a
Map

The output produced is:

```
    Total staff age: 68
```

◆

Finally, we show how we can also iterate through the characters that compose a `String`. In Example 06, name is processed character by character and inserted into a `List`.

```
    def name = 'Kenneth'
    def listOfCharacters = []

    for(letter in name)
        listOfCharacters << letter

    println "listOfCharacters: ${listOfCharacters}"
```

EXAMPLE 06
Looping through a
String

The output is:

```
    listOfCharacters: ["K", "e", "n", "n", "e", "t", "h"]
```

◆

8.3   IF STATEMENT

The general form of the *if statement* is:

```
    if(condition) {
        statement #1a
        statement #1b
        ...
    } else {
```

```
                statement #2a
                statement #2b
            ...
        }
```

where if and else are reserved words. If the *condition* evaluates to the Boolean value true, then the compound statement starting with statement #1a is executed and control is then passed to the statement following the if statement. If the value of the condition is false, then the compound statement starting with statement #2a is executed and again control continues with the statement after the if statement. As earlier, a single statement may replace either of the compound statements.

An if statement offers a means of selecting one of two distinct logical paths through a program. Sometimes, we wish to select whether to execute some program code. We achieve this through a shortened version of the if statement:

```
        if(condition) {
            statement #1
            statement #2
            ...
        }
```

If the condition evaluates to true, then the compound statement is executed and the program continues with the statement following the if statement. If the condition evaluates to false, then the compound statement is ignored and the program continues with the next statement. As before, a single statement may replace the compound statement.

In Example 07, the program reads two integers and prints them in ascending order. This is achieved by using an if-else statement to select the correct print statement:

EXAMPLE 07
A simple if
statement

```
import console.*

print 'Enter first value: '
def first = Console.readInteger()
print 'Enter second value: '
def second = Console.readInteger()

if(first < second)
    println "${first} and ${second}"
else
    println "${second} and ${first}"
```

An interactive session with this program might produce:

```
Enter first value: 34
Enter second value: 12
12 and 34
```

◆

Example 08 repeats this exercise. This time, the program employs the shortened version of the if statement. If the condition determines that the first value is greater than the second, then the values are interchanged.

```
import console.*

print 'Enter first value: '
def first = Console.readInteger()
print 'Enter second value: '
def second = Console.readInteger()

    // Exchange the order
if(first > second) {
    def temp = first
    first = second
    second = temp
}

println "${first} and ${second}"
```

EXAMPLE 08
Interchange two values

An execution of this program produces:

```
Enter first value: 34
Enter second value: 12
12 and 34
```

◆

Various combinations of if statements are allowed. For example, the statement associated with the else clause may be another if statement. This can be repeated any number of times. Such a construct is used to select from among a number of logical paths through the code. To illustrate this, consider a program fragment to read an examination score (any value from 0 to 100, inclusive) and assign a letter grade. The grading scheme that applies is shown by:

Score	Grade
70–100	A
60–69	B
50–59	C
40–49	D
0–39	E

A chain of if–else statements can then describe the necessary processing:

```
if(score>=70)
    grade='A'
else if(score>=60)
    grade='B'
else if(score>=50)
    grade='C'
else if(score>=40)
    grade='D'
else
    grade='E'
```

8.4 SWITCH STATEMENT

The if–else statement chain in the last section occurs so frequently that a special statement exists for this purpose. This is called the *switch statement* and its form is:

```
switch(expression) {
  case expression #1:
    statement #1a
    statement #1b
    ...
  case expression #2:
    statement #2a
    statement #2b
    ...


    ...
  case expression #N:
    statement #Na
    statement #Nb
    ...
  default:
    statement #Da
    statement #Db
    ...


}
```

where switch, case, and default are Groovy keywords. The default clause and its statements are optional. The control expression enclosed in parentheses is evaluated. This value is then compared, in turn, against each of the *case expressions*. If a match is made against one of the case expressions, then all statements from that case clause through to the end of the switch are executed. If no match is made, then the default statements are obeyed if a default clause is present. Example 09 illustrates the basic behavior of a switch statement.

```
def n = 2
switch(n) {
    case 1: println 'One'
    case 2: println 'Two'
    case 3: println 'Three'
    case 4: println 'Four'
    default: println 'Default'
}
println 'End of switch'
```

EXAMPLE 09
Basic switch
behavior

The control expression is simply the value of the variable n. When evaluated, it is compared, in turn, to the value of the case expressions. A match is found at case 2 and the output from the code is:

```
Two
Three
Four
Default
End of switch
```

◆

Normally, the statements of a case label are intended to be mutually exclusive. Having selected the matching case expression, we normally wish for only the corresponding statements to be obeyed, and then control passed to the statement following the switch statement. We achieve this with a *break statement* that, in the context of a switch statement, immediately terminates it and continues with the statement after the switch. Example 10 illustrates.

```
def n = 2
switch(n) {
  case 1:
    println 'One'
    break
  case 2:
    println 'Two'
    break
```

EXAMPLE 10
switch and
break statement

```
          case 3:
            println 'Three'
            break
          case 4:
            println 'Four'
            break
          default:
            println 'Default'
            break
        }
        println 'End of switch'
```

Running this program produces:

```
Two
End of switch
```

◆

A switch statement can be used as a replacement for the chain of if statements shown at the end of the previous section. The code in Example 11 shows a switch statement based on the value of the examination score. Each case clause matches against a range representing the grade. This time no default has been used.

EXAMPLE 11
switch and a range

```
import console.*

print 'Enter examination score: '
def score = Console.readInteger()
def grade

switch(score) {
  case 70..100:
    grade = 'A'
    break
  case 60..69:
    grade = 'B'
    break
  case 50..59:
    grade = 'C'
    break
  case 40..49:
    grade = 'D'
    break
```

```
    case 0..39:
      grade = 'E'
      break
}

println "Score: ${score}; grade: ${grade}"
```

Running this program produces:

```
Enter examination score: 50
Score: 50; grade: C
```

◆

The case expressions have been shown as an integer literal or a Range of integer values. In fact, the case expression might be a String, List, regular expression, or object of some class (see Chapter 12). Example 12 shows a switch statement in which the case expressions are Lists. A match is found if the value of the control expression is a member of the collection.

```
def number = 32

switch(number) {
  case [21, 22, 23, 24] :
    println 'number is a twenty something'
    break
  case [31, 32, 33, 34] :
    println 'number is a thirty something'
    break
  default :
    println 'number type is unknown'
    break
}
```

EXAMPLE 12
List case expressions

The output is:

```
number is a thirty something
```

◆

In Example 13, we show a switch statement in which the case expressions are regular expressions. Again, a match is made against the given patterns.

<table>
<tr><td>

EXAMPLE 13
Regular
expressions for
`case` labels

</td><td>

```
def number = '1234'

switch(number) {
  case ~'[0-9]{3}-[0-9]{4}' :
    println 'number is a telephone number'
    break
  case ~'[0-9]{4}' :
    println 'number is a 4-digit sequence'
    break
  default :
    println 'number type is unknown'
    break
}
```

</td></tr>
</table>

The output is:

```
number is a 4-digit sequence
```

◆

8.5   BREAK STATEMENT

The *break statement* is used to alter the flow of control inside loops and `switch` statements. We have already seen the break statement in action in conjunction with the `switch` statement. The break statement can also be used with `while` and `for` statements. Executing a break statement with any of these looping constructs causes immediate termination of the innermost enclosing loop.

Example 14 illustrates this idea. The program forms the sum of at most 100 positive integer values. The user provides the values as input. If, at any point, a negative value is entered, then the `for` loop immediately terminates and the value of the summation is printed.

<table>
<tr><td>

EXAMPLE 14
`for` loop and
`break` statement

</td><td>

```
import console.*

def MAX = 100
def sum = 0

for(k in 1..MAX) {
    print 'Enter next value: '
    def value = Console.readInteger()
    if(value < 0)
        break
```

</td></tr>
</table>

```
        sum += value
    }
    println "sum: ${sum}"
```

Running the program produces:

```
Enter next value: 11
Enter next value: 12
Enter next value: 13
Enter next value: 14
Enter next value: -1
sum: 50
```

◆

8.6 CONTINUE STATEMENT

The *continue statement* complements the break statement. Its use is restricted to while and for loops. When a continue statement is executed, control is immediately passed to the test condition of the nearest enclosing loop to determine whether the loop should continue. All subsequent statements in the body of the loop are ignored for that particular loop iteration.

In Example 15, the program finds the sum of 10 integers input by the user. If any negative value is entered, it is not included as part of the sum. It does, however, count as an input value.

```
import console.*

def MAX = 10
def sum = 0

for(k in 1..MAX) {
    print 'Enter next value: '
    def value = Console.readInteger()
    if(value < 0)
        continue
    sum += value
}

println "sum: ${sum}"
```

EXAMPLE 15
for loop and
continue
statement

An execution of the program is:

```
Enter next value: 1
Enter next value: 2
Enter next value: 3
Enter next value: 4
Enter next value: –5
Enter next value: –6
Enter next value: –7
Enter next value: 8
Enter next value: 9
Enter next value: 10
sum: 37
```

◆

8.7   EXERCISES

1. Write a method entitled quotient that finds the quotient of two positive integers using only the operations of additions and subtraction.

2. Write a program that reads a single positive integer data value and displays each individual digit from that value as a word. For example, the input value 932 should display:

    ```
    932: nine three two
    ```

3. Write a program that accepts a (24-hour) clock time expressed in hours, minutes, and seconds, and verbalizes the time as suggested by the following values:

    ```
    09:10:00     ten past nine
    10:45:00     quarter to eleven
    11:15:00     quarter past eleven
    17:30:00     half past five
    19:50:00     ten to eight
    06:12:29     just after ten past six
    06:12:30     just before quarter past six
    00:17:29     just after quarter past midnight
    ```

4. The Fibonacci sequence is defined by the following rule: The first two values in the sequence are both 1. Every subsequent value is the sum of the two preceding values. If fib(n) denotes the nth value in the sequence, then:

    $$fib(1) = 1$$
    $$fib(2) = 1$$
    $$fib(n) = fib(n–1) + fib(n–2)$$

Develop a method that implements fib(n), then exercise it by printing a table for the first 10 values from this sequence.

5. Rewrite the factorial method given in Appendix G, this time using a simple loop.

6. Given a Map that represents the staff and their telephone numbers, such as:

```
def staff=['Ken' : 2745, 'John' : 2746, 'Sally' : 2742]
```

develop a program to produce an alphabetical List of the staff with their telephone numbers.

7. To calculate the day of the week for a given date, Zeller's congruence can be used. The algorithm computes for any valid date an integer in the range of 0 to 6 inclusive, with 0 representing Sunday, 1 representing Monday, etc. The formula is:

$$Z = \left[\frac{26m-2}{10} + k + D + \frac{D}{4} + \frac{C}{4} - 2C + 77 \right] \bmod 7$$

In the formula:
   D = the year in the century
   C = the century
   k = the day of the month
   m = month number, with January and February taken as months 11 and 12 of the preceding year, and March is month 1, April is 2, ..., and December is 10.

Thus, for the date 16/11/2005, D = 5, C = 20, k = 16, and m = 9.
   Develop a program to read a date in the form DD/MM/YYYY and verbalize it. For example, the date 16/11/2005 is to produce the output Wednesday, 16 November 2005.

8. A playing card is represented by shorthand such as QS for the queen of spades, 10S for the ten of spades. The rank is A, 2...10, J, Q, or K. The suit is D, C, H, or S. Develop a program to read the shorthand, such as QS, and produce the longhand queen of spades.

9. Exercise 10 in Chapter 7 developed a method intToRoman which converted an Arabic value to its Roman equivalent. Develop its counterpart romanToInt.

10. Use the `intToRoman` and `romanToInt` methods to develop methods `addRoman` and `subtractRoman`. Both new methods receive two `String` parameters representing Roman values and return a `String` representing the result (also Roman). Develop an application to receive input such as VIIII + II.

11. Easter Sunday is the Sunday on or after March 21st. It is determined by the formula (integer arithmetic):

c = year / 100
n = year − 19 * (year / 19)
k = (c − 17) / 25
i = c − c / 4 − (c − k) / 3 + 19 * n + 15
i = i − 30 * (i / 30)
i = i − (i / 28) * (1 − i / 28) * (29 / (i + 1)) * ((21 − n) / 11)
j = year + year / 4 + i + 2 − c + c / 4
j = j − 7 * (j / 7)
l = i − j
m = 3 + (l + 40) / 44
d = l + 28 − 31 * m / 4

If the value for d exceeds 20, then Easter occurs in March; otherwise, it is in April.

12. The Julian date value is the number of days that have elapsed since some distant epoch date. For example, if today were Julian value 1000000, then tomorrow would be Julian value 1000001. A method to calculate the Julian value for a date is:

```
def julian(day, month, year) {
    def mm = month
    def yy = year

    if (mm > 2)
        mm -= 3
    else {
        mm += 9
        yy--
    }

    def cent = yy.intdiv(100)
    def yr = yy % 100

    return ((146097 * cent).intdiv(4)) + ((1461 * yr).intdiv(4))
    + (153 * mm + 2).intdiv(5) + day + 1721119

}
```

Develop a program to read a date in the form MM/YYYY and produce a calendar for that month. For example, the input value 11/2005 would produce:

November 2005

S	M	T	W	T	F	S
		1	2	3	4	5
6	7	8	9	10	11	12
13	14	15	16	17	18	19
20	21	22	23	24	25	26
27	28	29	30			

13. The Groovy language does not currently support the do statement as found in Java. Develop the Groovy program code that would realize a do statement.

CLOSURES

Groovy *closures* are a powerful way of representing blocks of executable code. Since closures are objects, they can be passed around as method parameters, for example. Because closures are code blocks, they can also be executed when required. Like methods, closures can be defined in terms of one or more parameters. A significant characteristic of closures is that they can access state information. This means that any variables in scope when the closure is defined can be used and modified by the closure.

One of the most common uses for a closure is processing a collection. For example, we can iterate across the elements of a collection and apply the closure to them. Groovy's closures are one feature that make developing scripts so easy.

This chapter introduces the general concepts of closures. Appendix H explores further features of closures, and Appendix J considers some advanced topics.

9.1   CLOSURES

The syntax for defining a closure is:

```
{comma-separated-formal-parameter-list -> statement-list}
```

If no formal parameters are required, then the parameter List and the -> separator are omitted. Here is a simple example of a closure with no parameters.

```
def clos={println 'Hello world'}
clos.call()
```

EXAMPLE 01

A closure and its invocation

Here, the closure has no parameters and consists of a single `println` statement. The closure is referenced by the identifier `clos`. The code block referenced by this identifier can be executed with the *call statement*, as shown in the example. The result is to print the message:

```
Hello world
```

◆

By introducing formal parameters into closure definitions, we can make them more useful, as we did with methods. Here is the same closure with the name of the individual receiving the greeting now provided as a parameter:

EXAMPLE 02
Parameterized
closure

```
def clos = {param -> println "Hello ${param}"}

clos.call('world')          // actual argument is 'world'
clos.call('again')          // actual argument is 'again'
clos('shortcut')            // abbreviated form
```

When we execute this script, the output produced is:

```
Hello world
Hello again
Hello shortcut
```

◆

Observe the third invocation in which the `call` has been omitted.

The next illustration repeats the previous example and produces the same result, but shows that an implicit single parameter referred to as `it` can be used.

EXAMPLE 03
Implicit single
parameter

```
def clos = {println "Hello ${it}"}

clos.call('world')
clos.call('again')

clos('shortcut')
```

We noted in the introduction that state information could be accessed by closures. More formally, closures can refer to variables at the time the closure is defined. Consider Example 04. Here, the variable `greeting` defines the salutation. This variable is in scope before `clos` is defined and, hence, its value can be used when the closure is called. Initially, the variable greeting has the value 'Hello'.

EXAMPLE 04
Closures and
enclosing scope

```
def greeting = 'Hello'
def clos = {param -> println "${greeting} ${param}"}
clos.call('world')

                // Now show that changes to this variable change the closure.
greeting = 'Welcome'
clos.call('world')
```

Before the second call to the closure, the value of the variable greeting is changed. This is reflected in the output produced by running the program:

```
Hello world
Welcome world
```

In the next example, we augment the previous code with a method entitled demo. It is passed a single argument clo, representing a closure. The method calls this closure with the argument 'Ken'. The method also introduces a new scope in which another variable greeting is bound to the value 'Bonjour'. This additional call generates the output:

```
Welcome Ken
```

and reveals that the state accessible to a closure is that in existence at the time the closure is defined and not when it is called. Here is the illustration:

EXAMPLE 05
Effect of scope

```
def greeting = 'Hello'
def clos = {param -> println "${greeting} ${param}"}
clos.call('world')

// Now show that changes to this variable change the closure.
greeting = 'Welcome'
clos.call('world')

def demo(clo) {
    def greeting = 'Bonjour'            // does not affect closure
    clo.call('Ken')
}

demo(clos)
```

The resulting output is:

```
Hello world
Welcome world
Welcome Ken
```

When calling methods that take a closure as the final parameter, Groovy offers a simplification that makes the code somewhat easier to read. In the last example, the method demo was called and the actual parameter was the closure. Where the final parameter to a method call is a closure, then it can be removed from the list of actual parameters and placed immediately after the closing parenthesis. Hence, the call to method demo could appear as either of the following:

```
demo(clos)        // closure parameter within the parentheses
demo() clos       // parameter removed from parentheses
```

This is demonstrated in the following example, where the closure is removed from the actual parameters in the call to demo and its empty parameter list is deleted.

EXAMPLE 06
Leave the closure
outside of the
actual argument
list

```
def greeting = 'Hello'
def clos = {param -> println "${greeting} ${param}"}

def demo(clo) {
    def greeting = 'Bonjour'                 // does not affect closure
    clo.call('Ken')
}

//demo() clos                                // 1: closure reference; include parentheses
demo() {param -> println "Welcome ${param}"} // 2: closure literal; include parentheses

demo clos                                    // 3: closure reference; omit parentheses
demo {param -> println "Welcome ${param}"}   // 4: closure literal; omit parentheses
```

The output is:

```
Welcome Ken
Hello Ken
Welcome Ken
```

◆

The final two program statements (numbered 3 and 4 in the comments) call the method demo and pass a closure as the actual parameter. The first of these two method calls uses a reference to a closure object while the second uses a closure literal. In both illustrations, the parentheses for the method call are omitted.

Observe also the statements numbered 1 and 2 in the comments. The second uses a closure literal and is acceptable to Groovy. However, the first uses a closure reference and is not successfully identified as part of the statement. This causes an execution error that reports that the method call is passed a null parameter.

More usually, closures are applied to collections (see Section 9.2). Effectively, we iterate over the elements in the collection and apply a closure to each element. For example, all numeric types support a method entitled upto. The signature for this method is:

```
void upto(Number to, Closure closure)
```

The programmer might call the method as in:

```
1.upto(10) {...}
```

This would call the closure literal 10 times. If the closure has a formal parameter p:

```
1.upto(10) {p -> ...}
```

then on each iteration, the parameter takes the value 1, 2, ..., 10.

The method upto iterates from the numeric value of the recipient number (1) to the given parameter value (10), calling the closure on each occasion. We can usefully employ this method to provide a way to compute the factorial of some value. We use upto to generate the series of integers 1, 2, 3, ... to a given limit. For each value, we compute the partial factorial until the series is complete. Here is the code:

EXAMPLE 07
Factorial with
closures

```
def factorial = 1
1.upto(5) {num -> factorial *= num}
println "Factorial(5): ${factorial}"
```

Running the script produces the output:

```
Factorial(5): 120
```

◆

9.2   CLOSURES, COLLECTIONS, AND STRINGS

Several List, Map, and String methods accept a closure as an argument (see also Appendix H). It is this combination of closures and collections that provides Groovy with some elegant solutions to common programming problems. For example, the each method with the signature:

```
void each(Closure closure)
```

is used to iterate through a List, Map, or String and apply the closure on every element. Example 08 presents a number of simple examples of the each method and a closure.

EXAMPLE 08
Illustrations of
the method **each**
and a closure

```
[1, 2, 3, 4].each {println it}

['Ken' : 21, 'John' : 22, 'Sally' : 25].each {println it}
['Ken' : 21, 'John' : 22, 'Sally' : 25].each {println "${it.key} maps to: ${it.value}"}

'Ken'.each {println it}
```

The first example prints the values 1, 2, 3, and 4 on separate lines. The final example prints each letter of the name on a separate line. In the second illustration, the keys and values from the Map are displayed in the style Ken = 21. The third demonstration separately accesses the key and value from the Map element and prints them as Ken maps to: 21. The output is:

```
1
2
3
4
Sally = 25
John = 22
Ken = 21
Sally maps to: 25
John maps to: 22
Ken maps to: 21
K
e
n
```

Often, we may wish to iterate across the members of a collection and apply some logic only when the element meets some criterion. This is readily handled with a conditional statement in the closure.

```
            // even values only
[1, 2, 3, 4].each {num -> if(num % 2 == 0) println num}

            // staff at least 25 years old
['Ken' : 21, 'John' : 22, 'Sally' : 25].each {staff ->
    if(staff.value >= 25) println staff.key
}
['Ken' : 21, 'John' : 22, 'Sally' : 25].each {staffName, staffAge ->
    if(staffAge >= 25) println staffName
}
            // only lowercase letters
'Ken'.each {letter -> if(letter >= 'a' && letter <= 'z') println letter}
```

EXAMPLE 09
Conditional
elements

The output from the script is:

```
2
4
Sally
Sally
e
n
```

Observe the two examples to find those staff members who are at least 25 years old. In both cases, we iterate over a Map and apply a closure to each member of the Map. In the first, the closure parameter staff is a Map.Entry that includes the key and the value pair. Hence, to check the age, we use staff.value in the Boolean expression. In the second example, the closure has two parameters representing the two Map.Entry elements, namely, the key (staffName) and the value (staffAge).

The find method finds the first value in a collection that matches some criterion. The condition to be met by the collection element is specified in the closure that must be some Boolean expression. The find method returns the first value found or null if no such element exists. The signature for this method is:

```
Object find(Closure closure)
```

EXAMPLE 10
Illustrations of
the find method
and closures

```
// locate the value 7
def value=[1, 3, 5, 7, 9].find {element->element>6}
println "Found: ${value}"

// locate no value (null)
value=[1, 3, 5, 7, 9].find {element->element>10}
println "Found: ${value}"

// first staff member over 21
value=['Ken' : 21, 'John' : 22, 'Sally' : 25].find {staff->staff.value>21}
println "Found: ${value}"
```

Output from this script is:

```
Found: 7
Found: null
Found: Sally=25
```

Notice that when we apply find to a Map, the return object is a Map.Entry. It would not, in this case, be appropriate to use a pair of parameters for the key and the value, as in:

```
value=['Ken' : 21, 'John' : 22, 'Sally' : 25].find {key, value -> value > 21}
```

since we are then not able to specify what is returned, the key or the value.

Whereas the find method locates the first item (if any) in a collection that meets some criterion, the method findAll finds all the elements, returning them as a List. The signature for this method is:

```
List findAll(Closure closure)
```

It finds all values in the receiving object matching the closure condition. Example 11 gives some examples of using findAll. The second illustration reveals how simple closures can be combined to implement more complex algorithms. The merit of this approach is that each closure is relatively simple to express.

```
               // Find all items that exceed the value 6
def values = [1, 3, 5, 7, 9].findAll {element -> element > 6}
values.each {println it}
```

EXAMPLE 11
Illustrations of
the method
findAll and
closures

```
               // Combine closures by piping the result of findAll
               // through to each
[1, 3, 5, 7, 9].findAll {element -> element > 6}.each {println it}
```

```
               // Apply a findAll to a Map finding all staff over the age of 24
values = ['Ken' : 21, 'John' : 22, 'Sally' : 25].findAll {staff -> staff.value > 24}
values.each {println it}
```

Again, applying findAll to a Map delivers a List of Map.Entry elements. This is shown by the final line of output from the script:

```
7
9
7
9
Sally = 25
```

Two other related methods that take a closure argument are any and every. Method any iterates through each element of a collection checking whether a Boolean predicate is valid for at least one element. The predicate is provided by the closure. Method every checks whether a predicate (a closure that returns a true or false value) is valid for all the elements of a collection, returning true if they do so and false otherwise. The signatures for these methods are:

```
boolean any(Closure closure)
boolean every(Closure closure)
```

◆

Example 12 shows some representative examples.

```
               // Any number over 12?
def anyElement = [11, 12, 13, 14].any {element -> element > 12}
println "anyElement: ${anyElement}"
```

EXAMPLE 12
Examples of
methods any and
every

```
               // Are all values over 10?
def allElements = [11, 12, 13, 14].every {element -> element > 10}
println "allElements: ${allElements}"
```

```
               // Any staff member over the age of 30?
def anyStaff = ['Ken' : 21, 'John' : 22, 'Sally' : 25].any {staff -> staff.value > 30}
println "anyStaff: ${anyStaff}"
```

When we run this script, we get the output:

```
anyElement: true
allElements: true
anyStaff: false
```

◆

Two further methods that we wish to consider are `collect` and `inject`. Again, both have a closure as a parameter. The method `collect` iterates through a collection, converting each element into a new value using the closure as the transformer. The method also returns a new `List` of the transformed values. It has the signature:

```
List collect(Closure closure)
```

Example 13 shows simple uses for this method.

EXAMPLE 13
Sample uses of
`collect` method

```
              // Square of the values
def list = [1, 2, 3, 4].collect {element -> return element * element}
println "list: ${list}"

              // Square of the values (no explicit return)
list = [1, 2, 3, 4].collect {element -> element * element}
println "list: ${list}"

              // Double of the values (no explicit return)
list = (0..<5).collect {element -> 2 * element}
println "list: ${list}"

              // Age by one year
def staff = ['Ken' : 21, 'John' : 22, 'Sally' : 25]
list = staff.collect {entry -> ++entry.value}
def olderStaff = staff.collect {entry -> ++entry.value; return entry}
println "staff: ${staff}"
println "list: ${list}"
println "olderStaff: ${olderStaff}"
```

Running this, we get the output:

```
list: [1, 4, 9, 16]
list: [1, 4, 9, 16]
list: [0, 2, 4, 6, 8]
staff: [Sally:27, John:24, Ken:23]
list: [26, 23, 22]
olderStaff: [Sally=27, John=24, Ken=23]
```

The third example of method `collect` is applied to a Range. This is permissible since the Range interface extends the List interface and can, therefore, be used in place of Lists. Observe also the illustration that iterates across the `staff` collection, increasing the age by 1. The returned value is a List of the new age values from the Map. The recipient Map object referred to as `staff` is also modified by the closure. The final example that assigns to `oldStaff` builds a List of Map.Entrys, with the age increased again.

◆

Example 14 further illustrates the `collect` method. Note the method `map`, which applies the closure parameter to the `collect` method over the list parameter. The `map` method is used for doubling, tripling, and for finding those that are even-valued elements of a list of integers. We shall find further uses for this map algorithm (see Appendix J).

```
                // A series of closures
    def doubles = {item -> 2 * item}
    def triples = {item -> 3 * item}
    def isEven = {item -> (item % 2 == 0)}

            // A method to apply a closure to a list
    def map(clos, list) {
        return list.collect(clos)
    }
            // Uses:
    println "Doubling: ${map(doubles, [1, 2, 3, 4])}"
    println "Tripling: ${map(triples, [1, 2, 3, 4])}"
    println "Evens: ${map(isEven, [1, 2, 3, 4])}"
```

EXAMPLE 14
Further examples
of `collect`

The output from the script is:

```
    Doubling: [2, 4, 6, 8]
    Tripling: [3, 6, 9, 12]
    Evens: [false, true, false, true]
```

◆

The final method that we explore in this section is entitled `inject`. This method iterates through a List, passing the initial value to the closure together with the first element, and then passing into the next iteration the computed value from the previous closure and the next element of the collection, and so on. Here is its signature:

```
    Object inject(Object value, Closure closure)
```

Here are three examples of finding the factorial of 5.

EXAMPLE 15

Factorial of 5

```
// Direct usage
def factorial = [2, 3, 4, 5].inject(1) {previous, element -> previous * element}
println "Factorial(5): ${factorial}"

// Equivalence
def fact = 1
[2, 3, 4, 5].each {number -> fact *= number}
println "fact: ${fact}"

// Named list
def list = [2, 3, 4, 5]
factorial = list.inject(1) {previous, element -> previous * element}
println "Factorial(5): ${factorial}"

// Named list and closure
list = [2, 3, 4, 5]
def closure = {previous, element -> previous * element}
factorial = list.inject(1, closure)
println "Factorial(5): ${factorial}"
```

The output is:

```
Factorial(5): 120
Fact: 120
Factorial(5): 120
Factorial(5): 120
```

◆

The segment of code that uses the variable fact aims to show that the result of method inject can be achieved using an each iterator method. First, the variable fact is assigned the value of the first parameter to inject (here, 1). Then, we iterate through each element of the List. For the first value (number = 2), the closure evaluates fact *= number, that is, fact = 1 * 2 = 2. For the second value (number = 3), the closure again evaluates fact *= number, that is, fact = 2 * 3 = 6, and so on.

9.3   OTHER CLOSURE FEATURES

Since a closure is an Object, it can be a parameter to a method. In Example 16, the simple filter method expects two parameters, a List and a closure. The method finds all those elements of the list that satisfy the condition specified by the closure using, of course, method findAll. The program then demonstrates two uses for the method.

```
              // Find those items that qualify
  def filter(list, predicate) {
      return list.findAll(predicate)
  }

              // Two predicate closure
  def isEven = {x -> return (x % 2 == 0)}
  def isOdd = {x -> return ! isEven(x)}

  def table = [11, 12, 13, 14]

              // Apply filter
  def evens = filter(table, isEven)
  println "evens: ${evens}"

  def odds = filter(table, isOdd)
  println "odds: ${odds}"
```

EXAMPLE 16
Closures as method
parameters

The output reveals that the variable evens is a List of all the even-valued integers from the table.

```
  evens: [12, 14]
  odds: [11, 13]
```

Closures can also be parameters to other closures. Example 17 introduces a closure takeWhile that delivers those elements from the beginning of a List that meets some criteria defined by the closure parameter named predicate.

```
              // Find initial list that conforms to predicate
  def takeWhile = {predicate, list ->
      def result = []
      for(element in list) {
          if(predicate(element)) {
              result << element
          } else
              return result
      }
      return result
  }

              // Two predicate closures
  def isEven = {x -> return (x % 2 == 0)}
  def isOdd = {x -> return ! isEven(x)}

  def table1 = [12, 14, 15, 18]
  def table2 = [11, 13, 15, 16, 18]

              // Apply takeWhile
  def evens = takeWhile.call(isEven, table1)
  println "evens: ${evens}"
```

EXAMPLE 17
Closures
as parameters to
closures

```
def odds = takeWhile(isOdd, table2)
println "odds: ${odds}"
```

The variable evens has the even-valued integer prefix from table1. This is shown by the program output:

```
evens: [12, 14]
odds: [11, 13, 15]
```

◆

In Example 18, the method multiply is defined. It accepts a single parameter and returns a closure. This closure multiplies two values, one of which is pre-set to the value of the method parameter. The variable twice is now a closure that returns double the value of its single parameter. In a similar manner, the closure multiplication accepts a single parameter and returns a closure. Like method multiply, the closure it returns multiplies its parameter by some predefined value. The closure quadruple multiplies its single parameter by the value 4.

EXAMPLE 18
Closures as return values

```
            // Method returning a closure
def multiply(x) {
    return {y -> return x * y}
}

def twice = multiply(2)

println "twice(4): ${twice(4)}"

            // Closure returning a closure
def multiplication = {x -> return {y -> return x * y}}

def quadruple = multiplication(4)

println "quadruple(3): ${quadruple(3)}"
```

The output demonstrates that the closure twice does indeed double its parameter while the closure quadruple multiplies its parameter by 4:

```
twice(4): 8
quadruple(3): 12
```

The final example we consider demonstrates that a closure may contain other nested closure definitions. In Example 19, we define the closure selectionSort, which sorts a list of integers into ascending order. To implement this closure, we are required to locate the smallest item of the unsorted tail region of the list and move it to the front. Moving the item to the front of the tail region actually involves swapping the front item with the smallest item. Hence, we implement the closure `selectionSort` with two local closures, `minimumPosition` and `swap`. The latter does the exchange we require, and the former finds the smallest item in the tail region of the `List`.

EXAMPLE 19
Selection sort

```
def selectionSort = {list ->

    def swap = {sList, p, q ->
        def temp = sList[p]
        sList[p] = sList[q]
        sList[q] = temp
    }
    def minimumPosition = {pList, from ->
        def mPos = from
        def nextFrom = 1 + from
        for(j in nextFrom..<pList.size()) {
            if(pList[j] < pList[mPos])
                mPos = j
        }
        return mPos
    }

    def size = list.size() -1
    for(k in 0..<size) {
        def minPos = minimumPosition(list, k)
        swap(list, minPos, k)
    }

    return list
}

def table = [13, 14, 12, 11, 14]

def sorted = selectionSort(table)

println "sorted: ${sorted}"
```

Running the program produces the desired result:

```
sorted: [11, 12, 13, 14, 14]
```

◆

We have to be especially diligent about the scope rules of variables and parameters when working with closures. See Appendices H and J for further discussion on these and other aspects of closures.

9.4   EXERCISES

1. Write a method intersect with two List parameters that find those elements that are common to both lists.

2. Write a method union with two List parameters that finds those elements that are in the first list, the second list, or both lists.

3. Write a method subtract with two List parameters that finds those elements that are in the first list but not in the second list.

4. Modify the code from the case study in Chapter 6 to use closures to format the output from the scripts.

5. Given a Map that represents the employees and their managers as in staff = ['Ken' : ['John', 'Peter'], 'Jon' : ['Ken', 'Jessie'], 'Jessie' : ['Jim', 'Tom']]. This shows that Ken supervises John and Peter, while Jessie is supervised by Jon. Develop the method findManagerOf(name, staff) that finds the manager of the employee with name. Use this to develop the method findNoManager(staff) to find a list of staff with no immediate manager.

6. A Map of nested Maps is used to represent a hotel. The outermost Map is indexed by an integer that represents a floor number. The value for each floor number key is an inner Map. Each inner Map is indexed by an integer representing a room number. The value for the room number key is a list of values detailing the hotel room. An example is hotel = [1 : [1 : ['Bedroom', 2], 2 : ['Bedroom', 4], 3 : ['Studyroom', 10]], 2 : [1 : ['Bedroom', 4], 2 : ['Bedroom', 4]], 3 : [1 : ['Bedroom', 4], 2 : ['Conferenceroom', 25, 'Balmoral']]]. Here, the first floor has three rooms: two bedrooms and a study room. One bedroom has a capacity of 2 while the other has a capacity of 4. The study room has a capacity of 10. On the top floor there is a conference room, entitled the Balmoral with a capacity of 25. Provide the method printAllRooms(hotel) that prints the floors and their rooms. Also, develop the method printRoomsOnFloor(hotel, floorNumber) that prints rooms occupying the given floor.

7. Offer an explanation for the purpose of the two closures lSubtract and rSubtract given as:

```
def lSubtract = {x -> return {y -> return x -y}}
def rSubtract = {y -> return {x -> return x -y}}
```

What kinds of object are p and q defined as:

```
def p = 1Subtract(100)
def q = rSubtract(1)
```

and what would be the effect of the following:

```
println "p(25): ${p(25)}"
println "q(9): ${q(9)}"
```

The closure comp is defined by:

```
def comp = {f, g -> return {x -> return f(g(x))}}
```

Provide a detailed explanation for its behavior. Now, discuss what is produced by the closure calls:

```
def r = comp(p, q)
def s = comp(q, p)
```

then predict the output from:

```
println "r(10): ${r(10)}"
println "s(10): ${s(10)}"
```

8. A software house is contracted to develop Groovy, Java, and C# projects. Each project has one or more programmers involved, with perhaps the same individual associated with more than one project. For example, the following shows Ken, John, and Jon involved with the Groovy project:

```
def softwareHouse = ['Groovy' : ['Ken', 'John', 'Jon'],
                     'Java' : ['Ken', 'John'],
                     'C#' : ['Andrew']
                    ]
```

Predict the effect of each of the following:

(a) softwareHouse.each {key, value -> if(value.size() >= 2) println "${value}"}

(b) softwareHouse['Groovy'].each {g ->
       softwareHouse['Java'].each {j ->
          if(g == j) println "${g}"
       }
    }

9. A university has a number of departments, each of which is responsible for one or more programs of study. For example, the following shows that the Computing Department has two programs, Computing and Information Systems. Respectively, they have 600 and 300 enrolled students.

```
def university = ['Computing' : ['Computing' : 600, 'Information Systems' : 300],
                  'Engineering' : ['Civil' : 200, 'Mechanical' : 100],
                  'Management' : ['Management' : 800]
                 ]
```

Predict the effect of the following:

```
university.each {k, v ->
    v.each {ke, va ->
        if(va>=300) println "${k}: ${ke}"
    }
}
```

10. Repeat exercise 14 from Chapter 7. This time, develop explode, implode, and reverseString as closures local to the closure isPalindrome.

FILES

The programs that we have studied have all produced some output and, in many cases, accepted some input. This has been achieved through using the *standard input* (keyboard) and *standard output* (screen). However, these simple programs are unrepresentative of many computer applications. In practice, most applications involve the permanent storage of data in a *computer file*. In this chapter, we consider applications that process files.

10.1   COMMAND LINE ARGUMENTS

A Groovy program exists in an environment established by the operating system. The environment supports passing *command line arguments* to a program when it begins execution. In a Groovy script, such as that in Example 01, these arguments can be accessed by the args variable, which is an array of Strings.

```
println "args: ${args}"
println "size: ${args.size()}"
println "First arg: ${args[0]}"
```

EXAMPLE 01
Command line arguments

If it is executed with the command:

```
groovy example01.groovy aaa bbb ccc
```

then the output produced is:

```
args: {"aaa", "bbb", "ccc"}
size: 3
First arg: aaa
```

We see that the args variable only includes the arguments. Method size can be used to obtain the number of items in the array variable args, which may be indexed in the usual manner.

10.2   FILE CLASS

Operating systems use system-dependent *pathname strings* to name files and directories. The File class presents an abstract, system-independent view of hierarchical pathnames. At its simplest, an *abstract pathname* is a sequence of zero or more String names. Except for the final String, the others represent directories. The last may represent a file or a directory. In an abstract pathname, a separator character separates each String name. Some example pathnames are:

```
myfile.txt                    // simple file
docs/report.doc               // file in docs subdirectory
src/groovy/example01.groovy   // file in nested subdirectories
src/groovy                    // directory
c:/windows                    // MS Windows directory and disk drive specifier
```

A File object can represent either a file or a directory. The methods in the File class provide operations whereby we can determine, among other things, whether the File object exists, whether it represents a file or a directory, whether the file is readable or writeable, and what the size of the file is. Further, Groovy has augmented the File class with methods that accept a closure as parameter. These methods prove particularly useful for traversing the content of a file or directory and processing it. Some common File methods are listed in Table 10.1. Again, methods marked with an asterisk are the augmented methods of the GDK. For example, method eachLine iterates through a text file, line by line, and applies a closure.

Example 02 is a program to tabulate the content of a file. The line parameter of the closure represents the next line from the file. The end-of-line character is not part of this line parameter. Hence, the println is required to display each line in the file on separate output lines. In the code, a new File object is created, processed, and closed when complete. Since the File object is otherwise not referenced, there is no requirement to reference it by a variable.

TABLE 10.1   Common File methods

Name	Signature/description
append *	`void append(String text)` Append the text at the end of this file.
createNewFile	`Boolean createNewFile()` Create a new, empty file named by this abstract pathname if and only if a file with this name does not yet exist.
delete	`Boolean delete()` Delete the file or directory denoted by this abstract pathname.
eachFile *	`void eachFile(Closure closure)` Invoke the closure for each file in the given directory.
eachFileRecurse *	`void eachFileRecurse(Closure closure)` Invoke the closure for each file in the given directory, and recursively to each subdirectory.
eachLine *	`void eachLine(Closure closure)` Iterate through the given file line by line.
exists	`Boolean exists()` Test whether the file or directory denoted by this abstract pathname exists.
getPath	`String getPath()` Convert this abstract pathname into a pathname String.
getText *	`String getText()` Read the content of this file and return it as a String.
isDirectory	`Boolean isDirectory()` Test whether the file denoted by this abstract pathname is a directory.
mkdir	`Boolean mkdir()` Create the directory named by this abstract pathname.
withPrintWriter *	`void withPrintWriter(Closure closure)` Helper method to create a new PrintWriter for this file, pass it into the closure, and ensure that it is closed again afterwards.

```
import java.io.File

if(args.size() != 1)
    println 'Usage: example02 filename'
else {
        // Print each line of the file
    new File(args[0]).eachLine { line ->
        println "Line: ${line}"
    }
}
```

EXAMPLE 02

Read and display a file, line-at-a-time

Note that if the file given as a command argument does not exist, then calling eachLine on it will raise an exception. If the input file contains:

```
This is the first line
This is the second line
This is the third line
This is the fourth line
```

then the output from the program is:

```
Line: This is the first line
Line: This is the second line
Line: This is the third line
Line: This is the fourth line
```

◆

A useful utility program from the Unix operating system is a program entitled "wc". This program scans a text file and obtains counts for the number of characters, words, and lines in the file. This is readily implemented in Groovy as shown in the following example.

EXAMPLE 03
WC utility

```
import java.io.File

            // Counters
def chars = 0
def words = 0
def lines = 0

if(args.size() != 1)
    println 'Usage: example03 filename'
else {
        // Process the file
    new File(args[0]).eachLine { line ->
        chars += 1 + line.length()
        words += line.tokenize().size()
        lines++
    }

        // Print the outcome
    println "chars: ${chars}; words: ${words}; lines: ${lines}"
}
```

Using the same file as previously produces:

```
chars: 94; words: 20; lines: 4
```

◆

Class File also includes the method eachFile. Normally, it is used for a File object that represents a directory. Once again, it accepts a closure as a parameter and invokes that closure for each file in the directory. In the following example, method printDir accepts the name of a directory as parameter. It simply invokes the support method listDir that expects a File object as first parameter and an integer as the second parameter. The File object represents a directory. The method listDir calls the eachFile method on that File object and the closure prints the names of the file in the directory. If any of these represent a subdirectory, then the listDir method recursively calls itself. The integer parameter is used to specify the level of indentation required by the listing. Each recursive call increases this value.

EXAMPLE 04

Directory listing

```
import java.io.File

        // List the content of a directory File
def listDir(dirFile, indent) {
    dirFile.eachFile { file ->
        (0..<indent).each { print " " }
        println "${file.getName()}"
        if(file.isDirectory())
            listDir(file, 2 + indent)
    }
}

        // Print the content of a named directory
def printDir(dirName) {
    listDir(new File(dirName), 0)
}

if(args.size() != 1 || new File(args[0]).isDirectory() == false)
    println 'Usage: example04 directory'
else {
        // Print the current directory
    printDir(args[0])
}
```

◆

Class File also supports the method eachFileRecurse. As its name suggests, the method iterates through all the files of a directory and recursively through any subdirectory. We might, for example, use this to identify those files that exceed a particular length. Example 05 shows this.

```
import java.io.File

            // List those files exceeding a given size
def printDir(dirName, size) {
    new File(dirName).eachFileRecurse { file ->
        if(file.length() > size)
            println "${file.getName()}"
    }
}

if(args.size() != 2 || new File(args[0]).isDirectory() == false)
    println 'Usage: example05 directory'
else {
        // List from the current directory
    printDir(args[0], args[1].toInteger())
}
```

◆

With the aid of a PrintWriter object, we can copy the contents of one file to another. The PrintWriter class is used to print formatted representations of objects to a file. Combining PrintWriter with File and eachLine produces an elegant implementation. First, we check for the existence of the destination file. If it exists, then it is removed. Class File has a method newPrintWriter that delivers a PrintWriter object for the given destination file. We then copy each line from the source file to the destination file.

```
import java.io.*

if(args.size() != 2)
    println 'Usage: example06 filename filename'
else {
        // Write to a destination file
    def outFile = new File(args[1])
    if(outFile.exists())
        outFile.delete()

        // Create a PrintWriter
    def printWriter = outFile.newPrintWriter()

        // Copy each line of the file
    new File(args[0]).eachLine { line ->
        printWriter.println(line)
    }
```

```
                   // Close up
            printWriter.flush()
            printWriter.close()
        }
```

◆

Class File also provides a number of helper methods to support input/output (see GDK documentation). For example, the method withPrintWriter creates a new PrintWriter for the file and then passes it into the closure and ensures that it is closed afterwards. Other such helper methods include withInputStream, withOutputStream, withReader, and withWriter. Example 07 repeats the previous example using a PrintWriter.

```
        import java.io.*

        if(args.size() != 2)
            println 'Usage: example07 filename filename'
        else {
                // Write to a destination file
            new File(args[1]).withPrintWriter { printWriter ->

                // Copy each line of the file
                new File(args[0]).eachLine { line ->
                    printWriter.println(line)
                }
            }
        }
```

EXAMPLE 07
File copying with
a PrintWriter

◆

A common task is to sort a text file. This is relatively simple to realize in Groovy for small- to medium-sized files since we already have the sort method for Lists. We can read each line from the file into a List, perform an internal sort, and then write the result back out to the same file. An implementation for this is given in Example 08.

```
        import java.io.*

        if(args.size() != 1)
            println 'Usage: example08 filename'
        else {
            def lines = []
```

EXAMPLE 08
Sorting a file

```
        // Read from the text file
new File(args[0]).eachLine { line ->
    lines << line
}

        // Sort the text
lines.sort()

        // Write back to text file
new File(args[0]).withPrintWriter { printWriter ->
    lines.each { line ->
        printWriter.println(line)
    }
}
}
```

Finally, consider a data file of the form:

```
John 2:30PM
Jon 10:30AM
// ...
```

that is used to maintain a List of events for a day diary. From this data, we wish to produce a report of that day's events in time order. If each entry from the file is placed into a List, then we can sort them on the time values. The sort method can accept a closure that operates as the comparator to find the ordering of the values. A regular expression can be used to extract the time from each line (see Chapter 3 and Appendix D). It might look like:

```
(\\d{1,2}):(\\d{2})([AP]M)
```

The digits and the suffix are grouped so that we can extract the individual elements to make the comparison. The complete regular expression for the diary entries is:

```
(\\w*)\\s((\\d{1,2}):(\\d{2})([AP]M))
```

◆

The code for this is given in Example 09. Note how we have used the compareTo operator <=> to great effect.

```
        if(args.size() != 1)
            println 'Usage: groovy9 filename'
        else {
            def TIME_PATTERN = '(\\w*)\\s((\\d{1,2}):(\\d{2})([AP]M))'
            def diary = []

                // read the file
            new File(args[0]).eachLine { entry ->
                diary << entry
            }

                // sort the entries
            diary.sort { entry1, entry2 ->
                def matcher1 = entry1 =~ TIME_PATTERN
                def matcher2 = entry2 =~ TIME_PATTERN
                matcher1.matches()
                matcher2.matches()

                def cmpMeridian = matcher1[0][5] <=> matcher2[0][5]
                def cmpHour = matcher1[0][3].toInteger() <=> matcher2[0][3].toInteger()
                def cmpMinute = matcher1[0][4].toInteger() <=> matcher2[0][4].toInteger()
                return ((cmpMeridian != 0) ? cmpMeridian : (cmpHour != 0) ? cmpHour : cmpMinute)
            }

            println 'Diary events'
            diary.each { entry -> println " ${entry}" }
        }
```

EXAMPLE 09
Diary report

10.3   EXERCISES

1. Rewrite Example 07 to perform file copying and double-space the text.

2. Write a program to copy one text file to another, removing any blank lines in the source file. The file names are given as command line arguments.

3. Write a program to number the lines in a text file. The input file name should be passed as a command line argument. The program should write to the standard output.

4. Write a program which concatenates a set of named input files on to the standard output. One or more file names are to be given as command line arguments.

5. Write a program that operates in a manner similar to the Unix grep utility. The program accepts two command line arguments: a pattern and a text file name. The program should print those lines of the file matching the pattern.

6. Prepare a variant of Example 08 with a command line option –r to reverse the direction of sorting.

11

CASE STUDY: A LIBRARY APPLICATION (METHODS, CLOSURES)

This chapter illustrates the power of Groovy methods and closures by constructing solutions to the small case study first introduced in Chapter 6. As before, we present a simple model of the loan data kept by a library. Our library maintains a record of the titles of the books in stock and the names of the borrowers who have been loaned one or more books.

As in the case study of Chapter 6, we develop the library application as a series of iterations. This lets us add functionality to the application in a controlled manner. It also ensures that we have a working (partial) solution as early as possible. The first iteration demonstrates that we can achieve the required functionality while the second implements a simple text-based, command-line user interface. In the third iteration, we simplify the coding of the second. Our aim is to make it easier to understand and maintain.

11.1 ITERATION 1: SPECIFICATION AND MAP IMPLEMENTATION

The problem specification requires that we manage and maintain the library loan stock. We are required to implement the following use cases:

- Add and remove books to/from the loan stock

- Record the loan and return of a book

- Display details of the current loan stock

- Display the number of books on loan to a given borrower

- Display the number of borrowers of a book

Having established an external view of the application in the use cases, there are various ways in which we can model it. We have already seen two possible solutions in Chapter 6, that is, using the List and Map data structures. For this iteration, we employ a Map to represent the library's stock of books. One reason for our choice is that the Map is ideally suited for the efficient storage and retrieval of information. We anticipate that this will be useful for implementing the library application.

Our intention is that the Map should be keyed by the title of each book and each corresponding value should be a List of the names of its borrowers. The assumption we have made is that there is a copy of each book for every borrower named in the List. Another useful feature of the Map is that its keys are unique. This eliminates the possibility of duplicate entries for a book title in the library's database.

In the Map, the value for each key is a List whose elements are zero or more Strings. Each String represents a borrower's name. Note that a List may contain duplicate elements. The assumption we have made is that a borrower may borrow several copies of a particular book. A List may also be empty. In this case, the book title that is its key represents a book not currently out on loan. A sample initialization of the loans database is:

```
def library = ['Groovy' : ['Ken', 'John'], 'OOD' : ['Ken'], 'Java' : ['John', 'Sally'], 'UML' : ['Sally'], 'Basic' : []]
```

The resulting Map data structure is illustrated diagrammatically in Figure 11.1. The figure shows that there are two Groovy books on loan to Ken and John, one OOD book to Ken, two Java books to John and Sally, and one UML book to Sally. Notice that the book titled Basic is not currently on loan, reflected by the fact that the value is an empty List.

The functionality required by this simple application is easily realized by Groovy methods. Each method implements one of the use cases identified from the specification. Had any of them proved particularly complicated, then, of course, we could have broken it down in to simpler methods. Note that although we use the term "method," we might just as well have used the term "procedure" in this context, because we are effectively taking a *procedural*

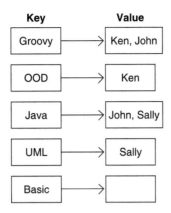

FIGURE 11.1   Sample Map data structure for the library application.

approach (Deitel, 2003) to the development of this case study. As with many scripting applications, we require no more than some simple procedural code to implement a solution.

To access the List of borrower names associated with a particular book title, we use the Map index operator [ ] (from the GDK) with the book title as the index value. This simplifies our coding task considerably. For example, to add a new book we have:

```
def addBook(library, bookTitle) {
    library[bookTitle] = []
}
```

and to determine the number of borrowers of a particular book, we have:

```
def readNumberBorrowers(library, bookTitle) {
    return library[bookTitle].size()
}
```

As in the partial listing of Library 01, most of the other methods are just as straightforward. For the sake of clarity, the various displays are intentionally simple but we remedy this in later chapters.

```
def addBook(library, bookTitle) {
    library[bookTitle] = []
}
```

LIBRARY 01

A Library
application—its
methods

```
def removeBook(library, bookTitle) {
    library.remove(bookTitle)
}

def lendBook(library, bookTitle, borrowerName) {
    library[bookTitle] << borrowerName
}

def returnBook(library, bookTitle, borrowerName) {
    library[bookTitle].remove(borrowerName)
}

def displayLoanStock(library) {
    println "Library stock: ${library} \n"
}

def readNumberBorrowedBooks(library, borrowerName) {
    //
    // get a List of each List of the borrower names from the library
    def borrowerNames = library.values().asList()
    //
    // create a single List of the borrower names
    borrowerNames = borrowerNames.flatten()
    //
    // return the number of borrower names in the List
    return borrowerNames.count(borrowerName)
}

def readNumberBorrowers(library, bookTitle) {
    return library[bookTitle].size()
}

// More code follows ...
```

◆

Notice that each method has library as a formal parameter. This is in keeping with a procedural style of software development in which procedures read or write from/to a central data structure. In our case study, it is, of course, the library database, implemented as a Map.

To test that our methods execute as expected, we develop a test case for each use case. In this simple version of the case study, we just check each output visually and assume perfect input data. For example, the test case for the display of the loan stock just prints the underlying Map on the console screen. We compare the output visually with that expected from the initialization of the Map. Clearly, this approach does work but it is not very realistic. Later in Chapter 15, we discuss testing in more detail. However, for the moment, this approach will suffice.

As with the iterative development of the application, it is often useful to introduce test-cases incrementally, that is, one at a time. This reduces the risk that the testing burden might overwhelm us and builds confidence in our software as testing progresses. For example, we might start with the script:

```
// methods as shown previously
// ...

    // Initialize the loan stock
def library = ['Groovy' : ['Ken', 'John'], 'OOD' : ['Ken'], 'Java' : ['John', 'Sally'], 'UML' : ['Sally'],
'Basic' : []]

    // Test Case: Display loan stock
println 'Test Case: Display loan stock'
displayLoanStock(library)
```

LIBRARY 01
A Library
application—the
first test case

◆

Happily, it produces the expected output:

```
Test Case: Display loan stock
Library stock: ["Groovy":["Ken", "John"], "UML":["Sally"], "Java":["John", "Sally"], "OOD":["Ken"],
"Basic":[]]
```

We now add another test case:

```
// methods, initialization and test case as shown previously
// ...

            // Test Case: Add a new book
println 'Test Case: Add a new book'
addBook(library, 'C#')
displayLoanStock(library)
```

LIBRARY 01
A Library
application—the
second test case

◆

Again, it produces the expected output:

```
Test Case: Display loan stock
Library stock: ["Groovy":["Ken", "John"], "UML":["Sally"], "Java":["John", "Sally"], "OOD":["Ken"],
"Basic":[]]
```

```
Test Case: Add a new book
Library stock: ["Groovy":["Ken", "John"], "UML":["Sally"], "Java":["John", "Sally"], "OOD":["Ken"],
"Basic":[], "C#":[]]
```

We continue in this manner, adding the remaining test cases one at a time, checking and correcting code as necessary.

```
// methods, initialization and test case as shown previously
// ...

    // Test Case: Remove a book
println 'Test Case: Remove a book'
removeBook(library, 'UML')
displayLoanStock(library)

    // Test Case: Record a book loan to a borrower
lendBook(library, 'Java', 'Ken')
println 'Test Case: Record a book loan to a borrower'
displayLoanStock(library)

    // Test Case: Record a book return by a borrower
returnBook(library, 'Java', 'Sally')
println 'Test Case: Record a book return by a borrower'
displayLoanStock(library)

    // Test Case: Display the number of books on loan to a borrower
println 'Test Case: Display the number of books on loan to a borrower'
println "Number of books on loan to Ken: ${readNumberBorrowedBooks(library, 'Ken')} \n"

    // Test Case: Display the number of borrowers of a book
println 'Test Case: Display the number of borrowers of a book'
println "Number of borrowers of Java: ${readNumberBorrowers(library, 'Java')} \n"
```

The final output is:

```
Test Case: Display loan stock
Library stock: ["Groovy":["Ken", "John"], "UML":["Sally"], "Java":["John", "Sally"], "OOD":["Ken"],
"Basic":[]]

Test Case: Add a new book
Library stock: ["Groovy":["Ken", "John"], "UML":["Sally"], "Java":["John", "Sally"], "OOD":["Ken"],
"Basic":[], "C#":[]]

Test Case: Remove a book
Library stock: ["Groovy":["Ken", "John"], "Java":["John", "Sally"], "OOD":["Ken"], "Basic":[], "C#":[]]
```

```
Test Case: Record a book loan to a borrower
Library stock: ["Groovy":["Ken", "John"], "Java":["John", "Sally", "Ken"], "OOD":["Ken"], "Basic":[],"C#":[]]

Test Case: Record a book return by a borrower
Library stock: ["Groovy":["Ken", "John"], "Java":["John", "Ken"], "OOD":["Ken"], "Basic":[], "C#":[]]

Test Case: Display the number of books on loan to a borrower
Number of books on loan to Ken: 3

Test Case: Display the number of borrowers of a book
Number of borrowers of Java: 2
```

At this point, we consider the first iteration to be complete. Full listings of the script are available on the book website.

II.2   ITERATION 2: IMPLEMENTATION OF A TEXT-BASED USER INTERFACE

Having demonstrated that the library application executes as expected, we now turn our attention to how a user might interact with it. Clearly, there are many possibilities. However, we choose the simplest: a text-based command line interface. In later chapters, we consider more elaborate alternatives.

For this iteration, we are required to present the user with a text-based menu of the options available. Having selected an option, it is actioned and the menu presented again so that another option can be selected and actioned. This continues until the user selects the Quit option.

We can use the Groovy flow of control constructs, discussed in Chapter 8, to good effect. For example, we have a while loop to control the repeated presentation of the menu and an if...else statement to select and action an option.

We can also introduce new methods as necessary. For example, we must elicit a book title, a borrower name, and a menu option from the user. These requirements are coded as the methods readBookTitle, readBorrowerName, and readMenuSelection, respectively. The partial listing of Library 02 illustrates. Complete listings are available on the book website.

LIBRARY 02

A Library
application—
additional methods
and control
structures

```
import console.*

// methods as shown previously
// ...

def readBookTitle(){
    print('\tEnter book title: ')
    return Console.readLine()
}


def readBorrowerName(){
    print('\tEnter borrower name: ')
    return Console.readLine()
}


def readMenuSelection(){
    println()
    println('0: Quit')
    println('1: Add new book')
    println('2: Remove book')
    println('3: Lend a book')
    println('4: Return a book')
    println('5: Display loan stock')
    println('6: Display number of books on loan to a borrower')
    println('7: Display number of borrowers of a book')

    print('\n\tEnter choice: ')
    return Console.readLine()
}
def library = [ 'Groovy' : ['Ken', 'John'], 'OOD' : ['Ken'], 'Java' : ['John', 'Sally'], 'UML' : ['Sally'],
'Basic' : [] ]

def choice = readMenuSelection()

while(choice != '0'){

    if(choice == '1')
        addBook(library, readBookTitle())
    else if(choice == '2')
        removeBook(library, readBookTitle())
```

```
    else if(choice == '3')
        lendBook(library, readBookTitle(), readBorrowerName())
    else if(choice == '4')
        returnBook(library, readBookTitle(), readBorrowerName())
    else if(choice == '5')
        displayLoanStock(library)
    else if(choice == '6') {
        def count = getNumberBorrowedBooks(library, readBorrowerName())
        println "\nNumber of books borrowed: ${count}\n"
    } else if(choice == '7') {
        def count = getNumberBorrowers(library, readBookTitle())
        println "\nNumber of borrowers: ${count}\n"
    } else
        println('\nUnknown selection\n')

        // next selection
    choice = readMenuSelection()
}

println('\nSystem closing\n')
```

Notice that the library initialization and supporting methods are unchanged from the previous iteration. However, we have no need for the test-case code. To test Library 02, we might select each menu option and then display the contents of the library to check the result. A typical interaction, with user input shown italicized and emboldened, is:

```
0: Quit
1: Add new book
2: Remove book
3: Lend a book
4: Return a book
5: Display loan stock
6: Display number of books on loan to a borrower
7: Display number of borrowers of a book


        Enter choice: 3
        Enter book title: Java
        Enter borrower name: Ken


0: Quit
1: Add new book
2: Remove book
3: Lend a book
4: Return a book
5: Display loan stock
```

```
6: Display number of books on loan to a borrower
7: Display number of borrowers of a book

     Enter choice: 5
Library stock: ["Groovy":["Ken", "John"], "UML":["Sally"], "Java":["John", "Sally", "Ken"], "OOD":["Ken"],
"Basic":[]]
```

◆

Since we have the expected outputs, at this point we consider this second iteration completed.

11.3   ITERATION 3: IMPLEMENTATION WITH CLOSURES

There are no new functional requirements for this iteration. Our aim is to recode the second iteration so that it is easier to understand and maintain. One potential problem with Library 02 is that the code, which controls its execution, that is, the if...else statement, may become increasingly difficult to understand as more and more options are added. Although we might replace it with a switch statement, this does not really help very much since all that we have done is to change the syntax slightly.

The closure, discussed in Chapter 9, is a particularly powerful feature of the Groovy language. It represents a block of executable code that is also an Object. Since it is an Object, it can be a value in a Map. If its key is a user choice, then we can locate and execute the associated closure without the need for complex control code.

For example, we might have a parameter-less closure, doAddBook, to execute the method addBook from Iteration 2.

```
def doAddBook = { addBook(library, readBookTitle()) }
```

If we have a similar closure for each possible action, then we can have a Map with each user choice as its key and the corresponding closure (actions) as its value.

```
def menu = ['1' : doAddBook,
            '2' : doRemoveBook,
            '3' : doLendBook,
            '4' : doReturnBook,
            '5' : doDisplayLoanStock,
            '6' : doDisplayNumberBooksOnLoanToBorrower,
            '7' : doDisplayNumberBorrowersOfBook
           ]
```

Such a structure is often called a *lookup table* or *dispatch table*. It is very useful because we can replace complex control code with a table lookup as in:

```
def choice = readMenuSelection()

while(choice != '0'){
    menu[choice].call()
    choice = readMenuSelection()
}
```

The partial listing of Library 03 combines these ideas. As with the previous examples, complete listings are available on the book website.

```
// methods and initialization as shown previously
// ...

def doAddBook = { addBook(library, readBookTitle()) }

def doRemoveBook = { removeBook(library, readBookTitle()) }

def doLendBook = { lendBook(library, readBookTitle(), readBorrowerName()) }

def doReturnBook = { returnBook(library, readBookTitle(), readBorrowerName()) }

def doDisplayLoanStock = { displayLoanStock(library) }

def doDisplayNumberBooksOnLoanToBorrower = {
        def count = getNumberBorrowedBooks(library, readBorrowerName())
        println "\nNumber of books borrowed: ${count}\n"
}

def doDisplayNumberBorrowersOfBook = {
        def count = getNumberBorrowers(library, readBookTitle())
        println "\nNumber of borrowers: ${count}\n"
}

def menu = ['1' : doAddBook,
            '2' : doRemoveBook,
            '3' : doLendBook,
            '4' : doReturnBook,
            '5' : doDisplayLoanStock,
            '6' : doDisplayNumberBooksOnLoanToBorrower,
            '7' : doDisplayNumberBorrowersOfBook
           ]
```

LIBRARY 03

A Library
application—a
recoded version

```
def choice = readMenuSelection()
while(choice != '0'){
    menu[choice].call()
    choice = readMenuSelection()
}


println('\nSystem closing\n')
```

◆

As expected, its execution is the same as Library 02. However, by recoding with closures, we have made it much easier to add extra functionality. For example, we may
be required to add an option to display an alphabetic list of the borrowers of a particular book. All we have to do is to develop a closure that calls a suitable method:

```
// method
def getBorrowers(library, bookTitle) {
    return library[bookTitle]
}


// closure
def doDisplayBorrowersOfBook = {
    def borrowerNames = getBorrowers(library, readBookTitle())
    println "\nBorrowers: ${borrowerNames.sort()}\n"
}
```

The closure is then added to the Map with a suitable key:

```
menu['8'] = doDisplayBorrowersOfBook
```

and the method readMenuSelection updated:

```
def readMenuSelection(){

    // As shown previously
    // ...

    println('8: Display borrowers of a book')
    // ...

}
```

The important point to realize is that the rest of the code is unchanged. In particular, there is no need to make code that was already complex even more complex. At this point, we consider this third iteration completed.

11.4 EXERCISES

1. Section 3.1 of Chapter 4 discussed the Groovy multiline text string. Recode the method `readMenuSelection` from Library 02 to make use of it. What are its advantages and disadvantages?

2. Amend the previous exercise so that it supports an option to display an alphabetical list of the borrowers of a particular book.

3. The JDK has the class `HashSet` that, like the `ArrayList`, can be initialized with a `List`. However, it does not hold duplicate elements. Use a `HashSet` to amend the previous exercise so that it supports an option to display an alphabetical list of all the books currently on loan. It should not contain duplicates.

4. Amend the previous exercise so that it supports an option to display an alphabetical list of all of the books in the library.

5. In Iteration 3, each closure called a method. Recast Library 03 so that each closure calls to a nested closure (see Section 9.3) which replaces the method. What are the advantages of this approach?

   The following exercises are intended to be miniprojects similar to the one discussed in this chapter.

6. Assume two `List`s exist that represent the names of staff involved in two separate project developments. A staff member may be involved in one or both projects. Find those staff involved in both projects. Find those involved in only one project. Develop methods to support such an application. Develop an additional method to find those staff involved in the first project but not in the second.

7. Consider the clock time program given in Example 05 of Chapter 7. As this program executes, the variables `hours`, `minutes`, `seconds`, and `totalSeconds` are created, in that order. After execution of the first two statements, the executing Groovy program would have created objects for the variables `hours` and `minutes`.

   The runtime environment for Groovy will maintain these objects as they are created. We might model this environment with a `Map` of the variable name and its value. Hence, after execution of the first two statements, we might have:

   ```
   environment = ['hours' : 1, 'minutes' : 2]
   ```

Provide methods add, getVariables, and getValue that:

(a) add a new variable and its value to the environment

(b) find all the variables in the current environment

(c) find the value for a named variable

8. Consider the word concordance program given in Example 12 of Appendix G. The runtime environment for this program needs to properly manage the block structure. The program executes by first declaring the doc variable. It then calls the concordance method. The first two lines of this method introduce the variables lineNumber and concord. These local variables only exist in the runtime environment while the concordance method is executing. Upon return from that method, these variables are removed from the environment. Continuing, the concord variable is added to the environment.

Model this application as a List in which each entry is a Map, as described in the preceding exercise. When we enter a new block, a new Map is appended to the List, and when we exit the block, that Map is removed. As variables are introduced into the environment, they are recorded in the most recent Map from the List.

Provide the following methods:

(a) addBlock: that introduces a new block in the environment

(b) removeBlock: that mimics exiting a block

(c) add: that introduces a new variable into the environment

(d) lookup: that obtains the value for a given variable

CLASSES

A Groovy *class* is a collection of data and the methods that operate on that data. Together, the data and methods of a class are used to represent some real world object from the problem domain. For example, if we are developing a banking application, we might expect to find classes to represent account objects, bank objects, and perhaps customer objects. Similarly, in a university student record system, we might require classes to represent student objects, course and module objects, as well as objects that represent programs of study.

Observe how these real-world objects may have a physical presence or may represent some well-understood conceptual entity in the application. In our examples, a student will most definitely exist, while a program of study has no physical existence.

12.1 CLASSES

A class in Groovy is used to represent some abstraction in the problem domain. As has been discussed, a class declares the state (data) and the behavior of objects defined by that class. Hence, a Groovy class describes both the instance fields and methods for that class. The properties specify the state information maintained by objects of the class. The methods define the behaviors we can expect from the objects.

Here is an example of a simple Groovy script that defines a class that describes a simple bank account together with some code to create an instance and display its state.

EXAMPLE 01

A simple Groovy
class

```
class Account {
    def number        // account number
    def balance       // current balance
}

        // create a new Account instance
def acc = new Account(number : 'ABC123', balance : 1200)

        // display its state values
println "Account ${acc.number} has balance ${acc.balance}"
```

The output from the script is:

```
Account ABC123 has balance 1200
```

◆

The Groovy keyword class is followed by the name of the class, namely, Account. The class declares two public properties and no methods. An instance of this class is created using the new operator, as in:

```
def acc = new Account(number : 'ABC123', balance : 1200)
```

The new keyword is followed by the name of the class of object we are creating. The remainder comprises a list of *named parameters* specifying how the properties of the instance are to be initialized. Here, the Account object, referenced as acc, has an account number of ABC123 and a balance of 1200. Observe how the properties of the instance are referenced in the print statement. The expression acc.number is used to access the number property of the Account object acc.

As simple as this class may appear, there is a great deal going on under the hood. First, the two properties introduced in the Account class are said to have *public access*. This means they can be used in any other part of the code to refer to the individual parts of the state of an instance of the Account class. This is how the print statement is able to access the state of the acc object.

Second, this simple example demonstrates how Groovy seeks to unify instance fields and methods. Properties remove the distinction between an instance field (sometimes also referred to as an *attribute*) and a method. From a view external to the Groovy class, a property is like both the instance field and its getter/setter methods. In effect, the usage of a property reference such as acc.number is implemented by acc.getNumber().

The class is a template for creating instances of objects defined by that class. In the next example, we create two Account objects and print their values.

```
class Account {
    def number          // account number
    def balance         // current balance
}

        // create two instances
def acc1 = new Account(number : 'ABC123', balance : 1200)
def acc2 = new Account(number : 'XYZ888', balance : 400)

        // report on both
println "Account ${acc1.number} has balance ${acc1.balance}"
println "Account ${acc2.number} has balance ${acc2.balance}"
```

EXAMPLE 02
Two object
instances

When we run the program, we get the output:

```
Account ABC123 has balance 1200
Account XYZ888 has balance 400
```

◆

We noted that the Groovy class corresponds to the equivalent Java class. This means that the getter and setter methods are implicitly part of the Groovy class. Hence, we can mix and match their usage, as shown in the next example.

```
class Account {
    def number          // account number
    def balance         // current balance
}

        // create two instances
def acc1 = new Account(number : 'ABC123', balance : 1200)
def acc2 = new Account(number : 'XYZ888', balance : 400)

        // access the state using properties
println "Account ${acc1.number} has balance ${acc1.balance}"

        // access the state using getters
println "Account ${acc2.getNumber()} has balance ${acc2.getBalance()}"

        // modify the state using a property
acc1.balance = 200
println "Account ${acc1.getNumber()} has balance ${acc1.getBalance()}"
```

EXAMPLE 03
Using the implicit
getter and setter
methods

```
                        // modify the state using a setter
            acc2.setBalance(600)
            println "Account ${acc2.number} has balance ${acc2.balance}"
```

The output is:

```
Account ABC123 has balance 1200
Account XYZ888 has balance 400
Account ABC123 has balance 200
Account XYZ888 has balance 600
```

◆

More usually, a class also has some methods to define the distinct behaviors of instances. In our simple Account class, we might expect methods to support making a deposit and making a withdrawal. We extend our Account class with the methods credit and debit for this purpose. Additionally, we include a method to display the state of an Account object. We show this in Example 04.

EXAMPLE 04
class methods

```
class Account {
    def number                    // account number
    def balance                   // current balance

    def credit(amount) {
        balance += amount
    }

    def debit(amount) {           // only if there are sufficient funds
        if(balance >= amount)
            balance = amount
    }

    def display() {
        println "Account: ${number} with balance: ${balance}"
    }

}

        // create a new instance
def acc = new Account(number : 'ABC123', balance : 1200)
acc.display()

        // credit transaction
acc.credit(200)                   // balance now 1400
acc.display()
```

```
                    // other transactions
    acc.debit(900)                    // balance now 500
    acc.debit(700)                    // balance remains unchanged at 500
    acc.display()
```

The output is:

```
    Account: ABC123 with balance: 1200
    Account: ABC123 with balance: 1400
    Account: ABC123 with balance: 500
```

◆

As an Account is an Object, instances of the Account class can be used as the elements of a List. In the next example, we create three instances of the Account class, place them in a List, and then display each. Note how this version of the Account class has replaced the display method with one entitled toString. This replacement method returns the state information as a String value.

EXAMPLE 05
lists of accounts

```
    class Account {
        def number               // account number
        def balance              // current balance

        def credit(amount) {
            balance += amount
        }

        def debit(amount) {            // only if there are sufficient funds
            if(balance >= amount)
                balance -= amount
        }

        def toString() {              // see also next example
            return "Account: ${number} with balance: ${balance}"
        }
    }

            // create some instances
    def acc1 = new Account(number : 'ABC123', balance : 1200)
    def acc2 = new Account(number : 'PQR456', balance : 200)
    def acc3 = new Account(number : 'XYZ789', balance : 123)

            // populate a list with the instances
    def accounts = [acc1, acc2, acc3]

            // now display each
    accounts.each { acc ->
        println acc.toString()
    }
```

The output is:

```
Account: ABC123 with balance: 1200
Account: PQR456 with balance: 200
Account: XYZ789 with balance: 123
```

◆

We define the toString method to give us a textual representation of an Account object and then use it in the expression acc.toString() as part of the print statement. To avoid an explicit call to toString, we record that we are *redefining* (see Chapter 14) toString. This requires that we repeat the full signature of the toString method and show that it returns a String value. Another version of this is shown next.

EXAMPLE 06
Redefining method
`toString`

```
class Account {
    def number                  // account number
    def balance                 // current balance

    def credit(amount) {
        balance += amount
    }

    def debit(amount) {         // only if there are sufficient funds
        if(balance >= amount)
            balance -= amount
    }

    String toString() {         // redefinition
        return "Account: ${number} with balance: ${balance}"
    }
}

        // populate a list with the instances
def accounts = [new Account(number : 'ABC123', balance : 1200),
                new Account(number : 'PQR456', balance : 200),
                new Account(number : 'XYZ789', balance : 123)]

        // now display each
accounts.each { acc ->
    println acc                 // automatically call toString
}
```

◆

The output from this example is the same as that shown in the last example.

The Java declaration for the Account class would normally include a *constructor method* for the initialization of objects of this class. We have not had to do this with our classes, choosing instead to use named parameters with the new operator. We can, of course, have constructor methods in our Groovy classes. Where we explicitly provide one, we would normally expect a class declaration to include a *parameterized constructor* for the proper initialization of the class properties. A constructor is distinguished as a method with the same name as the class. This is shown in Example 07.

```
class Account {

    def Account(number, balance) { // constructor method
        this.number = number
        this.balance = balance
    }

    def credit(amount) {
        balance += amount
    }

    def debit(amount) {              // only if there are sufficient funds
        if(balance >= amount)
            balance = amount
    }

    String toString() {             // redefinition
        return "Account: ${number} with balance: ${balance}"
    }

    def number                      // account number
    def balance                     // current balance
}

        // populate a list with the instances
def accounts = [new Account('ABC123', 1200),
            new Account('PQR456', 200),
            new Account('XYZ789', 123)]

        // now display each
accounts.each { acc ->
    println acc                     // automatically call toString
}

//def acc = new Account(number : 'ABC123', balance : 1200)    // No matching constructor
```

EXAMPLE 07
A constructor
method

Observe how we now create instances of this class. We invoke the constructor, passing two actual parameters for the account number and an initial balance. This time, they are presented using *positional parameters*. Further, note how the constructor method is defined. The formal parameters have been given the same name as the properties. To disambiguate this in the method body, we have used the this keyword to prefix the property. Hence, the statement this.number = number is interpreted as "assign to the number property of this object, the value of (the parameter) number."

Note also the final line of commented code. When a class includes a user-defined constructor, the auto-generated default constructor is not produced. The final statement tries to create a new Account object in the manner to which we have become accustomed. However, since this requires the default construc-tor, an error is reported stating that no matching constructor was available (see following text).

A final comment to make on this version of the Account class is that the properties have been shown at the end of the class declaration. This is perfectly acceptable in Groovy, even where the methods reference the properties before they are introduced. Our reason for doing this recognizes that a client program developed using such a class is more interested in the services supported by the class than its implementation.

We have preferred to use the named parameter scheme when creating an instance with the new operator. It is worth considering how they operate. Class properties result in auto-generated getter and setter methods. Further, where no constructor is declared, then the compiler will create the *default constructor.*

```
Account() {
}
```

Object creation with:

```
def acc = new Account(number : 'ABC123', balance : 1200)
```

is replaced with the following equivalent code (see Appendix B):

```
def acc = new Account()            // default constructor
acc.setNumber('ABC123')            // implicit setters
acc.setBalance(1200)
```

12.2 COMPOSITION

Examples 05 and 06 have shown how Account objects can be elements in a collection. We might use this technique to model a banking application in which accounts are opened with a bank and transactions are made on these accounts through the bank. The architecture for this application is described by a one-to-many relationship: one bank is associated with many accounts. This relationship is readily handled by a List or Map collection. Since some of the methods of the Bank class will require us to identify a particular account according to its account number, we choose to use a Map with the account number as the key and the Account object as the value. A sample Map with two Accounts is:

```
['ABC123' : new Account('ABC123', 1200), 'DEF456' : new Account('DEF456', 1000)]
```

where we use the constructor syntax new Account('ABC123', 1200) to create a new Account object.

This problem is modeled with the class diagram presented in Fig. 12.1. A composite *aggregation* relationship is defined between the Bank and Account class. The *multiplicity* indicator * shows that a single Bank object is related to none or more Account objects. Further, the *role* accounts is how the Bank refers to these many Accounts. This role name is realized as a property of the Bank class.

In our application, we wish to be able to open new accounts with the bank, make credit and debit transactions on particular accounts, obtain the balance for a particular account, and obtain the total assets for the bank (the sum of the balances for every opened account). The solution for this application is given in Example 08. Note how two classes are defined here. Pay particular attention to the Bank class. It initializes the accounts property to be an empty Map. Method openAccount populates this Map with an account number for the key and the Account object for its associated value. Methods findAccount and getTotalAssets use closures to good effect to implement their functionality.

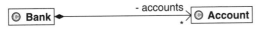

FIGURE 12.1 Class diagram.

```
class Account {

    def credit(amount) {
        balance += amount
    }
```

```
        def debit(amount) {              // only if there are sufficient funds
            if(balance >= amount)
                balance -= amount
        }

        String toString() {             // redefinition
            return "Account: ${number} with balance: ${balance}"
        }

// -----properties ----------------

        def number                      // account number
        def balance                     // current balance
}

class Bank {

    def openAccount(number, balance) {
        def acc = new Account(number : number, balance : balance)
        accounts[number] = acc
    }

    def creditAccount(number, amount) {
        def acc = this.findAccount(number)
        if(acc != null)
            acc.credit(amount)
    }

    def debitAccount(number, amount) {
        def acc = this.findAccount(number)
        if(acc != null)
            acc.debit(amount)
    }

    def getAccountBalance(number) {
        def acc = this.findAccount(number)
        return (acc == null) ? null : acc.balance
    }

    def getTotalAssets() {
        def total = 0
        accounts.each { number, account -> total += account.balance }
        return total
    }

    def findAccount(number) {
        def acc = accounts.find { entry -> entry.key == number }
        return (acc == null) ? null : acc.value
    }
```

```
// -----properties ----------------

    def name                    // name of bank
    def accounts = [ : ]        // accounts opened with the bank
}

    // open new bank
def bk = new Bank(name : 'Community')

    // Open new accounts
bk.openAccount('ABC123', 1200)
bk.openAccount('DEF456', 1000)
bk.openAccount('GHI789', 2000)

    // Perform transactions on a particular account
bk.creditAccount('ABC123', 200)    // balance now 1400
bk.debitAccount('ABC123', 900)     // balance now 500
bk.debitAccount('ABC123', 700)     // balance remains unchanged at 500

    // Display details of this account
println "Balance for account ABC123 is: ${bk.getAccountBalance('ABC123')}"

    // Calculate total bank assets
println "Total assets: ${bk.getTotalAssets()}"
```

Running the program produces:

```
Balance for account ABC123 is: 500
Total assets: 3500
```

◆

12.3 EXERCISES

1. Develop a class to represent an Employee, each having a staff number, a
   name, and a salary. Prepare an application to create a list of employees
   and to determine the total wage bill for these employees.

2. Develop a class to represent a Point in a two-dimensional space with an x
   and a y property. Include in the class the method moveBy, which moves
   the point by x and y displacements given as method parameters.

3. Build on the Point class developed in the last exercise to develop the class Line, defined by its start and end points. Include in the class the method moveBy, to displace the line by some given amount. Also, include the methods isHorizontal and isVertical to determine the nature of the line.

4. Build on the Point class developed earlier to develop the class Rectangle, defined by the position of its upper left corner, width, and height. Include in the class the methods moveBy, getArea, and getPerimeter. Method moveBy displaces the rectangle by a given amount. Methods getArea and getPerimeter calculate the area and the perimeter, respectively, of the rectangle.

5. Use the Employee class from the first exercise and develop a Company class with any number of employees. Introduce into the Company class methods hire(employee), display(), and getTotalSalaries(). Method hire introduces the new employee into the organization. Method display produces a list of each employee, while method getTotalSalaries computes the total wages bill for the company.

6. Further develop the last exercise so that the Company has any number of Departments and a Department has any number of Employees. Class Department has a name property, and is to have the methods add, display, and getTotalSalaries. Method add introduces a new employee into that division. Methods display and getTotalSalaries display all the employees in a department, and obtain the total wages bill for a department. Class Company should now have the methods open(department), hire(deptName, employee), display(), and getTotalSalaries().

7. A news agent maintains a list of customers, including their names. For each customer, the news agent has a list of newspapers to be delivered to their home. Develop a system to list each newspaper and the quantity required.

CASE STUDY: A LIBRARY APPLICATION (OBJECTS)

The library application first appeared in Chapter 6. In that chapter, we showed how combining Lists and Maps could produce complex data structures that can be used to manage the bookkeeping required by a library. The data maintained in these collections were simple strings. We revisited the application again in Chapter 11 and this time we included some procedural code that enhanced the capabilities of our system. For example, methods were provided to find those books that had been issued to a borrower and to record loans to a borrower.

This case study is applied to the same problem domain using the object-oriented concepts introduced in Chapter 12. Rather than have simple strings for the borrower and the book title, we can now use objects to represent the library, its borrowers, and the books. Since we use objects, they have more interesting state information and behaviors. As in the two earlier versions of this application, we use containers to model the complex relationships established between objects.

13.1 SPECIFICATION

We assume a sufficient familiarity with the operation of a library to understand the following description:

The library has a name, holds a number of books, each of which has a title, author, and unique catalog number. There are registered borrowers, each with a unique membership number and a name. A borrower may borrow a book and return it.

However, each book transaction must be recorded by a librarian. She is also expected to register a new borrower, add a new book, be able to display the entire loan stock, display those books available for loan, display those already out on loan, and display the details of each registered borrower.

These requirements are captured in the use cases:

- Add a new book to the loan stock

- Record the loan and return of a book

- Display the details of the current loan stock

- Register a new borrower

- Display details of the borrowers

The library system we are asked to develop is relatively nontrivial and so it merits developing it iteratively. For the first two iterations, we aim to demonstrate that our model is a good reflection of the problem domain. Clearly, if it is not, then the rest of the development effort is severely jeopardized. In the third iteration, we introduce a simple text-based user interface into the application. To help minimize the danger of "hacking," each iteration has stated aims that we demonstrate have been achieved.

13.2   ITERATION I: AN INITIAL MODEL

The specification mentions books that are borrowed from the library. This suggests a class diagram similar to that we met in Chapter 12 when we were concerned with a bank and its many accounts. The initial class diagram is given in Fig. 13.1. Class Book represents a book that may be borrowed from the library. It is a concrete class and carries the properties and behaviors common to all borrowed books, namely, the book catalog number, title, and name of the author. The class Library has a composite aggregation relationship with the Book class that represents its loan stock. This is implemented as a Map with the book catalog number as the key and the Book object as the value.

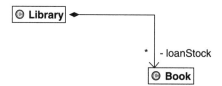

FIGURE 13.1   Initial class diagram.

In the banking example of Chapter 12, we demonstrated that the initial functionality of the classes was achieved by creating a number of objects, configuring the objects into the application architecture, and invoking various methods to ensure the integrity of our work. Here, we do likewise. We create a single Library object and a number of Book objects. We then add the books to the library's loan stock. Finally, we request the library to display its full stock. All of this is shown in Library 01.

LIBRARY 01
Initial object configuration

```groovy
class Book {

    String toString() {                    // redefinition
        return "Book: ${catalogNumber}: ${title} by: ${author}"
    }

// ------properties----------------

    def catalogNumber
    def title
    def author
}

class Library {

    def addBook(bk) {
        loanStock[bk.catalogNumber] = bk
    }

    def displayStock() {
        println "Library: ${name}"
        println '================='

        loanStock.each { catalogNumber, book -> println" ${book}" }
    }


// ------properties----------------

    def name
    def loanStock = [ : ]
}

        // Create a library object
def lib = new Library(name : 'Dunning')

        // Create some books...
def bk1 = new Book(catalogNumber : '111', title : 'Groovy', author : 'Ken')
def bk2 = new Book(catalogNumber : '222', title : 'OOD', author : 'Ken')
def bk3 = new Book(catalogNumber : '333', title : 'UML', author : 'John')
```

```
                // ...add them to the loan stock
lib.addBook(bk1)
lib.addBook(bk2)
lib.addBook(bk3)

                // See stock
lib.displayStock()
```

Note we have the closure's two formal parameters (the Map's key and its associated value) in:

```
    loanStock.each { catalogNumber, book -> println " ${book.value}" }
```

even though we make use of only one. This helps make it clear that loanStock references a Map, not a List, and so we adopt it as our standard practice.

When we execute this Groovy script, the results are as follows:

```
Library: Dunning
==============
      Book: 111: Groovy by: Ken
      Book: 222: OOD by: Ken
      Book: 333: UML by: John
```

◆

The display reveals that the correct architecture is established and that we have the correct behavior from our two classes. Therefore, we consider this iteration to be complete.

13.3   ITERATION 2: AUGMENT THE MODEL

We now need to introduce the notion of registered borrowers into our model. The specification states that they are identified by a unique membership number and have a name. The borrowers are permitted to borrow and return books. We capture this decision with the class diagram in Fig. 13.2. The Borrower objects are registered with the Library and they maintain a collection of borrowed books.

The realization of Fig. 13.2 involves introducing the Borrower class with membership number and name as properties. The Borrower class also has

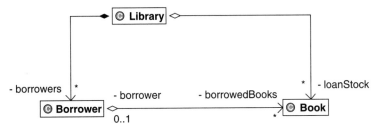

FIGURE 13.2 Introducing borrowers.

methods to add and remove a Book from the collection of those borrowed by the Borrower. Observe how a Book also refers to the Borrower (with the role name borrower) that has taken that item on loan. If this value is null, then it indicates that the Book is not on loan. If the value is not null, then the Borrower object referenced by this value is the Borrower who has the Book on loan.

The Library class is augmented with a method to register a new Borrower and a method to display each Borrower with the details of each Book they have borrowed. The class also includes operations to lend and return a Book. The full listing is given in Library 02.

```
class Book {

    def attachBorrower(borrower) {
        this.borrower = borrower
    }

    def detachBorrower() {
        borrower = null
    }

    String toString() {                    // redefinition
        return "Book: ${catalogNumber}: ${title} by: ${author}"
    }

//------properties----------------

    def catalogNumber
    def title
    def author
    def borrower = null
}
```

LIBRARY 02
Borrowers

```groovy
class Borrower {

    def attachBook(bk) {
        borrowedBooks[bk.catalogNumber] = bk
        bk.attachBorrower(this)
    }

    def detachBook(bk) {
        borrowedBooks.remove(bk.catalogNumber)
        bk.detachBorrower()
    }

    String toString() {
        return "Borrower: ${membershipNumber}; ${name}"
    }

// ------properties---------------

    def membershipNumber
    def name
    def borrowedBooks = [ : ]
}

class Library {

    def addBook(bk) {
        loanStock[bk.catalogNumber] = bk
    }

    def displayStock() {
        println "\n\nLibrary: ${name}"
        println '================'

        loanStock.each { catalogNumber, book -> println " ${book}" }
    }

    def displayBooksAvailableForLoan() {
        println "\n\nLibrary: ${name} : Available for loan"
        println '================'

        loanStock.each { catalogNumber, book -> if(book.borrower == null) println " ${book}" }
    }

    def displayBooksOnLoan() {
        println "\n\nLibrary: ${name} : On loan"
        println '================'

        loanStock.each { catalogNumber, book -> if(book.borrower != null) println " ${book}" }
    }
```

```groovy
    def registerBorrower(borrower) {
        borrowers[borrower.membershipNumber] = borrower
    }

    def displayBorrowers() {
        println "\n\nLibrary: ${name} : Borrower details"
        println '================='

        borrowers.each { membershipNumber, borrower ->
            println borrower
            borrower.borrowedBooks.each { catalogNumber, book -> println " ${book}" }
        }
    }

    def lendBook(catalogNumber, membershipNumber) {
        def loanStockEntry = loanStock.find { entry -> entry.key == catalogNumber }
        def borrowersEntry = borrowers.find { entry -> entry.key == membershipNumber }
        borrowersEntry.value.attachBook(loanStockEntry.value)
    }

    def returnBook(catalogNumber) {
        def loanStockEntry = loanStock.find { entry -> entry.key == catalogNumber }
        def bor = loanStockEntry.value.borrower
        bor.detachBook(loanStockEntry.value)
    }

// -----properties -----------------

    def name
    def loanStock = [ : ]
    def borrowers = [ : ]
}

        // Create a library object
def lib = new Library(name : 'Dunning')

        // Create some books...
def bk1 = new Book(catalogNumber : '111', title : 'Groovy', author : 'Ken')
def bk2 = new Book(catalogNumber : '222', title : 'OOD', author : 'Ken')
def bk3 = new Book(catalogNumber : '333', title : 'UML', author : 'John')

        // ...add them to the loan stock
lib.addBook(bk1)
lib.addBook(bk2)
lib.addBook(bk3)

        // See stock
lib.displayStock()
```

```
            // Now introduce some borrowers
bo1 = new Borrower(membershipNumber : '1234', name : 'Jessie')
bo2 = new Borrower(membershipNumber : '5678', name : 'Sally')

lib.registerBorrower(bo1)
lib.registerBorrower(bo2)

            // See borrowers
lib.displayBorrowers()

            // Finally, make some transactions
lib.displayBooksAvailableForLoan()

lib.lendBook('111', '1234')

lib.displayBooksAvailableForLoan()
lib.displayBooksOnLoan()
lib.displayBorrowers()

lib.returnBook('111')

lib.displayBooksAvailableForLoan()
lib.displayBooksOnLoan()
lib.displayBorrowers()
```

As with the previous iteration, when we run this script, the results reveal that the classes behave as expected.

```
Library: Dunning
================
    Book: 111: Groovy by: Ken
    Book: 222: OOD by: Ken
    Book: 333: UML by: John

Library: Dunning : Borrower details
================
    Borrower: 1234; Jessie
    Borrower: 5678; Sally

Library: Dunning : Available for loan
================
    Book: 111: Groovy by: Ken
    Book: 222: OOD by: Ken
    Book: 333: UML by: John
```

```
Library: Dunning : Available for loan
================
     Book: 222: OOD by: Ken
     Book: 333: UML by: John


Library: Dunning : On loan
================
     Book: 111: Groovy by: Ken


Library: Dunning : Borrower details
================
Borrower: 1234; Jessie
     Book: 111: Groovy by: Ken
Borrower: 5678; Sally


Library: Dunning : Available for loan
================
     Book: 111: Groovy by: Ken
     Book: 222: OOD by: Ken
     Book: 333: UML by: John


Library: Dunning : On loan
================


Library: Dunning : Borrower details
================
Borrower: 1234; Jessie
Borrower: 5678; Sally
```

◆

13.4 ITERATION 3: REINSTATE THE USER INTERFACE

The preceding implementation exercised the code by a "hard-wired" set of programmed instructions. In this final iteration, we give the application a text-based user interface controlled by a simple menu similar to the one developed in Iteration 2 of the Chapter 11 case study. Through the menu, we make the application more flexible since the functionality performed is determined by the selection made by the user.

The menu is readily implemented with some simple procedural code. The method readMenuSelection presents the user with the application menu, invites the user to make a selection, and then returns that value as its result to the caller.

A `while` loop ensures that the menu is repeated until the user indicates that the application is complete. A series of selections with a chain of `if..else` statements picks off the user choice and implements the required functionality.

Although this user interface is not especially difficult to implement, in the future, we may need to convert the application to have a graphical user interface or a web interface. If we consider the model developed in the previous iteration, then a design weakness becomes apparent. It is that the `Library` class has various display methods that output to the console. Unfortunately, a change of user interface would necessitate significant changes to it and possibly to other classes as well.

Our intention is that the classes such as `Book`, `Borrower`, and `Library` should have no responsibility for input or output. Collectively, we refer to these three classes as the *domain model.* This ensures that the domain model classes require no revisions to accommodate a change of user interface.

A useful approach is to have an object whose responsibility is to interact with the domain model and also to be responsible for input and output. For this reason, we introduce an `Action` class with a set of methods corresponding to each use case of the application. The relation of the `Action` class with the domain model classes is shown in Fig. 13.3.

The final listing is given in Library 03. The main application code handles the presentation of the menu and the selection made by the user. The user choice is then routed to one of the `Action` class methods. For example, the method `displayStock` in the class `Action` produces all the output from data obtained from the domain model `Library` class. Equally, the method `registerBorrower` from the class `Action` asks the user for the borrower details, constructs a `Borrower` object, and then registers that `Borrower` with the `Library`.

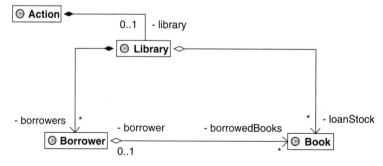

FIGURE 13.3 Incorporating the `Action` class.

```
import console.*
```

```
// The Book and Borrower classes are unchanged from the previous iteration

class Library {

    def addBook(bk) {
        loanStock[bk.catalogNumber] = bk
    }

    def registerBorrower(borrower) {
        borrowers[borrower.membershipNumber] = borrower
    }

    def lendBook(catalogNumber, membershipNumber) {
        def loanStockEntry = loanStock.find { entry -> entry.key == catalogNumber }
        def borrowersEntry = borrowers.find { entry -> entry.key == membershipNumber }
        borrowersEntry.value. attachBook(loanStockEntry.value)
    }

    def returnBook(catalogNumber) {
        def loanStockEntry = loanStock.find { entry -> entry.key == catalogNumber }
        def bor = loanStockEntry.value.borrower
        bor.detachBook(loanStockEntry.value)
    }
// -----properties ------------------

    def name
    def loanStock = [ : ]
    def borrowers = [ : ]
}

class Action {

    def addBook() {
        print('\nEnter book catalog number: ')
        def catalogNumber = Console.readLine()
        print('Enter book title: ')
        def title = Console.readLine()
        print('Enter book author: ')
        def author = Console.readLine()

        def bk = new Book(catalogNumber : catalogNumber, title : title, author : author)

        library.addBook(bk)
    }
```

```
def displayStock() {
    println "\n\nLibrary: ${library.name}"
    println '================='

    library.loanStock.each { catalogNumber, book -> println " ${book}" }
}

def displayBooksAvailableForLoan() {
    println "\n\nLibrary: ${library.name} : Available for loan"
    println '================='

    library.loanStock.each { catalogNumber, book -> if(book.borrower == null) println " ${book}" }
}

def displayBooksOnLoan() {
    println "\n\nLibrary: ${library.name} : On loan"
    println '================='

    library.loanStock.each { catalogNumber, book -> if(book.borrower != null) println " ${book}" }
}

def registerBorrower() {
    print('\nEnter borrower membership number: ')
    def membershipNumber = Console.readLine()
    print('Enter borrower name: ')
    def name = Console.readLine()

    def bor = new Borrower(membershipNumber : membershipNumber, name : name)

    library.registerBorrower(bor)
}

def displayBorrowers() {
    println "\n\nLibrary: ${library.name} : Borrower details"
    println '================='

    library.borrowers.each { membershipNumber, borrower ->
        println borrower
        borrower.borrowedBooks.each { catalogNumber, book -> println " ${book}" }
    }
}

def lendBook() {
    print('\nEnter book catalog number: ')
    def catalogNumber = Console.readLine()
    print('Enter borrower membership number: ')
    def membershipNumber = Console.readLine()
```

```
        library.lendBook(catalogNumber, membershipNumber)
    }

    def returnBook() {
        print('\nEnter book catalog number: ')
        def catalogNumber = Console.readLine()

        library.returnBook(catalogNumber)
    }

// -----properties ----------------

    def library
}

def readMenuSelection() {
    println()
    println('0: Quit')
    println('1: Add new book')
    println('2: Display stock')
    println('3: Display books available for loan')
    println('4: Display books on loan')
    println('5: Register new borrower')
    println('6: Display borrowers')
    println('7: Lend one book')
    println('8: Return one book')

    print('\n\tEnter choice>>> ')
    return Console.readString()
}

        // make the Action object
def action = new Action(library : new Library(name : 'Dunning'))

        // make first selection
def choice = readMenuSelection()
while(choice != '0') {

    if(choice == '1') {                        // Add new book
        action.addBook()
    } else if(choice == '2') {                 // Display stock
        action.displayStock()
    } else if(choice == '3') {                 // Display books available for loan
        action.displayBooksAvailableForLoan()
    } else if(choice == '4') {                 // Display books on loan
        action.displayBooksOnLoan()
    } else if(choice == '5') {                 // Register new borrower
```

```
        action.registerBorrower()
    } else if(choice == '6') {                    // Display borrowers
        action.displayBorrowers()
    } else if(choice == '7') {                    // Lend one book
        action.lendBook()
    } else if(choice == '8') {                    // Return one book
        action.returnBook()
    } else {
        println("Unknown selection")
    }
        // next selection
    choice = readMenuSelection()
}
println('System closing')
```

Of course, we should test that we have the same system functionality as before. This is easily accomplished by making menu choices that correspond to the "hard-wired" instructions of the previous iteration and then comparing the outputs. For example, with user input shown italicized and emboldened, we might have:

```
0: Quit
1: Add new book
2: Display stock
3: Display books available for loan
4: Display books on loan
5: Register new borrower
6: Display borrowers
7: Lend one book
8: Return one book

        Enter choice>>> 1

Enter book catalog number: 111
Enter book title: Groovy
Enter book author: Ken


// ...
// Present the menu to the user

        Enter choice>>> 2

Library: Dunning
================
    Book: 333: UML by: John
    Book: 111: Groovy by: Ken
    Book: 222: OOD by: Ken
```

```
// ...
// Present the menu to the user

        Enter choice>>> 6

Library: Dunning : Borrower details
=================
Borrower: 1234; Jessie
    Book: 111: Groovy by: Ken
Borrower: 5678; Sally

// ...
// Present the menu to the user

        Enter choice>>> 0


System closing
```

◆

Having established that we have the same outcomes, we consider this iteration complete.

13.5 EXERCISES

1. In Iteration 1 of this case study (listing Library 01), the Library adds a new Book to its stock with the method addBook(bk), where the single parameter bk represents a Book object created by the application client. Introduce a further variant of this method in which the Book details are given as method parameters as in addBook(catalogNumber, title, author).

2. The application script code in Library 01 first creates the Library object, and then some Book objects, adds the Books to the Library stock, and then displays the stock. What would have been the rationale for calling the method displayStock immediately after creating the Library object?

3. In Iteration 3, the code that presents a menu to the user, determines the choice made, and then actions that choice is rather repetitive. In keeping with the discussions in Section 11.3 of Chapter 11, replace this code with a lookup table that makes use of Groovy's closures.

4. Software developers usually recognize similarities between the systems they build. Although many of the details may be different, the overall design and implementation are often very similar. In our case study, we have a library with many books. However, we might have used a doctor with many patients or a university with many students. The design and the issues that arise from it would have been much the same.

Using this case study as a guide, consider the following:

- A car rental agency has several cars. Each car has a unique registration number, make and model name, and year of registration. Cars may be hired out to a customer registered with the company. Each customer has a name and a unique customer number. We are asked to support the company owner by logging which cars are rented to which customers.

- A video shop has a large number of videos for rent to customers. Each video has a unique title and each customer a unique registration number. As before, we are asked to log which videos are out on loan to which customers.

- A hospital has many doctors and patients. Each doctor and patient has a name and unique number. Doctors look after many patients but a patient has exactly one doctor. We are asked to develop a patient monitoring system by recording which patient is associated with a particular doctor.

- A university has many students, each with a unique matriculation number as well as a name and course of study. We are asked to be able to log each student and obtain a display of all students as well as those in a particular course.

Now develop a design and implementation based on one (or all) of them. You can include as much detail as you think is appropriate.

5. You are required to develop software to support the administration of a hotel. The major features of the hotel are:

- There are three floors numbered 1, 2, and 3, each of which has a variable number of rooms.

- Not all floors have the same combination of rooms.

- Each room has a room number, for example, 201 for room 1 on floor 2.

- Each room has a maximum occupancy, that is, the number of people who can use it.

Staff should be able to obtain details of each room on each floor in a variety of ways. As a minimum, the user must be able to request a report for:

- All the rooms on all floors

- All the rooms on a particular floor

- A particular room on a particular floor

and to decommission a room:

- Remove a particular room from a given floor

6. A software house employs programmers, each of whom has expertise in a particular programming language, for example, Groovy, C++, or Java. All programmers are paid a basic monthly salary of around 1000 pounds. However, the amount may vary from programmer to programmer.

Since they are in demand, a 10% enhancement of the basic salary is paid to each programmer who specializes in Groovy. However, programmers may change their specialist language and their salary enhancement should change accordingly. For example, after suitable training, a C++ programmer could become a Groovy programmer.

When a new programmer joins the staff, a more experienced programmer is assigned to him as a mentor. Both must specialize in the same programming language. The basic idea behind this practice is that the new recruit (the mentee) will benefit from the experience of the mentor. Since this is extra work for the mentor, he is awarded 5% of current salary enhancement for every mentee under his supervision. When a programmer no longer needs a mentor, the mentor's salary is changed accordingly.

For administrative purposes, each employee has a name and a unique payroll number.

You are required to develop software that supports the administration of the company. At a minimum, it should produce a detailed report on each programmer and a total monthly salary bill for the company.

The report should show for each programmer:

- Payroll number and name
- Specialist programming language and current monthly salary

together with:

- Details of any programmers that he is mentoring or is mentored by

14

INHERITANCE

In this chapter, we introduce the *inheritance* relationship that may exist between classes. It is widely used in object-oriented applications and brings to our designs and programs a powerful feature unique to object orientation.

Inheritance (also known as *specialization*) is a way to form new classes using classes that have already been defined. The former, known as *derived classes*, inherit properties and behaviors of the latter, which are referred to as *base classes*. The terms *parent class* and *child class* as well as *superclass* and *subclass* are also used in this context. Inheritance is intended to help reuse existing code with little or no modification.

Inheritance is also called *generalization*. For instance, an account is a generalization of current account (checking account) and deposit account (savings account). We say that "account" is an abstraction of current account, deposit account, and so on. Conversely, we can say that because current accounts are accounts, that is, a current account is an account, that they inherit all the properties common to all accounts, such as the account number or the account balance.

14.1 INHERITANCE

Consider a bank in which customers open various current (checking) accounts. Each current account is given a unique account number, as well as a balance and the permitted amount by which the account may be overdrawn. Using the knowledge from the preceding two chapters, we might arrive at the class CurrentAccount shown in Example 01.

EXAMPLE 01
CurrentAccount
class

```
class CurrentAccount {

    String toString() {
        return "Current Account: ${number}; balance: ${balance}; overdraft : ${overdraftLimit}"
    }

// -----properties ----------------

    def number
    def balance
    def overdraftLimit

}

        // populate a list with the instances
def accounts = [new CurrentAccount(number : 'AAA111', balance : 1000, overdraftLimit : 400),
            new CurrentAccount(number : 'BBB222', balance : 2500, overdraftLimit : 800)]

        // now display each
accounts.each { acc ->
    println acc                         // automatically call toString
}
```

When we execute this program, the output is as we expect. The two Account objects in the List variable accounts are printed using the definition of the toString method:

```
Current Account: AAA111; balance: 1000; overdraft : 400
Current Account: BBB222; balance: 2500; overdraft : 800
```

Although there is nothing intrinsically wrong with this class, we can improve it significantly. For example, it is likely that the bank also offers deposit (savings) accounts to its customers. If our bank has this new type of account, then we would also require a DepositAccount class. DepositAccounts are also given an account number and a balance, but no overdraft. DepositAccounts, however, earn interest. Both these types of accounts share some common characteristics, while each has additional properties.

We can think of a CurrentAccount (checking account) and a DepositAccount (savings account) as special kinds of Account. The Account class has the features common to both the CurrentAccount and DepositAccount class, namely, the account number and the balance. The CurrentAccount class is then related to the

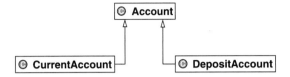

FIGURE 14.1   Inheritance.

Account class by inheritance. The DepositAccount class is also related to the Account class by inheritance. The Account class is usually referred to as the superclass and the CurrentAccount (and DepositAccount) class as the subclass.

The class diagram shown in Figure 14.1 is used to denote this arrangement of classes. An inheritance relation (directed arrow) relates the subclass CurrentAccount and DepositAccount to the superclass Account.

The Groovy reserved word extends specifies that a class inherits from another class. This leads to the code shown in Example 02. We will introduce the DepositAccount class shortly.

EXAMPLE 02
Class inheritance

```
class Account {

    String toString() {              // redefinition
        return "${number}; ${balance}"
    }

// -----properties ---------------

    def number
    def balance
}

class CurrentAccount extends Account {

    String toString() {
        return 'Current Account: ' + super.toString() + "; ${overdraftLimit}"
    }

// ------properties ---------------

    def overdraftLimit
}

        // populate a list with the instances
def accounts = [new Account(number : 'AAA111', balance : 1000),
            new CurrentAccount(number : 'BBB222', balance : 2000, overdraftLimit : 400),
            new CurrentAccount(number : 'CCC333', balance : 3000, overdraftLimit : 800)]
```

```
                // now display each
accounts.each { acc ->
    println acc                              // automatically call toString
}
```

Executing this program produces the output:

```
AAA111; 1000
Current Account: BBB222; 2000; 400
Current Account: CCC333; 3000; 800
```

◆

Here we see that the first line of output differs from the other two. This is because the first object in the accounts variable is an Account object while the other two are CurrentAccount objects. Since the first object in the List is an Account object, the implementation of the method toString in the Account class is responsible for what is displayed. The same message toString is also sent to the two CurrentAccount objects. However, in this class, the method toString has been redefined and is the reason for the last two lines of output.

The CurrentAccount class now has only those features special to it. Similarly, the Account class has only those relevant to accounts. This makes the CurrentAccount class much easier to develop. It is important to realize that the Account class can be reused in this application or any other. Later, we shall do exactly this and inherit class DepositAccount from it.

Note how the method toString is redefined in the subclass CurrentAccount. The behavior we require from it is to augment that produced by the toString method in the superclass Account. Hence, the method definition in CurrentAccount calls the method defined in the superclass with the expression super.toString(). The keyword super ensures that we invoke the method defined in the superclass. Without this keyword, the method toString in CurrentAccount would recursively call itself (see Appendix G).

14.2   INHERITED METHODS

In Groovy, all the features declared in a superclass are inherited by a subclass. This means that the CurrentAccount class (see preceding text) need declare only those methods and properties required by itself. In this case, it is the additional overdraftLimit property (we shall shortly discuss the method toString). In more complex examples, this would represent a significant savings in effort. Consider Example 03.

EXAMPLE 03
Inherited features

```
          class Account {

                  String toString() {                    // redefinition
                      return "${number}; ${balance}"
                  }

// -----properties ------------------

      def number
      def balance
}

class CurrentAccount extends Account {

      String toString() {
          return 'Current Account: ' + super.toString() + "; ${overdraftLimit}"
      }

// -----properties -----------------

      def overdraftLimit
}

          // populate a list with the instances
def accounts = [new Account(number : 'AAA111', balance : 1000),
                new CurrentAccount(number : 'BBB222', balance : 2000, overdraftLimit : 400),
                new CurrentAccount(number : 'CCC333', balance : 3000, overdraftLimit : 800)]

          // now display each
accounts.each { acc ->
      println acc                                      // automatically call toString
}

def ca = new CurrentAccount(number : 'DDD444', balance : 4000, overdraftLimit : 1200)

          // use methods and inherited methods
println "Overdraft: ${ca.overdraftLimit}"
println "Number: ${ca.number}"

def ac = new Account(number : 'EEE555', balance : 1234)

println "Number: ${ac.number}"                         // OK
//println "Overdraft: ${ac.overdraftLimit}"            // ERROR: no such property
```

Running this program delivers the output shown below. The first three lines
are as described for the preceding example. The next line is the overdraft limit
from the object ca. Because ca is an object of the class CurrentAccount, then

the message getOverdraftLimit is defined in its own class. The fifth line is the result of sending the message getNumber to the same CurrentAccount object. Since this class does not define this method, the system executes that inherited from its superclass Account.

```
AAA111; 1000
Current Account: BBB222; 2000; 400
Current Account: CCC333; 3000; 800
Overdraft: 1200
Number: DDD444
Number: EEE555
```

◆

Take note of the lines of code near the end of the listing in which the CurrentAccount object ca is created, and then the properties overdraftLimit and number are accessed. The overdraftLimit property is, of course, defined in the CurrentAccount class itself. However, the number property is inherited from the Account class. The remaining three lines in the code show that an Account object can be asked for its number (defined in the Account class), but we cannot reference the overdraftLimit for a Account object because there is no such property defined in that class.

14.3   REDEFINED METHODS

In Groovy, all the features declared in a superclass are inherited by a subclass. This means that if the CurrentAccount class did not define the toString method, then the one defined in the Account class would be inherited and used by all CurrentAccount objects. However, with Groovy, a method inherited by a subclass can be *redefined* to have a different behavior. An obvious strategy is for the toString method required in the CurrentAccount class to make use of the toString method in the Account superclass and to augment it with additional logic. Looking at Example 03, we see the toString method in class CurrentAccount as:

```
String toString() {
    return 'Current Account: ' + super.toString() + " by: ${overdraftLimit}"
}
```

Again, notice the use of the reserved keyword super. This time it is used to ensure that the toString method defined in its superclass is called to get part of the String returned by this CurrentAccount method.

14.4 POLYMORPHISM

A defining characteristic of object-oriented systems is the *polymorphic effect.* A message sent to an object of some class is received as normal. However, an object of a descendant class may also receive the same message. If the two classes of objects have their own definitions of the method for the message, then we may observe different behaviors. The use of the polymorphic effect results in systems that are apparently simple but that have complex execution patterns.

We can see this occurring in Example 03. The code fragment:

```
def accounts = [new Account(number : 'AAA111', balance : 1000),
                new CurrentAccount(number : 'BBB222', balance : 2000, overdraftLimit : 400),
                new CurrentAccount(number : 'CCC333', balance : 3000, overdraftLimit : 800)]

        // now display each
accounts.each { acc ->
    println acc                          // automatically call toString
}
```

produces the output:

```
AAA111; 1000
Current Account: BBB222; 2000; 400
Current Account: CCC333; 3000; 800
```

The print statement sends each acc object the toString message (implicitly). The first item taken from the List is an Account object and this produces the first output line. This, of course, is produced by the method toString defined in the Account class. The remaining two lines of output are, however, different from the first even when the same message is being sent. This is a consequence of the recipients being CurrentAccount objects for which the method toString has been redefined in the CurrentAccount subclass.

The full extent of this polymorphic effect is presented in Example 04. This application is concerned with modeling a Bank shown by the class diagram in Figure 14.2.

The Bank accounts comprise either CurrentAccounts or DepositAccounts. Methods are provided to open new accounts with the Bank and to obtain a report on the Bank and its accounts.

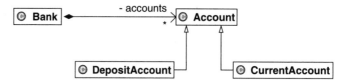

FIGURE 14.2   Bank application.

EXAMPLE 04

Bank example

```
class Account {

    String toString() {                    // redefinition
        return "${number}; ${balance}"
    }

// -----properties ---------------------

    def number
    def balance

}

class CurrentAccount extends Account {

    String toString() {
        return 'Current Account: ' + super.toString() + "; ${overdraftLimit}"
    }

// -----properties ---------------------

    def overdraftLimit
    }

class DepositAccount extends Account {

    String toString() {
        return 'Deposit Account: ' + super.toString() + "; ${interestRate}"
    }

// ------properties ---------------------

    def interestRate
}

class Bank {

    def openAccount(account) {
        accounts[account.numbergetNumber()] = account
    }
```

```
// ------properties --------------------

    def name
    def accounts = [ : ]

}

def displayBank(bk) {
    println "Bank: ${bk.name}"
    println '===================='

    bk.accounts.each { number, account -> println " ${account}" }
}

        // create a new Bank object
def bk = new Bank(name : 'Barclay')

        // create some accounts
def ca1 = new CurrentAccount(number : 'AAA111', balance : 2000, overdraftLimit : 400)
def ca2 = new CurrentAccount(number : 'BBB222', balance : 3000, overdraftLimit : 800)
def da1 = new DepositAccount(number : 'CCC333', balance : 4000, interestRate : 4)

        // add them to the bank
bk.openAccount(ca1)
bk.openAccount(ca2)
bk.openAccount(da1)

        // now display everything
displayBank(bk)
```

The output from this program is:

```
Bank: Barclay
====================
    Deposit Account: CCC333; 4000; 4
    Current Account: BBB222; 3000; 800
    Current Account: AAA111; 2000; 400
```

◆

Present in this example is the *principle of substitution*. This states that where in our code an object of a superclass is expected, an object of a subclass can be used. Method openAccount in class Bank has a single parameter representing some kind of Account object. In the application code, we send this method to the Bank object bk with CurrentAccount and DepositAccount objects. This is permissible, since the substitution principle ensures that when a superclass Account object is expected, then only methods of that class will be used on the parameter. Because the subclass objects automatically inherit that behavior, correct operation is guaranteed.

Finally, we should point out that since the `Bank` class is a domain model class, then we choose not to include any display methods for the reasons given in the previous chapter.

14.5   THE ABSTRACT CLASS

It is often useful to be able to define a class that acts only as a basis for establishing others. There is no intention to make an instance of it. It is a way of guaranteeing that all descendants share a common set of features. This kind of class is referred to as an *abstract class*.

For example, consider the bank application in Example 04. Assume that there will never be an instance of an `Account`; we have `CurrentAccounts` or `DepositAccounts` but never just `Accounts`. We intend that all accounts of the `Bank` share common features such as `number` and `balance`. Therefore, we decide that the class `Account` is *stereotypical* of an abstract class. In Figure 14.3, the `Account` class has been decorated with "A" to emphasize that the class is abstract.

We specify that a class is abstract with the keyword `abstract`, as shown for the `Account` class in Example 05. Otherwise, the remainder of the class and its subclasses remain the same. The key observation is that Groovy supports the notion that there is never any intention of creating instances of an abstract class.

EXAMPLE 05
No instances of abstract classes

```groovy
abstract class Account {

    String toString() {                 // redefinition
        return "${number}; ${balance}"
    }

// -----properties ------------------

    def number
    def balance

}

class CurrentAccount extends Account { ... }

class DepositAccount extends Account { ... }

class Bank { ... }

def displayBank(bk) { ... }
```

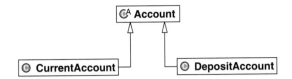

FIGURE 14.3   Abstract class.

```
        // create a new Bank object
def bk = new Bank(name : 'Barclay')

        // create some accounts
def ca1 = new CurrentAccount(number : 'AAA111', balance : 2000, overdraftLimit : 400)
def ca2 = new CurrentAccount(number : 'BBB222', balance : 3000, overdraftLimit : 800)
def da1 = new DepositAccount(number : 'CCC333', balance : 4000, interestRate : 4)

        // add them to the bank
bk.openAccount(ca1)
bk.openAccount(ca2)
bk.openAccount(da1)

        // now display everything
displayBank(bk)

//acc = new Account(number : 'DDD444', balance : 1234)     // ERROR
```

◆

The program delivers the same output as for the previous example. The final line of coding in Example 05 confirms that we are not permitted to create instances of the abstract class Account.

It is common for an abstract class to include a *deferred method*, that is, one for which no method definition is given. This usually arises because the class is too abstract to determine how the method should be implemented. The inclusion of a deferred method in an abstract class infers that subclasses must provide an implementation if they are to represent concrete classes from which instances can be created. In effect, the inclusion of a deferred method imposes a *protocol* on subclasses that must be respected if a concrete class is required. A deferred method in Groovy is known as an *abstract method* and is qualified with the abstract keyword. In Example 06, the abstract class Account includes an abstract method entitled isOverdrawn with the declaration:

```
        // class Account
def abstract isOverdrawn()
```

EXAMPLE 06
Abstract methods

```
abstract class Account {

    String toString() {                         // redefinition
        return "${number}; ${balance}"
    }

    def abstract isOverdrawn()                  // deferred method

// -----properties -----------------

    def number
    def balance

}

class CurrentAccount extends Account {

    String toString() {
        return 'Current Account: ' + super.toString() + "; ${overdraftLimit}"
    }

    def isOverdrawn() {                         // redefinition
        return balance < -overdraftLimit
    }

// ------properties ------------------

    def overdraftLimit
}

class DepositAccount extends Account {

    String toString() {
        return 'Deposit Account: ' + super.toString() + "; ${interestRate}"
    }

    def isOverdrawn() {                         // redefinition
        return balance < 0
    }

// ------properties ------------------

    def interestRate
}

class Bank {

    def openAccount(account) {
        accounts[account.number] = account
    }
```

```
// ------properties ------------------

    def name
    def accounts = [ : ]
}

def displayBank(bk) {
    println "Bank: ${bk.name}"
    println '===================='

    bk.accounts.each { number, account -> println " ${account}" }
}

        // create a new Bank object
def bk = new Bank(name : 'Barclay')

        // create some accounts
def ca1 = new CurrentAccount(number : 'AAA111', balance : 2000, overdraftLimit : 400)
def ca2 = new CurrentAccount(number : 'BBB222', balance : 3000, overdraftLimit : 800)
def da1 = new DepositAccount(number : 'CCC333', balance : 4000, interestRate : 4)

        // add them to the bank
bk.openAccount(ca1)
bk.openAccount(ca2)
bk.openAccount(da1)

        // now display everything
displayBank(bk)

        // check status of some accounts
println "Current account: ${ca1.number}; overdrawn?: ${ca1.isOverdrawn()}"
println "Deposit account: ${da1.number}; overdrawn?: ${da1.isOverdrawn()}"
```

◆

Again, the output from this program is the same as the previous two. Observe the definitions for the method isOverdrawn in both the CurrentAccount and DepositAccount classes. In the class CurrentAccount, the method checks the balance against the overdraftLimit. In the class DepositAccount, the balance is checked to see if it is negative.

14.6   THE INTERFACE CLASS

It is possible to have an abstract class in which none of its methods has been defined. They are all *deferred* to a subclass for their implementation. Such a class is referred to as an *interface class*. Since no method is actually defined, an interface presents only a specification of its behaviors. An interface proves extremely useful, acting as the *protocol* to which one or more subclasses must conform, that is, provide definitions for all its methods.

Groovy supports the concept of an interface class with the keyword inter-face. Although it is similar to an abstract class with no defined methods, it is important to realize that it is different in one important respect. It is that a class that implements the interface, that is, one that provides methods for its deferred operations, need not belong to the same class hierarchy. Although they may implement other methods and have different parents, if they implement those operations advertised by the interface, they can substitute for it. This simple fact makes the interface an extremely powerful facility that gives the designer more flexibility than the abstract class allows.

Consider the bank and its accounts. We can insist that we must be able to ask any account to determine whether it is overdrawn. Clearly, the class to which an account belongs must have implementations for the operation isOverdrawn. However, there is no requirement that each class is part of the same inheritance hierarchy. This is an important point that makes a critical difference to our design. All that matters is that the Bank is able to send the message isOverdrawn to each of its accounts. It may be possible to send other messages, but to be an account opened by the Bank, only the isOverdrawn operation is required.

We can model this situation with a Groovy interface as shown in Figure 14.4. The dashed inheritance arrows connecting AccountAB to AccountIF denote that (abstract) class AccountAB implements the interface AccountIF. The UML stereotype «interface» and/or the I adorns the AccountIF class.

The implementation for this is given in Example 07, where AccountIF is introduced as an interface class. An interface declares, but does not define, one or more abstract methods. The abstract class AccountAB conforms to the proto-col since it *implements* the AccountIF class. Notice that the AccountAB class offers a simple implementation for the isOverdrawn method. We must explicitly rede-fine it in the CurrentAccount class.

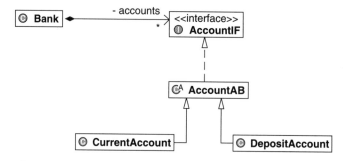

FIGURE 14.4   Interface class.

EXAMPLE 07

Interface class

```
interface AccountIF {

    def abstract isOverdrawn()                  // deferred method
}

abstract class AccountAB implements AccountIF {

    String toString() {                         // redefinition
        return "${number}; ${balance}"
    }

    def isOverdrawn() {                         // redefinition
        return balance < 0
    }

// -----properties -----------------

    def number
    def balance

}

class CurrentAccount extends AccountAB {

    String toString() {
        return 'Current Account: ' + super.toString() + "; ${overdraftLimit}"
    }

    def isOverdrawn() {                         // redefinition
        return balance <- overdraftLimit
    }

// ------properties ------------------

    def overdraftLimit
}

class DepositAccount extends AccountAB {

    String toString() {
        return 'Deposit Account: ' + super.toString() + "; ${interestRate}"
    }

// ------properties -----------------

    def interestRate
}
```

```groovy
class Bank {

    def openAccount(account) {
        accounts[account.number] = account
    }

// ------properties ------------------

    def name
    def accounts = [ : ]
}

def displayBank(bk) {
    println "Bank: ${bk.name}"
    println '===================='

    bk.accounts.each { number, account -> println " ${account}" }
}

        // create a new Bank object
def bk = new Bank(name : 'Barclay')

        // create some accounts
def ca1 = new CurrentAccount(number : 'AAA111', balance : 2000, overdraftLimit : 400)
def ca2 = new CurrentAccount(number : 'BBB222', balance : 3000, overdraftLimit : 800)
def da1 = new DepositAccount(number : 'CCC333', balance : 4000, interestRate : 4)

        // add them to the bank
bk.openAccount(ca1)
bk.openAccount(ca2)
bk.openAccount(da1)

        // now display everything
displayBank(bk)

        // check status of some accounts
println "Current account: ${ca1.number}; overdrawn?: ${ca1.isOverdrawn()}"
println "Deposit account: ${da1.number}; overdrawn?: ${da1.isOverdrawn()}"
```

Again, the output is the same as the most recent predecessors.

◆

Appendix B.5 briefly examines the place for interfaces in Groovy. Because of Groovy's dynamic typing, they are not actually required. With Groovy, polymorphism is simply a matter of matching method names and signatures. However, as in Java, interfaces provide the notion of a protocol that must be adhered to by all concrete subclasses. Further, Groovy code that includes an interface would more readily translate to Java, should that be necessary.

14.7   EXERCISES

1. Into Example 07, put an implementation for the method display in the Account class so that it not required in the subclasses CurrentAccount and DepositAccount.

2. Using Exercise 1 as a model, develop the classes StudentAB, Undergraduate, and Postgraduate. Class StudentAB is an abstract class and represents the general properties associated with students, namely, their names and their registration numbers. The other two classes are concrete specializations of class StudentAB. Class Undergraduate has the course name and year of study, while class Postgraduate has a research title. Establish a list of undergraduates and postgraduates and print their details.

3. The following class diagram describes the individuals who are employed by a software house. Consultants are temporary employees who receive a 500-pound monthly payment. A programmer receives an additional 10% bonus to the basic monthly payment if he specializes in Groovy.

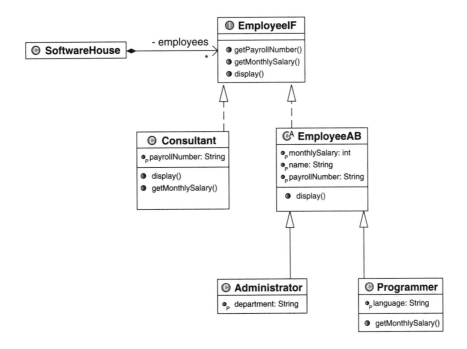

4. You are required to develop software to support the administration of a hotel. The major features of the hotel are:

- There are three floors numbered 1, 2, and 3, each of which has up to five rooms.

- Most rooms are ordinary bedrooms, but some are used for conferences.

- Conference rooms may have study rooms associated with them.

- Study rooms are simply modified bedrooms.

- Not all study rooms are associated with a conference room.

- Not all floors have the same combination of rooms.

- Each room has a room number, for example, 201 for room 1 on floor 2.

- Each room has a maximum occupancy, that is, the number of people who can use it.

- Conference rooms also have a name.

Staff should be able to obtain details of each room on each floor in a variety of ways. At a minimum, the user must be able to request for a report for:

- All the rooms on all floors

- All the rooms on a particular floor or

- A particular room on a particular floor

and to decommission a room:

- Remove a particular room from a given floor

If the room is a bedroom, then its number and maximum occupancy are displayed. However, if it is a conference room, then its name and the room number of each study room associated with it must also be given. A study room displays the same information as a bedroom.

5. In the following listing, class Point represents a point in a two-dimensional space. Complete the class hierarchy rooted on the interface QuadrilateralIF. A Rectangle is defined by the position of the upper left corner, width, and height.

```
class Point {

    def moveBy(deltaX, deltaY) {
        x += deltaX
        y += deltaY
    }

// -----properties ------------------

    def x
    def y
}

interface QuadrilateralIF {
    def abstract getArea()
    def abstract getPerimeter()
    def abstract moveBy(deltaX, deltaY)
}

class Rectangle implements QuadrilateralIF {

// ------properties -------------------

    def upperLeft
    def width
    def height
}

class Square extends Rectangle {
}

def rect = new Rectangle(upperLeft : new Point(x : 0, y : 10), width : 10, height : 5)
rect.moveBy(2, 4)

println "rect: ${rect.getArea()}, ${rect.getPerimeter()}"          // output: 50, 30

def sq = new Square(upperLeft : new Point(x : 0, y : 10), width : 10, height : 10)

println "sq: ${sq.getArea()}, ${sq.getPerimeter()}"          // output: 100, 40
```

6. Develop the classes SalariedEmployee and HourlyEmployee. A salaried
   employee has a salary, which is paid out monthly. An hourly employee
   has a fixed pay rate and a number of hours worked per month. Implement
   the method computeMonthlyPay for these two subclasses, then show that
   the monthly wages bill for the organization is 3300 pounds.

```
interface EmployeeIF {
    def abstract getName()
    def abstract getPayrollNumber()
}

abstract class EmployeeAB implements EmployeeIF {

    def abstract computeMonthlyPay()

// -----properties ------------------

    def name
    def payrollNumber
}

class SalariedEmployee extends EmployeeAB {

// ------properties ------------------

    def salary
}

class HourlyEmployee extends EmployeeAB {

// ------properties -------------------

    def payRate                           // per hour
    def hoursWorked                       // per month
}

class Company {

    def hire(employee) {
        employees[employee.payrollNumber] = employee
    }

    def getMonthlySalaryBill() {
        def total = 0

        employees.each { number, employee ->
            total += employee.computeMonthlyPay()
        }

        return total
    }
```

```
// ------properties ------------------

    def name
    def employees = [ : ]
}

def co = new Company(name : 'Napier')

def se1 = new SalariedEmployee(name : 'Ken', payrollNumber : 1111, salary : 12000)
def se2 = new SalariedEmployee(name : 'John', payrollNumber : 2222, salary : 18000)

def he1 = new HourlyEmployee(name : 'Sally', payrollNumber : 3333,
                  payRate : 5, hoursWorked : 160)

co.hire(se1)
co.hire(se2)
co.hire(he1)

println "Total monthly bill: ${co.getMonthlySalaryBill()}"       // output: 3300
```

UNIT TESTING (JUNIT)

This chapter explores the use of the JUnit testing framework within the Groovy environment. We use classes from the case study of Chapter 13 to illustrate how unit testing can be accomplished with the `GroovyTestCase` class. Next, we show how several `GroovyTestCases` can be combined into a `GroovyTestSuite`. Finally, we reflect on the role of unit testing in an iterative, incremental approach to application development. Throughout our discussion, we emphasize just how easy it is to benefit from unit testing with Groovy.

15.1 UNIT TESTING

The fundamental unit of an object-oriented system is the class. Therefore, an obvious candidate for a unit in *unit testing* is the class. The approach taken is to create an object of the class under testing and use it to check that selected methods execute as expected. Normally, we do not test every method, since it is not always possible or even desirable to do so. Our aim is to detect and correct any likely failures that might arise when a class is deployed in an application.

Unit testing is a programming activity, and so each unit test involves the internal coding details of the class under test. This is known as *white box testing* to suggest that we can "look inside" the class to see its inner workings. The alternative is *black box testing* which, as its name suggests, does not look inside the class. Its purpose is to check the overall effect of a method without any knowledge of how it is internally coded. The use case (functional) tests in Chapters 11 and 13 are examples of black box testing.

Perhaps the most obvious approach to unit testing is to build a test script that prints the expected results. Using the `Book` and `Library` classes from Example 01 of Chapter 13, we might have a test script, held in the file `runBookTest.groovy`, coded as:

```
class Book {

    def String toString() {
        return "Book: ${catalogNumber}: ${title} by: ${author}"
    }

// -----properties ----------------

    def catalogNumber
    def title
    def author

}

        //create the Book under test
def bk1 = new Book(catalogNumber : '111', title : 'Groovy', author: 'Ken')

        // test the method toString
println bk1
```

On execution, we have the output:

```
Book: 111: Groovy by: Ken
```

and we make a visual check of the actual output against the output expected.

Unfortunately, as the number of tests increases, our workload also increases. Every time the class under test is modified, the test script must be run to make sure that none of the tests fails. If we bear in mind that there may be a very large number of such tests, it is no surprise that this approach is not very successful. It is just too time consuming and—it has to be said—is rather boring.

There are several other alternatives, but most of them are flawed in some way. For example, inserting test code into a debugger is not much better than the test script approach. Such tests usually require the original author to interpret them, which means that they don't retain their benefit over time. When the original author is no longer available, such tests can be difficult or even impossible to apply. Another approach is to make assertions, as illustrated in Example 14 of Chapter 7. However, assertion checking can make our code unnecessarily complex and may adversely affect execution speed.

Using a commercial testing tool can also be problematic. Typically, such tools are expensive and require a considerable investment in time and effort to use them effectively. They are often too "heavyweight" for unit testing and are better suited to more demanding testing situations, for example, for the use-case (functional) testing of large applications.

15.2 THE GROOVYTESTCASE AND JUNIT TESTCASE CLASSES

JUnit is an open-source testing framework that is the accepted industry standard for the automated unit testing of Java code (see http://www.junit.org). It was originally written by Erich Gamma and Ken Beck, whose main goal was to write a unit testing framework that programmers would actually use. Two secondary goals were to encourage the writing of tests that retain their value over time and to use existing tests to create new ones.

Fortunately, the JUnit framework can be easily used for testing Groovy classes. All that is required is to extend the GroovyTestCase class that is part of the standard Groovy environment. It is based on the JUnit TestCase class.

Typically, a unit test case consists of several test methods, each of which tests a method declared in the class under test. For example, we might replace the previous test script with:

```
import groovy.util.GroovyTestCase

class BookTest extends GroovyTestCase {

    /**
     * Test that the expected String is returned from toString
     */
    def void testToString() {
        def bk1 = new Book(catalogNumber : '111', title : 'Groovy', author : 'Ken')
        def expected = 'Book: 111: Groovy by: Ken'

        assertToString(bk1, expected)
    }

}
```

The GroovyTestCase class has been carefully constructed to minimize the amount of work we have to do. For example, each method prefixed by test in BookTest is compiled and executed just like a normal Groovy script. This applies to any class that extends GroovyTestCase.

In the test methods, we make assertions about the state of the code. If during the execution of a test method an assertion is false, then it indicates there is a problem and the test fails. Groovy has an automatic mechanism for reporting on the location and nature of the failure. Alternatively, if the assertion is true, the test passes. There are several different assertions that can be made but, for our purposes, we need relatively few and they will be explained as we use them. Interested readers should consult the Groovy website for more extensive and detailed information.

For example, in testToString, we test that that when toString is called on the Book referenced by bk1, it should return the expected value. We accomplish this by making the assertion:

```
assertToString(bk1, expected)
```

The assertion is true and the test passes if the value of the String returned by bk1.toString() is equal to value of expected. Otherwise, the assertion is false and the test fails.

Execution of BookTest results in the test report:

```
.
Time: 0.05

OK (1 test)
```

Note that as the single test in BookTest has passed, the feedback given is minimal, that is, a dot representing the test and the execution time in seconds. This is intentional, since we just don't need to know any more than that the test passed. However, as we shall discover, if an assertion fails, we are given a more detailed report.

If we consider the Library class from Example 01 of Chapter 13, its unit tests are more interesting. For example, we might have:

```
import groovy.util.GroovyTestCase

class LibraryTest extends GroovyTestCase {

    /**
     * Set up the fixture
     */
    void setUp(){
        lib = new Library(name : 'Dunning')

        bk1 = new Book(catalogNumber : '111', title : 'Groovy', author :'Ken')
```

```
            bk2 = new Book(catalogNumber : '222', title : 'OOD', author : 'Ken')
    }


    /**
     * Test that addition of a Book to an empty Library results in one more Book
     * in the Library
     */
    void testAddBook_1() {
        def pre = lib.loanStock.size()
        lib.addBook(bk1)
        def post = lib.loanStock.size()

        assertTrue('one less book than expected', post == pre + 1)
    }


    /**
     * Test that the addition of two Books with different catalog numbers
     * to an empty Library results in two Books in the Library
     */
    void testAddBook_2() {
        lib.addBook(bk1)
        lib.addBook(bk2)
        def expected = 2
        def actual = lib.loanStock.size()

        assertTrue('unexpected number of books', expected == actual)
    }

// -----properties ----------------

    def lib

    def bk1
    def bk2
}
```

Notice that we use a numbering scheme with a suitable comment for a method
with several tests. However, the use of more meaningful method names, such as
testAddPublicationWithDifferentCatalogNumber, is a popular alternative.

The method setUp establishes the environment (context) in which each test
method executes. The test environment is known as the *test fixture* and it must
be initialized each time a test method executes. This ensures that there is no
interference between tests and that they can be run in any order. Groovy
arranges for setUp to be automatically executed before the execution of each test
method.

In our `LibraryTest` class, the test fixture is a `Library` object referenced by `lib` and two `Book` objects referenced by `bk1` and `bk2`, respectively. They are defined as properties of `LibraryTest` and all three are initialized by `setup`.

In each test method, we assert that something is true. If it is not, then the test fails and the failure is reported with a suitable message. For example, in `testAddBook_1`, we assert that on completion of the method, there should be one more `Book` in the `Library` with:

```
assertTrue('one less book than expected', post == pre + 1)
```

If the condition `post == pre + 1` evaluates to `true`, then the assertion is true. Otherwise, the assertion is false and a failure is reported with the text:

```
one less book than expected
```

incorporated into it to help identify the nature of the problem.

Similarly, in `testAddBook_2`, we assert that the addition of two `Books` with different catalog numbers to an empty `Library` should result in a `Library` with two `Books` in it. Execution of `LibraryTest` produces the output:

```
..
Time: 0.741

OK (2 tests)
```

and so we know that the two tests have passed. Although they appear to be rather simple, these tests give us confidence that the `Library` class is behaving as planned. There is no need to construct elaborate unit tests. In fact, it is normally much better to have several tests, each of which tests just one logical path through the method under test. They are not a burden since they are automatically compiled, executed, and checked. As we add more and more tests, we have more and more confidence in our code.

Unit testing is all about using our experience as programmers to detect and correct possible failures in our code. To illustrate, let's pose the question: What happens if we attempt to add a book with the same catalog number as one already in the library?

Perhaps we are not sure but suspect that it is not added. Therefore, a suitable test to add to `LibraryTest` is:

```
// class LibraryTest
/**
 * Set up the fixture
 */
```

```
void setUp(){
    // ...
    bk3 = new Book(catalogNumber : '222', title : 'UML', author : 'John')
}

/**
 * Test that addition of a Book with the same catalog number
 * as one already present in the Library results in no change
 * to the number of Books in the Library
 */
void testAddBook_3() {
        lib.addBook(bk1)
        lib.addBook(bk2)
        def pre = lib.loanStock.size()
        lib.addBook(bk3)
        def post = lib.loanStock.size()

    assertTrue('one more book than expected', post == pre)
}
```

On execution of LibraryTest, we have:

```
    ...
    Time: 0.772

    OK (3 tests)
```

However, the next question becomes, Is it the original or the new book that is in the library?

Let's assume we want it to be the original. Now, we can add another test method to LibraryTest:

```
/**
 * Test that addition of a Book with the same catalog number
 * as one already present in the Library results in no change
 * to the loan stock
 */
void testAddBook_4() {
    lib.addBook(bk2)
    lib.addBook(bk3)
    def expected = 'Book: 222: OOD by: Ken'
    def actual = lib.loanStock['222']

    assertToString(actual, expected)
}
```

On execution of `LibraryTest`, we get:

```
....F
Time: 0.901
There was 1 failure:
1) testAddBook_4(LibraryTest)junit.framework.AssertionFailedError:
toString() on value: Book: 222: UML by: John expected:<Book: 222: OOD
by: Ken> but was:<Book: 222: UML by: John>

FAILURES!!!
Tests run: 4, Failures: 1, Errors: 0
```

Now, the test report informs us that the fourth test method failed (hence, the four dots and `F`). It then goes on to give more information about the failure. Although it does not concern us here, note that if an unexpected exception occurs, an error, not a failure, is reported.

Having established that there is a problem with the `addBook` method in the `Library` class, we now recode the method as:

```
// class Library
def addBook(bk) {
    if(!loanStock.containsKey(bk.catalogNumber))
        loanStock[bk.catalogNumber] = bk
}
```

and execute the `LibraryTest` to give:

```
....
Time: 0.882

OK (4 tests)
```

Happily, all four tests pass and as a result we have more confidence in our code. Notice that we made the least number of changes to pass the fourth test and that previous tests have not been invalidated.

15.3   THE GROOVYTESTSUITE AND JUNIT TESTSUITE CLASSES

We anticipate that there will be one test case class for every class in an application. Therefore, it would be convenient if we could arrange to have all of our test cases gathered together as one entity. In the previous section, we discovered that the GroovyTestCase class makes it easy for us to write, compile, and execute a single JUnit TestCase. In a similar fashion, the GroovyTestSuite class makes it easy for us to use the JUnit TestSuite class designed to manage the execution of several JUnit TestCases.

Consider the following Groovy script, runAllTests.groovy:

```
import groovy.util.GroovyTestSuite
import junit.framework.Test
import junit.textui.TestRunner

class AllTests {

    static Test suite() {
        def allTests = new GroovyTestSuite()

        allTests.addTestSuite(BookTest.class)
        allTests.addTestSuite(LibraryTest.class)

        return allTests
    }

}

TestRunner.run(AllTests.suite())
```

The AllTests class has a static method, suite. It returns a GroovyTestSuite, referenced by allTests, to which the Class object for each GroovyTestCase has been added. Note that Test is an interface implemented by GroovyTestSuite. It just ensures that a GroovyTestSuite can be run.

On execution of the script, there is a call to the static run method of the TestRunner class. The actual parameter to this method call is the Test object returned by the suite method of the class AllTests. The run method automatically executes each GroovyTestCase in the GroovyTestSuite. In our case, they are the BookTest and LibraryTest classes developed previously. The details of how this is accomplished need not concern us here, but interested readers should consult the JUnit website (see http://www.junit.org) for more information.

Just as with a GroovyTestCase, we compile and execute runAllTests as normal to give a test report:

```
.....

Time: 0.861
OK (5 tests)
```

As before, all five tests (one from BookTest and four from LibraryTest) pass. Note that previously the TestRunner was executed "under the cover." Here, we find it convenient to make its presence explicit. Interested readers may like to consult the Groovy website (see http://groovy.codehaus.org) for alternatives.

To appreciate just how useful unit testing with Groovy is, if we return to the addBook method in the Library class, then we might decide that it should report on the success or failure of adding a Book. Therefore, we recode the method as:

```
// class Library

def addBook(bk) {
        if(!loanStock.containsKey(bk.catalogNumber)){
            loanStock[bk.catalogNumber] = bk
            return true
        } else
            return false
}
```

and add two new test methods to our LibraryTest class:

```
// class LibraryTest

/**
* Test that successfully adding a Book to the Library
 * is detected
 */
void testAddBook_5() {
    def success = lib.addBook(bk2)

    assertTrue('addition expected', success)
}


/**
 * Test that unsuccessfully attempting to add a Book with the same
 * catalog number as one already present in the Library is detected
 */
void testAddBook_6() {
    lib.addBook(bk2)
    def success = lib.addBook(bk3)

    assertFalse('no addition expected', success)
}
```

Now, all we have to do is to execute `runAllTests` to give the test report:

```
. . . . . . .
Time: 1.01

OK (7 tests)
```

Notice that `assertFalse` returns `true` if the condition evaluates to `false`. We find it more convenient than its equivalent:

```
assertTrue('no addition expected', success == false)
```

Because all of the previous tests have passed, we are reasonably confident that any changes made have not had a detrimental effect on the rest of our code. This has been achieved with minimal effort on our part. That is one of the reasons why unit testing is such a powerful tool in our armory!

15.4 THE ROLE OF UNIT TESTING

Unit testing is an integral part of our iterative, incremental approach to software development. Therefore, in Iteration 2 of the Chapter 13 case study, we would normally develop a `BorrowerTest` class for unit testing the `Borrower` class. For example, we might decide that a `Borrower` can only borrow a given `Book` once and have the following `BorrowerTest` class:

```
import groovy.util.GroovyTestCase

class BorrowerTest extends GroovyTestCase {

    /**
     * Set up the fixture
     */
    void setUp(){
        bor1 = new Borrower(membershipNumber : '1234', name : 'Jessie')

        bk1 = new Book(catalogNumber : '111', title : 'Groovy', author : 'Ken')
        bk2 = new Book(catalogNumber : '222', title : 'OOD', author : 'Ken')
        bk3 = new Book(catalogNumber : '222', title : 'UML', author : 'John')
    }
```

```
/**
 * Test that a Borrower with no Books on loan can borrow a Book
 */
void testAttachBook_1() {
    def pre = bor1.borrowedBooks.size()
    bor1.attachBook(bk1)
    def post = bor1.borrowedBooks.size()

    assertTrue('one less book than expected', post == pre + 1)
}


/**
 * Test that a Borrower with no Books on loan can borrow two Books
 * with different catalog numbers
 */
void testAttachBook_2() {
    bor1.attachBook(bk1)
    bor1.attachBook(bk2)
    def expected = 2
    def actual = bor1.borrowedBooks.size()

    assertTrue('unexpected number of books', expected == actual)
}


/**
 * Test that an attempt to borrow a Book with the same catalog number
 * as one already borrowed results in no change to the number of
 * Books borrowed
 */
void testAttachBook_3() {
    bor1.attachBook(bk2)
    def pre = bor1.borrowedBooks.size()
    bor1.attachBook(bk3)
    def post = bor1.borrowedBooks.size()

    assertTrue('one more book than expected', post == pre)
}


/**
 * Test that an attempt to borrow a Book with the same catalog number
 * as one already borrowed results in no change to the borrowed books
 */

void testAttachBook_4() {
    bor1.attachBook(bk2)
    bor1.attachBook(bk3)
    def expected = 'Book: 222: OOD by: Ken'
    def actual = bor1.borrowedBooks['222']
```

```
            assertToString(actual, expected)
    }

// -----properties ----------------

    def bor1

    def bk1
    def bk2
    def bk3

}
```

We discover that to make the Borrower class pass the tests, we must recode the attachBook method as:

```
    // class Borrower

    def attachBook(bk) {
        if(!borrowedBooks.containsKey(bk.catalogNumber)) {
            borrowedBooks[bk.catalogNumber] = bk
            bk.attachBorrower(this)
            return true
        }
        else
            return false
    }
```

Having done so, we add BorrowerTest.class to the GroovyTestSuite in AllTests:

```
    // ...

    class AllTests {

        static Test suite() {
            def allTests = new GroovyTestSuite()

            // ...
            allTests.addTestSuite(BorrowerTest.class)

            return allTests
        }
    }
    // ...
```

and then execute runAllTests as normal:

```
. . . . . . . . . . .
Time: 1.152

OK (11 tests)
```

Again, as part of Iteration 2, we should also update the LibraryTest and BookTest classes with new test methods that test changes made to the Library and Book classes, respectively. For example, we might have:

```
// class LibraryTest

/**
 * Set up the fixture
 */
void setUp(){

    // ...
    bor1 = new Borrower(membershipNumber : '1234', name : 'Jessie')
}


// ...


/**
 * Test that registering a Borrower with an empty Library results
 * in one more Borrower in the Library
 */
void testRegisterBorrower_1() {
    def pre = lib.borrowers.size()
    lib.registerBorrower(bor1)
    def post = lib.borrowers.size()

    assertTrue('one less borrower than expected', post == pre + 1)
}
// ...
def bor1

// ...
```

Execution of runAllTests gives the test report:

```
. . . . . . . . . . . .
Time: 1.412

OK (12 tests)
```

Normally, we continue in this manner, adding new test methods and test cases as the code develops. The ease of use of unit testing with Groovy makes effective unit testing a normal part of the software development process. The resulting benefits are enormous!

Complete listings for the GroovyTestCases and GroovyTestSuite developed in this chapter are supplied on the book website.

15.5 EXERCISES

Using the Book, Borrower, and Library classes from Iteration 2 of Chapter 13, you are required to develop three new test methods for the LibraryTest class developed in this chapter.

1. Test that registering two Borrowers with different membership numbers to an empty Library results in two Borrowers in the Library.

2. Test that an attempt to register a Borrower with the same membership number as one already in the Library results in no change to the number of Borrowers in the Library.

3. Test that an attempt to register a Borrower with the same membership number as one already in the Library results in no change to the Borrowers already registered.

4. An alternative to the GroovyTestSuite is to use a build tool such as Ant (see http://ant.apache.org) or Maven (see http://maven.apache.org). Unfortunately, a discussion of these powerful tools is outside the scope of this book. However, interested readers will benefit from a study of Groovy's XMLBuilder class, discussed in Chapter 19, before referring to the Groovy home website for the details of Groovy's AntBuilder class.

CASE STUDY: A LIBRARY APPLICATION (INHERITANCE)

The library application first appeared in Chapter 6. There, we showed how Lists and Maps can be combined to produce data structures to manage the book-keeping required by a library. In that chapter, the data maintained in these collections were simple strings. In Chapter 11, we enhanced the capabilities of the system by making use of procedural code and closures. A text-based menu was introduced to support user interaction. Later, in Chapter 13, we used objects with more interesting state information and behaviors to represent the library, its borrowers, and books. We also removed any input/output responsibilities from them and introduced another class for this purpose.

In the first two iterations in this chapter, we revisit the same case study and use class inheritance to model not just books and journals but publications in general. As with the earlier versions, we use containers to help model the relationships established among objects. Similarly, we continue to make use of unit tests. In the third iteration, we address the problem of error detection and user feedback as well as enhancing the functionality of the system. Finally, in the last iteration, we demonstrate how easy it is to use Groovy to police constraints placed on the model.

16.1 SPECIFICATION

As in the case study of Chapter 13, we assume a sufficient familiarity with the operation of a library to understand the following description:

TABLE 16.1 Use Cases for the Library Application

- Add new book
- Add new journal
- Display stock
- Display stock available for loan
- Display stock on loan
- Register new borrower
- Display borrowers
- Lend one book
- Lend one journal
- Return one book
- Return one journal

A library has a name and holds a number of stock items that may be either books or journals. Books and journals both have a title and a unique catalog number. However, each book has an author and each journal has the name of its editor. The system should be able to display the stock items available for loan and those that are out on loan. At some point in the future, the library will hold other stock items such as videos and compact disks.

There are registered borrowers, each with a name and unique membership number. A borrower may borrow and return a book or journal. The system should record each transaction. To record the borrowing of a book or journal, the membership number of the borrower and the catalog number for the publication are required. To record that a book or journal has been returned, only the catalog number is required.

The system should also be able to display details of the stock items out on loan to borrowers.

We are required to develop an application to support the librarian. The requirements are easily captured in a set of use-cases. The only difference is that we now add, display, lend, and return journals to/from the library. Here, we choose to simply tabulate our requirements in Table 16.1.

As with the previous case study, we develop a number of iterations, each with a stated aim that we demonstrate has been achieved.

16.2 ITERATION 1: CONFIRM THE POLYMORPHIC EFFECT

The specification mentions two kinds of stock items held in the library: books and journals. Further, we are advised that, in the future, videos and CDs will also be available. This suggests a class hierarchy for the various types of loan items. It should be capable of extending horizontally to include new categories of items and vertically to further specialize the items.

The initial class diagram is given in Figure 16.1. The Publication class represents any item that may be borrowed from the library. It is an abstract class and carries the properties and behaviors common to all borrowed items: the item catalog number and title as well as the provision of its textual representation. The two subclasses represent the actual items currently available in the library stock. In addition to the catalog number and title properties inherited from the superclass Publication, the subclass Book has an author property while subclass Journal has an editor property.

This leads us to develop the Groovy classes Publication, Book, and Journal held in the files Publication.groovy, Book.groovy, and Journal.groovy, respectively.

```groovy
abstract class Publication {

    String toString() {                        // redefinition
        return "${catalogNumber}: ${title}"
    }

// -----properties ----------------

    def catalogNumber
    def title
}

class Book extends Publication {

    String toString() {
        return 'Book: ' + super.toString() + " by: ${author}"
    }

// -----properties ----------------

    def author
}

class Journal extends Publication {

    String toString() {
        return 'Journal: ' + super.toString() + " edited by: ${editor}"
    }
```

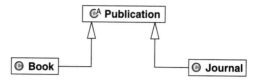

FIGURE 16.1   Initial class hierarchy.

```
// -----properties -----------------

    def editor
}
```

When deploying a class hierarchy, we need to be assured that we are correctly initializing the objects and that any polymorphic behavior operates as expected. This is the aim of this iteration. As all three classes redefine the toString method (Publication redefines toString from Object, Book and Journal redefines toString from Publication), we must ensure that we get the expected polymorphic behavior.

Following the discussions of the previous chapter, we create the GroovyTestCases, BookTest, and JournalTest for unit testing the Book and Journal classes. In the BookTest class, we have:

```
import groovy.util.GroovyTestCase

class BookTest extends GroovyTestCase {

    /*
     * Test that the expected String is returned
     */
    void testToString() {
        def bk1 = new Book(catalogNumber : '111', title : 'Groovy', author : 'K Barclay')
        def expected = 'Book: 111: Groovy by: K Barclay'

        assertToString(bk1, expected)

    }
}
```

The JournalTest class is similar. Notice that the unit tests also guarantee the constructor usage since the toString methods make use of all the object properties.

Because we also intend unit testing other classes, we have a runAllTests script to run a GroovyTestSuite, as described in Chapter 15.

```
import groovy.util.GroovyTestSuite
import junit.framework.Test
import junit.textui.TestRunner

class AllTests {

    static Test suite() {
        def allTests = new GroovyTestSuite()

        allTests.addTestSuite(BookTest.class)
        allTests.addTestSuite(JournalTest.class)

        return allTests
    }
}

TestRunner.run(AllTests.suite())
```

We can easily add other GroovyTestCases later.

As execution of the script results in the following test report:

```
..
Time: 0.39

OK (2 tests)
```

it confirms that we have the correct object initialization and polymorphic behavior. Therefore, we have achieved the aim of this iteration.

16.3 ITERATION 2: DEMONSTRATE THE REQUIRED FUNCTIONALITY

Having established that we can make use of the polymorphic effect, the aim of this iteration is to demonstrate that we can achieve the required system functionality described in the use cases of Section 16.1.

We have introduced the abstract class Publication with the properties and behaviors common to all borrowed items. Therefore, we adjust the class diagram in Figure 13.3 to reflect this decision. It is shown in Figure 16.2.

Clearly, we can base the implementation of these classes on those of the case study of Chapter 13. However, we can also incorporate the changes made to the Library and Borrower classes as a result of the unit testing in Chapter 15. Happily, we can also retain the Library and Borrower unit tests. We just add LibraryTest and BorrowerTest to the GroovyTestSuite in runAllTests.

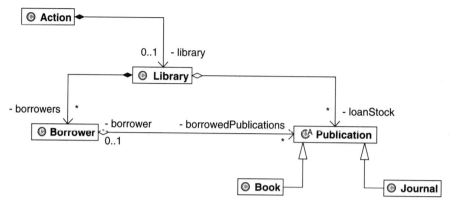

FIGURE 16.2   Class diagram.

Given the dynamic nature of Groovy, it makes no difference whether the Library and Borrower classes maintain a collection of Books or a collection of Publications. All that matters is that we send messages that correspond to methods declared in the recipient object's class or superclass(es). Therefore, all that is required are minor cosmetic name changes to the Library, Borrower, and GroovyTestCase classes. For example, we now have:

```
// class Library
def addPublication(publication) {
    if(!loanStock.containsKey(publication.catalogNumber)) {
        loanStock[publication.catalogNumber] = publication
        return true
    }
    else
        return false
}
```

and

```
// class Borrower
def attachPublication(publication) {
    if(!borrowedPublications.containsKey(publication.catalogNumber)) {
        borrowedPublications[publication.catalogNumber] = publication
        publication.attachBorrower(this)
        return true
    }
    else
    return false
}
```

and

```
/**
 * Test that addition of a Book to an empty Library results in one
 * more Publication in the Library
 */
void testAddPublication_1() {
    def pre = lib.loanStock.size()
    lib.addPublication(bk1)
    def post = lib.loanStock.size()

    assertTrue('one less publication than expected', post = pre + 1)
}
```

Of course, the Action class also needs minor changes. For example, as well as a method to read the details for a new Book, there is a similar method to read the details for a new Journal.

```
// class Action
def addJournal() {
    print('\nEnter journal catalog number: ')
    def catalogNumber = Console.readLine()
    print('Enter journal title: ')
    def title = Console.readLine()
    print('Enter journal editor: ')
    def editor = Console.readLine()

    def jo = new Journal(catalogNumber : catalogNumber, title : title, editor : editor)

    library.addPublication(jo)
}
```

Finally, we modify the Groovy script that presents a menu to a user and actions user choices. It is shown as Library 01.

```
import console.*

def readMenuSelection() {
    println()
    println('0: Quit')
    println('1: Add new book')
    println('2: Add new journal')
    println('3: Display stock')
    println('4: Display publications available for loan')
    println('5: Display publications on loan')
```

LIBRARY 01
A library of books and journals

```
        println('6: Register new borrower')
        println('7: Display borrowers')
        println('8: Lend one publication')
        println('9: Return one publication')

        print('\n\tEnter choice>>> ')
        return Console.readString()
}


        // make the Action object
def action = new Action(library : new Library(name : 'Dunning'))


        // make first selection
def choice = readMenuSelection()
while(choice != '0') {

    if(choice == '1') {                                // Add new book
        action.addBook()
    } else if(choice == '2'){                          // Add new journal
        action.addJournal()
    } else if(choice == '3') {                         // Display stock
        action.displayStock()
    } else if(choice == '4') {                         // Display publications available for loan
        action.displayPublicationsAvailableForLoan()
    } else if(choice == '5') {                         // Display publications on loan
        action.displayPublicationsOnLoan()
    } else if(choice == '6') {                         // Register new borrower
        action.registerBorrower()
    } else if(choice == '7') {                         // Display borrowers
        action.displayBorrowers()
    } else if(choice == '8') {                         // Lend one publication
        action.lendPublication()
    } else if(choice == '9') {                         // Return one publication
        action.returnPublication()
    } else {
        println("Unknown selection")
    }
        // next selection
    choice = readMenuSelection()
}
println('\nSystem closing')
```

◆

Complete listings for the script and supporting classes are given on the book website.

To complete this iteration, we run our unit tests. Happily, they all pass. Next, we use the menu to carry out functional testing. An obvious strategy is to make choices (assisted by the various display options) that correspond to the use-cases identified earlier. An illustrative session (with user data input shown emboldened and italized) is:

```
0: Quit
1: Add new book
2: Add new journal
3: Display stock
4: Display publications available for loan
5: Display publications on loan
6: Register new borrower
7: Display borrowers
8: Lend one publication
9: Return one publication

            Enter choice>>> 1

Enter book catalog number: 111
Enter book title: Groovy
Enter book author: K Barclay


// Present menu to the user

            Enter choice>>> 2

Enter journal catalog number: 333
Enter journal title: JOOP
Enter journal editor: S Smith


// Present menu to the user

            Enter choice>>> 3

Library: Dunning
==============
    Book: 111: Groovy by: K Barclay
    Journal: 333: JOOP edited by: S Smith


// Present menu to the user

            Enter choice>>> 0

System closing
```

Having encountered no problems, we consider this iteration to be complete.

16.4   ITERATION 3: PROVIDE USER FEEDBACK

Following a demonstration of the previous iteration, the librarian has asked for more feedback from the system and that commonly occurring errors be handled. She also wants the following use cases to be implemented:

- Remove a publication

- Display a particular publication

- Display selected publications

- Display a particular borrower

- Display selected borrowers

The aim of this iteration is to detect errors, give user feedback, and implement the additional use-cases.

We begin by addressing erroneous user data input. The librarian has advised us that users may attempt to:

- Add a duplicate publication

- Remove a nonexistent publication

- Register a duplicate borrower

- Remove a nonexistent borrower

- Lend a nonexistent publication

- Lend a publication already on loan

- Lend to a nonexistent borrower

- Return a nonexistent publication

- Return a publication that was not borrowed

- Display a nonexistent publication

- Display a nonexistent borrower

Clearly, we must check for these scenarios, take some appropriate action, and then inform the user. We decide that most of the checks should be the responsibility of the Library class. This is reasonable because it has methods to add, lend, remove, and return Publications as well as those to register a Borrower.

We also decide that it is the Library's responsibility to make a suitable textual message available to the Action class for display purposes. The idea is that
methods in the Library that are responsible for adding, removing, lending, or
returning Publications should return a String value to indicate the outcome.
Methods in the Library that register a borrower should do the same. The resulting code for the Library class is now:

```
class Library {

    def addPublication(publication) {
        def message
        if(loanStock.containsKey(publication.catalogNumber)== false){
            loanStock[publication.catalogNumber] = publication
            message = 'Publication added'
        }
        else
            message = 'Cannot add: publication already present'
        return message
    }

    def removePublication(catalogNumber) {
        def message
        if(loanStock.containsKey(catalogNumber)== true){
            def publication = loanStock[catalogNumber]
            //
            //note: use of safe navigation
            publication.borrower?.detachPublication(publication)
            publication.borrower = null
            loanStock.remove(catalogNumber)
            message = 'Publication removed'
        }
        else
            message = 'Cannot remove: publication not present'

        return message
    }
    def registerBorrower(borrower) {
        def message
        if(borrowers.containsKey(borrower.membershipNumber)== false){
            borrowers[borrower.membershipNumber] = borrower
            message = 'Borrower registered'
        }
        else
            message = 'Cannot register: borrower already registered'

        return message
    }
```

```
def lendPublication(catalogNumber, membershipNumber) {
    def message
    if(loanStock.containsKey(catalogNumber)== true) {
        def publication = loanStock[catalogNumber]
        if(publication.borrower == null) {
            if(borrowers.containsKey(membershipNumber) == true) {
                def borrower = borrowers[membershipNumber]
                borrower.attachPublication(publication)
                message = 'Publication loaned'
            }
            else
                message = 'Cannot lend: borrower not registered'
        }
        else
            message = 'Cannot lend: publication already on loan'
    }
    else
        message = 'Cannot lend: publication not present'

    return message
}

def returnPublication(catalogNumber) {
    def message
    if(loanStock.containsKey(catalogNumber) == true) {
        def publication = loanStock[catalogNumber]
        if(publication.borrower != null){
            publication.borrower.detachPublication(publication)
            message = 'Publication returned'
        }
        else
            message = 'Cannot return: publication not on loan'
    }
    else
        message = 'Cannot return: publication not present'
    return message
}

// ------properties ------------------

def name
def loanStock = [ : ]
def borrowers = [ : ]
}
```

As usual, we construct some unit tests to assure us that all is well. Typical examples of test methods in the LibraryTest class are:

```
// class LibraryTest
/**
 * Test that the Library has one less Publication after removal of
 * a Publication known to be in the Library
 */
void testRemovePublication_1() {
    //
    // bk1 is created in the fixture
    lib.addPublication(bk1)
    def pre = lib.loanStock.size()
    lib.removePublication(bk1.catalogNumber)
    def post = lib.loanStock.size()

    assertTrue('one more publication than expected', post == pre -1)
}


/**
 * Test that the correct message is available to a client
 */
void testRemovePublication_2() {
    //
    // bk1 is created in the fixture
    lib.addPublication(bk1)
    def actual = lib.removePublication(bk1.catalogNumber)
    def expected = 'Publication removed'

    assertTrue('unexpected message', actual == expected)
}
/**
 * Test that the correct message is available to a client
 */
void testRemovePublication_3() {
    def actual = lib.removePublication(bk1.catalogNumber)
    def expected = 'Cannot remove: publication not present'

    assertTrue('unexpected message', actual == expected)
}
```

Notice that we make use of safe navigation in the removePublication method. This means that we don't have to make an explicit check that the Publication to be removed is out on loan. If its borrower property is null, then the message detachPublication will not be sent and a null pointer exception will not be thrown.

We also decide that the Action class should be responsible for checking the existence of a specified Publication or Borrower before attempting to display it. It should inform the user about the nature of the problem encountered. This is a reasonable decision since it is an Action object that interacts with the user.

To implement the remaining new use cases, we introduce two more flexible display methods. Both make use of regular expressions with Strings, as discussed in Chapter 3. The first displaySelectedStock displays all Publications whose catalog numbers start with the String entered by the user. The second is similar since it displays all Borrowers whose membership numbers start with the String entered. An outline of the updated Action class is now:

```
import console.*

class Action {

    // ...

    def removePublication() {
        print('\nEnter publication catalog number: ')
        def catalogNumber = Console.readLine()
        def message = library.removePublication(catalogNumber)
        println "\nResult: ${message}\n"
    }

    // ...

    def displayOnePublication() {
        print('\nEnter publication catalog number: ')
        def catalogNumber = Console.readLine()

        def publication = library.loanStock[catalogNumber]
        if(publication != null) {
            this.printHeader('One publication display')
            println publication
        }
        else {
            println '\nCannot print: No such publication\n'
        }
    }

    // ...

    def displaySelectedStock() {
        print('\nEnter start of catalog numbers: ')
        def pattern = Console.readLine()
        pattern = '^' + pattern + '.*'
        def found = false

        this.printHeader('Selected publications display')
```

```
        library.loanStock.each { catalogNumber, publication -> if(catalogNumber =~ pattern){
            found= true
            println " ${publication}" }
        }

        if(found == false)
            println '\nCannot print: No such publications\n'
    }
```

```
// ...
```

```
    def displayOneBorrower() {
    print('\nEnter borrower membership number: ')
    def membershipNumber = Console.readLine()

    def bor = library.borrowers[membershipNumber]
    if(bor != null) {
        this.printHeader('One borrower display')
        println bor
        def publications = bor.borrowedPublications
        publications.each { catalogNumber, publication -> println " ${publication}" }
    } else
        println '\nCannot print: No such borrower\n'
}
```

```
// ...
```

```
def displaySelectedBorrowers() {
    print('\nEnter start of membership numbers: ')
    def pattern = Console.readLine()
    pattern = '^' + pattern + '.*'
    def found = false

        this.printHeader('Selected borrowers display')
        library.borrowers.each { membershipNumber, borrower ->
            if(membershipNumber =~ pattern){
                found = true
                println borrower
                def publications = borrower.borrowedPublications
                publications.each { catalogNumber, publication -> println " ${publication}" }
            }
        }

        if (found == false)
            println '\nCannot print: No such borrowers\n'
    }
```

```
// ...

private printHeader(detail) {
    println "\nLibrary: ${library.name}: ${detail}"
    println '================\n'
}

// -----properties ----------------

private library

}
```

Note the introduction of the private `printHeader` method. The kind of modification during iterative development is quite common. Provided that the change is documented and tested, all should be well.

All that remains is to modify the previous Groovy script to present and action a slightly different menu to the user. A partial listing is shown as Library 02.

LIBRARY 02

A library of books
and journals with
error detection
and user feedback

```
import console.*

def readMenuSelection() {

    // ...
    println('3: Remove a publication\n')

    // ...
    println('5: Display selected publications')
    println('6: Display one publication')

    // ...
    println('11: Display selected borrowers')
    println('12: Display one borrower\n')

    // ...
    print('\n\tEnter choice>>> ')
    return Console.readString()
}

        // make the Action object
def action = new Action(library : new Library(name : 'Dunning'))

        // make first selection
def choice = readMenuSelection()
while(choice != '0') {
```

```
        if(choice == '1') {
            // ...
        } else if(choice == '3') {
            action.removePublication()           // Remove a publication
            // ...
        } else if(choice == '5') {
            action.displaySelectedStock()        // Display selected stock
        } else if(choice == '6') {
            action.displayOnePublication()       // Display one publication
            // ...
        } else if(choice == '11') {
            action.displaySelectedBorrowers()    // Display selected borrowers
        } else if(choice == '12') {
            action.displayOneBorrower()          // Display one borrower
            // ...

            // next selection
        choice = readMenuSelection()
    }
    println('\nSystem closing\n')
```

We are now able to conduct functional tests based on the use-cases. An extract from a typical session with user data input shown emboldened and italized is:

```
    // ...

    0: Quit

    1: Add new book
    2: Add new journal
    3: Remove a publication

    4: Display stock
    5: Display selected publications
    6: Display one publication
    7: Display publications available for loan
    8: Display publications on loan

    9: Register new borrower
    10: Display all borrowers
    11: Display selected borrowers
    12: Display one borrower

    13: Lend one publication
    14: Return one publication
            Enter choice>>> 2

    Enter journal catalog number: 124
```

```
Enter journal title: JOOP
Enter journal editor: S Smith

Result: Publication added

// Present menu to the user

        Enter choice>>> 4

Library: Dunning: All publications display
=============
    Book: 111: Groovy by: K Barclay
    Journal: 124: JOOP edited by: S Smith
    Book: 123: OOD by: J Savage

// Present menu to the user

        Enter choice>>> 5

Enter start of catalog numbers: 12

Library: Dunning: Selected publications display
=============
    Journal: 124: JOOP edited by: S Smith
    Book: 123: OOD by: J Savage

// Present menu to the user

        Enter choice>>> 0

System closing
```

At this point, we consider this iteration to be complete.

◆

16.5   ITERATION 4: ENFORCE CONSTRAINTS

With graphical notations such as the UML, it is often difficult to record the finer details of a system's specification. The aim of this iteration is to demonstrate how Groovy can help us do this.

We can make assertions about our models by adding textual annotations to model elements. For example, Figure 16.3 is a class diagram that illustrates the constraint placed on the Borrower class such that no Borrower may have more than a certain number of Publications on loan.

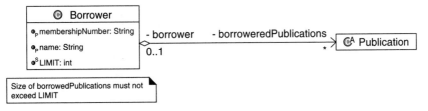

FIGURE 16.3   A constraint shown as a textual annotation.

The text in the note describes the constraint. It may be informal English, as is the case here, or it may be stated more formally. In any event, we must ensure in our implementation that this constraint is not violated. To accomplish this, we have updated the Borrower class to have a public static property LIMIT, initialized with the maximum number of Publications that may be on loan:

```
class Borrower {

    // ...

// -----properties ---------------
    def membershipNumber
    def name
    static public final LIMIT = 4
    private borrowedPublications = [ : ]
}
```

We can then make checks in the Library's methods so that we don't exceed that limit. A typical check in the lendPublication method is:

```
//class: Library
def lendPublication(catalogNumber, membershipNumber) {
    def message
    if(loanStock.containsKey(catalogNumber)== true) {
        def publication = loanStock[catalogNumber]
        if(publication.borrower == null) {
            if(borrowers.containsKey(membershipNumber)== true) {
                def borrower = borrowers[membershipNumber]
                if(borrower.borrowedPublications.size() < Borrower.LIMIT)  {
                    borrower.attachPublication(publication)
                    this.checkPublicationBorrowerLoopInvariant
                    ('Library.lendPublication')
                    message = 'Publication loaned'
                }
```

```
            else
                message = 'Cannot lend: borrower over limit'
        }
        else
            message = 'Cannot lend: borrower not registered'
    }
    else
        message = 'Cannot lend: publication already on loan'
}
else
    message = 'Cannot lend: publication not present'

return message
}
```

As usual, we update the Library's unit tests to confirm that the code executes as expected. For example, we have:

```
// class: LibraryTest
/**
 * Test that the correct message is available to a client
 */
void testLendPublication_7() {
    def bk4 = new Book(catalogNumber : '444', title : 'C++', author : 'S Smith')
    def bk5 = new Book(catalogNumber : '555', title : 'C', author :'A Cumming')
    def bk6 = new Book(catalogNumber : '666', title : 'C#', author : 'I Smith')
    //
    // bk1 and bk2 are created in the fixture
    def publicationList = [bk1, bk2, bk4, bk5, bk6]

    lib.registerBorrower(bor1)

    def actual
    publicationList.each{ publication ->
        lib.addPublication(publication)
        actual = lib.lendPublication(publication.catalogNumber, bor1.membershipNumber)
    }

    def expected = 'Cannot lend: borrower over limit'

    assertTrue('unexpected message', actual == expected)

}
```

Since Groovy's testing system is so easy to use, it encourages us to do more testing. For example, we can impose constraints on the relationships that exist among objects rather than just one object in isolation. These relational constraints start at some object and then follow architectural links to other objects before applying some test. For example, we can assert that if we navigate from any Publication on loan to its Borrower, then the borrowedPublications attribute of that Borrower must contain a reference to the Publication with which we started. In other words, a Publication on loan and its Borrower must be consistent with each other.

This is an example of a *loop invariant*. Although it does not concern us here, loop invariants are widely used in formal approaches to software development where proof of correctness is important. For our purposes, we just need to demonstrate that if we start at some object and follow a sequence of object links, that we then arrive back at the same object. The object diagram of Figure 16.4 illustrates this.

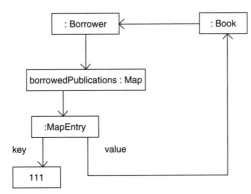

FIGURE 16.4   A Publication–Borrower loop invariant.

The figure shows that if we start from a given Book and navigate to its Borrower, then we should find that the Book's catalog number is a key in the Borrower's map of borrowed publications. For the model to be consistent, the associated value for that key should be the Book with which we started. We code the invariant check in Groovy as:

```
//class: Library
private checkPublicationBorrowerLoopInvariant(methodName) {
    def publications = loanStock.values().asList()

    def onLoanPublications = publications.findAll{ publication -> publication.borrower != null }

    def allOK = onLoanPublications.every { publication ->
        publication.borrower.borrowedPublications.containsKey(publication.catalogNumber)
    }
```

```
            if( allOK == false ) {
                throw new Exception("${methodName}: Invariant failed")
            }
        }
```

Since the violation of an invariant indicates that a serious error has occurred, we terminate the system by throwing an Exception with a suitable error message. Notice that we do not declare that the method throws an Exception (see Appendix B).

As before, we only check methods that are likely to cause a violation. In this case, it is just the method lendPublication.

```
// class: Library
def lendPublication(catalogNumber, membershipNumber) {
    // ...
                    if(borrower.borrowedPublications.size() < Borrower.LIMIT) {
                        borrower.attachPublication(publication)
                        this.checkPublicationBorrowerLoopInvariant('Library.lendPublication')
                        message = 'Publication loaned'
                    } else
                        message = 'Cannot lend: borrower over limit'

    // ...
}
```

Before we finish, we must create at least one unit test to check that the expected Exception is thrown. This turns out to be problematic since we have coded the attachPublication method in the Borrower class to ensure that the loop invariant is not violated.

One solution is to create a MockBorrower subclass whose redefined attachPublication method has the required abnormal behavior:

```
        class MockBorrower extends Borrower{

            def attachPublication(publication) {
                //
                // Normal behavior is commented out
                // borrowedPublications[publication.catalogNumber] = publication
                publication.attachBorrower(this)
            }
        }
```

We create a MockBorrower object in the unit test where a Borrower object would normally be expected.

```
// class LibraryTest {
void testCheckPublicationBorrowerLoopInvariant() {
    def mockBorrower = new MockBorrower(membershipNumber : '1234', name : 'P Thompson')
    lib.registerBorrower(mockBorrower)
    lib.addPublication(bk1)
    lib.addPublication(bk2)

    try {
        lib.lendPublication(bk1.catalogNumber, mockBorrower.membershipNumber)
        fail('Expected: Library.testPublicationBorrowerLoop: Invariant failed')
    } catch(Exception e){}
}

// ...
}
```

Note that the method fail reports a failure only if the Exception has not been thrown. The MockBorrower class is an example of the *mock object* testing design pattern (Massol, 2003). It avoids polluting normal code with abnormal behaviors.

Happily, all of the tests in the runAllTests script pass. Therefore, at this point, we conduct functional tests by executing a Groovy script from the previous iteration. As expected, no problems occur and we consider this iteration to be finished.

16.6 EXERCISES

1. The validation of data input by a user is an important part of any interactive system. Amend the Action class of the last iteration to validate the following:

    (a) A borrower's name should only contain letters of the alphabet and each part of the name must start with an upper-case letter, for example, K Barclay.

    (b) A borrower's membership number should consist of only digits, for example, 1234.

    (c) A publication's catalog number should consist of four digits followed by a lower-case letter, for example, 0012a.

2. The specification for the case study indicated that, at some point in the future, the library will hold other stock items such as videos and CDs.
    (a) Modify the class diagram of Figure 16.4 to include videos and CDs.

(b) Using the Groovy script of the last iteration and its supporting classes, develop an iteration that has books, journals, and videos in the library's loan stock. You can assume that a video has a catalog number, a title, and a duration that is measured in minutes.

3. Discuss the decisions made or approaches taken in the case study that made Exercise 2 easier or harder to accomplish.

4. (a) Implement the constraint that every `Publication` on loan to a Borrower is from the loan stock of the Library at which the borrower is registered.

    (b) Devise a suitable unit test for the constraint implemented in the preceding exercise.

5. (a) In Iteration 4, we have shown how to implement the `Publication–Borrower` invariant loop. Now, prepare an implementation for the `Borrower–Publication` invariant loop. It should start from each Borrower, navigate to each of its borrowed `Publications`, and check that it is the Borrower of each `Publication`.

    (b) Devise a suitable unit test for the constraint implement in the preceding exercise.

6. In this chapter, we have created and thrown an `Exception` when a constraint is broken. However, there are other occasions on which it might be useful to do the same.
    (a) Place constraints on a borrower's name, membership number, and publication catalog number to conform to the changes required in Exercise 1.

    (b) Implement these constraints by throwing an `Exception`.

    (c) Discuss the advantages and disadvantages of the approaches used in this exercise and in Exercise 1.

PERSISTENCE

In this chapter, we are concerned with persisting our data in a relational database (we assume a familiarity with the Structured Query Language (SQL) (Beaulieu, 2005; Molinaro, 2006). For the Java developer, this would involve programming to the Java Database Connectivity (JDBC) API. While ultimately, so too does the Groovy programmer, much of the burden of developing with this API is shifted to the Groovy framework, which makes light of the work involved in manipulating sets of data extracted from a database. For example, iterators and closures allow us to easily traverse the rows of a database table.

17.1 SIMPLE QUERIES

Consider a database with a single table having the details of a number of bank accounts. The table, known as accounts, might appear as shown in Figure 17.1. Each row represents a single account. The columns denote the account number and its current balance.

An API under the package name groovy.sql provides Groovy with simple access to SQL. The API makes extensive use of iterators and closures for manipulating the results from SQL queries. Example 01 demonstrates how we can query all the rows in the accounts table and display the details. For guidance on setting up the database, see Appendix A and the book website.

```
import groovy.sql.*

def DB = 'jdbc:derby:accountDB'
def USER = ''
```

EXAMPLE 01
Simple SQL query

accounts

number	balance
ABC123	1200
DEF456	400
...	...

FIGURE 17.1   Accounts table.

```
def PASSWORD = ''
def DRIVER = 'org.apache.derby.jdbc.EmbeddedDriver'

        // Connect to database
def sql = Sql.newInstance(DB, USER, PASSWORD, DRIVER)

        // Iterate over the result set
println 'Accounts'
println ' Number Balance '
println '+-----+-----+'
sql.eachRow('select * from accounts') { acc ->
    printf('| %-8s | %-8d |\n', [acc.number, acc.balance])
}
println '+-----+-----+'
```

Class Sql includes the method newInstance, which is used to connect to the required database. In this case, we create a Sql instance pointing to a Cloudscape database (see http://db.apache.org/derby/) (see Appendix A) on the local system. The database is identified by the JDBC connection URL jdbc:derby:accountDB. The driver class name is org.apache.derby.jdbc.EmbeddedDriver. The more significant part of the code follows next. The iterator method eachRow expects two parameters, namely, a String representing the SQL query and a closure to process each row from the result. Here, the closure simply prints each account number and balance.

The output from this program is:

```
Accounts
    Number          Balance
+--------------+-----------------+
| ABC123       |     1200        |
| DEF456       |     400         |
+--------------+-----------------+
```

◆

The next example performs the same query on the same database table. On this occasion, we use the results to create Account objects and add them to a list. Then, we simply display each object.

```
import groovy.sql.*

class Account {

    String toString() {
        return "Account: ${number} ${balance}"
    }
// -----properties ----------------
    def number
    def balance
}
def DB = 'jdbc:derby:accountDB'
def USER = ''
def PASSWORD = ''
def DRIVER = 'org.apache.derby.jdbc.EmbeddedDriver'


        // Collection of Account objects
def accounts = []


        // Connect to database and make query
def sql = Sql.newInstance(DB, USER, PASSWORD, DRIVER)
sql.eachRow('select * from accounts') { acc ->
    accounts << new Account(number : acc.number, balance : acc.balance)
}


        // Display accounts
accounts.each { acc ->
    println "${acc}"
}
```

EXAMPLE 02
Creating objects

The output reveals that the Account objects are correctly created:

```
Account: ABC123 1200
Account: DEF456 400
```

◆

17.2   RELATIONS

Consider a database with tables for both banks and their accounts. Once again, the accounts have a number and a balance. To identify the bank with which an account is associated, the accounts table also includes a *foreign key*. This uniquely identifies the bank and is achieved by including an identifier column into the bank table, acting as its *primary key*. Following this scheme, we also give

banks

id	name
RBS	Rich Bank of Scotland
BOS	Banque of Scotland
...	...

accounts

id	bankID	number	balance
1	RBS	ABC123	1200
2	RBS	DEF456	400
3	BOS	GHI789	600
...	...	...	...

FIGURE 17.2   Relations.

each account its own unique identifier. The tables might appear as in Figure 17.2. The banks table has the column id as its primary key. The accounts table is also given an id primary key. In the accounts table, the column bankID is the foreign key to identify the bank with which the account is opened.

Example 03 illustrates some processing of the database. The first two queries simply tabulate the data in the two tables. The final query includes a where clause, selecting only those accounts with the ID RBS bank.

EXAMPLE 03
Relations

```
import groovy.sql.*

def DB = 'jdbc:derby:bankDB'
def USER = ''
def PASSWORD = ''
def DRIVER = 'org.apache.derby.jdbc.EmbeddedDriver'

        // Connect to database
def sql = Sql.newInstance(DB, USER, PASSWORD, DRIVER)

        // Query the bank table
println 'Banks'
println ' Name '
println '+-----------------+'
sql.eachRow('select * from banks') { bk ->
    printf('| %-30s |\n', [bk.name])
}
println '+-----------------+'
println()

        // Query the accounts table
println 'Accounts'
```

```
println ' Number Balance Bank '
println '+-----+-----+---+'
sql.eachRow('select * from accounts') { acc ->
    printf('| %-8s | %-8d | %-4s |\n', [acc.number, acc.balance, acc.bankID])
}
println '+-----+-----+---+'
println()

         // Find the RBS accounts
println 'RBS accounts'
println ' Number Balance '
println '+-----+-----+'
sql.eachRow('select * from accounts where bankID = ?', ['RBS']) { acc ->
    printf('| %-8s | %-8d |\n', [acc.number, acc.balance])
}
println '+-----+-----+'
println()
```

Observe the statement:

```
sql.eachRow('select * from accounts where bankID = ?', ['RBS']) ...
```

◆

The where clause selects those accounts that have RBS as the bankID. In this example, the ? symbol is replaced by the value from the List. If the where clause includes more than one ? symbol, they are replaced, in order, by each value from the List.

The output produced by this application is shown in the following text. We see the two banks, the three accounts, and the two accounts associated with the RBS bank.

```
Banks
    Name
+----------------------+
|Rich Bank of Scotland |
|Banque of Scotland    |
+----------------------+

Accounts
    Number              Balance         Bank
+----------------+----------------+--------------+
|ABC123          |    1200        |  RBS         |
|DEF456          |    400         |  RBS         |
|GHI789          |    600         |  BOS         |
+----------------+----------------+--------------+
```

```
       RBS accounts
      Number      Balance
   +-------------+------------+
   | ABC123      |   1200     |
   | DEF456      |    400     |
   +-------------+------------+
```

17.3 DATABASE UPDATES

A database table can be updated with the SQL insert statement. This is used to inject a new row into the named table. In the same manner, the SQL delete statement is used to remove rows from a named table. Both are demonstrated in Example 04. Here, we use the original account database from the first three examples. In the sample code, we add two new rows to the accounts table, and then immediately remove them, leaving the database unchanged. At each stage, we print the content of the accounts table to monitor the effects.

EXAMPLE 04
Updates

```groovy
import groovy.sql.*

def DB = 'jdbc:derby:accountDB'
def USER = ''
def PASSWORD = ''
def DRIVER = 'org.apache.derby.jdbc.EmbeddedDriver'

def displayAccounts(banner, sql) {
    println banner
    sql.eachRow('select * from accounts') { acc ->
        println " Account: ${acc.number} ${acc.balance}"
    }
    println()
}

        // Connect to database
def sql = Sql.newInstance(DB, USER, PASSWORD, DRIVER)

        // Iterate over the result set
displayAccounts('Initial content', sql)

        // Now insert a new row...
sql.execute("insert into accounts(number, balance)values('GHI789', 600)")
```

```
        // ...and another
def newNumber = 'AAA111'
def newBalance = 1600
sql.execute("insert into accounts(number, balance) values(${newNumber}, ${newBalance})")

        // Now see what we have
displayAccounts('After inserts', sql)

        // Restore original
['GHI789', 'AAA111'].each { accNumber ->
    sql.execute('delete from accounts where number = ?',[accNumber])
}

        // Now see that they have gone
displayAccounts('After deletes', sql)
```

The output is:

```
    Initial content
        Account: ABC123 1200
        Account: DEF456 400

    After inserts
        Account: ABC123 1200
        Account: DEF456 400
        Account: GHI789 600
        Account: AAA111 1600

    After deletes
        Account: ABC123 1200
        Account: DEF456 400
```

◆

The groovy.sql package also includes the DataSet class. This class is an extension of the Sql class and acts as an object representation for a database table. With a DataSet, the programmer can iterate over the rows with the each method, add new rows with the add method, and perform any of the inherited methods from its superclass Sql such as execute, which obeys a given piece of SQL. This class type is shown in Example 05. It repeats the same logic as in Example 04.

```
import groovy.sql.*

def DB = 'jdbc:derby:accountDB'
```

EXAMPLE 05
DataSet updates

```
def USER = ''
def PASSWORD = ''
def DRIVER = 'org.apache.derby.jdbc.EmbeddedDriver'

def displayAccounts(banner, dSet) {
    println banner
    dSet.each { acc ->
        println " Account: ${acc.number} ${acc.balance}"
    }
    println()
}

        // Connect to database
def sql = Sql.newInstance(DB, USER, PASSWORD, DRIVER)
def accounts = sql.dataSet('accounts')

        // Iterate over the data set
displayAccounts('Initial content', accounts)

        // Now insert a new row...
accounts.add(number : 'GHI789', balance : 600)

        // ...and another
def newNumber = 'AAA111'
def newBalance = 1600
accounts.add(number : newNumber, balance : newBalance)

        // Now see what we have
displayAccounts('After inserts', accounts)

        // Restore original
['GHI789', 'AAA111'].each { accNumber ->
    accounts.execute('delete from accounts where number = ?',[accNumber])
}

        // Now see that they have gone
displayAccounts('After deletes', accounts)
```

◆

The final example in this section operates with the database containing the Banks and Accounts tables. As in the previous example, we add a new bank, then a new account associated with that bank, and then we undo the updates and leave the database unchanged.

EXAMPLE 06
Relation updates

```
import groovy.sql.*

def DB = 'jdbc:derby:bankDB'
def USER = ''
def PASSWORD = ''
def DRIVER = 'org.apache.derby.jdbc.EmbeddedDriver'

def displayBanks(banner, dSet) {
    println banner
    dSet.each { bk ->
        println " Bank: ${bk.id} ${bk.name}"
    }
    println()
}

def displayAccounts(banner, dSet) {
    println banner
    dSet.each { acc ->
        println " Account: ${acc.id} ${acc.bankID} ${acc.number} ${acc.balance}"
    }
    println()
}

        // Connect to database
def sql = Sql.newInstance(DB, USER, PASSWORD, DRIVER)
def banks = sql.dataSet('banks')
def accounts = sql.dataSet('accounts')

        // Query the bank table
displayBanks('Banks', banks)

        // Query the account table
displayAccounts('Accounts', accounts)

        // Now add a new bank...
banks.add(id : 'CB', name : 'Clydebank')

        // ...and check it is there
displayBanks('Banks (after add)', banks)

        // Now add a new account to this new bank...
accounts.add(bankID : 'CB', number : 'AAA111', balance : 1600)

        // ...and check it is there...
displayAccounts('Accounts (after add)', accounts)

                // ...then remove it...
accounts.execute('delete from accounts where number = ?', ['AAA111'])
```

```
        // ...and check it is gone
displayAccounts('Accounts (after delete)', accounts)

        // Now remove the new bank...
banks.execute('delete from banks where id=?', ['CB'])

        // ...and check it is gone
displayBanks('Banks (after delete)', banks)
```

The output is:

```
Banks
   Bank: RBS Rich Bank of Scotland
   Bank: BOS Banque of Scotland

Accounts
   Account: 1 RBS ABC123 1200
   Account: 2 RBS DEF456 400
   Account: 3 BOS GHI789 600

Banks (after add)
   Bank: RBS Rich Bank of Scotland
   Bank: BOS Banque of Scotland
   Bank: CB Clydebank

Accounts (after add)
   Account: 1 RBS ABC123 1200
   Account: 2 RBS DEF456 400
   Account: 3 BOS GHI789 600
   Account: 5 CB AAA111 1600

Accounts (after delete)
   Account: 1 RBS ABC123 1200
   Account: 2 RBS DEF456 400
   Account: 3 BOS GHI789 600

Banks (after delete)
   Bank: RBS Rich Bank of Scotland
   Bank: BOS Banque of Scotland
```

◆

17.4   OBJECTS FROM TABLES

Groovy is an object-oriented scripting language. One problem that arises is how to store objects for use at a later time by the same or another application. Using a relational database to persist our data is a natural and obvious choice. However, it poses the question of how we map the data in relational tables to objects. In this and the next sections, we develop a simple scheme for this mapping. In the final section, we use Groovy as a "glue" technology and exploit an established framework for this purpose.

We consider how to create Account objects from the accounts table in the accountDB database used in the first two examples of this chapter. We might simply consider using the eachRow iterator and create Account objects from each row in the table. However, given that a database may contain various tables with various structures, we require a more generic scheme for creating objects from tables.

Consider the abstract class SqlQuery shown in the listing below. Its two properties are an Sql object and a string representing an SQL query to retrieve all the elements in a table. The class employs the *template method* (Gamma et al., 1995) mapRow to deliver an object of the required type from a single row from the database table. The execute method uses mapRow to deliver a List of objects constructed from all the rows of the table. This is achieved by invoking the rows method on the sql object, passing the query string as parameter. This produces a List of the result sets from the query. Each entry is then processed to convert each row into an object.

```
abstract class SqlQuery {

    def SqlQuery(sql, query) {
        this.sql = sql
        this.query = query
    }

    def execute() {
        def rowsList = sql.rows(query)
        def results = []
        def size = rowsList.size()
        0.upto(size -1) { index ->
            results << this.mapRow(rowsList[index])
        }
        return results
    }

    def abstract mapRow(row)

// -----properties ----------------

    def sql
    def query
}
```

We can now specialize this generic solution to retrieve a List of Account objects formed from the rows in the accounts table, which is the class AccountQuery:

```
class AccountQuery extends SqlQuery {

    def AccountQuery(sql) {
        super(sql, 'select * from accounts')
    }

    def mapRow(row) {
        def acc = new Account(number : row.getProperty('number'),
                                     balance : row.getProperty('balance'))
        return acc
    }
}
```

Method mapRow has a single GroovyRowResult (see GDK) parameter. It represents a single row from the table. We can access the columns of this row by name or by index using, respectively, the methods getProperty and getAt. Here, we use getProperty to access the individual columns and to initialize an Account object.

Finally, Example 07 illustrates how we recreate the Account objects from the data in the accounts table, and then display their properties.

EXAMPLE 07
Objects from
tables

```
import groovy.sql.*

def DB = 'jdbc:derby:accountDB'
def USER = ''
def PASSWORD = ''
def DRIVER = 'org.apache.derby.jdbc.EmbeddedDriver'

        // Connect to database
def sql = Sql.newInstance(DB, USER, PASSWORD, DRIVER)

        // Prepare the query object
def accQuery = new AccountQuery(sql)

        // Get the Accounts
def accs = accQuery.execute()

accs.each { acc ->
    println "${acc}"
}
```

◆

17.5   INHERITANCE

Where an application model includes inheritance, we need to be able to represent every concrete type in the database. Consider the bank account class hierarchy shown in Example 04 of Chapter 14. Classes CurrentAccount and DepositAccount are the concrete classes we wish to persist. To handle both types of accounts, one solution is to develop a database table with all the properties used in all subclasses. Here, this would include the account number, balance, overdraft limit, and interest rate. To distinguish a row for the two types of accounts, we include an additional column in our table to denote the account type (Figure 17.3). Example 08 illustrates reading such a database, constructing objects, and displaying them.

EXAMPLE 08
Inheritance

```
import groovy.sql.*

def DB = 'jdbc:derby:specialDB'
def USER = ''
def PASSWORD = ''
def DRIVER = 'org.apache.derby.jdbc.EmbeddedDriver'

        // Connect to database
def sql = Sql.newInstance(DB, USER, PASSWORD, DRIVER)

        // Prepare the query object
def accQuery = new SpecialAccountQuery(sql)

        // Get the Accounts
def accs = accQuery.execute()

accs.each { acc ->
    println "${acc}"
}
```

◆

Once again, we inherit from class SqlQuery. This time, the method mapRow in the class SpecialAccountQuery needs to distinguish the kind of Account object to create, using the column type in the table.

accounts

type	number	balance	overdraftlimit	interestrate
CURRENT	AAA111	2000	400	null
CURRENT	BBB222	3000	800	null
DEPOSIT	CCC333	4000	null	4
...	...	...	...	...

FIGURE 17.3 Accounts table.

```
class SpecialAccountQuery extends SqlQuery {

    def SpecialAccountQuery(sql) {
        super(sql, 'select * from accounts')
    }

    def mapRow(row) {
        def acc = null

    if(row.getProperty('type') == 'CURRENT')
        acc = new CurrentAccount(number : row.getProperty('number'),
            balance : row.getProperty('balance'), overdraftLimit :row.getProperty('overdraftlimit'))
    else
        acc = new DepositAccount(number : row.getProperty('number'),
            balance : row.getProperty('balance'), interestRate : row.getProperty ('interestrate'))
    return acc
    }
}
```

17.6   THE SPRING FRAMEWORK

The Spring framework (Johnson et al., 2005; Wall et al., 2004) is an important open- source application development framework designed to make Java/J2EE development easier and more productive. Spring aims to help structure complete applications. A detailed discussion of Spring is beyond the scope of this book. The reader is referred to the references. However, as we develop ever more complex applications, it is worth considering exploiting this framework.

One advantage of adopting Spring is to gain leverage from its support for the Data Access Object (DAO) design pattern. The primary purpose of the DAO pattern is to separate issues of persistence from the general application classes and application logic. Like our earlier discussion of MVC, the DAO pattern separates knowledge of the database technology used from the remainder of the code.

The problem that we model is described by the class diagram shown in Figure 17.4. A one-to-many relationship exists between a Bank and its Accounts. The Account class includes the number and balance properties with matching getters and setters.

Figure 17.5 describes the accounts table used to maintain the data for the various accounts. It is organized in a manner similar to that described in the previous section. The table is included in the accountDB database.

FIGURE 17.4   Banking application.

accounts

number	balance
AAA111	2000
BBB222	3000
CCC333	4000
...	...

FIGURE 17.5   Accounts table.

Spring uses a DataSource object to obtain a connection to the database. Specifically, we shall use a DriverManagerDataSource implementation that is useful for test or standalone environments. An instance is created with code such as:

```
ds = new DriverManagerDataSource(driverClassName : 'org.apache.derby.jdbc.EmbeddedDriver',
            url : 'jdbc:derby:accountDB', username : '', password : '')
```

To execute SQL queries and map the results to Groovy classes, Spring provides a set of classes in the org.springframework.jdbc.object package. For example, the class MappingSqlQuery is used to run a query and obtain objects from the result. Consider the class AccountQuery that extends the MappingSqlQuery class:

```
import java.sql.*
import org.springframework.jdbc.object.*

class AccountQuery extends MappingSqlQuery {

    def AccountQuery(ds) {
        super(ds, 'select * from accounts')
        this.compile()
    }
    protected Object mapRow(ResultSet rs, int rowNumber) {
        def acc = new Account(number : rs.getString('number'), balance : rs.getInt('balance'))

        return acc
    }
}
```

The central idea of the superclass MappingSqlQuery is that we specify an SQL query that can be run with the execute method. The query is specified in the constructor of the subclass AccountQuery. Execution of this query produces a database ResultSet. The subclass must also include an implementation for the (protected; see Appendix I) mapRow method to map the data from each row of the query result into an object that represents the entities retrieved by the query. Hence, the method execute will return a List of Account objects.

In a similar manner, the class AccountInsert is used to insert a new row into the database table:

```
import java.sql.*
import org.springframework.jdbc.object.*
import org.springframework.jdbc.core.*

class AccountInsert extends SqlUpdate {

    def AccountInsert(ds) {
        super(ds, 'insert into accounts(number, balance) values(?, ?)')
        this.declareParameter(new SqlParameter(Types.VARCHAR))
        this.declareParameter(new SqlParameter(Types.INTEGER))
        this.compile()
    }
}
```

We now create an interface that describes the functionality required by our DAO. In this simple example, we retrieve all the Accounts from the database and add a new Account to the database:

```
interface BankDaoIF {

    def abstract getAccounts()
    def abstract addAccount(acc)
}
```

The class BankDaoJdbc is the JDBC implementation for this interface. This is readily achieved by using the AccountQuery and the AccountInsert classes. For example, method getAccounts simply invokes the execute method on an instance of the AccountQuery class and delivers a List of Accounts.

```
import org.springframework.jdbc.object.*
import org.springfOramework.jdbc.core.*

class BankDaoJdbc implements BankDaoIF {
```

```
        def getAccounts() {
            def aQuery = new AccountQuery(dataSource)
            return aQuery.execute()
    }

    def addAccount(acc) {
        def params = [acc.number, acc.balance]
        def aInsert = new AccountInsert(dataSource)
        aInsert.update(params as Object[])
    }

// -----properties ----------------

    def dataSource
}
```

We only have to change the Bank class to take advantage of the database persistence. We add a reference to a BankDaoIF, which the Bank class constructor initializes. The constructor also invokes the getAccounts method on the DAO and initializes its accounts property with the List. As a simple illustration, we also include the method openAccount. Its implementation uses the method addAccount on the DAO and then appends the account to the accounts collection.

```
class Bank {

    def Bank(name, dao) {
        this.name = name
        this.dao = dao

        accounts = dao.getAccounts()
    }

    def openAccount(account) {
        dao.addAccount(account)
        accounts << account
    }

// -----properties ----------------

    def name
    def accounts

    def dao
}
```

Finally, we develop a simple illustrative script. Here, we create a Bank object that is initialized with the content of the database, open a new account, and then tabulate all the accounts in the Bank. If we were to run this script to only perform the update, then run a second version which performs the display, we would see the persistence in action.

EXAMPLE 09

Spring framework

```
import groovy.sql.*
import org.springframework.jdbc.datasource.*

def DB = 'jdbc:derby:accountDB'
def USER = ''
def PASSWORD = ''
def DRIVER = 'org.apache.derby.jdbc.EmbeddedDriver'

def displayBank(bk) {
    println "Bank: ${bk.name}"
    println '===================='

    bk.accounts.each { account -> println " ${account}" }
    println()
}

def ds = new DriverManagerDataSource(driverClassName : DRIVER, url : DB,
                        username : USER, password : PASSWORD)
def dao = new BankDaoJdbc(dataSource : ds)
def bk = new Bank('Napier', dao)

def da = new Account(number : 'DDD444', balance : 5000)
bk.openAccount(da)

        // now display everything
displayBank(bk)
```

The output produced is:

```
Bank: Napier
====================
  Account: AAA111; 2000
  Account: BBB222; 3000
  Account: CCC333; 4000
  Account: DDD444; 5000
```

◆

17.7 EXERCISES

1. Using Example 01 as a template, produce a list of those accounts whose balance exceeds 1000. Place a simple if statement within the eachRow iterator.

2. Repeat the first exercise but this time use the SQL select statement to retrieve the desired accounts.

3. Our usage of the method eachRow involved a query String and the closure representing the action. This method is overloaded with a second version eachRow(query, params, closure) in which params is a List of parameter values in the manner of Example 03. Use this style of eachRow to list all accounts with a balance above a value given as program input.

4. An alternative scheme to handle inheritance is to use one table per class. Hence, for the example in Section 17.5, we might have three tables: accounts, currentaccounts, and depositaccounts. Each table has the same information as the properties of the corresponding classes. Of course, we must use foreign keys in the currentaccounts and depositaccounts tables to link with the data from the accounts table. Develop a program to read such a database and tabulate the details of the current and deposit accounts.

5. Develop further the example given in Section 17.6 to have an account class hierarchy similar to that shown in Chapter 14.

CASE STUDY: A LIBRARY APPLICATION (PERSISTENCE)

In this chapter, we extend the final iteration of the application developed in Chapter 16 so that the library, its borrowers, and publications (the domain model) persist in a database. Earlier, we made use of an `Action` object to implement a model–view–controller (MVC) architecture and, as a consequence, keep the domain model separate from the user interaction code. In this case study, we introduce a data access object (DAO) to keep the domain model separate from database persistence code. It is implemented with the Spring framework and the Cloudscape DBMS.

The `Publication`, `Book`, and `Journal` classes are unchanged and only a minor change is required in the `Borrower` class. However, there are significant changes made to the `Library` class and the main Groovy script that runs the application. Both rely on the construction of a DAO using the Spring framework. In the first iteration, we detail the changes required.

In the second iteration, we consider the impact of persistence on unit testing. Happily, we find that all of our earlier unit tests can be run without too much trouble. We also find that is surprisingly easy to introduce new unit tests aimed at testing our implementation of persistence. Finally, we reflect on the role of automated unit testing and Groovy.

18.1 ITERATION 1: PERSIST THE DOMAIN MODEL

For this case study, we use the functional specification of the case study from the final iteration of Chapter 16. However, we are required to amend the application so that the domain model persists in a database. In keeping with the discussions of Chapter 17, we decide to make use of the Cloudscape relational DBMS and the Spring framework. Cloudscape is a modern, Java-based DBMS and Spring is an elegant framework that brings discipline to the implementation of the DAO. Therefore, we readily take advantage of the fact that Groovy makes both easily accessible to us.

As the aim of this iteration is to demonstrate that we can persist the application in a database, we start by developing a database comprising two tables. The first, borrowers, represents the library's borrowers and the second, publications, represents the publications it holds. Both tables are illustrated in Figure 18.1. Each table has a primary key shown as membershipNumber and catalogNumber, respectively. They provide unique entries. In the publications table, there is also a foreign key, shown as borrowerID, that connects to the borrowers table. It is used when a publication is on loan to a borrower. Finally, the publications table handles inheritance in the manner described in Section 17.5, that is, one table represents the classes Publication, Book, and Journal.

Note that in the publications table, there are two books (type = BOOK) and one journal (type = JOURNAL). For consistency, we use only upper-case letters to denote each type of publication. Further, the Groovy book is on loan to Jessie (borrowerID = 1234).

Next, we amend the classes previously developed. Happily, the Publication, Book, and Journal classes require no changes. In the Borrower class, we declare the Map used to hold borrowed Publications as a property rather than a private attribute. This avoids the need to provide explicit getter and setter methods. Similarly, the two Maps used in the Library class to maintain its collection of Borrowers and Publications are now declared as properties.

borrowers

membershipNumber	name
1234	Jessie
...	...

publications

catalogNumber	title	author	editor	type	borrowerID
111	Groovy	Ken Barclay		BOOK	1234
222	UML	John Savage		BOOK	null
333	OOD		Jon Kerridge	JOURNAL	null
...	...	...	...	...	...

FIGURE 18.1   Library database tables.

Our first major change is to introduce a DAO to the Library. Just like the Bank class discussed in Section 17.6, it uses a DAO to handle its database access requirements. By adopting the DAO design pattern, the Library has no knowledge of the underlying database. Notice that the hallmark of a good design is to separate major concerns. Here, we have separated the business logic, that is, the model, and the database persistence code.

The functionality we require from the DAO is easily described by the interface LibraryDaoIF:

```
interface LibraryDaoIF {

    def abstract getBorrowers()
    def abstract getPublications(borrowers)

    def abstract addPublication(publication)
    def abstract removePublication(publication)

    def abstract registerBorrower(borrower)

    def abstract lendPublication(catalogNumber, membershipNumber)
    def abstract returnPublication(catalogNumber)


}
```

It just specifies those methods used previously by the Action class to access and update the Library's "database." Of course, the database was just two simple Maps. Now, it includes a fully functional relational database.

Because we intend to communicate with the database using the JDBC API, we name the class that implements this interface LibraryDaoJdbc. Its detailed coding is as follows:

```
import org.springframework.jdbc.object.*
import org.springframework.jdbc.core.*

class LibraryDaoJdbc implements LibraryDaoIF {

    def getBorrowers() {
        def bQuery = new BorrowerQuery(dataSource)
        return bQuery.execute()
    }

    def getPublications(borrowers) {
        def pQuery = new PublicationQuery(dataSource, borrowers)
        return pQuery.execute()
    }
```

```
def addPublication(publication) {
  def params = null
  if(publication instanceof Book)
    params = [publication.catalogNumber, publication.title, publication.author, '', 'BOOK', null]
  else
    params = [publication.catalogNumber, publication.title, '', publication.editor, 'JOURNAL', null]

  def pInsert = new PublicationInsert(dataSource)
  pInsert.update(params as Object[])
}

def removePublication(publication) {
  def params = [publication.catalogNumber]
  def pRemove = new PublicationRemove(dataSource)
  pRemove.update(params as Object[])
}

def registerBorrower(borrower) {
  def params = [borrower.membershipNumber, borrower.name]

  def bInsert = new BorrowerInsert(dataSource)
  bInsert.update(params as Object[])
}

def lendPublication(catalogNumber, membershipNumber) {
  def params = [membershipNumber, catalogNumber]

  def pUpdate = new PublicationUpdate(dataSource)
  pUpdate.update(params as Object[])
}

def returnPublication(catalogNumber) {
  def params = [null, catalogNumber]

  def pUpdate = new PublicationUpdate(dataSource)
  pUpdate.update(params as Object[])
}

// -----properties ----------------

  def dataSource
}
```

In the implementation of the getBorrowers and getPublications methods, we have introduced the classes BorrowerQuery and PublicationQuery. They are subclasses to the MappingSqlQuery class imported from the Spring framework and behave in a manner similar to the AccountQuery class discussed in Section 17.6.

Both classes are invaluable because they enable us to query the database (in the constructors) and then create domain model objects (in the redefined mapRow method) based on the results of the query. Of course, the Spring framework takes care of the details of the communication with the underlying database. Their coding is as follows:

```
// class: BorrowerQuery
import java.sql.*
import org.springframework.jdbc.object.*

class BorrowerQuery extends MappingSqlQuery {

    def BorrowerQuery(ds) {
        super(ds, 'select * from borrowers')
        this.compile()
    }

    protected Object mapRow(ResultSet rs, int rowNumber) {
        def bor = new Borrower(membershipNumber : rs.getString('membershipNumber'),
                                        name : rs.getString('name'))
        return bor
    }
}

// class: PublicationQuery
import java.sql.*
import org.springframework.jdbc.object.*

class PublicationQuery extends MappingSqlQuery {

    def PublicationQuery(ds, borrowers) {
        super(ds, 'select * from publications')
        this.compile()

        this.borrowers = borrowers          // used by mapRow to update the model
    }
```

```
    protected Object mapRow(ResultSet rs, int rowNumber) {
        def pub = null

        if(rs.getString('type') == 'BOOK')
            pub = new Book(catalogNumber : rs.getString('catalogNumber'),
                            title : rs.getString('title'), author : rs.getString('author'))
        else
            pub = new Journal(catalogNumber : rs.getString('catalogNumber'),
                            title : rs.getString('title'), editor : rs.getString('editor'))

        def borID = rs.getString('borrowerID')

        if(borID != null) {
            def bor = borrowers[borID]
            if(bor != null)
                bor.attachPublication(pub)

        }

        return pub
    }

// -----properties ----------------

    def borrowers                           // an alias for borrowers in the Library

}
```

Notice how the method mapRow in PublicationQuery arranges for a Publication to be attached to its Borrower and for its Borrower to be attached to it. The call to the Borrower's attachPublication method mimics the approach taken in earlier case studies. This brings a strong element of consistency to our work.

In this method, we locate a Borrower as usual by using its membershipNumber (borrowerID in the database) as an index into the Map, borrowers. Unfortunately, since we must redefine Spring's mapRow method, borrowers cannot be a formal parameter. Therefore, we alias borrowers with a property set by the PublicationQuery constructor. Our intention is that the Library will supply it as an actual parameter when it calls its DAO's getPublications method.

The classes BorrowerInsert, PublicationInsert, PublicationUpdate, and PublicationRemove all subclass the SqlUpdate class imported from the Spring framework. They are modeled on the AccountInsert class discussed in Section 17.6. Again, these classes are invaluable, as we can easily update the database from the domain model without having to concern ourselves with the details of communicating with the database.

```
// class: BorrowerInsert
import java.sql.*
import org.springframework.jdbc.object.*

import org.springframework.jdbc.core.*

class BorrowerInsert extends SqlUpdate {

    def BorrowerInsert(ds) {
        super(ds, 'insert into borrowers(membershipNumber, name) values(?, ?)')
        this.declareParameter(new SqlParameter(Types.VARCHAR))
        this.declareParameter(new SqlParameter(Types.VARCHAR))
        this.compile()
    }
}


// class: PublicationInsert
import java.sql.*
import org.springframework.jdbc.object.*
import org.springframework.jdbc.core.*

class BorrowerInsert extends SqlUpdate {

    def BorrowerInsert(ds) {
        super(ds, 'insert into borrowers(membershipNumber, name) values(?, ?)')
        this.declareParameter(new SqlParameter(Types.VARCHAR))
        this.declareParameter(new SqlParameter(Types.VARCHAR))
        this.compile()
    }
}


// class: PublicationUpdate
import java.sql.*
import org.springframework.jdbc.object.*
import org.springframework.jdbc.core.*

class PublicationUpdate extends SqlUpdate {

    def PublicationUpdate(ds) {
        super(ds, 'update publications set borrowerID = ? where catalogNumber = ?')
        this.declareParameter(new SqlParameter(Types.VARCHAR))
        this.declareParameter(new SqlParameter(Types.VARCHAR))
        this.compile()
    }
}
```

```
// class: PublicationRemove
import java.sql.*
import org.springframework.jdbc.object.*
import org.springframework.jdbc.core.*

class PublicationRemove extends SqlUpdate {

    def PublicationRemove(ds) {
        super(ds, 'delete from publications where catalogNumber = ?')
        this.declareParameter(new SqlParameter(Types.VARCHAR))
        this.compile()
    }
}
```

Notice that in the PublicationUpdate class, the borrowerID field of the publications table is changed when a Publication is on loan to a Borrower.

Pleasingly, the changes required in the Library class required are minimal
and easily accomplished. The Library continues to be responsible for maintaining its collection of Borrowers and Publications in two Maps, referenced by borrowers and loanStock, respectively. Of course, all of the error checking code
previously developed is unchanged as a consequence of introducing the database.

The first change is that the Library should make appropriate calls to its DAO
when changes are made to its two Maps. This ensures that there is consistency
between the domain model and the database during the execution of the application. The second is that the Library's constructor should initialize its DAO and
use it to initialize its two Maps. This ensures consistency between the database and
the model on application startup. Outline code for the Library is now:

```
class Library {

    def Library(name, dao) {
        this.name = name
        this.dao = dao

        def bors = dao.getBorrowers()
        bors.each { bor ->
            borrowers[bor.membershipNumber] = bor
        }

        def pubs = dao.getPublications(borrowers)
        pubs.each { pub ->
            loanStock[pub.catalogNumber] = pub
        }
    }
```

```
def addPublication(publication) {
    def message
    if(loanStock.containsKey(publication.catalogNumber) == false) {
        //
        // update database
        dao.addPublication(publication)
        //
        // update model
        loanStock[publication.catalogNumber] = publication
        message = 'Publication added'
    }
    else
        message = 'Cannot add: publication already present'

    return message

}

// As for iteration 4 of Chapter 16

// ...

// ------properties --------------------

def name
def loanStock = [ : ]
def borrowers = [ : ]
def dao

}
```

Notice how the combination of Groovy and the Spring framework have made the underlying database virtually transparent. For example, code such as:

```
def bors = dao.getBorrowers()
bors.each { bor ->
    borrowers[bor.membershipNumber] = bor
}

def pubs = dao.getPublications(borrowers)
pubs.each { pub ->
    loanStock[pub.catalogNumber] = pub
}
```

in the constructor is beautifully elegant and remarkably effective. Similarly, code such as:

```
dao.addPublication(publication)
```

used in the addPublication method to update the underlying database just could not be simpler.

As the functional specification has not changed, the Action class continues to have the same responsibilities. For example, the method displayStock produces a list of all the publications in the library's stock by delegating to a Library object. Similarly, the method registerBorrower communicates with the librarian through a text-based menu. She is prompted to supply the borrower's membership number and name as before. Happily, this means that no changes are required to the Action class.

The final task is to develop a Groovy script to run the application. Most of the code is the controller logic that presents the menu, obtains the user choice, and then calls the appropriate method in the Action class. It is unchanged from the previous version.

However, there is one major difference between this version and the one developed in Chapter 16. It is that we exploit the inversion of control (IoC) design pattern (see http://www.martinfowler.com/articles/injection.html) supported by the Spring framework. Its aim is to eliminate the coupling between classes that can be the source of difficult programming problems.

In earlier case studies, we created and assembled component objects directly. For example, we created a Library object, created an Action object, and then attached the Library object to it as an aggregate component. However, experience has shown that as we develop ever more complex architectures, this approach becomes untenable. Fortunately, Spring provides us with a *lightweight container* responsible for "wiring together" components.

With Spring, the class ClassPathXmlApplicationContext is used to create and assemble related objects. Its constructor expects a configuration file that defines the required objects that are required and how they are to be wired together. Specifically, we have the configuration file config.xml:

```xml
<?xml version="1.0" encoding="UTF-8"?>
<!DOCTYPE beans PUBLIC "-//SPRING//DTD BEAN//EN"
                "http://www.springframework.org/dtd/spring-beans.dtd">

<beans>
    <bean id="dataSource" class="org.springframework.jdbc.datasource.DriverManagerDataSource">
        <constructor-arg index="0"><value>org.apache.derby.jdbc.EmbeddedDriver</value></constructor-arg>
        <constructor-arg index="1"><value>jdbc:derby:libraryDB</value></constructor-arg>
        <constructor-arg index="2"><value></value></constructor-arg>
        <constructor-arg index="3"><value></value></constructor-arg>
    </bean>
```

```
    <bean id="libDao" class="LibraryDaoJdbc">
        <property name="dataSource">
            <ref local="dataSource"/>
        </property>
    </bean>

    <bean id="lib" class="Library">
        <constructor-arg index="0"><value>Napier</value></constructor-arg>
        <constructor-arg index="1"><ref local="libDao"/></constructor-arg>
    </bean>

    <bean id="act" class="Action">
        <property name="library">
            <ref local="lib"/>
        </property>
    </bean>
</beans>
```

As described in Chapter 17, in this XML file, a bean is introduced with the bean element, identified with an id attribute. Its class is defined with the class attribute and a property with the property name attribute. There is also an attribute constructor-arg index to specify a constructor's parameter.

For example, the bean identified as libDao and class LibraryDaoJdbc has a property dataSource. It refers to another local bean also identified as dataSource. This implies that the class LibraryDaoJdbc requires the setter method setDataSource to initialize that relationship property.

The XML also tells us that constructor arguments specified for the object identified as dataSource should be used. The object in question is a DriverManagerDataSource object whose class is imported from the Spring framework. The constructor parameters allow the Library to communicate with a local Cloudscape database.

The important point for us to understand is that any necessary code is generated automatically, and so the description of the LibraryDaoJdbc class given earlier is simplified. For example, we don't have to develop the setDataSource method. It also makes the use of this class much easier since we don't have to create and configure LibraryDaoJdbc and DriverManagerDataSource objects directly.

The creation of Action and Library beans is similar. They are created and configured automatically. It makes a real difference to know that, given a suitable configuration file, the Spring framework allows us to make use of a relational database.

To complete the main Groovy script, we create a suitable application context and get an `Action` object from it. The coding required is refreshingly straightforward:

```
def applicationContext = new ClassPathXmlApplicationContext('config.xml')
def action = applicationContext.getBean('act')
```

Outline code for this iteration is presented as Library 01:

LIBRARY 01

Main script

```
import org.springframework.context.support.*
import console.*

def readMenuSelection() {
    println()
    println('0: Quit\n')
    println('1: Add new book')

    // As for iteration 4 of Chapter 16
    // ...

    print('\n\tEnter choice>>> ')
    return Console.readString()
}

def applicationContext = new ClassPathXmlApplicationContext('config.xml')
def action = applicationContext.getBean('act')

// make first selection
def choice = readMenuSelection()
while(choice != '0') {

    if(choice == '1') {
        action.addBook()                    // Add new book
    }
    // As for iteration 4 of Chapter 16
    // ...
    } else {
        println("\nUnknown selection")
    }
        // next selection
    choice = readMenuSelection()
}
println('\nSystem closing\n')
```

◆

To complete this iteration, we must demonstrate that we have the same functionality as the previous iteration. Functional testing using the text-based menu to exercise each use-case will suffice in this iteration but we revisit this decision in the next. Therefore, we repeat the functional tests carried out in iteration 4 of Chapter 16. Happily, we find that the results are exactly the same.

We must also demonstrate that changes to the domain model persist in the database. Again, this is relatively easy to accomplish. We just note the state of the domain model by selecting the options:

- Display stock

- Display publications available for loan

- Display publications on loan

- Display all borrowers

then close the application and then rerun it. As before, we find that the results of the four display options are the same. At this point, we consider that the iteration has met its aims.

18.2   ITERATION 2: THE IMPACT OF PERSISTENCE

In the previous case studies, unit testing has been an integral part of our software development. In this iteration, we consider the impact of persistence. Clearly, by introducing a database, we have made a significant change to our software. Therefore, we try to ensure that all of our previous unit tests execute without failure and that we can develop new unit tests pertinent to persistence.

Starting with the Book, Journal, and Borrower classes, there is no problem. Their respective GroovyTestCase classes, that is, BookTest, JournalTest, and BorrowerTest, all execute without reporting any failures or errors. Therefore, we add their class files to the runAllTests script. This is reassuring but not unexpected since these classes have no involvement with the database.

With the Library class, the situation changes as it interacts with the database through its DAO. In addition, it is created by the Spring framework as part of an Action object. Before running the previous Library unit tests, we must ensure that we can clear the database to avoid interference between tests. To accomplish this, we update the LibraryDaoIF interface with a clearAllMethod:

```
interface LibraryDaoIF {

    // ...
    def abstract clearAll()
}
```

and implement it in LibraryDaoJdbc as:

```
// class: LibraryDaoJdbc
def clearAll()  {
    def pClear = new PublicationsClear(dataSource)
    pClear.update()
    def bClear = new BorrowersClear(dataSource)
    bClear.update()
}
```

The classes PublicationsClear and BorrowersClear are coded as:

```
import java.sql.*
import org.springframework.jdbc.object.*
import org.springframework.jdbc.core.*

class BorrowersClear extends SqlUpdate {

    def BorrowersClear(ds) {
        super(ds, 'delete from borrowers')
        this.compile()
    }
}
```

and

```
import java.sql.*
import org.springframework.jdbc.object.*
import org.springframework.jdbc.core.*

class PublicationsClear extends SqlUpdate {

    def PublicationsClear(ds) {
        super(ds, 'delete from publications')
        this.compile()
    }
}
```

Now, we can update the setUp method of the previous LibraryTest class:

```
// class: LibraryTest
void setUp() {
    // Create the Action object
    def applicationContext = new ClassPathXmlApplicationContext ('config.xml')
    action = applicationContext.getBean('act')

    // Clear the model
    action.library.loanStock = [:]
    action.library.borrowers = [:]
```

```
    // Clear the database
    action.library.dao.clearAll()

    // As for iteration 4 of Chapter 16
    // ...
}
```

Notice that the property lib has been replaced with the property action. As its name suggests, it references the Action object created by the Spring framework. We access the Library created by the Spring framework through it. For example, we ensure the each test starts with an empty Library with:

```
        action.library.loanStock = [:]
        action.library.borrowers = [:]
```

and so any initializations made by the Spring framework are undone.

Similarly, we clear the database before starting each test with:

```
        action.library.dao.clearAll()
```

and make calls to the Library in the test methods with action.library, as in:

```
        void testAddPublication_1() {
            def pre = action.library.loanStock.size()
            action.library.addPublication(bk1)
            def post = action.library.loanStock.size()

            assertTrue('one less publication than expected', post == pre + 1)
        }
```

Otherwise, the LibraryTest class is unchanged. Happily, all tests pass and we add the LibraryTest class file to the runAllTests script. This give us confidence that the Book, Journal, Borrower, and Library classes have been unaffected by the introduction of the database to the Library and the construction of the Library by the Spring framework. At this point, we are confident that we have not "broken anything."

If we turn our attention to unit testing those classes that make use of the database, then the LibraryDaoJdbc class is the only candidate. An outline of the LibraryDaoJdbcTest class is:

```
    import groovy.util.GroovyTestCase
    import org.springframework.context.support.*
```

```groovy
class LibraryDaoJdbcTest extends GroovyTestCase {

    /**
     * Set up the fixture
     */
    void setUp(){

        action = this.getActionObject()

        action.library.loanStock = [:]
        action.library.borrowers = [:]

        action.library.dao.clearAll()
        bk1 = new Book(catalogNumber : '111', title : 'Groovy', author :'Ken')
        jo1 = new Journal(catalogNumber : '333', title : 'JOOP', editor :'Sally')
        bor1 = new Borrower(membershipNumber : '1234', name : 'Jessie')
    }

    /**
     * Test that the addition of a Book is stored in the database
     */
    void testAddPublication_1() {
        // update the model and the database
        action.library.addPublication(bk1)
        //
        // reset the model
        action.library.loanStock = [:]
        //
        // restore the Action object from the database
        action = this.getActionObject()

        def expected = 1
        def actual = action.library.loanStock.size()
        def book = action.library.loanStock[bk1.catalogNumber]

        assertTrue('unexpected number of publications', actual == expected)
        assertNotNull('book not present', book)
    }

    /**
     * Test that the addition of a Journal is stored in the database
     */
    void testAddPublication_2(){
        // ...
    }
```

```
/**
 * Test that the removal of a Publication is stored in the database
 */
void testRemovePublication(){
    // ...
}


/**
 * Test that a new Borrower is stored in the database
 */
void testRegisterBorrower(){
    // update the model and the database
    action.library.registerBorrower(bor1)
    //
    // reset the model
    action.library.borrowers = [:]
    //
    // restore the Action object from the database
    action = this.getActionObject()

    def expected = 1
    def actual = action.library.borrowers.size()
    def borrower = action.library.borrowers[bor1.membershipNumber]

    assertTrue('unexpected number of borrowers', actual == expected)
    assertNotNull('borrower not present', borrower)
}

/**
 * Test that the lending of a Publication to a Borrower is stored in the database
 */
void testLendPublication(){
    // ...
}


/**
 * Test that the return of a Publication is stored in the database
 */
void testReturnPublication(){
    // ...
}


/**
 * Test that the database tables, borrowers and publications are empty
 */
```

```
void testClearAll(){
    // update the model and the database
    action.library.addPublication(bk1)
    action.library.addPublication(jo1)
    action.library.registerBorrower(bor1)
    //
    // reset the model and the database
    action.library.loanStock = [:]
    action.library.borrowers = [:]
    action.library.dao.clearAll()
    //
    // restore the Action object from the database
    action = this.getActionObject()

    def actual = (action.library.loanStock.size() == 0) &&
                     (action.library.borrowers.size() == 0)
    assertTrue('unexpected Publications or Borrowers', actual == true)
}


/**
  * Get an Action object composed of a Library with its Borrowers and Publications
  * updated from the database
  */
private getActionObject() {
    def applicationContext = new ClassPathXmlApplicationContext('config.xml')
    return applicationContext.getBean('act')
}


// -----properties ------------------

def action
def bk1
def jo1
def bor1
}
```

When we add the corresponding class file to the runAllTests script and execute it, then all (38) tests pass. Although we might add more tests later, at this point, we are reasonably confident that the database is behaving as expected. Full listings are given on the book website.

Note that as well as inheriting a setUp method from the GroovyTestCase class, a subclass also inherits a tearDown method. It executes on completion of each test method and is normally redefined to reclaim or close major resources used in a test. Otherwise, it has no effect. Closing the connection to a database is an obvious use for it but is unnecessary here. Also, an excellent JUnit-based framework, DbUnit (see http://dbunit.sourceforge.net) is available for testing database applications. However, we can assume that the Cloudscape database has been rigorously tested!

Before leaving this iteration, we take the opportunity to reflect on the relationship between unit testing and Groovy. Clearly, for any developer, unit testing is an important activity. However, we believe that for the Groovy programmer, it is not just important, it is essential. This is because Groovy is a dynamic language and that means that the compiler can't make all the type checks that are possible in a statically typed language. There is no guarantee that a Groovy script that compiles cleanly will execute cleanly. For example, execution may be prematurely terminated because some object cannot execute a particular method or does not have a particular property.

An obvious solution is to execute Groovy code as often and as thoroughly as possible. Hopefully, problems can be fixed as they arise. Of course, to do this manually is impractical, but it is made possible with automated unit tests. For example, when we execute the `runAllTests` script we have a guarantee that the code in these (38) tests not only compiles but executes cleanly.

One final point to make is that a unit test often does more than a compiler check could. It checks that something makes sense. There is even a view that the combination of a dynamic language such as Groovy and unit testing is more useful than just a traditionally compiled programming language (see `http://www.mindview.net/WebLog/log-0025`) on its own. For example, a compiler might report that an `int` is returned from a method where a `String` is expected. Groovy will not do this. However, a compiler cannot check that the `String` returned makes sense.

We can easily accomplish this with a unit test. For example, in the `LibraryTest` class, we have:

```
// class: LibraryTest
void testRemovePublication_2() {
    action.library.addPublication(bk1)
    def actual = action.library.removePublication(bk1.catalogNumber)
    def expected = 'Publication removed'

    assertTrue('unexpected message', actual == expected)
}
```

The test checks that the `String` correctly informs that a `Publication` has been removed, not just that a `String` is made available. Therefore, we strongly advocate the use of unit testing, but stress that with Groovy, it is no hardship. On the contrary, it is fun!

18.3   EXERCISES

1. From time to time, borrowers leave the library. Therefore, our software must support a deregistration facility. Introduce a method:

   ```
   removeBorrower(membershipNumber)
   ```

   to the Library class that removes a Borrower from the Library. Update the final iteration of the case study so that users have this option available.

2. Devise and implement tests for the removeBorrower method. For example, you should test that a Borrower removed has no outstanding loans and that no Publication is attached to it. Also, you should check that the database is updated accordingly. Finally, consider erroneous user input, for example, removing a Borrower who is not registered.

3. Discuss how the design decisions made in this and earlier chapters have affected the ease or difficulty of the changes made.

4. Discuss how Groovy has affected the ease or difficulty of the changes made.

5. In the case study, there is one database table publications for the classes Book and Journal. Discuss the assertion that this decision is pragmatic but not object oriented. Suggest an alternative and give an outline implementation.

6. The database in the case study is held locally. How does the use of a DAO design pattern affect accessing a database on a remote server? Give an outline implementation.

XML BUILDERS AND PARSERS

XML has quickly established itself as a technology that can be used for a variety of applications. As simple XML markup, it can represent both data and its structure. This is illustrated in the output produced from Example 01. XML is so adaptable that it also finds uses for object configuration (see Chapters 18 and 22), GUI architecting (see Chapter 20), and application building and deploying (see Appendix K).

Groovy supports a tree-based *markup generator,* BuilderSupport, that can be subclassed to make a variety of tree-structured object representations. Commonly, these *builders* are used to represent XML markup, HTML markup, or, as we shall see in the next chapter, Swing user interfaces. Groovy's markup generator catches calls to pseudomethods and converts them into elements or *nodes* of a tree structure. Parameters to these pseudomethods are treated as attributes of the nodes. Closures as part of the method call are considered as nested subcontent for the resulting tree node.

These pseudomethods are an illustration of the meta-object protocol (MOP) described in Section I.5 of Appendix I. The BuilderSupport class, from which concrete builder classes are derived, includes an implementation of the MOP method invokeMethod, which translates the pseudomethods into the nodes of the resulting tree.

19.1 GROOVY MARKUP

Whichever kind of builder object is used, the Groovy markup syntax is always the same. For example, consider the following fragment:

```
staffBuilder = ...                    // create a builder object
staffBuilder.staff(department : 'Computing', campus : 'Merchiston') {
    academic(name : 'Ken Barclay', office : 'C48', telephone : '2745') {
        module(number : 'C012002', name : 'Software Development 1')
        module(number : 'C012005', name : 'Software Development 2')
    }
    academic(name : 'John Savage, office : 'C48', telephone : '2746') {
        module(number : 'C022002', name : 'Software Development 3')
        module(number : 'C032005', name : 'Design Patterns)
    }
}
```

Here, the tree structure is presented by nested elements. Both academic elements have two distinct module elements. The staff element comprises two academic elements. Figure 19.1 is a tree representation of this data.

The interpretation is that the staffBuilder object calls the pseudomethod staff invoked with two parameters. The first parameter is the Map of objects [department : 'Computing', campus : 'Merchiston']. The second parameter is a Closure object representing the nested subelements. When invoked, this closure will make two calls on the pseudomethod academic. These pseudomethod calls then repeat the same pattern. For example, the first academic method call has the Map parameter [name : 'Ken Barclay', office : 'C48', telephone : '2745'].

It is important to recognize that all this is native Groovy syntax being used to represent any arbitrarily nested markup. Since this is native markup, then we can also mix in any other Groovy constructs such as variables, control flow such as branching, or method calls. In this chapter, we discuss a builder for XML structures. In later chapters, we will see builders for other kinds of tree-shaped structures, including GUI objects.

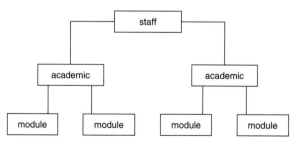

FIGURE 19.1   Tree representation of builder.

19.2   MARKUPBUILDER

Our first illustration is a `MarkupBuilder` for an XML document to represent a book with its title, author, publisher, and ISBN. The pseudomethod `author('Ken Barclay')` will produce the XML element in which the parameter becomes the content:

```
<author>Ken Barclay</author>
```

If the parameter appears as a named parameter, then this is translated into an attribute of an XML element. For example, `isbn(number : '1234567890')` produces:

```
<isbn number='1234567890'/>
```

EXAMPLE 01
A first example

```
import groovy.xml.MarkupBuilder

        // Create a builder
def mB = new MarkupBuilder()

        // Compose the builder
mB.book() {
    author('Ken Barclay')        // producing <author>Ken Barclay</author>
    title('Groovy')
    publisher('Elsevier')
    isbn(number : '1234567890')  // producing <isbn number='1234567890'/>
}
```

◆

Executing this script produces the output sent directly to the standard output stream:

```
<book>
  <author>Ken Barclay</author>
  <title>Groovy</title>
  <publisher>Elsevier</publisher>
  <isbn number='1234567890'/>
</book>
```

Here, the `MarkupBuilder` class is used to construct the application. The builder object `mB` is called with the pseudomethod `book` to establish a `<book>` element. The absence of parameters for this method call specifies an element with content. The closure contains pseudomethod calls that produce the book content such as the `<author>` element.

The builder object mB is called with the pseudomethod book. Further, the nested elements author, title, and so on are also considered pseudomethods applied to the builder object mB.

The default constructor for the class MarkupBuilder is initialized so that the generated XML is issued to the standard output stream. We can use a parameterized constructor call to specify a file to which to send the XML. This is shown in Example 02. Here, the parameter to the MarkupBuilder constructor is a PrintWriter (see JDK) and is obtained from the File object. The output to file book.xml is the same as the XML previously cited.

EXAMPLE 02
File output

```
import groovy.xml.MarkupBuilder
import java.io.*

        // Create a builder
def mB = new MarkupBuilder(new File('book.xml').newPrintWriter())

        // Compose the builder
mB.book() {
        author('Ken Barclay')         // producing <author>Ken Barclay</author>
        title('Groovy')
        publisher('Elsevier')
        isbn(number : '1234567890')   // producing <isbn number='1234567890'/>
}
```

◆

We can now be more ambitious and construct a much larger XML document. A Map provides the data used to populate the XML. Each key entry in the Map represents a book ISBN. The value is a List object containing the remaining book details. The listing is shown in Example 03.

EXAMPLE 03
A Library of Books

```
import groovy.xml.MarkupBuilder
import java.io.*

def data = ['1111111111' :    ['Groovy',                 'Ken Barclay', 'Elsevier'],
            '2222222222' :    ['Object Oriented Design', 'John Savage', 'Elsevier'],
            '3333333333' :    ['C Programming',          'Ken Barclay', 'Prentice Hall']
           ]
```

```
        // Create a builder
def mB = new MarkupBuilder(new File('library.xml').newPrintWriter())

        // Compose the builder
def lib = mB.library() {
    data.each { bk ->
        mB.book() {
            title(bk.value[0])
            author(bk.value[1])
            publisher(bk.value[2])
            isbn(number : bk.key)
        }
    }
}
```

Note how, in this example, we have to repeat the mB prefix on mB.book() to distinguish this as further markup and not normal Groovy script as part of the closure. Without this qualifier, book() { ... } would result in an error from the Groovy compiler. The output from the program is written to the file and contains:

```
<library>
  <book>
    <title>Object Oriented Design</title>
    <author>John Savage</author>
    <publisher>Elsevier</publisher>
    <isbn number='2222222222'/>
  </book>
  <book>
    <title>C Programming</title>
    <author>Ken Barclay</author>
    <publisher>Prentice Hall</publisher>
    <isbn number='3333333333' />
  </book>
  <book>
    <title>Groovy</title>
    <author>Ken Barclay</author>
    <publisher>Elsevier</publisher>
    <isbn number='1111111111' />
  </book>
</library>
```

◆

Note that the books are not in the same order as the data in the Map. Of course, this is a consequence of a Map as an unordered collection of key/value pairs. Should we require them in the same order, then see Exercise 5.

19.3   XML PARSING

The Groovy XmlParser class employs a simple model for parsing an XML document into a tree of Node (see GDK documentation) instances. This parser ignores any comments and processing instructions in the XML document and converts the XML into a Node for each element in the XML. Each Node has the name of the XML element, the attributes of the element, and references to any child Nodes. This model is sufficient for most simple XML processing.

The resulting tree of Node objects can be traversed using the object navigation scheme introduced in Appendix I. If doc represents the root of the <library> example given previously, then doc.book selects all the <book> elements in the <library>. The List of <book> elements is delivered as a List of Node objects representing the <book> elements. Equally, doc.book[0] selects the first <book> in the <library>. In our <library>, a <book> element has a single <title> element. However, since there may be many <title> elements enclosed by a <book> element, in the same way that many <book> elements are enclosed by the <library> element, then doc.book[0].title[0] obtains the first <title> for the first <book>.

Example 04 illustrates the XmlParser class and the navigation of an XML document. Note how the text method defined in the Node class is used to obtain the String value for the <title> element.

<table>
<tr><td>EXAMPLE 04
XML parsing and
navigation</td><td>

```
import groovy.util.*

def parser = new XmlParser()
def doc = parser.parse('library.xml')

println "${doc.book[0].title[0].text()}"
```
</td></tr>
</table>

The program output is as expected:

```
Object Oriented Design
```

Since doc.book delivers a List of Nodes, then we can use an iterator method and a closure to process all the <book> elements in the <library>. In Example 05, we use the each iterator to print the title of every book.

```
import groovy.util.*

def parser = new XmlParser()
def doc = parser.parse('library.xml')

doc.book.each { bk ->
    println "${bk.title[0].text()}"
}
```

EXAMPLE 05
Iterating through
XML content

Again, the expected outcome is:

```
Object Oriented Design
C Programming
Groovy
```

◆

The preceding example could take advantage of doc.book.title navigating to all book titles. Example 06 simplifies the previous code.

```
import groovy.util.*

def parser = new XmlParser()
def doc = parser.parse('library.xml')

doc.book.title.each { title ->
    println "${title.text()}"
}
```

EXAMPLE 06
Simplification
through navigation

The notation ['@number'] can be applied to an <isbn> element to obtain its number attribute. Consider then, the following XML file that lists some academic staff and the grades they assigned to the students they tutor. The staff are recorded by their name, and the students by their names and grades. The file contains:

```
<staff>
    <lecturer name='Ken Barclay'>
        <student name='David' grade='55'/>
        <student name='Angus' grade='75'/>
    </lecturer>
    <lecturer name='John Savage'>
        <student name='Jack' grade='60'/>
        <student name='Todd' grade='44'/>
        <student name='Mary' grade='62'/>
    </lecturer>
```

```
        <lecturer name='Jessie Kennedy'>
            <student name='Mike' grade='50'/>
            <student name='Ruth' grade='70'/>
        </lecturer>
    </staff>
```

◆

Example 07 demonstrates selecting entries from this file based on various criteria.

EXAMPLE 07
Attributes

```
import groovy.util.*

def parser = new XmlParser()
def doc = parser.parse('staff.xml')

println doc.lecturer.student['@name']

println doc.lecturer.student.findAll { stu ->
    stu['@grade'].toInteger() >= 65
} ['@name']

doc.lecturer.student.each { stu ->
    if(stu['@grade'].toInteger() >= 65)
        println stu['@name']
}
```

◆

The first print statement obtains a List of all the student names:

```
[David, Angus, Jack, Todd, Mary, Mike, Ruth]
```

The second print statement is used to obtain a List of those students with a grade not less than 65. For each such student, we then print their name.

```
[Angus, Ruth]
```

The each iterator at the end of the listing achieves the same as the last example. This time, no List object is generated, but those same student names are printed, one per line:

```
Angus
Ruth
```

Consider the development of a large database application. This might involve producing many interlinked tables to capture the entities and relations in the problem domain. Producing the SQL instructions to create these tables might prove an expensive and time-consuming activity. In the next example, we show how an XML document can be used to describe the tables and their relations and how from the XML, it is a relatively simple task to convert it into SQL instructions.

The XML document (in the file tables.xml) contains:

```
<?xml version="1.0" encoding="UTF-8"?>

<tables>
    <table name="Book">
        <field name="title" type="text"/>
        <field name="isbn" type="text"/>
        <field name="price" type="integer"/>
        <field name="author" type="id"/>
        <field name="publisher" type="id"/>
    </table>
    <table name="Author">
        <field name="surname" type="text"/>
        <field name="forename" type="text"/>
    </table>
    <table name="Publisher">
        <field name="name" type="text"/>
        <field name="url" type="text"/>
    </table>
</tables>
```

Each <table> element describes a table in a relational database. The <field> subelements represent the fields of the table with its name and type. The basic types supported in this small example are text, integer, and id. An id type denotes a relationship with another table and is a foreign key for another table. The program to process this information is given in Example 08.

EXAMPLE 08
XML to SQL

```
import groovy.util.*

def typeToSQL = ['text'      : 'TEXT NOT NULL',
                 'id'        : 'INTEGER NOT NULL',
                 'integer'   : 'INTEGER NOT NULL'
                ]
def parser = new XmlParser()
def doc = parser.parse('tables.xml')
```

```
doc.table.each { tab ->
    println "DROP TABLE IF EXISTS ${tab['@name']};"
    println "CREATE TABLE ${tab['@name']}("
    println " ${tab['@name']}_ID ${typeToSQL['id']},"
    tab.field.each { col ->
        println " ${col['@name']} ${typeToSQL[col['@type']]},"
    }
    println " PRIMARY KEY (${tab['@name']}_ID)"
    println ");"
}
```

◆

When we run this application against the data in `tables.xml`, we produce the SQL to establish the tables in the database:

```
DROP TABLE IF EXISTS Book;
CREATE TABLE Book(
    Book_ID INTEGER NOT NULL,
    title TEXT NOT NULL,
    isbn TEXT NOT NULL,
    price INTEGER NOT NULL,
    author INTEGER NOT NULL,
    publisher INTEGER NOT NULL,
    PRIMARY KEY (Book_ID)
);
DROP TABLE IF EXISTS Author;
CREATE TABLE Author(
    Author_ID INTEGER NOT NULL,
    surname TEXT NOT NULL,
    forename TEXT NOT NULL,
    PRIMARY KEY (Author_ID)
);
DROP TABLE IF EXISTS Publisher;
CREATE TABLE Publisher(
    Publisher_ID INTEGER NOT NULL,
    name TEXT NOT NULL,
    url TEXT NOT NULL,
    PRIMARY KEY (Publisher_ID)
);
```

Combining our XML parsing and navigation of an XML structure with a `MarkupBuilder` provides a mechanism whereby we can apply a transformation to some input XML and deliver some new output, either XML or some other form. This kind of transformation is often the preserve of XSLT (Fitzgerald,

2003; Tidwell, 2001). However, many transformations are arguably easier to capture as Groovy. This is shown by Example 09, in which we take the weather file (all temperatures are Fahrenheit and all dates are MM/DD/YYYY):

```
<weather>
  <temperatures city="Paris">
    <temperature date="01/21/2001">67</temperature>
    <temperature date="01/22/2001">70</temperature>
    <temperature date="01/23/2001">72</temperature>
    <temperature date="01/24/2001">62</temperature>
    <temperature date="01/25/2001">65</temperature>
    <temperature date="01/26/2001">65</temperature>
    <temperature date="01/27/2001">66</temperature>
    <temperature date="01/28/2001">78</temperature>
  </temperatures>
  <temperatures city="London">
    <temperature date="01/21/2001">42</temperature>
    <temperature date="01/22/2001">41</temperature>
    <temperature date="01/23/2001">45</temperature>
    <temperature date="01/24/2001">50</temperature>
    <temperature date="01/25/2001">31</temperature>
    <temperature date="01/26/2001">40</temperature>
    <temperature date="01/27/2001">42</temperature>
    <temperature date="01/28/2001">47</temperature>
  </temperatures>
  <temperatures city="Edinburgh">
    <temperature date="01/21/2001">22</temperature>
    <temperature date="01/22/2001">24</temperature>
    <temperature date="01/23/2001">23</temperature>
    <temperature date="01/24/2001">30</temperature>
    <temperature date="01/25/2001">12</temperature>
    <temperature date="01/26/2001">10</temperature>
    <temperature date="01/27/2001">28</temperature>
    <temperature date="01/28/2001">22</temperature>
  </temperatures>
</weather>
```

and produce a table of the temperatures for each city and determine the lowest recorded value for each city. This latter task, although simple to describe, is not the simplest to express in XSLT. However, with Groovy object navigation, it is a relatively simple exercise.

```
import groovy.util.*

def parser = new XmlParser()
def doc = parser.parse('weather.xml')
```

EXAMPLE 09
Transforming XML

```
doc.temperatures.each { temps ->
    def lowest = 200
    println "City: ${temps['@city']}"

    println '+------+--+'
    temps.temperature.each { temp ->
        def tmp = temp.text().toInteger()
        printf('| %10s | %2d |\n', [temp['@date'], tmp])
        if(tmp < lowest)
            lowest = tmp
    }
    println '+------+--+'

    println "Lowest recorded temperature is: ${lowest}"
    println()
}
```

When we run this script, the output is:

```
City: Paris
+------+--+
| 01/21/2001 | 67 |
| 01/22/2001 | 70 |
| 01/23/2001 | 72 |
| 01/24/2001 | 62 |
| 01/25/2001 | 65 |
| 01/26/2001 | 65 |
| 01/27/2001 | 66 |
| 01/28/2001 | 78 |
+------+--+
Lowest recorded temperature is: 62

City: London
+------+--+
| 01/21/2001 | 42 |
| 01/22/2001 | 41 |
| 01/23/2001 | 45 |
| 01/24/2001 | 50 |
| 01/25/2001 | 31 |
| 01/26/2001 | 40 |
| 01/27/2001 | 42 |
| 01/28/2001 | 47 |
+------+--+
Lowest recorded temperature is: 31
```

```
City: Edinburgh
+------+--+
| 01/21/2001 | 22 |
| 01/22/2001 | 24 |
| 01/23/2001 | 23 |
| 01/24/2001 | 30 |
| 01/25/2001 | 12 |
| 01/26/2001 | 10 |
| 01/27/2001 | 28 |
| 01/28/2001 | 22 |
+------+--+
Lowest recorded temperature is: 10
```

◆

Some XSLT transformations are extremely difficult to express (see http://www.
oracle.com/technology/pub/articles/wang_xslt.html, http://www.javaworld.
com/javaworld/jw-12-2001/jw-1221-xslt.html). For some, we would have to
resort to nonportable XSLT extensions. Groovy's support for an XPath-like
notation (see http://www.w3.org/TR/xpath20/) to traverse complex structures
generally yields a simpler implementation than using XSLT.

For example, consider an XML document for a CD catalog:

```
<catalog>
  <cd>
    <title>Empire Burlesque</title>
    <artist>Bob Dylan</artist>
    <country>USA</country>
    <company>Columbia</company>
    <price>10.90</price>
    <year>1985</year>
  </cd>
  <cd>
    <title>Hide your heart</title>
    <artist>Bonnie Tyler</artist>
    <country>UK</country>
    <company>CBS Records</company>
    <price>9.90</price>
    <year>1988</year>
  </cd>
  <cd>
```

```
      <title>Still got the blues</title>
      <artist>Gary More</artist>
      <country>UK</country>
      <company>Virgin Records</company>
      <price>10.20</price>
      <year>1990</year>
   </cd>
   <cd>
     <title>This is US</title>
     <artist>Gary Lee</artist>
     <country>UK</country>
     <company>Virgin Records</company>
     <price>12.20</price>
     <year>1990</year>
   </cd>
</catalog>
```

We plan to publish this data, grouping the CDs by their country of origin, then further grouped by year of publication. The final form we seek is:

```
<grouping>
  <country name='UK'>
    <year year='1988'>
      <title>Hide your heart</title>
    </year>
    <year year='1990'>
      <title>Still got the blues</title>
      <title>This is US</title>
    </year>
  </country>
  <country name='USA'>
    <year year='1985'>
      <title>Empire Burlesque</title>
    </year>
  </country>
</grouping>
```

We exploit the ease whereby we can traverse an XML structure. Further, we use Groovy's native language support for Lists and Maps to make the necessary transformations. We convert the XML into a Map in which the key is the country of origin:

```
['UK' : ...,
 'USA' : ...
 ]
```

The value for each key is another Map in which the key is the year of publication:

```
['UK' : [1988 : ..., 1990 : ...],
 'USA' : [1985 : ...]
 ]
```

Finally, the values for these inner Maps are Lists of titles:

```
['UK' : [1988 : ['Hide your heart'], 1990 : ['Still got the blues', 'This is US']],
 'USA' : [1985 : ['Empire Burlesque']]
]
```

From this structure, we can readily make the transformation into the required XML. Example 10 is the script for this task. The conversion from the XML into the Map of Maps is performed by the countryGrouping method.

EXAMPLE 10
Grouping

```
import groovy.util.*
import groovy.xml.*

def countryGrouping(catalog) {
    countryMap = [:]

    catalog.cd.each { cd ->
        if(countryMap.containsKey(cd.country[0].text())) {
            def yearMap = countryMap[cd.country[0].text()]
            if(yearMap.containsKey(cd.year[0].text()))
                yearMap[cd.year[0].text()] << cd.title[0].text()
            else
                yearMap[cd.year[0].text()] = [cd.title[0].text()]
        } else {
            countryMap[cd.country[0].text()] = [(cd.year[0].text()) : [cd.title[0].text()]]
        }
    }

    return countryMap
}

def parser = new XmlParser()
def doc = parser.parse('catalog.xml')

        // Create a builder
def mB = new MarkupBuilder(new File('catalog.countries.xml').newPrintWriter())
def groupings = countryGrouping(doc)
```

```
mB.grouping() {
    groupings.each { country, yearMap ->
        mB.country(name : country) {
            yearMap.each { year, titleList ->
                mB.year(year : year) {
                    titleList.each { title ->
                        mB.title(title)
                    }
                }
            }
        }
    }
}
```

As a final example of making transformations to an XML data file, consider one that represents a report of customers' orders. The original file content might be:

```
<orderinfo>
  <customer group="exclusive">
    <id>234</id>
    <serviceorders>
      <order>
        <productid>1231</productid>
        <price>100</price>
        <timestamp>2004-06-05:14:40:05</timestamp>
      </order>
      <order>
        <productid>2001</productid>
        <price>20</price>
        <timestamp>2004-06-12:15:00:44</timestamp>
      </order>
    </serviceorders>
  </customer>
  <customer group="regular">
    <id>111</id>
    <serviceorders>
      <order>
        <productid>1001</productid>
        <price>10</price>
        <timestamp>2004-06-07:10:00:56</timestamp>
      </order>
      <order>
        <productid>1231</productid>
        <price>10</price>
        <timestamp>2004-06-01:09:42:15</timestamp>
      </order>
```

```
        <order>
          <productid>2001</productid>
          <price>20</price>
          <timestamp>2004-06-16:22:11:19</timestamp>
        </order>
      </serviceorders>
    </customer>
    <customer group="regular">
      <id>112</id>
      <serviceorders/>
    </customer>
  </orderinfo>
```

◆

Observe how each customer is identified by the <id> element such as
<id>234</id> and each order identifies the product by examples such as
<productid>1231</productid>. A requirement might be to transform the XML
into one in which the <timestamp> element is removed and the customer and
product identifiers are replaced by their names taken from a database. Again,
this is not the kind of transformation undertaken by XSLT. Example 11 is the
simple Groovy script to make this change.

EXAMPLE 11
Replacing ids

```
import groovy.sql.*
import groovy.util.*
import groovy.xml.*

def DB = 'jdbc:derby:orderinfoDB'
def USER = ''
def PASSWORD = ''
def DRIVER = 'org.apache.derby.jdbc.EmbeddedDriver'

        // Connect to database
def sql = Sql.newInstance(DB, USER, PASSWORD, DRIVER)

def parser = new XmlParser()
def doc = parser.parse('orderinfo.xml')

        // Create a builder
def mB = new MarkupBuilder(new File('orderinfo.details.xml').newPrintWriter())

mB.orderinfo() {
    doc.customer.each { cust ->
        mB.customer(group : cust['@group']) {
```

```
        def customer = sql.firstRow('select * from customers'+
                                    'where id = ?', [cust.id[0].text()])
    mB.id(customer.name)
    mB.serviceorders() {
        cust.serviceorders.order.each { order ->
            mB.order() {
                def product = sql.firstRow('select * from products
                                where id = ?', [order.productid[0].text()])
                mB.productid(product.name)
                mB.price(order.price[0].text())
            }
        }
    }
}
}
}
```

◆

19.4 EXERCISES

1. Use a `MarkupBuilder` to construct the weather file illustrated in Example 09.

2. Using the `library.xml` file from Examples 04, 05, and 06, produce a list of the titles and the ISBNs of books published by Elsevier.

3. Modify Example 09 and transform the XML into HTML that can be rendered by a browser.

4. Extend Example 10 to handle configuration files as shown at the end of Chapter 18.

5. Modify Example 03 so that the output is in ISBN order.

GUI BUILDERS

The preceding chapter described how Groovy markup can be used to assemble XML structures. A graphical application is an assembly of Swing components, nested one within another in a hierarchical manner. For example, we might have panels nested within other panels to construct a user interface. Equally, we might have text fields and buttons in a user dialog. Hence, the native syntax of Groovy markup can also be used for Swing applications.

20.1 SWINGBUILDER

A graphical application can be developed using the Swing framework (Eckstein et al., 2002; Topley, 1998). This is a large and complex library consisting of over 300 classes and interfaces. The software engineers that developed it made full use of leading edge technologies, such as *design patterns* (Gamma et al., 1995; Grand, 2002), and this further complicates its usage.

With the `SwingBuilder` class, the pseudomethods represent Swing components. In most cases, these pseudomethods are named after the Swing class with the prefix "J" removed and the first letter given as lowercase. Hence, pseudomethod `frame` is used to construct a `JFrame` widget and `textField` for a `JTextField` widget. The pseudomethod parameters are used to initialize the component. The closure defines the subcomponent widgets.

The first illustration is a graphical application that displays the text "Hello world." Objects of the class `JLabel` represent fixed text elements in Swing. Objects of the class `JFrame` are used to represent an application's top-level window. In this first application, we populate a `JFrame` object with an enclosed `JLabel` object. This immediately suggests Groovy markup with a `frame` and a contained `label`. Example 01 presents the code.

EXAMPLE 01
A first frame

```
import groovy.swing.SwingBuilder
import javax.swing.*

        // Create a builder
def sB = new SwingBuilder()

        // Compose the builder
def frame = sB.frame(title : 'Example01', location : [100, 100],
        size : [400, 300], defaultCloseOperation : WindowConstants.EXIT_ON_CLOSE) {
    label(text : 'Hello world')
}

        // Now show it
frame.pack()
frame.setVisible(true)
```

◆

Here, the SwingBuilder class is used to construct the application. The builder object sB is called with the pseudomethod frame to establish a JFrame object. The named parameters of the method call specify the title in the caption bar, the position of the upper left of the window, the size of the window, and that the application exits the Java runtime when the close button on the frame is selected. The closure contains a single pseudomethod call label that creates the JLabel object decorated with the required text. Figure 20.1 shows the application running.

We quickly become more ambitious, populating the frame with a panel that maintains six components. Pairs of labels and text fields are used to invite the user to supply their full name. The panel employs a GridLayout manager to arrange the subcomponents that are organized in a 3-by-2 grid (with a 5-pixel gap between each). The code for this is given in Example 02.

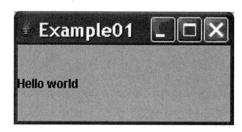

FIGURE 20.1　The first frame.

EXAMPLE 02
Using a layout
manager

```
import groovy.swing.SwingBuilder
import javax.swing.*
import java.awt.*

        // Create a builder
def sB = new SwingBuilder()

        // Compose the builder
def frame = sB.frame(title : 'Example02', location : [100, 100],
        size : [400, 300], defaultCloseOperation : WindowConstants.EXIT_ON_CLOSE) {
    panel(layout : new GridLayout(3, 2, 5, 5)) {
        label(text : 'Last Name:', horizontalAlignment : JLabel.RIGHT)
        textField(text : '', columns : 10)
        label(text : 'Middle Name:', horizontalAlignment : JLabel.RIGHT)
        textField(text : '', columns : 10)
        label(text : 'First Name:', horizontalAlignment : JLabel.RIGHT)
        textField(text : '', columns : 10)
    }
}

        // Now show it
frame.pack()
frame.setVisible(true)
```

◆

Figure 20.2 shows this code executing. Notice how the six components are presented as three rows of two elements. Each row has a label and a text field.

Continuing in this manner can lead to deeply nested structures that can be difficult to construct and maintain. Often, it is better to construct separate substructures, and then compose them into a larger structure. This is shown in Example 03, which repeats the previous illustration. Note how the subpanel is defined separately and then incorporated into the frame.

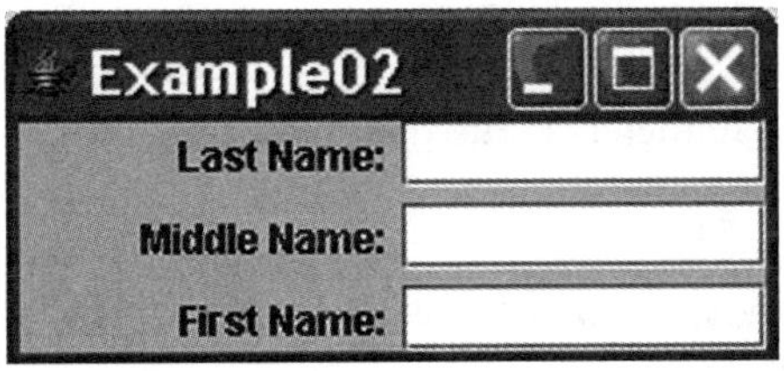

FIGURE 20.2 GridLayout manager.

EXAMPLE 03

Incremental
assembly

```groovy
import groovy.swing.SwingBuilder
import javax.swing.*
import java.awt.*

        // Create a builder
def sB = new SwingBuilder()

        // Build the panel...
def mainPanel = {
    sB.panel(layout : new GridLayout(3, 2, 5, 5)) {
        label(text : 'Last name:', horizontalAlignment : JLabel.RIGHT)
        textField(text : '', columns : 10)
        label(text : 'Middle name:', horizontalAlignment : JLabel.RIGHT)
        textField(text : '', columns : 10)
        label(text : 'First name:', horizontalAlignment : JLabel.RIGHT)
        textField(text : '', columns : 10)
    }
}

        // ...and the frame
def frame = sB.frame(title : 'Example03', location : [100, 100],
        size : [400, 300], defaultCloseOperation : WindowConstants.EXIT_ON_CLOSE) {
    mainPanel()
}

        // Now show it
frame.pack()
frame.setVisible(true)
```

◆

It is now relatively easy to incorporate more Swing components into the application canvas. Example 04 includes two buttons. Pay attention to how the main panel uses a BorderLayout manager. A BorderLayout manager employs a NORTH, EAST, WEST, SOUTH, and CENTER arrangement to position, at most, five components. In this case, we must specify where the subcomponents are to be placed. The constraints parameter is used for this purpose, appearing on the subassemblies.

EXAMPLE 04

Buttons

```groovy
import groovy.swing.SwingBuilder
import javax.swing.*
import java.awt.*
```

```
        // Create a builder
def sB = new SwingBuilder()

        // Build the button panel...
def buttonPanel = {
    sB.panel(constraints : BorderLayout.SOUTH) {
        button(text : 'OK')
        button(text : 'Cancel')
    }
}

        // ...then the main panel...
def mainPanel = {
    sB.panel(layout : new BorderLayout()) {
        label(text : 'Is this OK?', horizontalAlignment : JLabel.CENTER, constraints :
BorderLayout.CENTER)
        buttonPanel()
    }
}

        // ...and the frame
def frame = sB.frame(title : 'Example04', location : [100, 100],
        size : [400, 300], defaultCloseOperation : WindowConstants.EXIT_ON_CLOSE) {
    mainPanel()
}

        // Now show it
frame.pack()
frame.setVisible(true)
```

◆

Figure 20.3 shows how this example appears. The text is placed in the central region (with a default FlowLayout), while the buttons are given the SOUTH constraint.

FIGURE 20.3   BorderLayout manager and buttons.

In the next example, we attach *event handlers* to the buttons. An event handler represents the action to perform when the button is pressed. Each `button` pseudomethod call includes the `actionPerformed` parameter. This represents a code block presented as a closure. In both cases, this is a simple `print` statement. For example, when the OK button is pressed, the text "OK pressed" appears in the console.

EXAMPLE 05
Event handlers

```groovy
import groovy.swing.SwingBuilder
import javax.swing.*
import java.awt.*

def sB = new SwingBuilder()

        // Build the button panel...
def buttonPanel = {
    sB.panel(constraints : BorderLayout.SOUTH) {
        button(text : 'OK', actionPerformed : {
            println 'OK pressed'
        })
        button(text : 'Cancel', actionPerformed : {
            println 'Cancel pressed'
        })
    }
}

        // ...then the main panel...
def mainPanel = {
    sB.panel(layout : new BorderLayout()) {
        label(text : 'Is this OK?', horizontalAlignment : JLabel.CENTER,
                    constraints : BorderLayout.CENTER)
        buttonPanel()
    }
}

        // ...and the frame
def frame = sB.frame(title : 'Example05', location : [100, 100],
        size : [400, 300], defaultCloseOperation : WindowConstants.EXIT_ON_CLOSE) {
    mainPanel()
}

        // Now show it
frame.pack()
frame.setVisible(true)
```

◆

We take this further in Example 06 by using a closure to handle the event. This can help to simplify the actionPerformed parameter by moving the code into this handler. Here, we provide two handler closures, one for each button. The two buttons are assembled from data in a List object. The two sub-Lists of buttons have the text that decorates a button and the closure object that acts as the button event handler.

```groovy
import groovy.swing.SwingBuilder
import javax.swing.*
import java.awt.*

        // Handlers
def okHandler = {
    println 'OK pressed'
}

def cancelHandler = {
    println 'Cancel pressed'
}

        // Buttons
def buttons = [['OK', okHandler], ['Cancel', cancelHandler]]

        // Create a builder
def sB = new SwingBuilder()

        // Build the button panel...
def buttonPanel = {
    sB.panel(constraints : BorderLayout.SOUTH) {
        buttons.each { but ->
            sB.button(text : but[0], actionPerformed : but[1])
        }
    }
}

        // ...then the main panel...
def mainPanel = {
    sB.panel(layout : new BorderLayout()) {
        label(text : 'Is this OK?', horizontalAlignment : JLabel.CENTER,
                    constraints : BorderLayout.CENTER)
        buttonPanel()
    }
}

        // ...and the frame
def frame = sB.frame(title : 'Example06', location : [100, 100],
        size : [400, 300], defaultCloseOperation : WindowConstants.EXIT_ON_CLOSE) {
    mainPanel()
}
```

EXAMPLE 06
Event handler
methods

```
                                // Now show it
                        frame.pack()
                        frame.setVisible(true)
```

◆

Observe how the buttonPanel uses the each iterator to assemble the buttons from the buttons object (a List of Lists). Here, we are mixing in normal Groovy code with the builder markup. The closure associated with each can comprise further Groovy statements or further builder markup. For the latter, we must refer to the builder object sB to disambiguate it from other Groovy code.

In the next example, we develop a simple application to convert a distance measured in inches to the equivalent amount in centimeters. The program operates with two text fields and a button. The number of inches is entered into one of the text fields, the button is pressed, and the conversion is displayed in the other text field. Example 07 is the code listing.

EXAMPLE 07

Imperial to metric
converter

```
import groovy.swing.SwingBuilder
import javax.swing.*
import java.awt.*

        // Create a builder
def sB = new SwingBuilder()

        // properties
def inputText = null
def outputText = null

        // Handlers
def doConvert = {
    def text = inputText.getText()
    def inches = text.toInteger()
    def centimetres = 2.54 * inches
    outputText.setText(centimeters.toString())
}

        // Build the input panel...
def inputPanel = {
    sB.panel() {
        label(text : 'Input the length in inches:', horizontalAlignment : JLabel.RIGHT)
        inputText = textField(text : '', columns : 10)
    }
}
```

```
        // ...then the output panel...
def outputPanel = {
    sB.panel() {
        label(text : 'Converted length in centimeters:', horizontalAlignment : JLabel.RIGHT)
        outputText = textField(text : '', columns : 10, enabled : false)
        button(text : 'Convert', actionPerformed : doConvert)
    }
}

        // ...and now the main panel
def mainPanel = {
    sB.panel(layout : new GridLayout(2, 3, 5, 5)) {
        inputPanel()
        outputPanel()
    }
}

        // ...and the frame
def frame = sB.frame(title : 'Example07', location : [100, 100],
        size : [400, 300], defaultCloseOperation : WindowConstants.EXIT_ON_CLOSE) {
    mainPanel()
}

        // Now show it
frame.pack()
frame.setVisible(true)
```

◆

Observe how, in the inputPanel, the textField is referenced by the variable inputText. Similarly, the text field for the converted value is referenced by the variable outputText. The actionPerformed parameter for the button invokes the event handler closure doConvert, accessing these two values. The values are two JTextField objects, representing the source of the input and the destination for the output. Closure doConvert extracts the String from the input JTextField using the method getText, does the conversion, and puts a String into the output JTextField using the method setText. Figure 20.4 shows this program executing.

It is also worth also recalling (see Appendix B) how this script is enclosed by a Java class. Variables defined in the script, such as inputText, are properties of the enclosing class. Methods defined in the script, such as doConvert, are methods of the enclosing class. As ever, the methods of a class can refer to the properties defined in that same class. Hence, the method doConvert can refer to the variables inputText and outputText.

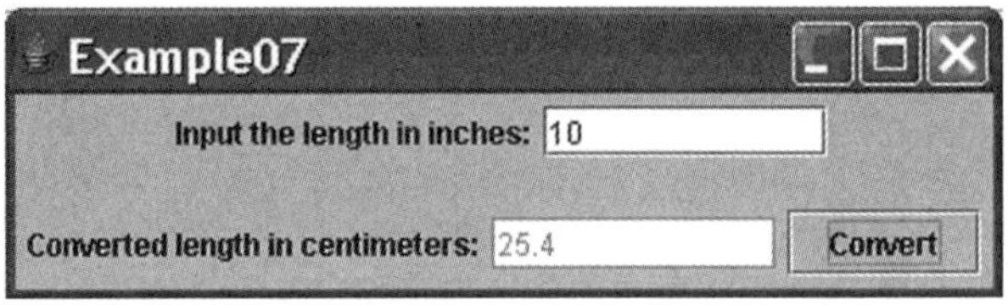

FIGURE 20.4   Imperial to metric converter.

20.2   LISTS AND TABLES

A graphical application often employs lists and tables to present its data. The Swing class JList represents a component for selecting one or more items from a set of choices. The content of a list component is dynamic in that we may add or remove items from the list. Two aspects of a JList are that it uses a data model to represent the list data, and a selection model to determine how many items may be picked from the list. When we add or remove items from the list, we actually remove them from the underlying data model.

A demonstration of the next example is shown in Figure 20.5. The JList component is wrapped by a JScrollPane to reduce the presentation size of the list. On this occasion, the Remove button is active while the Add button is disabled. If the Remove button is pressed, the selected item in the list is deleted. If any text is entered into the text field, the Add button is enabled and, when pressed, the content of the text field is inserted into the list.

The code for this is given in Example 08. Note the two button handlers doRemove and doAdd. Their action is to remove the selected item from the list or insert an item into the list. Both achieve this by removing from or adding to the data model an object of the class DefaultListModel. Initially, this is populated from a preset Groovy List entitled staffList.

Using a data model to back up a graphical component is a common scheme and is referred to as the model–view–controller (the familiar MVC)

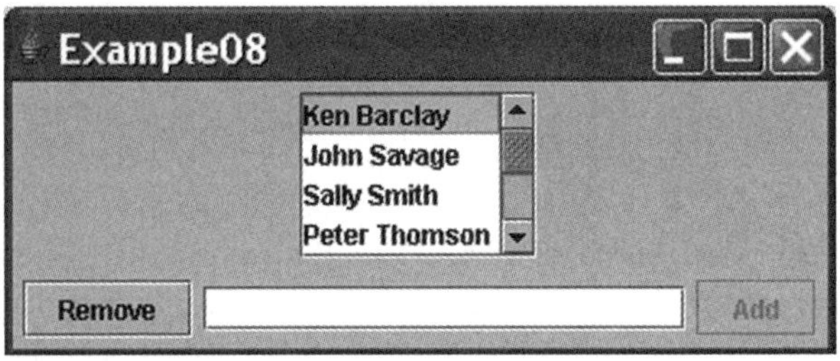

FIGURE 20.5   Lists.

architecture. The *model* part represents the data for the component. The *view* part is the visual appearance of the component, while the *controller* represents the user interaction with the component. This MVC architecture also applies to text fields. The model part is referred to as its *document*. Here, we initialize our `staffNameTextField` with an object of the class `PlainDocument`. An object of the class `StaffDocumentListener` is registered with the document to receive notifications of changes. Specifically, when text is entered into the field, the Add button is enabled. When the text is removed, the Add button is disabled.

```groovy
import groovy.swing.SwingBuilder
import javax.swing.*
import javax.swing.event.*
import javax.swing.text.*
import java.awt.*

        // properties
def staffList = null
def removeButton = null
def staffNameTextField = null

        // Event handler for the Remove button
def doRemove = {
    def listModel = staffList.getModel()
    def index = staffList.getSelectedIndex()
    def size = listModel.size()

    listModel.remove(index)
    if(size == 0)
        removeButton.setEnabled(false)
    else {
        if(index == listModel.getSize())
            index--

        staffList.setSelectedIndex(index)
        staffList.ensureIndexIsVisible(index)
    }
}

        // Event handler for the Add button
def doAdd = {
    def listModel = staffList.getModel()
    def staffName = staffNameTextField.getText()

    if(staffName == '' || listModel.contains(staffName)) {
        Toolkit.getDefaultToolkit().beep()
```

```
                    staffNameTextField.requestFocusInWindow()
                    staffNameTextField.selectAll()
                    return
                }

                def index = staffList.getSelectedIndex()
                index = (index == -1) ? 0 : 1 + index

                listModel.insertElementAt(staffName, index)

                staffNameTextField.requestFocusInWindow()
                staffNameTextField.setText('')

                staffList.setSelectedIndex(index)
                staffList.ensureIndexIsVisible(index)
            }

                // ---------------------------------------------------
                // Implementation for an observer to register to receive
                // notifications of changes to a text document.
        class StaffDocumentListener implements DocumentListener {

                void    changedUpdate(DocumentEvent event) {
                    if(event.document.length <= 0)
                        button.setEnabled(false)
                }

                void    insertUpdate(DocumentEvent event) {
                    button.setEnabled(true)
                }

                void    removeUpdate(DocumentEvent event) {
                    if(event.document.length <= 0)
                        button.setEnabled(false)
                }
            }

        // -----properties ----------------

            def     button

        }

                // -----------------------------------------------
                // Specialized DefaultListModel with a parameterized
                // constructor
```

```groovy
class StaffListModel extends DefaultListModel {

    StaffListModel(list) {
        super()
        list.each { item -> this.addElement(item) }
    }
}


        // Create a builder
def sB = new SwingBuilder()

        // Panel carrying the staff list
def listPanel = {
    sB.panel(constraints : BorderLayout.CENTER) {
        scrollPane() {

            def sList = ['Ken Barclay',      'John Savage',
                         'Sally Smith',      'Peter Thomson',
                         'John Owens',       'Neil Urquhart',
                         'Jessie Kennedy',   'Jon Kerridge'
                        ]
            staffList = list(model : new StaffListModel(sList),
                    selectionMode : ListSelectionModel.SINGLE_SELECTION,
                    selectedIndex : 0, visibleRowCount : 4)
        }
    }
}


        // Add/Remove buttons and text field
def buttonPanel = {
    sB.panel(constraints : BorderLayout.SOUTH) {
        removeButton = button(text : 'Remove', actionPerformed : doRemove)
        def plainDocument = new PlainDocument()
        staffNameTextField = textField(text : '', columns : 20,
                document : plainDocument, actionPerformed : doAdd)
        def addButton = button(text : 'Add', enabled : false, actionPerformed : doAdd)
        def documentListener = new StaffDocumentListener(button : addButton)
        plainDocument.addDocumentListener(documentListener)
    }
}


        // Now the main panel...
def mainPanel = {
    sB.panel(layout : new BorderLayout()) {
        listPanel()
        buttonPanel()
    }
}
```

```
            // ...and the frame
    def frame = sB.frame(title : 'Example08', location : [100, 100],
            size : [400, 300], defaultCloseOperation : WindowConstants.EXIT_ON_CLOSE) {
        mainPanel()
    }


            // Now show it
    frame.pack()
    frame.setVisible(true)
```

◆

The next example demonstrates setting up a JTable. A JTable is used to present its data as a two-dimensional grid. Like the JList component, a JTable relies on various other classes to support its operation. Again, an MVC architecture is employed. The class DefaultTableModel realizes the data for a JTable. In fact, the SwingBuilder object uses a specialized version of groovy.model.DefaultTableModel for this purpose. In Example 09, we see that this is initialized with a List of Maps entitled staffList. A JTable also requires labels for the columns, and this is provided by the elements closureColumn. The closure columns are added to the special table model. The closure columns specify the column name and how elements are accessed from a column. Here, closures simply extract from the row the map value according to the key. Figure 20.6 shows Example 09 executing.

EXAMPLE 09
A table component

```
import groovy.swing.SwingBuilder
import javax.swing.*
import javax.swing.table.*
import java.awt.*


        // Create a builder
def sB = new SwingBuilder()


        // Panel carrying the staff list
def tablePanel = {
    sB.panel(constraints : BorderLayout.CENTER) {
        scrollPane() {
            table(selectionMode : ListSelectionModel.SINGLE_SELECTION) {
                def staffList = [[forename : 'Ken', surname : 'Barclay', room : 'C48', telephone : 2745],
                        [forename : 'John', surname : 'Savage', room : 'C48', telephone : 2746],
                        [forename : 'Sally', surname : 'Smith', room : 'C46', [telephone : 2742],
                        [forename : 'Peter', surname : 'Thomson', room : 'D51', telephone : 2781],
```

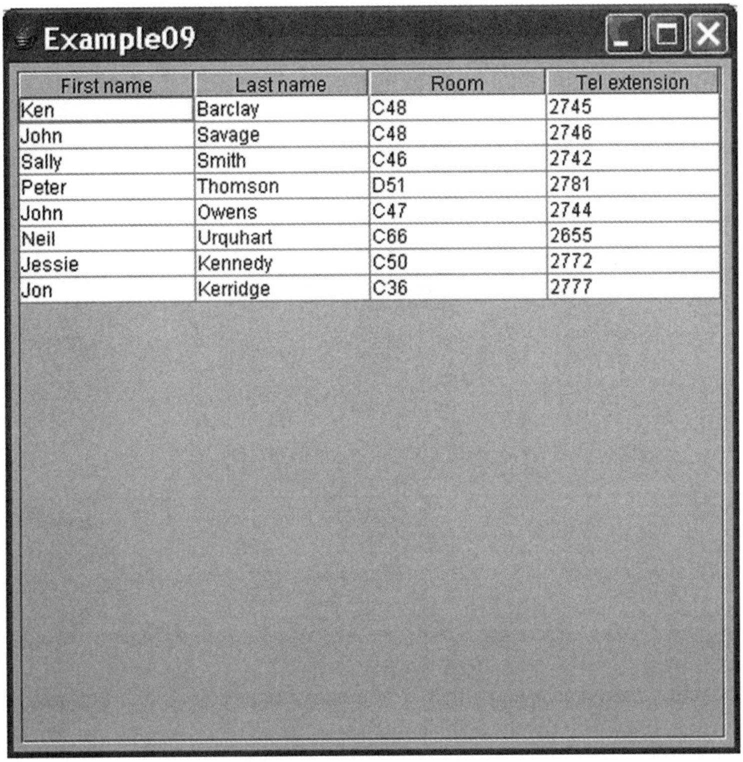

FIGURE 20.6 JTable component.

```
                    [forename : 'John', surname : 'Owens', roo : 'C47',telephone : 2744],
                    [forename : 'Neil', surname : 'Urquhart', room : 'C66', telephone : 2655],
                    [forename : 'Jessie', surname : 'Kennedy', room : 'C50', telephone : 2772],
                    [forename : 'Jon', surname : 'Kerridge', room : 'C36', telephone : 2777]
                    ]

        tableModel(list : staffList) {
            closureColumn(header : 'First name', read : {row -> return row.forename})
            closureColumn(header : 'Last name', read : {row -> return row.surname})
            closureColumn(header : 'Room', read : {row -> return row.room})
            closureColumn(header : 'Tel extension', read : {row -> return row.telephone})
        }
      }
    }
  }
}
```

```
        // Now the main panel...
def mainPanel = {
    sB.panel(layout : new BorderLayout()) {
        tablePanel()
    }
}


        // ...and the frame
def frame = sB.frame(title : 'Example09', location : [100, 100],
        size : [400, 300], defaultCloseOperation : WindowConstants.EXIT_ON_CLOSE) {
    mainPanel()
}


        // Now show it
frame.pack()
frame.setVisible(true)
```

◆

20.3   BOX AND BOXLAYOUT CLASSES

The BoxLayout class is a layout manager that produces one row or column of components. It is especially useful for producing ribbons of buttons. The Box class is a light-weight container prepared with a BoxLayout manager. The Box class provides several conveniences for including components in a boxed layout. Using a Box is generally more convenient than creating a panel that is controlled with a BoxLayout manager. The pseudomethods hbox and vbox are used to create a Box of horizontal components and a Box of vertical components, respectively. Figure 20.7 demonstrates a vertical Box holding a strip of buttons.

In the listing given in Example 10, the class FixedButton (FixedTextArea) is used to create a specialized JButton (JTextArea) of a fixed size. Observe how we create instances of these classes and wrap them in the pseudomethod widget. The widget method is used to create a specialized Swing component.

The figure is also populated with a multiline text area. It is anticipated that the buttons will provide some application functionality, producing output into this area. The text area in this example is disabled, so it simply acts as a display panel.

EXAMPLE 10
Buttons and text area

```
import groovy.swing.SwingBuilder
import javax.swing.*
import java.awt.*


        // Button of set size
class FixedButton extends JButton {
```

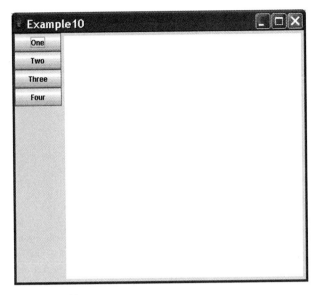

FIGURE 20.7   Box of buttons.

```
    Dimension getMinimumSize() { return BUTTONSIZE }
    Dimension getMaximumSize() { return BUTTONSIZE }
    Dimension getPreferredSize() { return BUTTONSIZE }

    private static final BUTTONSIZE = new Dimension(80, 30)
}

        // Text area of set size
class FixedTextArea extends JTextArea {

    Dimension getMinimumSize() { return TEXTAREASIZE }
    Dimension getMaximumSize() { return TEXTAREASIZE }
    Dimension getPreferredSize() { return TEXTAREASIZE }

    private static final TEXTAREASIZE = new Dimension(400, 400)
}

        // Create a builder
def sB = new SwingBuilder()

        // Now the main panel...
def mainPanel = {
    sB.panel(layout : new BorderLayout()) {
        vbox(constraints : BorderLayout.WEST) {
```

```
            def buttons = ['One', 'Two', 'Three', 'Four']
                buttons.each { but ->
                sB.widget(new FixedButton(text : but))
                }
        }
        panel(constraints : BorderLayout.CENTER) {
            widget(new FixedTextArea(enabled : false))
        }
    }
}


        // ...and finally the frame
def frame = sB.frame(title : 'Example10', location : [100, 100],
        size : [400, 300], defaultCloseOperation : WindowConstants.EXIT_ON_CLOSE) {
    mainPanel()
}


        // Now show it
frame.pack()
frame.setVisible(true)
```

◆

Appendix L illustrates other Swing components presented through the SwingBuilder. Together they illustrate how easy it is to develop a graphical application using Groovy's SwingBuilder.

20.4   EXERCISES

The following exercises are presented as use cases for a small project. The user should read further aspects of the SwingBuilder class described in Appendix L before proceeding.

1. Using the knowledge described here and in Appendix L, develop a graphical application to act as an integrated development environment (IDE) for preparing, compiling, and running Groovy scripts. The IDE should appear as shown in Figure 20.8. In this first version, put simple print statements in each of the event handlers, as shown in Example 06. Use System.exit(0) as the code for the Exit handler (see Example 01, Appendix L), so that the application closes correctly.

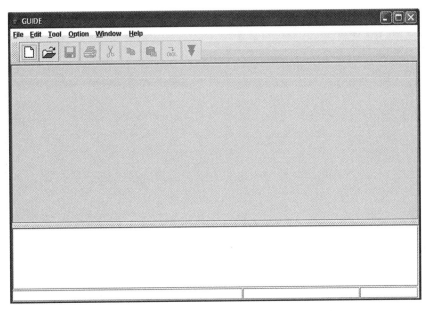

FIGURE 20.8 Initial IDE.

The main panel should be organized as a split pane. The upper panel will act as the editor panel. It will be organized as a tabbed pane, where each tab will be associated with a Groovy source file to be edited, compiled, or executed. The lower panel is the console in which the running script interacts with the user.

2. Now implement the handler for the menu File + New. The text area for preparing the Groovy script should be a scrolled editor pane. Initially, the tab is decorated as Edit1, Edit2, and so on. Add a specialized DocumentListener to the editor pane so that if the content of the text document is modified, then the tab is decorated with an * as in *Edit1. See Figure 20.9.

Now implement the handler for File + Open. Here, use a JFileChooser to invite the user to nominate the *.groovy file to open. The file is presented in a scrolled editor pane with the tab having the file name. Again, associate a DocumentListener as for a new file.

Continue by implementing File + SaveAs and File + Save menus. The handler for File + Save will call the File + SaveAs handler if the tab includes Edit or *Edit as the tab prefix. Again, a JFileChooser will invite the user to nominate the name and location of the file. This will

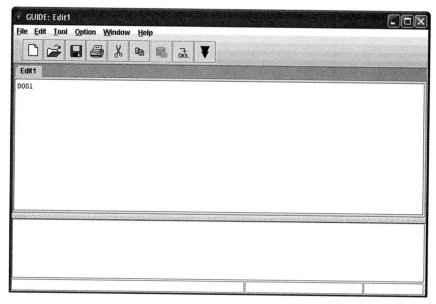

FIGURE 20.9   Editor tab.

apply if the tab is Edit or *Edit. Otherwise, the name in the tab is used to update the current file.

3. Arrange for the application to include the file name and its location in the title bar. Add a ChangeListener to the tabbed pane, so that when a different tab is selected by the user, the title bar is updated to reflect the new file that is activated. Additionally, add a MouseListener to the tabbed pane, so that when the user presses the right mouse over a tab, then a popup menu invites the user to close the tab and its file.

4. Introduce handlers for Edit + Cut, Edit + Copy and Edit + Paste.

5. Introduce a specialized version of the class DropTarget so that we can drag and drop *.groovy files onto the IDE.

    A finished version for this project is given in the distribution src\guide directory.

TEMPLATE ENGINES

The mail merge features found in a word processor are used to merge form letters with names and addresses from a mailing list. A form letter consists of static text, such as the body of the letter, and place-holders for those parts of the letter that are to be replaced. Typically, this might include the name and address of the recipient. The data source includes the values for the place-holders for each individual to receive the letter. Such merge facilities can greatly reduce the burden on the user, especially when the amount of data is large and comprises various elements.

Groovy's *template engine* operates like a mail merge but is much more general. Essentially, there is no restriction on the nature of the form document or the source of the merged data.

21.1 STRINGS

We know from Chapter 3 that a String enclosed in single quotes is taken literally, while a String in double quotes is interpreted. Hence, the following comments demonstrate the output from the two print statements:

```
def name = "Ken"
println 'My name is: ${name}'        // My name is: ${name}
println "My name is: ${name}"        // My name is: Ken
```

In effect, the interpretation of double-quoted strings is similar to the action of a template engine. Here, the expression ${name} is replaced by the actual value of the name variable.

21.2   TEMPLATES

Consider the simple template appearing in the file book.template. This file contains the form for an XML element describing a single book:

```
<book>
    <author>${author}</author>
    <title>${title}</title>
    <publisher>${publisher}</publisher>
    <isbn number="${isbn}"/>
</book>
```

As usual, the substituted values are declared using the ${ } notation. Mapping of the place-holders to actual values is relatively simple through a *binding* and a SimpleTemplateEngine. The binding is a Map with the place-holders as keys and the replacements as the values. The code for its usage is shown in Example 01.

EXAMPLE 01

Mapping values for
a simple template

```
import groovy.text.*
import java.io.*

def file = new File('book.template')
def binding = ['author'        : 'Ken Barclay',
               'title'         : 'Groovy',
               'publisher'     : 'Elsevier',
               'isbn'          : '1234567890'
              ]
def engine = new SimpleTemplateEngine()
def template = engine.createTemplate(file)
def writable = template.make(binding)
println writable
```

When we execute this program, we replace ${author} in the template with the value Ken Barclay. The final output produced by the application is:

```
<book>
    <author>Ken Barclay</author>
    <title>Groovy</title>
    <publisher>Elsevier</publisher>
    <isbn number="1234567890"/>
</book>
```

◆

A variation on this example delivers the merged result to a file. In Example 01, the template object is of the class Writable. In the print statement, the message

toString is called implicitly on this object to display its value. As we show in
Example 02, we can also send the message writeTo to persist the result in a file.

EXAMPLE 02
Persisting a
merged template

```
import groovy.text.*
import java.io.*

def file = new File('book.template')
def binding = ['author'          :'Ken Barclay',
               'title'           :'Groovy',
               'publisher'       :'Elsevier',
               'isbn'            :'1234567890'
              ]
def writable = new SimpleTemplateEngine().createTemplate(file).make(binding)
def destination = new FileWriter('book.xml')
writable.writeTo(destination)
destination.flush()
destination.close()
```

◆

We can also call upon the scripting syntax used by JavaServer Pages (JSP)
(Bergsten, 2003). Two scripting elements from JSP that we can use are JSP
scriplets (denoted by <% ... %>) and JSP *expressions* (denoted as <%= ... %>).
The scriplet is used to add a block of code, including control flow statements,
print statements, and variables. Consider the file library.template:

```
<library>
<% for(bk in books) { %>
  <book>
    <author>${bk.value[0]}</author>
    <title>${bk.value[1]}</title>
    <publisher>${bk.value[2]}</publisher>
    <isbn number='${bk.key}'/>
  </book>"
<% } %>
</library>
```

Here, the scriplet includes a loop that iterates through the books collection. It is a
Map collection and, for each key/value entry, the key is the book's ISBN, and the
corresponding value is a list carrying the author, title, and publisher, in that order.

To bind values, we need to provide such a Map as that shown in Example 03.
Note how a binding for 'books' associates with the Map referenced by the
variable books.

EXAMPLE 03
Merging a
collection

```
import groovy.text.*
import java.io.*

def file = new File('library.template')
def books = ['1234567890' : ['Ken Barclay', 'Groovy', 'Elsevier'],
             '0750660989' : ['John Savage', 'OOD with UML and JAVA', 'Elsevier'],
             '0130373265' : ['Ken Barclay', 'C Programming', 'Prentice Hall']
             ]
def writable = new SimpleTemplateEngine().createTemplate(file).make(['books' : books])
println writable
```

When we execute this program against the template file, the output produced is:

```
<library>
    <book>
        <author>Ken Barclay</author>
        <title>C Programming</title>
        <publisher>Prentice Hall</publisher>
        <isbn number='0130373265'/>
    </book>
    <book>
        <author>John Savage</author>
        <title>OOD with UML and JAVA</title>
        <publisher>Elsevier</publisher>
        <isbn number='0750660989'/>
    </book>
    <book>
        <author>Ken Barclay</author>
        <title>Groovy</title>
        <publisher>Elsevier</publisher>
        <isbn number='1234567890'/>
    </book>

</library>
```

◆

A simple adaptation of the preceding example is to make the bindings from a database. The books table in the booksDB database has rows containing a book ISBN, author, title, and publisher. Additionally, we have a template for generating HTML in the file library.html.template:

```
<html>
  <head>
    <title>Library</title>
  </head>
  <body>
    <table border="1">
      <% sql.eachRow('select * from books') { bk -> %>
        <tr>
          <td>${bk.author}</td>
          <td>${bk.title}</td>
          <td>${bk.publisher}</td>
          <td>${bk.isbn}</td>
        </tr>
      <% } %>
    </table>
  </body>
</html>
```

The revised code is:

```
import groovy.sql.*
import groovy.text.*

import java.io.*

def DB = 'jdbc:derby:booksDB'
def USER = ''
def PASSWORD = ''
def DRIVER = 'org.apache.derby.jdbc.EmbeddedDriver'

      // Connect to database
def sql = Sql.newInstance(DB, USER, PASSWORD, DRIVER)

      // Create the template
def file = new File('library.html.template')
def writable = new SimpleTemplateEngine().createTemplate(file).make(['sql' : sql])
println writable
```

◆

EXAMPLE 04

Template
instantiation from
a database

Class Sql has no suitable constructor to initialize an instance from a JDBC connection URL, username, password, and driver class name. Here, we use the
helper method newInstance. The output we get is:

```
<html>
  <head>
    <title>Library</title>
  </head>
  <body>
    <table border="1">
        <tr>
          <td>Ken Barclay</td>
          <td>C Programming</td>
          <td>Prentice Hall</td>
          <td>0130373265</td>
        </tr>
        <tr>
          <td>John Savage</td>
          <td>OOD with UML and JAVA</td>
          <td>Elsevier</td>
          <td>0750660989</td>
        </tr>
        <tr>
          <td>Ken Barclay</td>
          <td>Groovy</td>
          <td>Elsevier</td>
          <td>1234567890</td>
        </tr>
    </table>
  </body>
</html>
```

21.3   EXERCISES

1. Modify the code in Example 01 and comment out the binding for the author as shown in the following example. Now, execute the program and explain its effect.

```
def binding = [//'author'      :'Ken Barclay',
```

2. Using the original code from Example 01, modify the data file as shown in the following example. Now, execute the program and explain its effect.

```
<author>${authorname}</author>
```

CASE STUDY: A LIBRARY APPLICATION (GUI)

Using knowledge gained in Chapter 20 and Appendix L, in this chapter, we revisit the library case study of Chapter 18. Our aim is to give the application a more modern look and feel by adding a GUI. Happily, we reap the benefit of its MVC architecture by not having to change any of the model classes. Similarly, the decision to use a DAO means that no changes to classes that access the database are required. Finally, Groovy's `SwingBuilder` makes the construction of the GUI relatively easy.

22.1 ITERATION 1: PROTOTYPE THE GUI

The aim of this iteration is to demonstrate that we can replace the text-based menu developed in the case study of Chapter 18 with a GUI. Our intention is that it should mirror the GUI developed in Example 10 of Chapter 20. Therefore, we replace the options presented by the menu with suitably labeled `FixedButtons` and replace `Action` class methods with event handlers.

The model classes (`Library`, `Publication`, `Book`, `Journal`, `Borrower`) and the DAO implementation (`LibraryDaoJdbc`) require no changes. This makes the coding task relatively straightforward. The code for the GUI is shown the listing of Library 01.

```
import groovy.swing.*
import groovy.sql.*
import javax.swing.*
import java.awt.*
```

LIBRARY 01
User interface

```
class FixedButton extends JButton {

    Dimension getMaximumSize() { return BUTTONSIZE }
    Dimension getMinimumSize() { return BUTTONSIZE }
    Dimension getPreferredSize() { return BUTTONSIZE }

    private static final BUTTONSIZE = new Dimension(250, 30)
}


class FixedTextArea extends JTextArea {

    Dimension getMaximumSize() { return TEXTAREASIZE }
    Dimension getMinimumSize() { return TEXTAREASIZE }
    Dimension getPreferredSize() { return TEXTAREASIZE }

    private static final TEXTAREASIZE = new Dimension(600, 400)
}


        // Event handlers
def doExit = {
    System.exit(0)
}


        // Create the builder
def sB = new SwingBuilder()


        // Create the button panel
def buttonPanel = {
    sB.panel(constraints : BorderLayout.WEST) {
        vbox() {
            widget(new FixedButton(text : 'Exit'), actionPerformed : doExit )
            widget(new FixedButton(text : 'Add new publication'))
            widget(new FixedButton(text : 'Display stock'))
            widget(new FixedButton(text : 'Display publications available for loan'))
            widget(new FixedButton(text : 'Display publications on loan'))
            widget(new FixedButton(text : 'Register new borrower'))
            widget(new FixedButton(text : 'Display borrowers'))
            widget(new FixedButton(text : 'Lend one publication'))
            widget(new FixedButton(text : 'Return one publication'))
        }
    }
}
        // Create display panel
def displayPanel = {
    sB.panel(constraints : BorderLayout.CENTER) {
        widget(new FixedTextArea(enabled : false))
    }
}
```

```
        // Create status panel
def statusPanel = {
    sB.panel(constraints : BorderLayout.SOUTH) {
        label(text : 'Status')
        textField(text : '', columns : 60, enabled : false)
    }
}


        // Assemble main panel
def mainPanel = {
    sB.panel(layout : new BorderLayout()) {
        sB.panel(layout : new BorderLayout(), constraints : BorderLayout.CENTER) {
            buttonPanel()
            displayPanel()
        }
        statusPanel()
    }
}


        // Main frame
def frame = sB.frame(title : 'Library application', location : [50, 50], size : [800, 500],
        defaultCloseOperation : WindowConstants.EXIT_ON_CLOSE) {
    mainPanel()
}

frame.pack()
frame.setVisible(true)
```

Notice that much of the complexity of the construction of the GUI is simplified by using panels of panels to assemble its various components and that we use BorderLayout managers to position the elements.

When we execute this script, we see that the GUI comprises a vertical strip of buttons that correspond to the menu items in the simple text interface of the previous case study. To the right is a text area into which the program can deliver the output. At the bottom of the window is a status panel used to present any user information. Figure 22.1 illustrates its appearance.

To complete this iteration, we put a single event handler behind the Exit button. Happily, it behaves as expected, and we proceed to the next iteration where we provide more handlers.

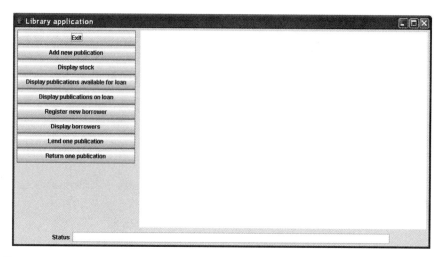

FIGURE 22.1   Visual interface.

22.2   ITERATION 2: IMPLEMENT THE HANDLERS

The application now requires event handlers to provide the required functionality. The aim of this iteration is to put most of them in place. The remainder are left as an exercise for the reader. Similarly, we display error messages in the status panel that originate from the Library, but we leave error detection by the GUI as an exercise for the reader (see Section 22.3).

In the previous iteration, we were satisfied that we could correctly introduce an event handler for the Exit button. The other buttons, of course, are labeled to correspond to the application use cases. We anticipate that a button's handler will send messages to the Library just as the Action object in the previous case study. In effect, the logic of the Action class methods becomes the code for the application event handlers. The listing for Library 02 illustrates.

LIBRARY 02
Event handlers

```
import groovy.swing.*
import groovy.sql.*
import javax.swing.*
import java.awt.*

import org.springframework.context.support.*

def applicationContext = new ClassPathXmlApplicationContext ('config.xml')
def library = applicationContext.getBean('lib')
```

```
              // properties
def statusTextField = null
def displayTextArea = null

              // helper closure

def displayPublication = { indent, pub ->
    displayTextArea.append(indent)
    if(pub instanceof Book)
        displayTextArea.append("Book: ${pub.catalogNumber}: ${pub.title} by: ${pub.author}" + '\n')
    else
        displayTextArea.append("Journal : ${pub.catalogNumber}: ${pub.title} edited by:"+
                                          "${pub.editor}" + '\n')
    statusTextField.setText('')
}

              // Event handlers
def doExit = {
    System.exit(0)
}

def doAddNewPublication = {
    def message
    def pubType = JOptionPane.showInputDialog(null, 'Add a book (B) or journal (J)',
                                          'Add new publication', JOptionPane.QUESTION_MESSAGE)
    if(pubType == 'B' || pubType == 'b') {
        def catalogNumber = JOptionPane.showInputDialog(null, 'Enter book catalog number',
                                          'Add new publication', JOptionPane.QUESTION_MESSAGE)
        def title = JOptionPane.showInputDialog(null, 'Enter book title','Add new publication',
                                          JOptionPane.QUESTION_MESSAGE)
        def author = JOptionPane.showInputDialog(null, 'Enter book author', 'Add new publication',
                                          JOptionPane.QUESTION_MESSAGE)

        message = library.addPublication(new Book(catalogNumber : catalogNumber, title : title,
                                          author : author))

        statusTextField.setText(message)

    } else if(pubType == 'J' || pubType == 'j') {
        def catalogNumber = JOptionPane.showInputDialog(null, 'Enter journal catalog number',
                                          'Add new publication', JOptionPane.QUESTION_MESSAGE)
        def title = JOptionPane.showInputDialog(null, 'Enter journal title', 'Add new publication',
                                          JOptionPane.QUESTION_MESSAGE)
        def editor = JOptionPane.showInputDialog(null, 'Enter journal editor', 'Add new publication',
                                          JOptionPane.QUESTION_MESSAGE)

        message = library.addPublication(new Journal(catalogNumber : catalogNumber, title: title,
                                          editor : editor))
```

```groovy
            statusTextField.setText(message)

    } else
        JOptionPane.showMessageDialog(null, 'Incorrect response (B or J)', 'Add new publication',
                                                    JOptionPane.ERROR_MESSAGE)
}


def doDisplayStock = {
    def stock = library.loanStock
    displayTextArea.append('Library (full stock inventory):' + '\n')
    displayTextArea.append('================================' + '\n')

    stock.each { catNo, pub ->
        displayPublication('', pub)
    }

    statusTextField.setText('')
}


def doDisplayPublicationsAvailableForLoan = {
    def stock = library.loanStock
    displayTextArea.append('Library (publications available for loan):' + '\n')
    displayTextArea.append('==========================================' + '\n')

    stock.each { catNo, pub ->
        if(pub.borrower != null) {
            displayPublication('', pub)
        }
    }

    statusTextField.setText('')
}


def doDisplayPublicationsOnLoan = {
    def stock = library.loanStock
    displayTextArea.append('Library (publications on loan):' + '\n')
    displayTextArea.append('================================' + '\n')

    stock.each { catNo, pub ->
        if(pub.borrower != null) {
            displayPublication('', pub)
        }
    }

    statusTextField.setText('')
}
```

```
def doRegisterNewBorrower = {
    def message
    def membershipNumber = JOptionPane.showInputDialog(null,
                                'Enter borrower membership number','Register new borrower',
                                JOptionPane.QUESTION_MESSAGE)
    def name = JOptionPane.showInputDialog(null, 'Enter borrower name', 'Register new borrower',
                                JOptionPane.QUESTION_MESSAGE)

    message = library.registerBorrower(new Borrower(membershipNumber: membershipNumber, name : name))

    statusTextField.setText(message)
}

def doDisplayBorrowers = {
    def stock = library.loanStock
    def borrowers = library.borrowers
    displayTextArea.append('Library (all borrowers):' + '\n')
    displayTextArea.append('========================' + '\n')

    borrowers.each { memNo, bor ->
        if(bor.membershipNumber != 0) {
            displayTextArea.append("Borrower: ${bor.membershipNumber}; ${bor.name}" + '\n')

                def displayed = false
                stock.each { catNo, pub ->
                    if(pub.borrower == bor)
                        displayPublication(' ', pub)
                        displayed = true
                }
                if(displayed == false)
                    displayTextArea.append(' None')
        }
    }

    statusTextField.setText('')
}

def doLendPublication = {
    def message
    def catalogNumber = JOptionPane.showInputDialog(null, 'Enter publication catalog number',
                                'Lend publication', JOptionPane.QUESTION_MESSAGE)
    def membershipNumber = JOptionPane.showInputDialog(null,
                                'Enter borrower membership number', 'Lend publication',
                                JOptionPane.QUESTION_MESSAGE)

    message = library.lendPublication(catalogNumber, membershipNumber)

    statusTextField.setText(message)
}
```

```groovy
def doReturnPublication = {
    def message
    def catalogNumber = JOptionPane.showInputDialog(null, 'Enter publication catalog number',
                                    'Return publication', JOptionPane.QUESTION_MESSAGE)

    library.returnPublication(catalogNumber)

    statusTextField.setText(message)
}


        // Create the builder
def sB = new SwingBuilder()

        // Create the button panel
def buttonPanel = {
    sB.panel(constraints : BorderLayout.WEST) {
        vbox() {
            widget(new FixedButton(text : 'Exit'), actionPerformed : doExit)
            widget(new FixedButton(text : 'Add new publication'),
                                    actionPerformed : doAddNewPublication)
            widget(new FixedButton(text : 'Display stock'),
                                    actionPerformed : doDisplayStock)
            widget(new FixedButton(text : 'Display publications available for loan'),
                                    actionPerformed : doDisplayPublicationsAvailableForLoan)
            widget(new FixedButton(text : 'Display publications on loan'),
                                    actionPerformed : doDisplayPublicationsOnLoan)
            widget(new FixedButton(text : 'Register new borrower'),
                                    actionPerformed : doRegisterNewBorrower)
            widget(new FixedButton(text : 'Display borrowers'),
                                    actionPerformed : doDisplayBorrowers)
            widget(new FixedButton(text : 'Lend one publication'),
                                    actionPerformed : doLendPublication)
            widget(new FixedButton(text : 'Return one publication'),
                                    actionPerformed : doReturnPublication)
        }
    }
}


        // Create display panel
def displayPanel = {
    sB.panel(constraints : BorderLayout.CENTER) {
        sB.scrollPane() {
            def displayTextArea = new FixedTextArea(enabled : false)
            sB.widget(new JScrollPane(displayTextArea))
        }
    }
```

```
}

        // Create status panel
def statusPanel = {
    sB.panel(constraints : BorderLayout.SOUTH) {
        label(text : 'Status')
        def statusTextField = textField(text : '', columns : 60, enabled : false)
    }
}

        // Assemble main panel
def mainPanel = {
    sB.panel(layout : new BorderLayout()) {
        sB.panel(layout : new BorderLayout(), constraints : BorderLayout.CENTER) {
            buttonPanel()
            displayPanel()
        }
        statusPanel()
    }
}

        // Main frame
def frame = sB.frame(title : 'Library application', location : [50, 50], size : [800, 500],
                            defaultCloseOperation : WindowConstants.EXIT_ON_CLOSE) {
    mainPanel()
}

frame.pack()



frame.setVisible(true)
```

Notice that we have an Add new publication button rather than one to add a book and another to add a journal. This is just a pragmatic decision to decrease the number of buttons on the GUI and makes no real difference to the underlying software. However, we must amend the configuration file to reflect the fact that we no longer have an Action object (the event handlers replace it). This is easily accomplished by removing:

```
<bean id="act" class="Action">
        <property name="library">
            <ref local="lib"/>
        </property>
```

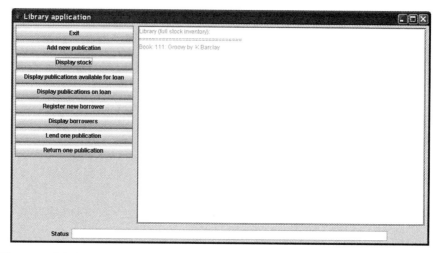

FIGURE 22.2   The GUI with handlers in place.

```
</bean>
```

from the file. Otherwise, the logic is unchanged from the case study of Chapter 18. A typical output is shown in Figure 22.2.

As usual, our last task is to test the application. Functional use case testing is just as before, that is, we visually check that the various outputs are as expected. However, there is a small problem that arises with the unit tests. Rather than access the Library through an Action object as in the previous case study, we now access it directly (the Action object does not exist). This requires a few small changes to the LibraryTest and LibraryDaoJdbcTest classes. For example, we now have:

```
// class: LibraryTest
void setUp(){
    def applicationContext = new ClassPathXmlApplicationContext ('config.xml')
    library = applicationContext.getBean('lib')

    library.loanStock = [:]
    library.borrowers = [:]

    library.dao.clearAll()
    // ...
}
```

and

```
// class: LibraryDaoJdbcTest
private getLibraryObject() {
    def applicationContext = new ClassPathXmlApplicationContext ('config.xml')
    return applicationContext.getBean('lib')
}
```

Happily, all of the tests pass and we consider this application complete. Full listings of the Groovy scripts and classes are available on the book website.

22.3   EXERCISES

1. In the second iteration, we omitted some important use cases. For example, the GUI should support the following:

   • Remove a publication

   • Display a particular publication

   • Display selected publications

   • Display a particular borrower

   • Display selected borrowers

   Using the code from the Action class of Chapter 18, implement one or more of these use cases.

2. In the second iteration, we omitted some error detection code in the GUI. For example, the GUI should report an error when:

   • A particular publication for display does not exist.

   • No publication in publications selected for display exists.

   • A particular borrower for display does not exist.

   • No borrower in borrowers selected for display exists

   Using the code from the Action class of Chapter 18, implement one or more of these error checks.

3. Reflect on the effort required to make updates. Give a least four good reasons why Groovy is useful in this context.

4. In Library 01, we create the button panel with the following code:

```
def buttonPanel = {
    sB.panel(constraints : BorderLayout.WEST) {
        vbox() {
            widget(new FixedButton(text : 'Exit'), actionPerformed : doExit)
            widget(new FixedButton(text : 'Add new publication'))
            widget(new FixedButton(text : 'Display stock'))
            widget(new FixedButton(text : 'Display publications available for loan'))
            widget(new FixedButton(text : 'Display publications on loan'))
            widget(new FixedButton(text : 'Register new borrower'))
            widget(new FixedButton(text : 'Display borrowers'))

            widget(new FixedButton(text : 'Lend one publication'))
            widget(new FixedButton(text : 'Return one publication'))
        }
    }
}
```

Although it makes our intention obvious, it is rather repetitive. Recode it using the approach illustrated in Example 06 of Chapter 20. It uses a data structure that is a List of Lists, each of which holds a button's text as a String and a closure object that acts as its event handler.

SERVER-SIDE PROGRAMMING

Java servlets are a central technology of server-side Java development. A *servlet* is a small pluggable extension to a web server that enhances the server's functionality. A servlet is used to create dynamic content for a webpage, in effect creating a *web application*. Many organizations have redeployed their business applications as web applications using servlet technology.

A servlet is a server extension provided by a Java class that can be loaded dynamically by the web server. Today, all major web servers provide support for servlets. As a consequence, servlets are portable across web servers, as well operating environments due to the universal availability of Java on all operating systems.

JavaServer Pages (JSP) is closely associated with servlets. A JSP page is a regular web page combining static markup with JSP elements that generate the parts that differ among requests. When a JSP page is requested, the static content is merged with the dynamic content produced from the JSP elements. The result is then returned to the browser. A web server that supports JSP first converts the JSP page into a servlet, in what is known as the translation phase. All static content essentially remains unchanged. All JSP elements are converted to Java code, which provides for the dynamic behavior.

In this chapter, we consider Groovlets and GSPs, Groovy's equivalents to Java servlets and JSPs. Once again, we note how Groovy simplifies servlets and JSPs.

23.1 SERVLETS

Because servlets are written in Java, they are portable across operating systems and across server implementations. Servlets can harness all the features of the

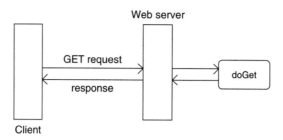

FIGURE 23.1   Servlet handling a GET request.

core Java APIs, such as networking and database connectivity. Servlets also provide an efficient implementation of web applications. Once a servlet is loaded, it remains in existence as an object instance. Further requests by the server are simple method calls to that object. Servlet code offers an elegant object-oriented implementation, supported by its API classes.

When a client connects to a web server and makes an HTTP request, it is realized as GET or POST requests. The GET is designed for getting information (a document, a database query, etc.). The POST is for posting information (a credit card number, information to be stored in a database, etc.). This is outlined in Figure 23.1.

A GET request from a client is forwarded by the web server to the servlet object. Specifically, the server object will conform to a Java interface, and redefine the behavior for the doGet method. This method operates as the handler for the GET request. A similar scheme applies to PUT requests, handled by the doPut method of the servlet object.

Writing a Java servlet then involves subclassing javax.servlet.http. HttpServlet to override the doGet and/or the doPut method (see Figure 23.1). Both methods have HttpServletRequest and HttpServletResponse parameters. As their names suggest, they represent, respectively, the client's request data and the servlet's response.

23.2   GROOVLETS

As has been indicated, developing a servlet involves some sophisticated Java programming. With Groovy, things are much simpler. The Groovlet framework provides an elegant and simplified platform for building web applications. This simplicity is achieved by the GroovyServlet class. This servlet will run Groovy scripts as Groovlets.

With a Groovlet, there is no need to subclass HttpServlet and redefine doGet or doPut. In fact, there is no need to even develop a class. The Groovlet simply delivers the response for the client. This simplicity is demonstrated in Example 01 where the code prints the HTML content for the browser to render.

```
println """
<html>
    <head>
        <title>Hello world groovlet</title>
        <link rel="stylesheet" type="text/css" href="groovy.css"/>
    </head>
    <body>
        <p class="redarial20">Hello world groovlet</p>
    </body>
</html>
"""
```

EXAMPLE 01
Hello world

◆

The effect of executing this web application is given in Figure 23.2. The Groovlet framework maps all URLs of a chosen pattern to a specific servlet according to the deployment descriptor file web.xml. The <servlet> element registers the servlet name with its class. The <servlet-mapping> entry indicates that GroovyServlet should handle all *.groovy requests. An extract of the web.xml file is:

```
<?xml version="1.0"?>

<web-app>

    <servlet>
        <servlet-name>GroovyServlet</servlet-name>
        <servlet-class>groovy.servlet.GroovyServlet</servlet-class>
    </servlet>

    <servlet-mapping>
        <servlet-name>GroovyServlet</servlet-name>
        <url-pattern>*.groovy</url-pattern>
    </servlet-mapping>

    ...

</web-app>
```

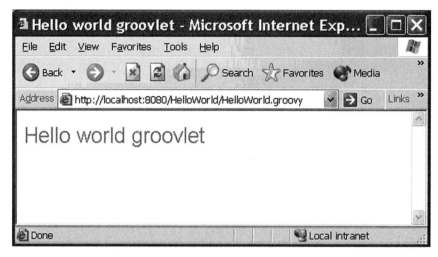

FIGURE 23.2   Hello world in a browser.

Deploying a web application to, say, the Apache Tomcat (Brittain and Darwin, 2003) servlet container typically involves compiling application code files and distributing Java archive files, HTML files, and so on. This is obviously a role served by build tools such as Ant (Holzner, 2005). Equally, we might consider using a specialized `AntBuilder` as described in Appendix K.1.

We noted earlier that the `doGet` and `doPut` methods of a Java servlet are passed request and response parameters. These and other objects available to a Java servlet are implicitly available to a Groovlet. The variables that can be used in a Groovlet are listed in Table 23.1.

Example 02 uses some of these variables to produce the output shown in Figure 23.3. Here, we prepare a table showing details about the server and values for two initialization values.

TABLE 23.1   Implicit Groovlet Variables

Variable Name	Bound To
request	ServletRequest
response	ServletResponse
context	ServletContext
application	ServletContext
session	request.getSession(true)
out	response.getWriter()
sout	response.getOutputStream()
html	new MarkupBuilder(out)

EXAMPLE 02
Implicit variables

```
println """
<html>
    <head>
        <title>Hello system groovlet</title>
        <link rel="stylesheet" type="text/css" href="groovy.css"/>
    </head>
    <body>
        <p class="redarial20">Hello system groovlet</p>

        <table border="1" class="arial10">
            <tr>
                <td>Servlet container:</td>
                <td>${application.getServerInfo()}</td>
            </tr>
            <tr>
                <td>User init parameter:</td>
                <td>${application.getInitParameter("user")}</td>
            </tr>
            <tr>
                <td>Project init parameter:</td>
                <td>${application.getInitParameter("project")}</td>
            </tr>
        </table>
    </body>
</html>
"""
```

◆

The method `getInitParameter` is used to get the value for the so-called `Init` parameters. These initial values are specified in the `web.xml` file:

```
<web-app>

    ...

    <context-param>
        <param-name>user</param-name>
        <param-value>KenB</param-value>
    </context-param>
    <context-param>
        <param-name>project</param-name>
        <param-value>Groovy</param-value>
    </context-param>

</web-app>
```

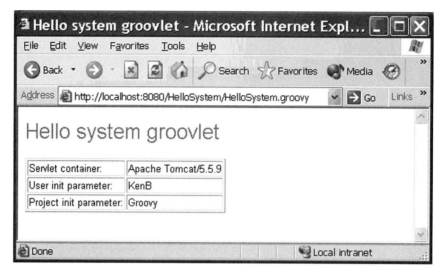

FIGURE 23.3   Information access.

Chapter 19 introduced builders for XML content. They, of course, are exactly what are required to construct the HTML content. We repeat the last illustration as Example 03. Observe how the predefined variable html is used. This is a MarkupBuilder object (see Chapter 19) with the generated HTML response sent through the out variable.

EXAMPLE 03
Using builders to compose HTML content

```
import groovy.xml.MarkupBuilder

html.html() {
    head() {
        title("Hello system groovlet")
        link(rel : "stylesheet", type : "text/css", href : "groovy.css")
    }
    body() {
        div(class : "redarial20") {
            p("Hello system groovlet")
        }

        table(border : "1", class : "arial10") {
            tr() {
                td("Servlet container:")
                td("${application.getServerInfo()}")
            }
            tr() {
                td("User init parameter:")
                td("${application.getInitParameter('user')}")
            }
```

```
            tr() {
                td("Project init parameter:")
                td("${application.getInitParameter('project')}")
            }
        }
    }
}
```

◆

The next application demonstrates handling form data. The static page
Introduction.html is a form that requests the user's first name and surname.
The action attribute points to the Groovlet Hello.groovy. The form page
appears as:

```
<html>
    <head>
        <title>Introduction</title>
        <link rel="stylesheet" type="text/css" href="groovy.css"/>
    </head>
    <body>
        <form method="get" action="Hello.groovy">

            <div class="redarial20">Please enter your name<br/></div>
            <table class="arial10">
                <tr>
                    <td>Firstname:</td>
                    <td><input type="text" name="firstname"/></td>
                </tr>
                <tr>
                    <td>Surname:</td>
                    <td><input type="text" name="surname"/></td>
                </tr>
                <tr>
                    <td><input type="submit"/></td>
                </tr>
            </table>

        </form>
    </body>
</html>
```

Example 04 lists the Groovlet.

EXAMPLE 04
Request parameters

```
import groovy.xml.MarkupBuilder

html.html() {
    head() {
        title("Hello groovlet")
        link(rel : "stylesheet", type : "text/css", href : "groovy.css")
    }
    body() {
        div(class : "redarial20") {
            p("Hello groovlet")
        }

        div(class : "arial10") {
            p("Hello, ${request.getParameter('firstname')} ${request.getParameter('surname')}")
        }

    }
}
```

◆

In the final example from this section, we show how a Groovlet can access a database (Figure 23.4). We use a markup builder to assemble a table to display the details of bank accounts. For each account, we tabulate its number and its balance. The code is given in Example 05.

EXAMPLE 05
Database access

```
import groovy.xml.MarkupBuilder
import groovy.sql.*

def DB = "jdbc:derby:C:/Books/groovy/src/Chapter23.Groovlets/Example05/accountDB"
def USER = ""
def PASSWORD = ""
def DRIVER = "org.apache.derby.jdbc.EmbeddedDriver"

        // Connect to database
def sql = Sql.newInstance(DB, USER, PASSWORD, DRIVER)
```

```
html.html() {
    head() {
        title("Account groovlet")
        link(rel : "stylesheet", type : "text/css", href : "groovy.css")
    }
    body() {
        div(class : "redarial20") {
            p("Account groovlet")
        }

        table(border : "1", class : "arial10") {
            sql.eachRow("select * from account") { acc ->
                html.tr() {
                    td("${acc.number}")
                    td("${acc.balance}")
                }
            }
        }
    }
}
```

◆

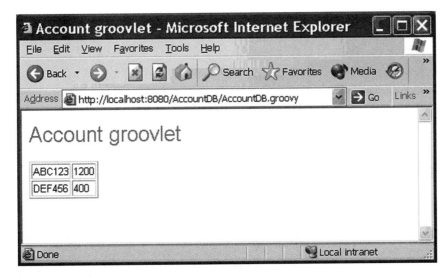

FIGURE 23.4 Database access.

23.3 GSP PAGES

JSP pages are used primarily for the presentation of content. This is, of course, a mixture of static and dynamic content. A stated purpose of JSP is to enable the separation of dynamic and static content. However, because of the functionality provided by JSP, it is more a case that JSP enables the separation rather than enforces it.

Superficially, GroovyServer Pages (GSP) look very similar to JSPs. The primary distinction is that the GSP framework is actually a template engine (see Chapter 21). A consequence is that GSPs have less functionality than their JSP counterparts and, in some sense, are better suited to the task of simply merging static and dynamic content.

GSPs are well suited to the task of presenting web content. Since the GSP framework is that of a template technology, its role is firmly focused on the view aspect of an MVC architecture. The examples later in this section will blend Groovlets and GSPs, with the former concerned with business logic and the latter responsible for viewing information content.

A GSP page is a regular web page with interwoven dynamic content. GSPs allow for the inclusion of Groovlet code into an otherwise static HTML file. Each block of code (usually called a *scriptlet*) is embedded in <% and %>. As with Groovlets, we can reference servlet objects such as session. The listing given in Example 06 is a simple GSP that displays the content Hello three times. Observe how the scriptlet manages the loop.

EXAMPLE 06
A simple GSP

```
<html>
    <head>
        <title>Hello GSP</title>
        <link rel="stylesheet" type="text/css" href="groovy.css"/>
    </head>
    <body>
        <p class="redarial20">Hello GSP</p>

        <p class="arial10">
            <% 3.times() { %>
                Hello
            <% } %>
        </p>
    </body>
</html>
```

◆

When loaded into the browser, we have Figure 23.5.

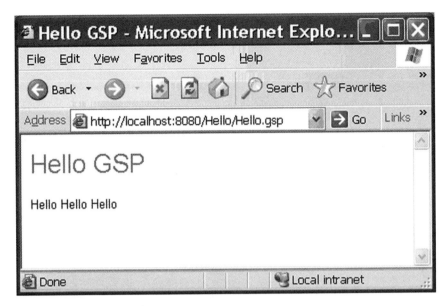

FIGURE 23.5 A simple GSP.

Next, we revisit Example 4. An HTML form accepts the user's first name and surname, then output the values on a separate page. Here, we do this by setting the action element of the form to refer to the Groovlet:

```
def dispatcher = request.getRequestDispatcher("Hello.gsp")
dispatcher.forward(request, response)
```

The Groovlet simply forwards the request to the GSP that will perform the presentation. The request parameters are carried from the Groovlet to the GSP, where they can be obtained as shown in Example 07.

EXAMPLE 07
Request parameters in a GSP

```
<html>
    <head>
        <title>Hello GSP</title>
        <link rel="stylesheet" type="text/css" href="groovy.css"/>
    </head>
    <body>
        <p class="redarial20">Hello GSP</p>

        <p class="arial10">
            Hello <% print "${request.getParameter('firstname')}";
                    print "${request.getParameter('surname')}" %>
```

```
        </p>
      </body>
    </html>
```

◆

The result is given in Figure 23.6.

FIGURE 23.6 Request parameters.

The final example illustrates how a Groovlet might be tasked with any application processing and GSPs would simply have responsibility for presentation. Once again, we use our bank account database. The Groovlet is responsible for the code to open and access the account table. In the code, the accounts data set is bound to the request object using the method setAttribute. This effectively is a binding between a name and the accounts object.

```
import groovy.xml.MarkupBuilder
import groovy.sql.*

      // Forwards to specified page
def forward(page, req, res) {
    def dispatcher = req.getRequestDispatcher(page)
    dispatcher.forward(req, res)
}
```

```
def DB = "jdbc:derby:C:/Books/groovy/src/Chapter23.Groovlets/Example08/accountDB"
def USER = ""
def PASSWORD = ""
def DRIVER = "org.apache.derby.jdbc.EmbeddedDriver"

        // Connect to database
def sql = Sql.newInstance(DB, USER, PASSWORD, DRIVER)
def accounts = sql.dataSet("account")

request.setAttribute("accounts", accounts)

forward("AccountDB.gsp", request, response)
```

The Groovlet then forwards to the GSP, which accesses the same accounts object
and employs an iterator and closure to present each account number and balance
in a table. Note the use of an expression enclosed by <%= and %>. The expression
enclosed by these tags is evaluated and the result is included in the page.

EXAMPLE 08
GSP to display a
database table

```
<html>
    <head>
        <title>Account GSP</title>
        <link rel="stylesheet" type="text/css" href="groovy.css"/>
    </head>
    <body>
        <p class="redarial20">Account GSP</p>

        <table border="1" class="arial10">
            <% def accounts = request.getAttribute('accounts')
                accounts.each { acc -> %>
                <tr>
                    <td> <%= acc.number %> </td>
                    <td> <%= acc.balance %> </td>
                </tr>
            <% } %>
        </table>
    </body>
</html>
```

◆

Figure 23.7 is the screenshot when the GSP is displayed.

FIGURE 23.7 Database view.

23.4 EXERCISES

1. Repeat Example 02 using the MarkupBuilder class shown in Example 03.

2. Repeat Example 07 using only Groovlets, as shown in Example 01.

3. Extend Example 04 and validate that the inputs for the user's first and last name are non-null. If so, return to the input form and additionally report a suitable error message.

4. Prepare a simple GSP that welcomes the user with the message "Good Morning," "Good Afternoon," or "Good Evening," as appropriate.

CASE STUDY: A LIBRARY APPLICATION (WEB)

This is our final consideration of the library case study. Here, we replace the graphical user interface (GUI) developed in Chapter 22 with a web browser interface, transforming the system into a web application. From the preceding chapter, we use a combination of Groovlets and GSPs.

As described in previous versions of this case study, we sought to separate our logic using an MVC architecture. Adopting this framework in Chapter 13, we were able to separate the business logic of our domain model classes from the text-based user interface classes. Maintaining this architecture into Chapter 22 meant that it was a relatively simple task to replace the text-based user interface classes with Swing classes, giving the application a GUI.

Once again, our investment in establishing an MVC architecture demonstrates the ease with which we can substitute a new user interface. GSPs are well suited to the task of presenting web content. Since the GSP framework is a template technology, its role is firmly focused on the view aspect of an MVC architecture. In turn, Groovlets provide the controller logic we require in the application, such as adding a new publication or lending a publication to a borrower. Finally, we continue with an unchanged domain model, using data access objects to interact with the database.

24.1 ITERATION I: WEB IMPLEMENTATION

The graphical interface for this application will mirror that developed in Chapter 20. Visually, it appears as shown in Figure 24.1. It comprises a vertical strip of buttons with an explanatory label to the left of each button.

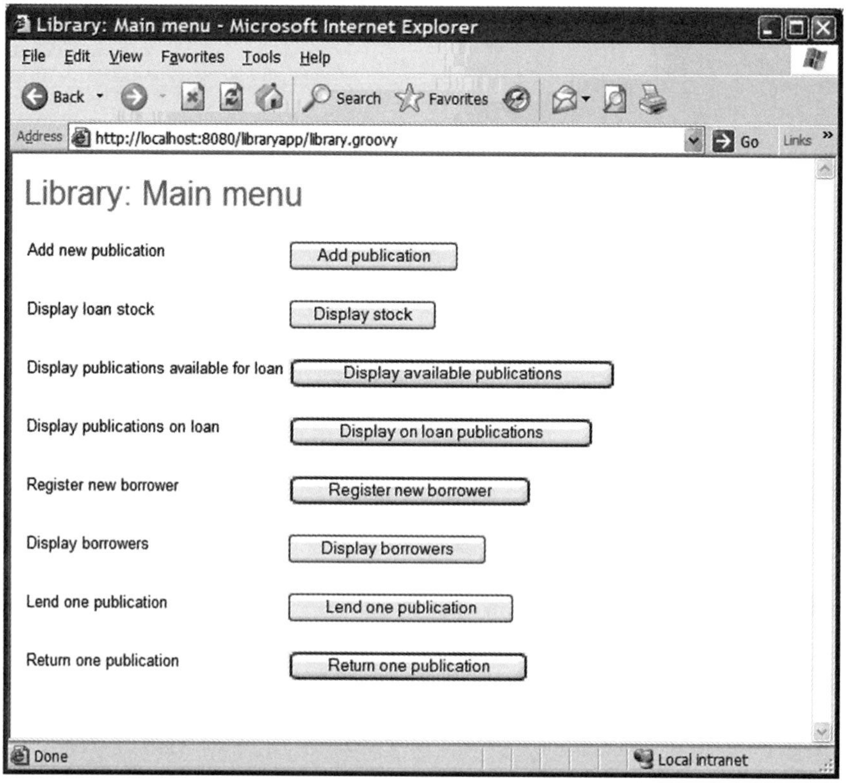

FIGURE 24.1   Visual interface.

As was demonstrated in Example 08 of Chapter 23, a Groovlet is used to start the application. Once again, we use the Spring framework to configure the application beans. We then bind the Library object referenced by the lib variable to the name 'lib' so that we can refer to that object elsewhere in the application. The code for this is in library.groovy:

```
import java.io.*
import org.springframework.context.support.*

def applicationContext = new FileSystemXmlApplicationContext(context.getRealPath('/') + 'config.xml')
def lib = applicationContext.getBean('lib')

application.setAttribute('lib', lib)

Utility.forward('mainmenu.gsp', request, response)
```

The forward method introduced in Example 08 of Chapter 23 has been made a static method of the Utility class since we use it throughout the application.

The GSP `mainmenu.gsp` renders the menu we see in Figure 24.1. It is assembled using an HTML table with two columns. The left column is an explanatory note for the use case. The right column is a button to select that service. A segment of the code for this is:

```
<html>
  <head>
    <title>Library: Main menu</title>
    <link rel="stylesheet" type="text/css" href="groovy.css"/>
  </head>

  <body>
    <p class="redarial20">Library: Main menu</p>

    <table>

      <tr>
        <td class="arial10" valign="top">Add new publication</td>
        <td>
          <form action="addpublication.gsp">
            <input type="submit" value="Add publication"/>
          </form>
        </td>
      </tr>

      <tr>
        <td class="arial10" valign="top">Display loan stock</td>
        <td>
          <form action="displaystock.gsp">
            <input type="submit" value="Display stock"/>
          </form>
        </td>
      </tr>

// ...

    </table>
  </body>
</html>
```

To display the complete loan stock belonging to the library, the action for the use-case button invokes the GSP `displaystock.gsp`. It produces an output similar to that in Figure 24.2. The GSP references the `Library` object set in the startup Groovlet, and then iterates over each `Publication` in the `loanStock` using the each iterator. The associated closure assembles the table rows, selectively printing a `Book` or `Journal`.

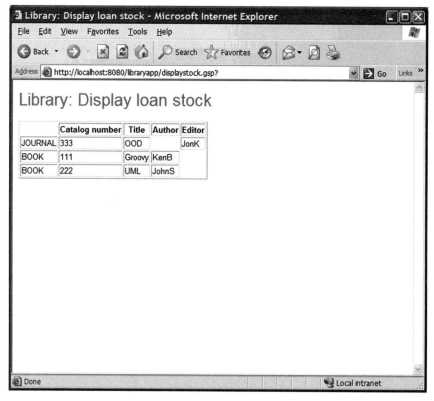

FIGURE 24.2   Loan stock display.

Many of the other use-cases for this project are provided by a GSP and its matching Groovlet. For example, when a publication is to be returned, the publication's catalog number is required, and we get this from the GSP:

```
<html>
  <head>
    <title>Library: Return one publication</title>
    <link rel="stylesheet" type="text/css" href="groovy.css"/>
  </head>

  <body>
    <p class="redarial20">Library: Return one publication</p>

    <form action="returnpublication.groovy">
      <table>
        <tr>
          <td class="arial10">Catalog number: </td>
```

```
          <td><input type="text" name="catalognumber"/></td>
        </tr>
      </table>
      <input type="submit" value="Submit"/>
    </form>
  </body>
</html>
```

The catalog number entered by the user is then transferred as a request parameter to the Groovlet that implements the service:

```
def lib = application.getAttribute('lib')

def catalogNumber request.getParameter('catalognumber')
lib.returnPublication(catalogNumber)

Utility.forward('mainmenu.gsp', request, response)
```

24.2   EXERCISE

1. Consider the main menu provided by `mainmenu.gsp`. Each application use case is presented in a table row, with the left column having the use-case descriptor and the right column being a button to activate the service. Consider revising this implementation and using a `MarkupBuilder` to assemble the HTML.

EPILOGUE

This chapter signals the end of our journey into programming with Groovy. We believe that it also marks the period in which Groovy will make major contributions to the Java platform. We expect to see growth in the usage of Groovy, which mirrors that of Java when it was first announced. Groovy's role will be as a flexible, agile scripting language that complements Java.

It is recognized that Groovy represents an immature technology. However, this is only partly true. It is accepted that the current reference implementation (JSR 06) has a number of imperfections to correct. Notwithstanding, it is a robust implementation that will be at the core of official releases. Full support for Groovy is under development from IDE builders (see `http://groovy.code-haus.org/Eclipse+Plugin,http://groovy.codehaus.org/IntelliJ+IDEA+Plugin`).

The relative immaturity of Groovy is offset by reminding ourselves that Groovy derives most of its capabilities from the extensive collection of Java APIs. In much the same way as Java represents a relatively small and simple programming language that is then enriched with APIs, so is Groovy. Groovy goes one step further by offering an agile environment that can fully exploit this reservoir of code. Groovy and Java are partners, with Java as the systems programming language for developing these frameworks and infrastructures, and Groovy for gluing them into applications.

As the Groovy momentum grows, we will undoubtedly see greater integration with existing products as well as new products developed for Groovy. We used parts of the Spring framework throughout this text. We expect Groovy to find a place in several areas of Spring, such as unit testing, bean definition, and perhaps even a view in SpringMVC, exploiting Groovy's support for templates. A separate development, entitled Grails (see `http://grails.codehaus.org/`), aims to repeat the success of Ruby on Rails (see `http://www.rubyonrails.org/`) on the Ruby platform. Rails is an open-source Ruby framework for developing database-backed web applications.

Web services (Erl, 2004; Topley, 2003) is a related area in which Groovy might also contribute. In addition to simplifying access to services, Groovy could make a contribution to the related Business Process Execution Language for web services, BPEL (see `http://www-128.ibm.com/developerworks/webservices/library/ws-bpelwp/`). BPEL makes extensive use of XML in which Groovy has strong support. Further, as observed elsewhere (see `http://www.martinfowler.com/articles/languageWorkbench.html`), Groovy's builders might be the basis of a domain-specific language (DSL) for BPEL.

Groovy also offers new educational opportunities. Computing and software engineering students should find Groovy attractive since it makes it easy to get started writing Javalike software without having to address complex issues too soon. Although such students will almost inevitably migrate to Java, they should also find Groovy's "gluing" abilities useful in more ambitious applications later in their careers.

Groovy can also assist specialist academic studies that involve software development. Groovy's light touch allows the specialty to shine through and not be obscured by detailed Java programming.

Let's get Groovy.

SOFTWARE DISTRIBUTION

The materials presented in this textbook are supplied under various open-source licenses. The binary and source code are freely available and, as a consequence, evolve rapidly by the input of the programming community. The materials are of extremely high quality and are free to users.

The examples used in this book were developed on the MS Windows platform. The descriptions given here, therefore, pertain to that environment. Most of the discussion is, however, generally applicable and can be readily adapted for other platforms.

The following sections are necessarily brief and may be subject to change. However, readers should consult the website for the book and the website for the tool for more details and updates.

A.1 THE JAVA DEVELOPMENT KIT

The Java Development Kit (JDK) is available from the website at http://java.sun.com/j2se/1.5.0/download.jsp. It is downloaded as a self-extracting compressed file, and available for a variety of platforms. From the same website, a ZIP file containing the documentation can also be obtained. Under MS Windows, double-click the executable (say, jdk-1_5_04-windows-i586-p.exe) to start the unpacking procedure. The default is to locate the JDK in the folder C:\Program Files\. A space in a folder name is often the source of many subtle bugs, and it is recommended that one nominate the directory (say, C:\jdk-1_5_04) as the destination.

Unpack the ZIP documentation file into the same location so that the JDK is all in one directory.

A.2   THE GROOVY DEVELOPMENT KIT

The Groovy Development Kit (GDK) is available from the website (see http://groovy.codehaus.org/). It is downloaded as a ZIP file and is a complete package, including the tools and the documentation. Unpack this into a suitable location; once again, observe the caution of folders with embedded spaces in their names. The distribution includes a number of subfolders such as bin (for executables, batch files, and so on) and the lib folder containing the Groovy JAR files.

A.3   ANT

Apache Ant is a Java-based build tool. It is available at http://ant.apache.org/bindownload.cgi. It is downloaded as a ZIP file and is a complete package, including the tools and the documentation. Unpack this into a suitable location; once again, observe the caution of folders with embedded spaces in their names. The distribution includes a number of subfolders such as bin (for executables, batch files, and so on) and the lib folder containing the JAR files.

The docs folder of the distribution includes an index.html welcome page. From here, follow the manual link to extensive documentation for installing, using, and running Ant as well as documentation on the various Ant tasks.

A.4   THE DERBY/CLOUDSCAPE DATABASE

The Cloudscape database was originally developed at IBM. It has been donated to the open source community under the new name Derby. It is available from the website at http://db.apache.org/derby/. Unpack this into a suitable location. The distribution includes the lib folder containing its supporting JAR files.

The doc/pdf folder includes a number of documentation files. The "getting started" document is invaluable for those new to DBMS tools. The developer's guide discusses installing and deploying Cloudscape, while the reference and tools documents address such matters as SQL and Cloudscape tools such as ij, the interactive JDBC scripting tool.

A.5   THE SPRING FRAMEWORK

The Spring framework is available form the website (see `http://www.`
`springframework.org/`). It is supplied as a complete ZIP file, including supporting documentation. Unpack this into a suitable location. The distribution
includes the `dist` folder, which contains its supporting JAR files.

The `docs/reference` folder has an enormously informative book on Spring
delivered as a PDF file. The `docs/api` folder is a reference for the classes provided by Spring.

A.6   THE TOMCAT SERVER

The Tomcat server is available from the website at `http://tomcat.apache.org/`.
It is distributed in a number of common formats. Download a binary edition
and unpack this into a suitable location. The distribution includes the `bin` folder
for executables, batch files, and so on. The supplied documentation (in `webs\`
`tomcat-docs`) refers to the batch files `bin\startup.bat` and `bin\shutdown.bat`
for starting and stopping Tomcat. The folder `webapps` is the folder in which we
deploy web applications. A subfolder off the latter, `tomcat-docs`, includes a
Tomcat user guide covering introduction, setup, and deployment.

A.7   ECLIPSE IDE

The Eclipse IDE is an open-source integrated development environment (see
`http://www.eclipse.org/`). Its unique plug-in–based architecture makes it easy
to create, integrate, and utilize software tools. It has rapidly developed and now
has an extensive collection of tools. The class diagrams used in this book were
developed using the Omondo UML tool (see `http://www.eclipse-`
`plugins.info/eclipse/plugins.jsp`; follow the categories and UML links).
A Groovy plug-in is currently a work in progress (see `http://groovy.code`
`haus.org/Eclipse+Plugin`).

A.8   THE TEXTBOOK SOURCES

The examples and exercises are available at the book website. The examples are
located in the `src` folder and the exercises in the `solutions` folder. In both, the
code files are in subdirectories, with names reflecting the chapters and appendices to which they belong. Hence, the subdirectory `AppendixI.Classes` in the
`src` folder contains the `*.groovy` example files for Appendix I. The subdirectory

Chapter12.Classes in the solutions folder contains the *.groovy exercises for Chapter 12. The structure of the src folder, for example, is illustrated as:

```
src
      AppendixB.Groovy
      AppendixD.Strings
      ...
      Chapter07.Methods
            example01.groovy
            example02.groovy
            ...
      Chapter08.Control.Flow
      ...
      guide
      lib
      utils
      setgroovy.bat
```

In all cases, files that represent a class declaration follow the usual Java naming convention. Hence, the file containing the Account class is found in the Account.groovy file. Those files that represent scripts are given names such as example01.groovy or exercise02.groovy.

Within the src folder, the utils subdirectory includes the source code for the classes Console (Chapter 5 and Appendix F), Build (Appendix K), and Functor (Appendix J). An Ant build file compiles this code, and then creates and deploys the file utils.jar into the src\lib subdirectory. The guide subdirectory has all the source files for the GUIDE tool. Again, an Ant build file is provided to compile and archive the code.

The src folder also includes the file setgroovy.bat. This MS Windows batch file sets the environment for using Groovy on this platform. It will, of course, need to be edited to reflect the local settings of the reader. Used as a template, a similar configuration file can be prepared for other platforms.

As new features are regularly added to the website, the reader is advised to consult it for any up-to-date information.

GROOVY

The syntax of Groovy is based on the Java programming language syntax. This makes for a relatively short learning curve for Java developers. Groovy makes writing scripts and applications for the Java platform fast and easy. It includes language features found in Python, Ruby, and Smalltalk, but uses syntax more natural to Java developers. Because Groovy is based on Java, applications written in Groovy can use the full complement of Java APIs, and Groovy works seamlessly with other components and applications written in the Java programming language.

In this appendix, we seek to demonstrate how Groovy implements a variety of its features using Java. We hope to show how the authors of Groovy use simple and elegant designs that are pure Java. Hence, as pure Java, they are also able to fully exploit the Java APIs.

B.1 SIMPLE AND ELEGANT

The authors of Groovy sought to develop a language that was sympathetic with Java. The aim was to introduce a language that would offer no surprises to the Java developer. So, for example, Groovy has classes that can be presented as normal Java code. Syntactically, a Groovy class can appear as if it were a Java class. It is compiled into standard Java byte code that conforms to the Java Virtual Machine Specification (JVM). To the JVM, there is no difference between a class file compiled from the Groovy language and one compiled from the Java programming language.

Tradition has it that the first program should be the "hello, world" program (Kernighan and Ritchie, 1988). The program simply prints the text hello, world on to the standard output. In Groovy, this would appear as:

```
println 'hello, world'
```

A Java programmer might expect to see a class with a method called main. The main method would involve some statement to produce the required output. Somewhat surprisingly, at the bytecode level, this Groovy code is pure Java! If we were to compile the code using the Groovy compiler into a .class file, then disassemble the bytecode represented by that .class file, we would discover the Java code that would be expected.

If this Groovy code is placed in the Groovy source file Hello.groovy, then when we explore the bytecode produced by the Groovy compiler, we have the following (much simplified and incomplete) equivalent:

```
public class Hello ... {

    public static void main(String[] args) {
        Hello h = new Hello();
        h.run(args);
    }

    public void run(String[] args) {
        this.println('hello, world');
    }

}
```

This time, we do have a class that is named Hello. The class includes the expected startup method, main. In main, an object of the class Hello is created and invokes its run method. The run method is defined by this class and invokes the println method on itself, passing the string we wish displayed. Of course, println is not defined in the class Hello. It is inherited from the class Object that Hello indirectly extends.

This explanation leads us to infer that the Java class Object defines the method println, but this is not the case. Further, there is no Groovy variant of the class that extends Object and includes the println method. In fact, the Groovy interpreter intercepts this method call and implements it itself, giving the impression that println is indeed a method of class Object.

Groovy describes these apparently augmented classes as part of the Groovy Development Kit (GDK). The classes are documented (see http://groovy. codehaus.org/groovy-jdk.html) as if the Java classes in the JDK (Java

Development Kit) do indeed include additional methods. One needs, therefore, to be alert to the role of the Groovy interpreter in these matters. Significantly, the JDK is not changed.

B.2 METHODS

All methods ultimately belong to a class. This is also true for those defined (at the top level) in a Groovy script (see Chapter 7 and Appendix G). As has been demonstrated, the script code is enclosed in a class. A top-level method is then a method of that class. Hence, the Groovy script (from the file Demo.groovy):

```
def times(x, y) {
    return x * y
}

def p = times(3, 4)
println p
```

is incorporated into a class in a manner equivalent to:

```
public class Demo ... {

    public static void main(String[] args) {
        Demo h = new Demo();
        h.run(args);
    }

    public void run(String[] args) {
        Object p = this.times(new Integer(3), new Integer(4));
        this.println(p);
    }

    public Object times(Object x, Object y) {
        return x.multiply(y);
    }
}
```

First, note the signature of method times. Since most of our Groovy code employs dynamic typing, then the parameter types and the return type are Object. The method itself is implemented by invoking the multiply method on the object referenced by x and passing y as the method parameter. Of course, multiply is the method implementation for the * operator (see Chapter 2, Appendix C, and Appendix G).

In the run method, the variable p is assigned the value returned from the call of method times. The actual parameters are Integers initialized with the integer literals. Note how p is a local variable of method run.

B.3   LISTS

Groovy provides native syntax support for Lists and Maps (see Chapter 4 and Appendix E). For example, a List of three integer values is:

```
def numbers = [11, 12, 13]
```

As has been shown, Groovy has a [] shorthand for constructing Lists directly. We see that this is implemented with a createList method. It is given all the Objects we pass to it, and returns a new ArrayList (see JDK) containing them.

```
public class Demo ... {

    public static void main(String[] args) {
        Demo d = new Demo();
        d.run(args);
    }

    public Object run(String[] args) {
        Object numbers = createList(new Object[] {new Integer(11), new Integer(12), new Integer(13)});
        return numbers;
    }
}
```

B.4   CLASSES

A Groovy class (see Chapter 12 and Appendix I) significantly simplifies its Java equivalent. The use of the def keyword seeks to unify the notion of an attribute (instance field) and a method. In Groovy, a property is equivalent to the instance field and its getter/setter methods.

```
class Account {

// -----properties --------------------

    def number
    def balance
}
```

The Java version for this class might appear as:

```
public class Account ... {
    public Account() { ... }

    public Object getNumber() { return number; }
    public void setNumber(number) { this.number = number; }

    public Object getBalance () { return balance; }
    public void setBalance(Object balance) { this. balance = balance; }

// ------properties ----------------
    Object number;
    Object balance;
}
```

The inclusion of the default constructor and the setter methods for each property also supports Groovy's use of named parameters when creating an object. For example:

```
def acc = new Account(number : 'ABC123', balance : 1200)
```

is simply a contraction for:

```
Account acc = new Account();
acc.setNumber('ABC123');
acc.setBalance(new Integer(1200));
```

B.5   POLYMORPHISM

Although Groovy includes support for interfaces (see Chapter 14), it does not really require them because of its dynamic typing. An interface is used to specify a protocol that other classes implement. With an object of a class that implements the interface, we can then call whatever methods exist on that interface.

In Groovy, polymorphism is simply a matter of matching method names. Two objects belonging to two unrelated classes can be sent the same message, provided that the method is defined by each class. The following example illustrates:

```
class Account {

    def display() {
        println "Account: ${number} ${balance}"
    }

    def number
    def balance
}

class Student {

    def display() {
        println "Student: ${registrationNumber} ${name}"
    }

    def registrationNumber
    def name
}

def group = [new Account(number : 'ABC123', balance : 1200),
                    new Student(registrationNumber : '2006.1234', name : 'Ken Barclay')
            ]

group.each { item -> item.display() }
```

The two classes Account and Student do not share a common superclass or implement the same interface. When we iterate over the collection, we can call the display method on every object referenced in the group.

B.6 CLOSURES

A Groovy closure (see Chapter 9 and Appendix H) is implemented using an inner class (Eckel, 2003). Consider the following script in which the product of two values is defined by a parameterized closure named times. The closure gets called, and the result assigned to the variable z.

```
def times = { x, y ->
    return x * y
}

def z = times(3, 4)
```

The run method includes the definition of a local inner class, here arbitrarily named as TimesClosure, that extends the Groovy class Closure. Local classes can use the properties and methods of the enclosing class. Further, code in a local inner class can use local variables and parameters in the method that defines the class. This is how the scoping rules that apply to closures are derived. An instance of this class is then created and the closure invoked, passing the two integer literals as instances of the class Integer.

```
public class Demo ... {

    public static void main(String[] args) {
        Demo d = new Demo();
        d.run(args);
    }

    public Object run(String[] args) {
        class TimesClosure extends Closure { ... }
        TimesClosure clos = new TimesClosure(this);
        Object z = invokeClosure(clos, new Object[] {new Integer(3), new Integer(4)});
        return z;
    }
}
```

The inner class is defined in a manner somewhat like the following listing. When a closure is called, then its call method is invoked. Here, the body for this method is the body for the closure definition, invoking method multiply.

```
class TimesClosure ... {

    public TimesClosure(Object obj) {
        super(obj);
        owner = Demo.this;
    }

    public Object call(Object obj1, Object obj2) {
        return invokeMethod(this, "multiply", new Object[] {obj1, obj2})
    }
}
```

B.7 EXCEPTIONS

The Java programming language uses exceptions to provide error-handling capabilities for its programs. An exception is an event that occurs during the execution of a program that disrupts the normal flow of execution. The Java runtime system requires that a method either catch or specify all checked exceptions that can be thrown by that method. A method can catch an exception by providing an exception handler for that type of exception or specify that it can throw exceptions by using the throws clause in the method declaration.

Classes that extend the JDK Exception class are known as *checked exceptions*. The Java compiler checks to see whether two things occur in a program using these classes:

- Every method that throws a checked exception must advertise it in the throws clause in its method definition.

- Every method that calls a method that advertises a checked exception must either handle that exception (with try and catch) or must, in turn, advertise that exception in its own throws clause.

There are other errors that can occur, such as when memory is exhausted, that are outside programmer control. They prevent the Java virtual machine from fulfilling its specification. Since it is not possible to plan for such errors, it would be necessary to catch them everywhere. This defeats the principle of maintaining uncluttered code. Therefore, these errors are *unchecked exceptions*, meaning exceptions that you don't have to include in a throws clause.

Since Groovy does not distinguish between checked and unchecked exceptions, then the throws clause in method heads is not supported. As a consequence, the Groovy compiler does not enforce the rules described previously. By default, Groovy assumes that all exceptions are unchecked, unless the programmer chooses to indicate otherwise.

C

MORE ON NUMBERS AND EXPRESSIONS

The Groovy interpreter plays an important role in the evaluation of an expression. For example, in Chapter 2, we discussed operators in the context of the evaluation expressions such as 123 + 456. The assumption made was that it was possible to send the message plus to an Integer object. This is not strictly true because there is no class in the Groovy environment with that method. The Groovy interpreter recognizes that two integers are being added and arranges matters so that it appears that the method call 123.plus(456) is executed. The attraction of this approach is that the core Java classes such as Integer, on which Groovy is built, are unchanged, yet they give us a more Groovy-like functionality.

C.1 CLASSES

Recall from our earlier discussions that everything in Groovy is an object. It is not surprising, therefore, that an integer value is an instance of the class Integer and a floating-point value is an instance of the class BigDecimal. In effect, a Groovy definition such as:

```
def age = 25
```

is equivalent to:

```
Integer age = new Integer(25)
```

in which the variable age refers to an instance of an Integer object.

Chapter 2 also introduced the relational and equality operators. These produce a `boolean` value of `false` or `true`. In, for example:

```
def age1 = 25
def age2 = 35
def isYounger = age1 < age2
```

the variable `isYounger` refers to an instance of the class `Boolean` with the value `true`.

C.2   EXPRESSIONS

We have stressed that the arithmetic expression 123 + 456 is actually implemented by Groovy as the `plus` method call as if it were `123.plus(456)`. Either is then a valid expression in Groovy. Following what we stated in the preceding section, it means we may also express this as `new Integer(123).plus(new Integer(456))`. Although legal in Groovy, this is probably not a wise decision, but it does illustrate the equivalence of these constructs.

It is perhaps worth noting that we can chain together multiple assignments. The following is perfectly valid Groovy:

```
def p = 10
def q = 20
p = q = 30        // p is 30, q is 30
```

C.3   OPERATOR ASSOCIATIVITY

An expression involving operators of equal precedence is resolved by the *associativity* of the operators. This defines the direction in which operators possessing the same precedences are executed. For example, the expression:

```
2 + 3 * 4 + 5
```

is evaluated in the following manner. Multiplication has the highest precedence of the three operators and is evaluated first. The expression now reduces to 2 + 12 + 5 with the two addition operators having equal precedence. The associativity is left to right, and so the 2 and 12 are first added to give 14 before finally the 14 and 5 are summed to produce 19 as the final result.

If, in the expression 2 + 3 * 4 + 5, it is required to perform both the additions before executing the multiplication, then this is indicated by employing parentheses (and) around the subexpressions. The expression would then be presented as (2 + 3) * (4 + 5), and it evaluates to 5 * 9 or 45.

The full table of operator precedence and associativity is given in Table C.1.

TABLE C.1   Operator Precedence and Associativity

Category	Operators	Example	Associativity
Array subscript	[ ]	a[2]	Left to right
Member access	.	a.b()	
Postfix operators	expr++ expr--	x++	Right to left
Unary operators	++expr --expr + - ≈ !	-x	Right to left
Multiplicative	* / %	x * y	Left to right
Additive	+ -	x + y	Left to right
Shift	<< >> >>>	x << y	Left to right
Relational	< <= > >= instanceof	x <= y	Left to right
Equality	== != <=>	x != y	Left to right
Bitwise and	&	x & y	Left to right
Bitwise exclusive or	^	x ^ y	Left to right
Bitwise inclusive or	|	x | y	Left to right
Logical and	&&	x && y	Left to right
Logical or	||	x || y	Left to right
Conditional	:?	a < b ? x : y	Left to right
Assignment	= += -= *= /= %= &=	x += y	Right to left
	^= |= <<= >>= >>>=		

C.4   VARIABLE DEFINITIONS

A variable definition introduces a variable and optionally initializes it with a given value. It also determines the *scope* or extent over which the variable can be referenced. This is defined as the block of code in which the definition occurs. The following are valid definitions:

```
def a = 10
def b = 20, c = 30
```

Observe how the second example defines and initializes two variables.

It is also possible to define a variable without initializing it. In that case, since the variable will be a reference to an object, it is implicitly initialized to null. The following all have the same effect:

```
def d = null          // explicitly null
def e, f              // both implicitly null
```

It is illegal in Groovy to define a variable twice in the same code block. Thus, the following would elicit an error reporting that the variable p has already been defined:

```
def p = 20
def p = 30            // error: p already defined
```

Equally, if a variable has not been defined and then is used in an expression, an error reports that no variable is defined:

```
def pp = qq           // error: qq not defined
```

Section 2.4 specified the rule for creating valid identifiers in Groovy. Identifiers must not conflict with the Groovy keywords that are reserved for use by the language. The list of Groovy keywords is given in Table C.2.

TABLE C.2   Groovy Keywords

abstract	any	as	assert	boolean
break	byte	case	catch	char
class	continue	def	default	do
double	else	enum	extends	false
final	finally	float	for	if
implements	import	in	instanceof	int
interface	long	native	new	null
package	private	protected	public	return
short	static	strictfp	super	switch
synchronized	this	threadsafe	throw	throws
transient	true	try	void	volatile
while	with			

C.5 COMPOUND ASSIGNMENT OPERATORS

Groovy supports *compound assignment operators* for abbreviating some assignment expressions. Any statement of the form:

```
variable = variable operator expression
```

can be written as:

```
variable operator = expression
```

provided that operator is one of the binary operators shown in Table C.1. Some examples are:

```
balance += 15        // balance = balance + 15
balance -= 15        // balance = balance - 15
interest *= 1.5      // interest = interest * 1.5
interest /= 2.5      // interest = interest / 2.5
value %= 4           // value = value % 4
```

In these examples, since the variable is being updated, it should have been previously defined and initialized.

C.6 LOGICAL OPERATORS

The *logical* operators are given in Table C.3. The logical *and* operator (represented as &&) and the logical *or* operator (||) are binary operators. They are applied to a pair of Boolean values and produce a Boolean result. The logical negation operator (!) is a unary operator, applied to a single Boolean value that delivers a Boolean result.

TABLE C.3 Logical Operators

Operator	Description	Associativity
&&	Logical and	Left to right
||	Logical or	Left to right
!	(Unary) logical negation	Right to left

The effect of applying these operators is shown in Table C.4.

TABLE C.4   Evaluation of Logical Expressions

P	Q	$P\&\&Q$	$P||Q$	S	$!S$
false	false	false	false	false	true
False	true	false	true	true	false
True	false	false	true		
True	true	true	true		

There is one subtlety about the logical *and* operator and the logical *or* operator that is worthy of note. In the evaluation of the subexpressions that are the operands of the && and || operators, the evaluation stops as soon as the outcome is determinable. Suppose expr1 and expr2 are the subexpression operands. Then, in:

```
expr1 && expr2
```

expr2 will not be evaluated if expr1 is determined to be false. Consider the following:

```
def a = 10
def b = 20
def c = 30
def d = (b < a) && (c = 40)
```

Since the subexpression b < a is false, then variable c is not assigned the new value 40.

Equally, if expr1 is true, then in:

```
expr1 || expr2
```

expr2 will not be evaluated since the value of the logical expression is already known to be true.

C.7   CONDITIONAL OPERATOR

The *conditional operator* (also called the *ternary operator*) produces a value and is of the form:

```
expr ? expr#1 : expr#2
```

If the expr evaluates to the Boolean value true, then the value of expr#1 is the result produced. If expr evaluates to false, the value of expr#2 is the result. Commonly, this operator is used to produce a value for assignment or a return value. Examples of the conditional operator are:

```
def positive = x < 0 ? -x : x

def min(x, y) {
    return x < y ? x : y
}
```

C.8   QUALIFIED NUMERIC LITERALS

So far, we have used the default decimal notation to represent integer literals. However, we can qualify an integer literal as an octal or hexadecimal representation by prefixing it with 0 or 0x, respectively. For example, we might have 0xAB and 0177 to represent decimal 171 and 127, respectively. Additionally, we can append an integral suffix (I, L, or G) to an integer literal. The integer is then an instance of the class Integer, Long, or BigInteger, respectively. Each is capable of representing an increasing range of values. Where no suffix is given, the literal is an instance of the class into which the value will fit.

Floating-point literals are, by default, instances of the class BigDecimal. Normally, we use the decimal notation but we may also use scientific notation. In this case, the floating literal is appended with a letter E (or letter e) followed by an optionally signed integer. This suffix represents some power of ten that is applied to the value. For example, we might have 123E2 and 1.23e-2 to represent 12300.0 and 0.0123, respectively. As with integer literals, the suffixes F, D, or G can be applied to floating point literals to qualify them as instances of the class Float, Double, or BigDecimal, respectively.

Here are some valid examples:

```
123L        // Long
456G        // BigInteger
1.23F       // Float
4.56D       // Double
7.89G       // BigDecimal
```

C.9   CONVERSIONS

When a Groovy variable is introduced, it must be defined with the keyword def. We can also use an explicit *primitive type* that introduces a *statically typed*

variable (see Section 10). In the following code fragment, the variable temperature is statically typed as a Double, while the age variable is untyped but its value
is determined at runtime to be an Integer.

```
double temperature = 32.0
def age = 25
```

Notice that temperature is actually a Double. We will discuss this shortly. Other
primitive types used in this book are int and boolean. For example, we might
have:

```
int age = 25
```

and

```
boolean result = age > 21
```

Now, age is statically typed to be an Integer and result statically typed to be a
Boolean.

Recall from our earlier discussions that everything in Groovy is an object
and so it is not surprising that each of the types int, double, and boolean ultimately become Java classes Integer, Double, and Boolean. Therefore, temperature becomes an instance of the class Double, age an instance of the class
Integer, and result an instance of the class Boolean. In effect, a Groovy declaration such as:

```
int age = 25
```

is equivalent to:

```
Integer age = new Integer(25)
```

However, expression evaluation with Groovy is more complex than just
making these changes. Recall that an integer accurately stores the value, but the
range of values available is limited. This applies to the int primitive as well as
its wrapper Integer class. It is also true that a floating-point value represented
in a binary form is not (usually) held accurately, although the range of values
available is greatly extended. This applies to the float and double primitives as
well as to their wrapper classes Float and Double.

An alternative is to use some other representation that allows numbers to be
held with arbitrary precision and range. The Java API provides the classes
BigInteger and BigDecimal for this purpose. Although we are not concerned

with the details of such representations, we should be aware that they are normally inefficient when compared to their binary equivalents. Therefore, calculations with them take longer and require more computer memory.

Of course, Groovy provides access to all Java math classes and operations. However, to make Groovy scripts with literal numeric values as intuitive as possible, a "least surprising" approach has been adopted. Therefore, a Groovy literal with a decimal point is, by default, a BigDecimal rather than a Float or a Double. If required, Float and Double types can be created explicitly or by using a suffix (see Section 8). The scientific notation is also available should it be necessary.

Similarly, an integral numeric literal (without a suffix) is, by default, the smallest type into which the value will fit; that is, it is an Integer, Long, or BigInteger. As before, Integer and Long types can be created explicitly or by using a suffix. The hexadecimal and octal notations are also available.

Another outcome of the "least surprising" approach is that Groovy never automatically promotes a binary floating-point number to a BigDecimal. To do so would imply a level of exactness to a result that is not guaranteed to be exact. It is also true that performance is better with a binary representation and so once it is introduced, it is kept. Therefore, binary operations involving BigDecimals, BigIntegers, Doubles, Floats, Longs, and Integers automatically convert their arguments according to Table C.5. The exception is division, which is discussed next in the following text.

The division operators / and /= produce a Double result if either operand is a Float or a Double. Otherwise, a BigDecimal is produced. In other words, the operators behave normally. However, if integer division is required, it can be performed on the integral types by casting the result of the division, as in:

```
(int) (3/2)      // gives a result of 1
```

or by using the intdiv operation, as in:

```
3.intdiv(2)      // gives a result of 1
```

TABLE C.5 Argument Conversion Matrix

	BigDecimal	BigInteger	Double	Float	Long	Integer
BigDecimal	BigDecimal	BigDecimal	Double	Double	BigDecimal	BigDecimal
BigInteger	BigDecimal	BigInteger	Double	Double	BigInteger	BigInteger
Double	Double	Double	Double	Double	Double	Double
Float	Double	Double	Double	Double	Double	Double
Long	BigDecimal	BigInteger	Double	Double	Long	Long
Integer	BigDecimal	BigInteger	Double	Double	Long	Integer

C.10 STATIC TYPING

We are also permitted to statically type a variable in Groovy. We replace the key-word def with one of the fundamental type names such as int or double, or with a user-defined class name. Hence, we might have:

```
int age = 25
double temperature = 98.4
boolean isAdult = true
```

Statically typed variables can then be checked for their correct usage. For example, in the context of the previously mentioned variable definitions, the following would generate a cast class exception as a consequence of trying to assign a string value to an int variable:

```
age = "Ken"
```

C.11 TESTING

The representation of numeric literal values and the evaluation of arithmetic expressions is an important part of Groovy. However, it is potentially difficult and confusing. Therefore, it is wise to be sure that Groovy behaves as we expect it to. The following code for the GroovyMathTest class has some representative unit tests (see Chapter 15) that help us achieve this aim. The tests are based on assertions made in the Groovy home website (see http://groovy.codehaus.org). Interested readers may add others as appropriate.

```
import groovy.util.GroovyTestCase

class GroovyMathTest extends GroovyTestCase {

    void testExactLiteralDefaultCalculations() {
        assertTrue( 1.1 + 0.1 == 1.2 )
    }

    void testOctal() {
        assertTrue( 0177 == 127 )
    }
```

```
void testHexadecimal() {
    assertTrue( 0xAB == 171 )


}

void testSuffixes() {
    assertTrue( "I suffix", 42I == new Integer("42") )
    assertTrue( "L suffix", 123L == new Long("123") )
    assertTrue( "Long type", 2147483648 == new Long("2147483648") )
    assertTrue( "G suffix #1", 456G == new java.math.BigInteger("456") )
    assertTrue( "G suffix #2", 123.45G == new java.math.BigDecimal("123.45") )
    assertTrue( "G suffix #3", 123.45G == new Double("123.45") )
    assertTrue( "Default BigDecimal type", 123.45 == new java.math.BigDecimal("123.45") )
    assertTrue( "D suffix", 1.200065D == new Double("1.200065") )
    assertTrue( "F suffix", 1.234F == new Float("1.234") )
    assertTrue( "E suffix", 1.23E23D == new Double("1.23E23") )
    assertTrue( "e suffix", 1.23e23D == new Double("1.23e23") )
}

void testDivision() {
    assertTrue( "Trailing zeros removed", 1/2 == new java.math.BigDecimal("0.5") )
    assertTrue( "Normalized to 10 places #1", 1/3 == new java.math.BigDecimal("0.3333333333") )
    assertTrue( "Normalized to 10 places #2", 2/3 == new java.math.BigDecimal("0.6666666667") )
}

void testIntegerDivisionByCasting() {
    assertTrue( (int)(3/2) == 1I )
}

void testIntegerDivisionByIntdiv() {
    assertTrue( 3.intdiv(2) == 1I )
}

void testBinaryOperationConvertionMatrix() {
    // Many more assertions could be made.
    //
    assertTrue( "#1 G+G #1", (123.45 + 67.8).getClass().getName() == "java.math.BigDecimal" )
    assertTrue( "#1 G + G #2", (123.45 + 67G).getClass().getName() == "java.math.BigDecimal" )
    assertTrue( "#1 G + D", (123.45 + 67.8D).getClass().getName() == "java.lang.Double" )
    assertTrue( "#1 G+F", (123.45 + 67.8F).getClass().getName() == "java.lang.Double" )
    assertTrue( "#1 G+L", (123.45 + 67L).getClass().getName() == "java.math.BigDecimal" )
    assertTrue( "#1 G+I", (123.45 + 67I).getClass().getName() == "java.math.BigDecimal" )
    //
    assertTrue( "#2 G+G #1", (123 + 67.8).getClass().getName() == "java.math.BigDecimal" )
    assertTrue( "#2 G+G #2", (123 + 67G).getClass().getName() == "java.math.BigInteger" )
    assertTrue( "#2 G+D", (123 + 67.8D).getClass().getName() == "java.lang.Double" )
    assertTrue( "#2 G+F", (123 + 67.8F).getClass().getName() == "java.lang.Double" )
```

```
        assertTrue( "#2 G + L", (123G + 67L).getClass().getName() == "java.math.BigInteger" )
        assertTrue( "#2 G + I", (123G + 67I).getClass().getName() == "java.math.BigInteger" )
        //
        assertTrue( "#3 L + L", (123 + 67L).getClass().getName() == "java.lang.Long" )
        assertTrue( "#3 I + I", (123 + 67I).getClass().getName() == "java.lang.Integer" )
    }

}
```

MORE ON STRINGS AND REGULAR EXPRESSIONS

A regular expression is a formula for matching strings to some pattern. They can provide very powerful mechanisms for describing the pattern, for splitting a string according to the pattern, or for modifying the string around the pattern. At first sight, they can appear daunting because of their complicated construction. However, a little practice can greatly ease matters.

D.1 REGULAR EXPRESSIONS

Regular expressions are essentially a specialized programming language hosted within Groovy. They provide a means of determining whether a string matches some pattern. For example, we might wish to determine whether a string has the pattern of a social security number. We can also use regular expressions to split a string in various ways or to modify a string.

A regular expression is presented as a `String`. However, some characters are given special roles and are known as *metacharacters*. Much of this appendix is devoted to demonstrating their effect within a regular expression. The metacharacters we shall discuss are:

```
. ^ $ * + ? [ ] { } \ | ( )
```

A short explanation of their meaning is given in Table D.1.

TABLE D.1   Metacharacters

Metacharacter	Description
.	Matches any single character. For example, the regular expression b.t would match the strings bat, bet, but not beat.
^	Matches the beginning of a line. For example, the regular expression ^Mat would match the beginning of the string Matches, but would not match Football Matches.
$	Matches the end of a line. For example, the regular expression ball$ would match the end of the string Football, but would not match Football Matches.
*	Matches zero or more occurrences of the immediately preceding character or regular expression. For example, the regular expression A* matches any number of occurrences of A, that is, A, AA, AAA, and so on.
+	Matches one or more occurrences of the immediately preceding character or regular expression. For example, the regular expression A+ matches any number of occurrences of A, that is, A, AA, AAA, etc.
?	Matches zero or one occurrence of the immediately preceding character or regular expression.
[ ]	Matches any one of the characters listed between the brackets. For example, the regular expression B[aeu]t matches Bat, Bet, and But.
{ }	Matches a specific number within a range of the immediately preceding character or regular expression. For example, the regular expression [0-9]{3} matches exactly three digits.
\	The escape character, used to make the following character act as itself, even where it is a metacharacter. For example, \$ represents the dollar sign.
|	Or together two expressions. For example, the regular expression (He|She) said matches both He said and She said.
( )	Consider the enclosed expression as a group, saving the matched characters.

D.2   SINGLE CHARACTER MATCH

The period character (.) in regular expressions matches any single character. Example 01 illustrates with a set of assertions that are all true.

EXAMPLE 01
Single character match

```
assert 'Bat' =~ 'B.t'
assert 'Bet' =~ 'B.t'
assert 'But' =~ 'B.t'
```

```
assert 'Batter' =~ 'B.tt.r'
assert 'Better' =~ 'B.tt.r'
assert 'Butter' =~ 'B.tt.r'

assert 'B.t' =~ 'B\\.t'
assert !('Bat' =~ 'B\\.t')
```

◆

D.3   MATCH AT THE BEGINNING

The caret character (^) in regular expressions matches only at the beginning of the string. Example 02 illustrates with a set of assertions that are all true.

```
assert 'Batter' =~ '^Bat'
assert 'Batter' =~ '^Batt'
assert !('batter' =~ '^Bat')
```

EXAMPLE 02
Match at the beginning

◆

D.4   MATCH AT THE END

The dollar sign character ($) in regular expressions matches only at the end of the string. Example 03 illustrates with a set of assertions that are all true.

```
assert 'Football' =~ 'ball$'
assert 'Mothball' =~ 'ball$'
assert !('Dancehall' =~ 'ball$')
```

EXAMPLE 03
Match at the end

◆

D.5   MATCH ZERO OR MORE

The asterisk character (*) in regular expressions matches zero or more occurrences of the immediately preceding character or regular expression. Example 04 illustrates with a set of assertions that are all true.

EXAMPLE 04
Match zero or more

```
assert 'Ft' =~ 'Fo*t'
assert 'Fot' =~ 'Fo*t'
assert 'Foot' =~ 'Fo*t'
assert 'Fooot' =~ 'Fo*t'
```

◆

D.6   MATCH ONE OR MORE

The plus character (+) in regular expressions matches one or more occurrences of the immediately preceding character or regular expression. Example 05 illustrates with a set of assertions that are all true.

EXAMPLE 05
Match one or more

```
assert !('Ft' =~ 'Fo+t')
assert 'Fot' =~ 'Fo+t'
assert 'Foot' =~ 'Fo+t'
assert 'Fooot' =~ 'Fo+t'
```

◆

D.7   MATCH NONE OR ONE

The question mark character (?) in regular expressions matches none or one occurrence of the immediately preceding character or regular expression. Example 06 illustrates with a set of assertions that are all true.

EXAMPLE 06
Match none or one

```
assert 'Shoe-shine' =~ 'Shoe-?shine'
assert 'Shoeshine' =~ 'Shoe-?shine'
```

◆

D.8   MATCH NUMBER

The repeating qualifier {m,n} in regular expressions matches at least m but not more than n occurrences of the immediately preceding character or regular expression. Both m and n are positive integer values. If n is omitted but the preceding comma is present, then this is interpreted as meaning at least m times. If only one value n is given, it means exactly n occurrences. Example 07 illustrates with a set of assertions that are all true.

```
assert 'abc' =~ 'ab{1,3}c'
assert 'abbc' =~ 'ab{1,3}c'
assert 'abbbc' =~ 'ab{1,3}c'

assert !('ac' =~ 'ab{1,3}c')
assert !('abbbbc' =~ 'ab{1,3}c')

assert 'abbbc' =~ 'ab{3}c'
assert !('abbc' =~ 'ab{3}c')

assert 'abbbc' =~ 'ab{3,}c'
assert 'abbbbc' =~ 'ab{3,}c'
assert !('abbc' =~ 'ab{3,}c')
```

EXAMPLE 07
Match number

◆

Note that the * modifier is equivalent to {0,}, the + modifier to {1,}, and the ? modifier to {0,1}.

D.9   CHARACTER CLASSES

Character classes match a single character from a group of characters. The characters are listed between the brackets [and]. Individual characters can be given as [aeiou] (the vowels) or given as a range [a-z] (the lowercase letters). Multiple ranges are also permitted as in [a-zA-Z] (the letters). To match any character except those in the range, the complement character is used as in [^0-9] (i.e., any character other than a digit).

```
assert '0' =~ '[0-9]{1,3}'
assert '01' =~ '[0-9]{1,3}'
assert '012' =~ '[0-9]{1,3}'
assert !('0123' ==~ '[0-9]{1,3}')
assert !('A45' =~ '[0-9]{3}')

assert 'tan' =~ 't[aeiou]n'
assert 'ten' =~ 't[aeiou]n'
assert 'tin' =~ 't[aeiou]n'
assert 'ton' =~ 't[aeiou]n'
assert 'tun' =~ 't[aeiou]n'
assert !('Tan' =~ 't[aeiou]n')
```

EXAMPLE 08
Character classes

◆

If you wish to match a dash (-) in a character group, it has to be the first character, as in [-ab], so that it is not interpreted as the range-making character.

D.10   ALTERNATION

Alternative patterns are expressed with the metacharacter |. Usually, the alternatives use parentheses for groupings.

Alternation

```
assert 'tan' =~ 't(a|e|i|o|u)n'
assert 'ten' =~ 't(a|e|i|o|u)n'
assert 'tin' =~ 't(a|e|i|o|u)n'
assert 'ton' =~ 't(a|e|i|o|u)n'
assert 'tun' =~ 't(a|e|i|o|u)n'
assert 'toon' =~ 't(a|e|i|oo|u)n'
```

◆

D.11   MISCELLANEOUS NOTATIONS

Some shorthand notations for commonly used regular expressions have been developed. Table D.2 lists some of these.

Regular expressions use the backslash character \ to cancel the meaning of special characters. Unfortunately, this conflicts with Groovy's usage of the same character as an escape character in string literals. The consequence is that we must escape any backslash character with a further backslash. This is shown in the following:

EXAMPLE 10
Miscellaneous
notations

```
assert '12:34' =~ '\\d{2}:\\d{2}'
assert !('2:34' =~ '\\d{2}:\\d{2}')

assert 'Hello world' =~ '\\w*\\s*\\w*'
assert !('Hello world Groovy' ==~ '\\w*\\s*\\w*')
```

◆

TABLE D.2   Shorthand Notations

Shorthand	Equivalent Notation	Description
\d	[0-9]	Digit
\D	[^0-9]	Non-digit
\w	[a-zA-Z0-9]	A word character
\W	[^a-zA-Z0-9]	A non-word character
\s	[\t\n\f\r\v]	A whitespace character
\S	[^\s]	A non-whitespace character

D.12   GROUPING

Parentheses around some part of a regular expression establish a *group* that can be later retrieved from the matched string. That way, a regular expression can be used to dissect a string into subgroups. For example, a U.S. social security number is of the form 999-99-9999, meaning three digits, a hyphen, two digits, another hyphen, and four digits. Example 11 includes a regular expression for this, which also retrieves the three numeric subgroups.

```
def SSNPATTERN = '([0-9]{3})-([0-9]{2})-([0-9]{4})'
def ssN = '123-45-6789'

def matcher = ssN =~ SSNPATTERN
matcher.matches()

println "matcher[0]: <${matcher[0]}>"
println "matcher[0][0]: <${matcher[0][0]}>"
println "matcher[0][1]: <${matcher[0][1]}>"
println "matcher[0][2]: <${matcher[0][2]}>"
println "matcher[0][3]: <${matcher[0][3]}>"
```

EXAMPLE 11
U.S. social
security number

◆

The variable matcher is an object of the Matcher class (see the JDK documentation). It is used to perform differing kinds of matching operations. For example, method matches attempts to match the entire text against the pattern. The GDK augments this class with the method getAt to provide support for the indexing operator. Then, for example, matcher[0][1] represents the 0th match of the whole pattern and the first group within that match. Output from this program is:

```
matcher[0]: <["123-45-6789", "123", "45", "6789"]>
matcher[0][0]: <123-45-6789>
matcher[0][1]: <123>
matcher[0][2]: <45>
matcher[0][3]: <6789>
```

Example 12 illustrates groupings get the parts of a United Kingdom car registration (license) plate. Its form is XX99 XXX. The two digits can be used to determine the date of registration. For example, 01 represents April 2001, 51 is September 2001, 02 is April 2002, and so on.

EXAMPLE 12

U.K. car
registration plate

```
def UKPATTERN = '([A-Z]{2})([0-9]{2})\\s([A-Z]{3})'
def ukPlate = 'SK51 PIQ'

def matcher = ukPlate =~ UKPATTERN
matcher.matches()

println "matcher[0]: <${matcher[0]}>"
println "matcher[0][0]: <${matcher[0][0]}>"
println "matcher[0][1]: <${matcher[0][1]}>"
println "matcher[0][2]: <${matcher[0][2]}>"
println "matcher[0][3]: <${matcher[0][3]}>"
```

The output is:

```
matcher[0]: <["SK51 PIQ", "SK", "51", "PIQ"]>
matcher[0][0]: <SK51 PIQ>
matcher[0][1]: <SK>
matcher[0][2]: <51>
matcher[0][3]: <PIQ>
```

◆

The final illustration is of a date expressed as MMM DD, YYYY. An example is NOV 28, 2005. Example 13 produces the output:

EXAMPLE 13

Dates

```
matcher[0]: <["NOV 28, 2005", "NOV", "28", "2005"]>
matcher[0][0]: <NOV 28, 2005>
matcher[0][1]: <NOV>
matcher[0][2]: <28>
matcher[0][3]: <2005>
```

```
def DATEPATTERN = '([A-Z]{3})\\s([0-9]{1,2}),\\s([0-9]{4})'
def date = 'NOV 28, 2005'

def matcher = date =~ DATEPATTERN
matcher.matches()

println "matcher[0]: <${matcher[0]}>"
println "matcher[0][0]: <${matcher[0][0]}>"
println "matcher[0][1]: <${matcher[0][1]}>"
println "matcher[0][2]: <${matcher[0][2]}>"
println "matcher[0][3]: <${matcher[0][3]}>"
```

◆

MORE ON LISTS, MAPS, AND RANGES

The Groovy interpreter plays an important role when we invoke methods on an object declared in a Groovy script. Essentially, the interpreter intercepts these method calls so that it can add behaviors not present in the Java core classes. In this manner, Groovy designers have been able to extend the functionality of the Java core classes (the JDK) so that they are more Groovy-like. However, it is important to understand that the JDK itself is unchanged. For example, if we call the method each (see Chapter 9) on a List, as in:

```
def numbers = [11, 12, 13, 14]
numbers.each {it -> println it*2}
```

then we should appreciate that no such method exists in any class in the JDK. The interpreter makes it look as if a List object has this method present, even though it is absent at the JVM level. In a similar manner, the functionality of the Map class has been extended. We will describe this extra functionality as the Groovy GDK methods.

We should also understand that when we define a List, as in:

```
def numbers = [11, 12, 13, 14]
```

then Groovy's dynamic typing ability comes into play. As we have assigned a literal List value, numbers is made to reference an ArrayList at runtime.

However, even though it is a normal JDK ArrayList, it can, by virtue of the Groovy GDK methods, respond to additional methods such as each. Similarly, when we define a Map with:

```
def names = ['Ken' : 'Barclay', 'John' : 'Savage']
```

then, at runtime, names references a HashMap. As before, its behavior is extended by the Groovy GDK methods.

E.1   CLASSES

When we refer to a List, we mean an object that behaves according to the interface List but whose actual type does not concern us. We further qualify this last statement by extending the behavior to include Groovy GDK methods associated with Lists. We have noted that the default implementation is an ArrayList:

```
def numbers = [1, 2, 3]
println "numbers: ${numbers.getClass().getName()}"          // java.util.ArrayList
```

If required, we can nominate a different representation with the as clause:

```
def numbers = [] as LinkedList
numbers.addAll([1, 2, 3])
println "numbers: ${numbers.getClass().getName()}"          // java.util.LinkedList
```

We must be careful, however, with statements such as:

```
def numbers = [] as LinkedList
numbers = numbers + [1, 2, 3]
println "numbers: ${numbers.getClass().getName()}"          // java.util.ArrayList
```

Here, the assignment to the variable numbers does so using the default ArrayList implementation. In the earlier illustration, the variable numbers remains as a LinkedList since we are simply invoking the addAll method on it.

The as clause can only be applied to an empty List. Were we to use:

```
def numbers = [1, 2, 3] as LinkedList
```

this would raise a class cast exception since we are attempting to coerce an ArrayList object into a LinkedList object, and this is not possible since the class LinkedList does not subclass ArrayList.

The as clause can be usefully employed when a method, such as a method from the JDK, requires an array of values for its actual parameter. If our code has a List with the values to pass to that method, we do the following:

```
def names = ['Ken', 'John', 'Jessie']

def someMethod(String[] args) { ... }

someMethod(names as String[])      // convert to required type
```

E.2 LISTS

Chapter 4 identified that the List methods getAt and putAt support using the indexing operator on, respectively, the right and left sides of an assignment. Hence:

```
def numbers = [1, 2, 3]
def  x = numbers[1]                // x = numbers.getAt(1)
numbers[1] = 22                    // numbers.putAt(1, 22)
```

If we make an assignment using the indexing operator to an index beyond the current size of a List, then the null value is auto-generated for the other indices. In the following example, the variable numbers is originally of size 3. The assignment then increases it to size 10, with the indices 3 through 8, inclusive, representing the null value.

```
def numbers = [0, 1, 2]
println "numbers: ${numbers}"      // numbers: [0, 1, 2]
numbers[9] = 9
println "numbers: ${numbers}"      // numbers: [0, 1, 2, null, null, null, null, null, null, 9]
```

Additionally, an index value beyond the size of a List returns null:

```
println "numbers[20]: ${numbers[20]}"      // numbers[20]: null
```

E.3   RANGES

A Range literal such as 1..10 is an instance of the class IntRange. This class implements the Range interface and extends the AbstractList class. The Range interface introduces the methods getFrom, getTo, and isReverse. Extending AbstractList means that a Range also supports List methods. This is illustrated in the following fragment:

```
def rng = 1..10
println "rng: ${rng.getClass().getName()}"              // groovy.lang.IntRange
println "to, from: ${rng.getFrom()} ${rng.getTo()}"     // to, from: 1 10
println "get: ${rng.get(0)}"                            // get: 1
```

Not all List methods are appropriate for a Range, and they should not be used. For example, rng.set(0, 99) will generate an unsupported operation exception.

There are a small number of special cases that require care. These are shown in the listing:

```
println "1..1: ${1..1}"      // 1..1: [1]
println "1..0: ${1..0}"      // 1..0: [1, 0]
println "1..<2: ${1..<2}"    // 1..<2: [1]
println "1..<1: ${1..<1}"    // 1..<1: []
```

The first and third examples are Ranges with a single value. The second example is a Range of two values in reverse order. The final example is the potential pitfall since it a Range with no values.

E.4   THE SPREAD OPERATOR

The *spread operator* is provided to spread the elements of a List into another List or spread the elements of a Map into another Map. The spread operator for a List is denoted by the * symbol. Consider the code:

```
def x = [2, 3]
def y = [0, 1, *x, 4, *[5, 6, 7]]
println "y: ${y}"            // y: [0, 1, 2, 3, 4, 5, 6, 7]
```

The variable y represents a List in which the elements of the List denoted by the variable x and the literal [5, 6, 7] are spread into y.

In a similar manner, the symbol `*:` is the spread operator for use with Maps. In the following, Map `x` and literal Map `[6 : 'f', 7 : 'g']` are absorbed into the Map `y`.

```
def x = [3 : 'c', 4 : 'd']
def y = [1 : 'a', 2 : 'b', *:x, 5 : 'e', *:[6 : 'f', 7 : 'g']]
println "y: ${y}"
            // y: [2:"b", 4:"d", 6:"f", 1:"a", 3:"c", 7:"g", 5:"e"]
```

E.5   TESTING

It is always worthwhile conducting a few simple tests even if they just confirm that our understanding of a particular aspect of Groovy is correct. The following `GroovyTestCase` is an example of these kinds of tests. Others can be easily added.

```
import groovy.util.GroovyTestCase

class GroovyJDKTests extends GroovyTestCase {

// Establish the fixture
    def obj
    def table
    def count

void setUp() {
    obj = new Object();
    table = [11,12,13,14]
    count = 0
}

// ****************************************************************
// Object tests
// ****************************************************************

    // Show that we have an Object
    void testObjectClassName() {
        def className = obj.getClass().getName()
        assertTrue(className == "java.lang.Object")
    }
```

```
    // Show that we have a toString method
    void testObjecttoStringMethodName() {
        def methods = obj.getClass().getMethods()
        def methodNames = methods.collect{ element -> return element.getName() }
        assertTrue( methodNames.contains("toString") )
    }


    // Show that we have the correct number of public methods from JDK Object
    void testObjectMethodNumber() {
        def methods = obj.getClass().getMethods()
        assertTrue( methods.length == 9 )
    }

    // Show that we don't have an each method
    void testObjectEachMethodName() {
        def methods = obj.getClass().getMethods()
        def methodNames = methods.collect{ element -> return element.getName() }
        assertFalse( methodNames.contains("each") )
    }

    // Show that we can send the each message
    void testEachMethodCallForAnObject() {
        obj.each {element -> count++ }
        assertTrue( count == 1 )
    }

// *****************************************************************
// List tests
// *****************************************************************

    // Show that we have an ArrayList
    void testListClassName() {
        def className = table.getClass().getName()
        assertTrue( className == "java.util.ArrayList" )
    }

    // Show that we have a size method
    void testListSizeMethodName() {
        def methods = table.getClass().getMethods()
        def methodNames = methods.collect{ element -> return element.getName() }
        assertTrue( methodNames.contains("size") )
    }

    // Show that we have the correct number of public methods from JDK ArrayList
    void testArrayListMethodNumber() {
        def methods = table.getClass().getMethods()
```

```
        assertTrue( methods.length == 35 )
}

// Show that we don't have an each method
void testListEachMethodName() {
    def methods = obj.getClass().getMethods()
    def methodNames = methods.collect{ element -> return element.getName() }
    assertFalse( methodNames.contains("each") )
}

// Show that we can send the each message
void testEachMethodCallForAList() {
    table.each {element -> count++ }
    assertTrue( count == 4 )
    }
}
```

MORE ON SIMPLE INPUT AND OUTPUT

In this appendix, we provide some further examples of formatted output and consider the input class Console, introduced in Chapter 5.

F.1 FORMATTED OUTPUT

A conversion specification in the format string is introduced with the percent (%) character. Then, there is a series of options to the conversion. The specification ends with the conversion operation expressed as a single character. The general definition for a conversion specification is then:

```
%[index$][flags][width][.precision]conversion
```

The optional index is an unsigned integer indicating the position of the parameter in the parameter list. The first argument is referenced by 1$, the second by 2$, and so on. We shall not illustrate this option. The optional flags is a set of characters that modify the output format. The set of valid flags will depend on the conversion. The optional width is a non-negative decimal integer indicating the minimum number of characters to be written to the output. The optional precision is a non-negative decimal integer usually used to restrict the number of characters. The specific behavior depends on the conversion. Finally, the required conversion is a character indicating how the argument should be formatted. The set of valid conversions for a given argument depends on the parameter type.

Not all possible combinations are explored in this appendix. There are simply too many. Here, we provide an explanation for a range of common examples. The reader is referred to the documentation for the Formatter class (JDK) for a complete description.

In all our examples, the actual output value is surrounded with [and] to emphasize what is actually produced by the conversion. The actual effect is given alongside the printf statement as a comment.

Example 01 illustrates using the %d conversion to print integer values. The %d conversion is for the signed decimal conversion of an integer value. Observe how the – flag left justifies the output, while the + flag guarantees a preceding sign on the value. The 0 flag specifies that leading spaces are to be replaced with leading zeros.

EXAMPLE 01
%d conversion

```
def j = 45
def k = -123
def jj = 123456780

printf("[%d]\n", [k])          // [-123]
printf("[%4d]\n", [j])         // [  45]
printf("[%-5d]\n", [j])        // [45  ]
printf("[%05d]\n", [j])        // [00045]
printf("[%2d]\n", [k])         // [-123]
printf("[%+4d]\n", [j])        // [ +45]
printf("[%+05d]\n", [j])       // [+0045]
printf("[%d]", [jj])           // [123456789]
```

◆

Example 02 uses the %f for the signed decimal conversion of floating-point values. The specifications include examples such as 10.2, which denote a total field width of 10 character places and a precision of 2 decimal places.

EXAMPLE 02
%f conversion

```
def x = 12.345
def y = -678.9

printf("[%f]\n", [y])          // [-678.900000]
printf("[%-10.2f]\n", [x])     // [12.35     ]
printf("[%+8.1f]\n", [x])      // [   +12.3]
printf("[%.2f]\n", [y])        // [-678.90]
printf("[%08.2f]\n", [x])      // [00012.35]
printf("[%+06.1f]\n", [x])     // [+012.3]
```

◆

The %e and %E conversions are used to present floating-point values in scientific notation. The form for this is d.dddddde+dd (for %e conversion) and d.ddddddE+dd (for %E conversion). The optional precision specifies the number of decimal places (six is the default). Example 03 presents some illustrations.

EXAMPLE 03
%e and %E
conversions

```
def x = 12.345
def y = -678.9

printf("[%e]\n", [x])              // [1.234500e+01]
printf("[%E]\n", [x])              // [1.234500E+01]
printf("[%14.4e]\n", [x])          // [  1.2345e+01]
printf("[%-12.1E]\n", [y])         // [-6.8E+02    ]
printf("[%+12.2E]\n", [x])         // [  +1.23E+01]
printf("[%.2e]\n", [y])            // [-6.79e+02]
printf("[%10.0e]\n", [x])          // [    1e+01]
```

◆

In Example 04, we show how to format a String value with the %s conversion. Some care is required where the optional precision denotes how many characters of the String to output.

EXAMPLE 04
%S conversion

```
def message = "Hello"

printf("[%s]\n", [message])        // [Hello]
printf("[%8s]\n", [message])       // [   Hello]
printf("[%-8s]\n", [message])      // [Hello   ]
printf("[%6.2s]\n", [message])     // [    He]
printf("[%-10.6s]\n", [message])   // [Hello     ]
```

◆

The last example in this section illustrates what happens when too many or too few values are available to the format string. In the second illustration, the extra values are simply ignored. In the final illustration, an exception is raised when there are insufficient values provided.

EXAMPLE 05
Too many and too
few values

```
def x = 21
def y = 22
def z = 23

printf('First: %d, second: %d\n', [x, y])       // ok
printf('First: %d, second: %d\n', [x, y, z])    // extras ignored
//printf('First: %d, second: %d\n', [x])        // raise exception
```

◆

F.2   CONSOLE CLASS

Chapter 5 introduced the user class Console to read various kinds of values from the user console. Essentially, it is a series of static methods which obtain the next input value from a line buffer. When the buffered line is exhausted, it is refreshed with new user input. Here is the class:

```
package console

class Console {

    def static readLine() {
        return getNextLine()
    }

    def static readString() {
        return getNextToken()
    }

    def static readInteger() {
        return getNextToken().toInteger()
    }

    def static readDouble() {
        return getNextToken().toDouble()
    }

    def static readBoolean() {
        return (getNextToken() == "true")
    }

    private static String getNextToken() {
        if(inputLine == null)
            readInputLine()

        while(inputIndex == numberOfTokens)
            readInputLine()

        return inputTokens[inputIndex++]
    }

    private static String getNextLine() {
        if(inputLine == null)
            readInputLine()
```

```
            while(inputIndex == numberOfTokens)
                readInputLine()

            def line = inputTokens[inputIndex..<numberOfTokens].join(' ')
            inputIndex = numberOfTokens
            return line
        }

        private static void readInputLine() {
            inputLine = System.in.readLine()
            inputTokens = inputLine.tokenize()
            numberOfTokens = inputTokens.size()
            inputIndex = 0
        }

    // -----properties -----------------

        private static String inputLine          = null
        private static List inputTokens          = null
        private static int numberOfTokens        = 0
        private static int inputIndex            = -1
    }
```

Clearly, it could be more elaborate. However, we have deliberately chosen to keep things simple. An example of its usage is shown in the following example:

```
import console.*

def lastName = Console.readString()     // input: Barclay
println "lastName: ${lastName}"         // lastName: Barclay

def name = Console.readString()         // input: Ken Barclay
println "name: ${name}"                 // name: Ken

name = Console.readLine()               // input: NONE!!!
println "name: ${name}"                 // name: Barclay
```

When the program executes, the following is produced:

```
Barclay
lastName: Barclay
Ken Barclay
name: Ken
name: Barclay
```

The first line is the input value given by the user. This is the input consumed by the first call to readString. The value is stored in the lastName variable, and then output as the second line. The second call to readString buffers the input shown as the third line. From this, it obtains Ken as the input, assigns it to the variable name, and prints it as line four. Finally, the readLine method call requires no further user input since the buffer stills holds the remainder from line three. The name is printed as shown on the final line

MORE ON METHODS

A method that can make a call on itself is known as a *recursive method*. When the method makes a direct call on itself from within its own method body, we refer to this as *direct recursion*. When one method calls another that, in turn, calls the first again, we refer to this as *indirect recursion*. Recursion is an extremely powerful approach for expressing many elegant programming solutions.

In this appendix, we demonstrate recursive methods as well as other aspects of methods such as statically typed parameters and return values.

G.1 RECURSIVE METHODS

A method may invoke any other method. Programmers exploit this facility to build programs hierarchically, in which one method invokes submethods to perform subsidiary tasks. These submethods might invoke further submethods to perform simpler tasks, and so on.

This is not the only way of using methods. In particular, a method may call (or invoke) itself. Such a method is said to be *recursive*. Many programming problems have solutions that are expressible *directly* or *indirectly* through recursion. The ability to map these solutions on to recursive methods often leads to elegant and natural implementations.

To illustrate, consider a method to evaluate the *factorial* of a number. The factorial of a positive integer n, written n!, is defined as the product of the successive integers 1 through n inclusive. The factorial of 0 is treated as a special case and is defined as equal to 1. Therefore:

$$n! = n * (n - 1) * (n - 2) * \ldots * 3 * 2 * 1$$

and

$$0! = 1$$

It follows that:

$$n! = n * ((n - 1) * (n - 2) * \ldots * 3 * 2 * 1)$$

and thus:

$$n! = n * (n - 1)!$$

Example 01 demonstrates a factorial method for this purpose. Observe how the
if statement selects the return value according to the value of the parameter n.

```
def factorial(n) {
    if(n == 0)
        return 1
    else
        return n * factorial(n - 1)
}

def fact5 = factorial(5)
println "factorial(5): ${fact5}"
```

EXAMPLE 01
Recursive
factorial method

The output from the program is:

```
factorial(5): 120
```

◆

For many List processing applications, it is common to have methods head,
tail, and cons. Respectively, they return the first item in a list (or null if the list
is empty), return a new list with the first item removed, and return a new list
with a new item at its head. These methods are shown in Example 02. They are
then used to develop the methods upTo and prod. Method upTo returns a list of
integers as given by the method parameters. Method prod multiplies all the integers in a list of integers. Both upTo and prod are defined recursively. Finally, upTo
and prod can be used to define another version of factorial.

EXAMPLE 02

List handling

```
def head(list) {
    return (list.size() == 0) ? null : list[0]
}

def tail(list) {
    def size = list.size()
    return (size == 0) ? [] : list[1..<size]
}

def cons(item, list) {
    def copy = list
    copy.add(0, item)
    return copy
}

def upTo(m, n) {
    if(m > n)
        return []
    else
        return cons(m, upTo(m + 1, n))
}

def prod(list) {
    if(head(list) == null)
        return 1
    else
        return head(list) * prod(tail(list))
}

def factorial(n) {
    return prod(upTo(1, n))
}

println "factorial(5): ${factorial(5)}"
```

This program produces the same output as the previous program.

◆

G.2   STATIC TYPING

Our methods have been defined with dynamic typing for both the method
parameters and the method return. This feature makes the methods more
generic, as demonstrated in Example 03. Here, method times returns the result
of multiplying its two parameters. Three calls are made to this method with

various actual parameter types. Since the * operator is applicable in all the given situations, everything executes as expected.

```
def times(x, y) {
    return x * y
}


println "times(3, 4): ${times(3, 4)}"
println "times(3.1, 4.2): ${times(3.1, 4.2)}"
println "times('Hello', 4): ${times('Hello', 4)}"
```

EXAMPLE 03
Dynamically typed methods

The output from this program is:

```
times(3, 4): 12
times(3.1, 4.2): 13.02
times('Hello', 4): HelloHelloHelloHello
```

◆

The return type and the types for the formal parameters of a method can also be given statically. This is sometimes necessary when we wish to redefine a method from a Java superclass. In this case, we must specify the actual types involved. Such *statically typed* methods also introduce an element of security since they cannot be called without actual parameters of the required type.

Example 04 repeats the previous example, but this time the method times has its types statically defined. The last two calls then generate errors since the actual parameters are of the incorrect types.

```
int times(int x, int y) {
    return x * y
}

println "times(3, 4): ${times(3, 4)}"
//println "times(3.1, 4.2): ${times(3.1, 4.2)}"      // missing method exception
//println "times('Hello', 4): ${times('Hello', 4)}"  // missing method exception
```

EXAMPLE 04
Statically typed methods

◆

Had we wished to allow method times to accept numeric types, then we would relax the constraint that the parameters and return type are integers and replace with the class name Number, the superclass for all numeric types. Example 05 is an update for the previous example.

EXAMPLE 05
Typed method

```
Number times(Number x, Number y) {
    return x * y
}

println "times(3, 4): ${times(3, 4)}"
println "times(3.1, 4.2): ${times(3.1, 4.2)}"
```

◆

This then makes a compelling case for redefining the factorial method introduced in Example 01 as one with a single integer parameter and returning an integer result. This we show in Example 06, where the call factorial(5.1) reports that
no method entitled factorial is defined with a BigDecimal formal parameter.

EXAMPLE 06
Statically typed
factorial method

```
int factorial(int n) {
    if(n == 0)
        return 1
    else
        return n * factorial(n − 1)
}

println "factorial(5): ${factorial(5)}"
println "factorial(5.1): ${factorial(5.1)}"        // missing method exception
```

◆

G.3   ACTUAL PARAMETER AGREEMENT

The actual parameters in a method call must match exactly the number of formal
parameters given in the method definition. Otherwise, Groovy will report a missing
method exception. The final two method calls in Example 07 report this error. The
first of these has too few actual parameters. The second has too many parameters.

EXAMPLE 07
Missing method

```
def meth(a, b, c ) {
    println "meth(${a}, ${b}, ${c})"
}

meth(1, 2, 3)
meth(1, 2)                      // missing method
meth(1, 2, 3, 4)                // missing method
```

◆

G.4   METHOD OVERLOADING

Groovy supports *method overloading*. An overloaded method is one within the same scope as another, with the same name but with a different number of parameters. When such a method is called, then the correct method is resolved by a process of *parameter matching*. The number of actual parameters is used to determine which method to invoke. This is demonstrated in Example 08.

```
def times(x, y) {
    return x * y
}

def times(x) {
    return 2 * x
}

println "times(3, 4): ${times(3, 4)}"
println "times(3): ${times(3)}"
```

EXAMPLE 08
Method overloading

Here, method `times` is overloaded to take two or one parameter(s). The first call provides two actual parameters and this is resolved to the first implementation. The second call is resolved to the second definition. Output from this program confirms this behavior:

```
times(3, 4): 12
times(3): 6
```

◆

G.5   DEFAULT PARAMETER AMBIGUITY

Default method parameters and overloaded methods introduce a possible ambiguity. Consider Example 09.

```
def times(x, y = 4) {
    return x * y
}

def times(x) {
    return 2 * x
}

println "times(3, 5): ${times(3, 5)}"
println "times(3): ${times(3)}"
```

EXAMPLE 09
Default parameter
ambiguity

In this example, the method times has been overloaded and method calls would be resolved by the number of actual parameters. Additionally, the first version of this method has a default value for its second parameter. This could, potentially, conflict with the second method definition. The first call, times(3, 5), is resolved to the first method definition. The second call, times(3), might be interpreted as the first method with the second value defaulted or to the second method with its single parameter. Groovy resolves this potential ambiguity by giving preference to the method with the exact number of parameters. This is shown by the program output:

```
times(3, 5): 15
times(3): 6
```

◆

This kind of ambiguity can, of course, be clarified by the use of static typing of the parameters. Consider Example 10:

EXAMPLE 10
Statically typed
method parameters

```
def times(String str, num = 1) {
        return str * num
}

def times(x) {
    return 2 * x
}

println "times('Hello', 3): ${times('Hello', 3)}"
println "times('Hello'): ${times('Hello')}"
println "times(3): ${times(3)}"
println "times(1.2): ${times(1.2)}"
```

When this script is executed, the output is:

```
times('Hello', 3): HelloHelloHello
times('Hello'): Hello
times(3): 6
times(1.2): 2.4
```

Note how the second line of output reveals that there is no ambiguity where the only parameter is a String.

◆

G.6 COLLECTIONS AS METHOD PARAMETERS AND RETURN VALUES

The next illustration introduces the method `split` that accepts a `List` of lines of text as input and splits each line into its individual words. The program then sorts the words into alphabetic order.

```
def split(lines) {
    def words = []
    lines.each { line ->
        def wordsInLine = line.tokenize()
        words.addAll(wordsInLine)
    }
    return words
}

def doc = ['This is the first line', 'This is the second line', 'This is the third line']
def words = split(doc).sort()

words.each { word ->
    println "${word}"
}
```

EXAMPLE 11
Word split a list
of lines

Running this program produces:

```
This
This
This
first
is
is
is
line
line
line
second
the
the
the
third
```

◆

A word concordance is an alphabetical list of words from a piece of text. The text is represented as a series of lines containing the individual words. The concordance lists each word and the set of line numbers in which the word occurs.

EXAMPLE 12
Word concordance

```
import java.util.*

def concordance(lines) {
    def lineNumber = 1
    def concord = [ : ]
    lines.each { line ->
        def wordsInLine = line.tokenize()
        wordsInLine.each { word ->
            if(concord[word] == null)
                concord[word] = [lineNumber]
            else
                concord[word] << lineNumber
        }
        lineNumber++
    }
    return concord
}

def printConcordance(concordance) {
    def words = concordance.keySet().sort()
    words.each { word ->
        print "${word} "
        concordance[word].each { lineNumber -> print "${lineNumber} "}
        println()
    }
}

def doc = ["This is the first line", "This is the second line","This is the third line"]
def concord = concordance(doc)
printConcordance(concord)
```

The concordance method operates on each line of text. Each line is split into individual words using the tokenize method. If the word is presently not part of the concordance, then the word and its line number are put into the concordance Map. If the word is already present, then the line number is appended on to the existing list of line numbers for this word. When this processing is completed the method printConcordance arranges the output in alphabetical order. We do this by getting the keys from the Map, sorting them, and then accessing the Map with the sorted keys. The program output is:

```
This: 1 2 3
first: 1
is: 1 2 3
line: 1 2 3
second: 2
the: 1 2 3
third: 3
```

◆

In the next example, a series of data values (perhaps obtained from a data file), represent individual expense claims made by staff members. The data are represented in the following text, with the name of the claimant, the amount claimed, and the reason for the expenditure.

```
John    45.00   Train
Ken     102.20  Air
etc
```

A method to process this data and obtain the total amount claimed is shown in Example 13.

```
def totalExpenses(expenseLines) {
    def total = 0
    expenseLines.each { expenseLine ->
        def expense = expenseLine.tokenize()
        total += expense[1].toDouble()
    }
    return total
}

def expensesData = ['John         45.00    Train',
                    'Ken          102.20   Air',
                    'Sally        22.20    Supplies'
                   ]
println "Total expenses: ${totalExpenses(expensesData)}"
```

EXAMPLE 13
Expenses

◆

We might consider separating the expense amount, such as 102.20, into two separate values 102 and 20, representing the dollars and cents, and doing all the arithmetic with integer values. In that case, we could first tokenize each expense line into its three constituents, and then use a regular expression to obtain the groups of digits representing the dollar and cent value. This is shown next.

EXAMPLE 14
Expenses

```
def totalExpenses(expenseLines) {
    def total = 0
    expenseLines.each { expenseLine ->
        def expense = expenseLine.tokenize()
        def matcher = expense[1] =~ '([0-9]*)\\.([0-9]*)'
        matcher.matches()
        total += 100 * matcher[0][1].toInteger() + matcher[0][2].toInteger()
    }
    return total / 100
}

def expensesData = ['John      45.00      Train',
                    'Ken       102.20     Air',
                    'Sally     22.20      Supplies'
                   ]
println "Total expenses: ${totalExpenses(expensesData)}"
```

◆

MORE ON CLOSURES

Chapter 9 introduced closures and demonstrated their importance when iterating over collections. We also described general aspects of closures including closure parameters. Here, we consider other details concerning closures including default parameters, the distinction between closures and methods, and closures and scope rules. We also tabulate and describe the methods for Lists, Maps, and Ranges that take a closure as parameter.

H.1 CLOSURES AND AMBIGUITY

Example 06 in Chapter 9 outlined how a closure appearing as the final actual parameter to a method call may be removed from the list of actual parameters and placed immediately following the closing parenthesis. If meth represents a method with three parameters:

```
def meth(a, b, c) {...}
```

and clos is a closure variable, {...} a closure literal, and x and y two arbitrary values, then the following observations are made:

```
meth(x, y, {...})              // OK
meth(x, y) {...}               // OK
meth(x, y, clos)               // OK
meth(x, y) clos                // ERROR: no such method
```

The second line illustrates placing the closure literal after the method call parameters. The fourth line demonstrates that this same technique may not be used with a closure variable. The Groovy interpreter is unable to recognize that the clos identifier is part of the method call. Groovy will report that it is unable to find a method named meth with two parameters.

If meth represents a method with one parameter:

```
def meth(c) {...}
```

clos is a closure variable, and {...} a closure literal, the following observations are made:

```
meth({...})             // OK
meth() {...}            // OK
meth {...}              // OK
meth(clos)              // OK
meth() clos             // ERROR: null pointer exception
meth clos               // OK
```

In the fifth line, the call to meth is made but with no actual parameter. Within the method body, the formal parameter will be initialized as null, and any usage within the method issues the error shown. Somewhat confusingly, the final example works.

H.2   CLOSURES AND METHODS

We need to be absolutely clear about the following two Groovy constructs:

```
def double = {n -> return 2 * n}
def double(n) {return 2 * n}
```

The former defines a closure and the latter is a method definition. Section 7.6 discusses the notion of scope. Any closure reference will occur in some scope. Hence, the following two closures could not appear together:

```
def divide = {x, y -> return x / y }
def divide = {x -> return 1 / x }
```

An error would report that the name divide has already been defined. In contrast, we know that Groovy supports method overloading, and that the following is permissible:

```
def multiply(x, y) {return x * y}
def multiply(x) {return 2 * x}
```

H.3 DEFAULT PARAMETERS

Like methods, the formal parameters to a closure may be assigned default values. Here is a simple illustration:

```
def greeting = {message, name = "world" -> println "${message} ${name}" }

greeting("Hello", "world")
greeting("Hello")
```

Both closure calls produce the output `Hello world`.

H.4 CLOSURES AND SCOPE

The effect of scope on closures was introduced in Section 9.1 and illustrated in Examples 04 to 07, inclusive. Example 19 in Chapter 9 presented a selection sort as a closure with local closures to support its implementation. A similar arrangement is given in the `bubbleSort` closure shown in Example 01:

```
def bubbleSort = { list ->

    def swap = {values, j, k ->
        def temp = values[j]
        values[j] = values[k]
        values[k] = temp
    }

    def size = list.size()
    def numberSorted = 0

    while(numberSorted < size) {
        for(index in 1..<(size -numberSorted)) {
            if(list[index] < list[index -1])
                swap(list, index, index -1)
        }
        numberSorted ++
    }

    return list
}
```

EXAMPLE 01
Bubblesort as a closure

```
def numbers = [13, 14, 11, 12, 14]
println "Sorted numbers: ${bubbleSort(numbers)}"
```

◆

A variable cannot be defined twice in the same scope. Hence, we could not define the local closure swap as shown in the following text, since its formal parameter list would introduce a variable of the same name into the current scope, the body of the bubbleSort closure.

```
def swap = {list, j, k ->
    def temp = list[j]
    list[j] = list[k]
    list[k] = temp
}
```

These same scope rules would, however, permit us to define swap as shown in the following text. This time, the behavior is described in terms of the two parameters and the list variable is defined in the enclosing scope.

```
def swap = {j, k ->
    def temp = list[j]
    list[j] = list[k]
    list[k] = temp
}
```

A final observation to make is that closures must consist of only statements. This means that the local closure swap could not be replaced by a method definition.

H.5   RECURSIVE CLOSURES

Appendix G (Section G.1) introduced the recursive method, that is, a method that calls or invokes itself. This is made possible because the body of a method can reference itself. The ability to directly reference a closure in its definition is not supported in Groovy. However, when we recognize that a closure is an object of the class Closure, then the body of the closure can refer to itself with the this keyword. A consequence of this is that recursive closures are possible, as shown by Example 02, which reprograms factorial as a closure.

EXAMPLE 02
Recursive
factorial closure

```
def factorial = { n ->
    return (n == 0) ? 1 : n * this.call(n - 1)
}

println "Factorial(5): ${factorial(5)}"
```

The output is:

```
Factorial(5): 120
```

◆

Since the factorial closure cannot reference itself within the body of the closure, this means that the following is illegal in Groovy:

```
def factorial = { n ->
    return (n == 0) ? 1 : n * factorial(n - 1)
}
```

H.6 STATIC TYPING

Closures have been defined with dynamic typing for both the parameters and the return value. This feature renders closures more generic, as demonstrated in Example 03. Here, the closure times returns the result of multiplying its two parameters. Three calls are made to this closure with various actual parameter types. Since the * operator is applicable in all the given situations, everything is correct.

```
def times = {x, y ->
    return x * y
}

println "times(3, 4): ${times(3, 4)}"
println "times(3.1, 4.2): ${times(3.1, 4.2)}"
println "times('Hello', 4): ${times('Hello', 4)}"
```

EXAMPLE 03
Dynamically typed closures

◆

The return type and the types for the formal parameters of a closure can also be given statically. Such statically typed closures introduce an element of security since they cannot be called without actual parameters of the required type or subtype.

Example 04 repeats the previous example, but this time the closure times has its parameters statically defined. The third call will generate an error, since the actual parameters are of the incorrect types.

EXAMPLE 04
Statically typed
closure

```
def times = {Number x, Number y ->
    return x * y
}

println "times(3, 4): ${times(3, 4)}"
println "times(3.1, 4.2): ${times(3.1, 4.2)}"
//println "times('Hello', 4): ${times('Hello', 4)}"
```

◆

H.7   ACTUAL PARAMETER AGREEMENT

The actual parameters in a closure call must match exactly the number of formal parameters given in the definition. Otherwise, Groovy will report incorrect arguments. The final two closure calls in Example 05 report this error. The first of these has too few actual parameters. The second has too many parameters.

EXAMPLE 05
Missing closure

```
def clos = {a, b, c ->
    "clos(${a}, ${b}, ${c})"
}

clos(1, 2, 3)
//clos(1, 2)                    // missing closure
//clos(1, 2, 3, 4)             // missing closure
```

◆

H.8   CLOSURES, COLLECTIONS, AND RANGES

Lists, Maps, and Ranges include a number of methods that have a closure parameter, which makes it easy to iterate over the elements of the collection or range and perform a task. The more common of these methods are tabulated in Table H.1. The methods inject and reverseEach are applicable only to Lists and Ranges. Again, the asterisk symbols inform us that these are augmented GDK methods.

TABLE H.1 Iterator methods

Name	Signature/description
any *	`boolean any(Closure clos)` Iterate over every element of this collection, and check whether the predicate denoted by `clos` is valid for at least one element.
collect *	`List collect(Closure clos)` Iterate through this collection and transform each element into a new value using `clos` as the transformer, and then returning a `List` of transformed values.
collect *	`List collect(Collection collection, Closure clos)` Iterate through this collection and transform each element into a new value using `clos` as the transformer and then add it to the `collection`, returning the resulting collection.
each *	`void each(Closure clos)` Iterate through this collection and apply the closure `clos` to each element.
every *	`boolean every(Closure clos)` Iterate over every element of this collection, and check whether the predicate denoted by `clos` is valid for all elements.
find *	`Object find(Closure clos)` Find the first element in this collection which conforms to the predicate denoted by `clos`.
findAll *	`List findAll(Closure clos)` Find all the elements in this collection that match the predicate denoted by `clos`.
findIndexOf *	`int findIndexOf(Closure clos)` Iterate over every element of this collection and return the index of the first element that matches the condition specified by the closure `clos`.
inject *	`Object inject(Object value, Closure clos)` Iterate through this collection, and pass the initial value to the closure `clos` along with the first iterated element, then pass this result into the next iteration.
reverseEach *	`void reverseEach(Closure clos)` Iterate through this collection in the reverse order and apply the closure `clos` to each element.
sort *	`List sort(Closure clos)` Sort this collection, using the closure `clos` as comparator.

H.9 RETURN STATEMENT

We need to be aware of the semantics of the return statement when used within a closure body. For example, to determine whether an item is a member of a List, we would normally use method find. However, consider the two variations of isMember as shown in Example 06. The first version, isMemberA, uses a simple for loop to iterate across all the elements of the List. If a match is found, the method exits immediately, returning the true value. If the loop is exhausted and no match is found, then the method returns false. This implementation behaves correctly, as shown by the first two print statements.

```
def isMemberA(item, list) {
    def size = list.size()
    for(index in 0..<size) {
        if(list[index] == item)
            return true
    }
    return false
}

def isMemberB(item, list) {
    list.each { element ->
        //println "searching: ${element}"
        if(element == item)
            return true
    }
    return false
}

def numbers = [11, 12, 13, 14]
println "isMemberA(15, numbers): ${isMemberA(15, numbers)}"    // OK: false
println "isMemberA(13, numbers): ${isMemberA(13, numbers)}"    // OK: true

println "isMemberB(15, numbers): ${isMemberB(15, numbers)}"    // OK: false
println "isMemberB(13, numbers): ${isMemberB(13, numbers)}"    // ERROR: false
```

◆

We might consider being more Groovy-like and using the each iterator method with a closure to perform the searching. This implementation is given in the method isMemberB. However, as shown by the final two print statements, this version always returns false. The explanation for this lies in understanding how method each is implemented. As shown in the following text, an iterator is used to retrieve references to the objects in the list and to call the closure clos, passing each obj as actual parameter.

```
def each(list, clos) {
    def iter = list.iterator()
    while(iter.hasNext()) {
        def obj = iter.next()
        clos.call(obj)
    }
}
```

In our example, the actual closure contains the return statement. This makes a return from the closure `call` and the `while` loop continues with the next object in the `list`. We can see this effect if we uncomment the print statement in method `isMemberB`. We discover that every element is processed, the loop is completed, and the method `isMemberB` finishes by always returning `false`.

H.10   TESTING

It is always worthwhile conducting a few simple tests, even if they just confirm that our understanding of a particular aspect of Groovy is correct. The following `GroovyTestCase` is an example of these kinds of tests. Others can be easily added. Here, we confirm our understanding of closures and collections.

```
import groovy.util.*
import java.util.regex.*

class GroovyIteratorTests extends GroovyTestCase {

    void setUp() {
        numbers = [11, 12, 13, 14]
        staffTelephones = ['Ken' : 2745, 'John' : 2746, 'Sally' : 2742]
        century = 2000..2099
    }

        // method any
    void testAny() {
        assertTrue('One even value', numbers.any {element -> return (element % 2 == 0)})
        assertTrue('Ken is staff member', staffTelephones.any {entry -> return (entry.key == 'Ken')})
        assertTrue('This century all correct', century.any {element -> return
                                    (element >= 2000 && element < 2100)})
    }

    void testCollect() {
        assertTrue('Doubled numbers',
                [22, 24, 26, 28] == numbers.collect {element -> return 2 * element})
```

```
        assertTrue('Incremented telephone number',
                [2746, 2747, 2743].containsAll(staffTelephones.collect {entry ->
                        return ++ entry.value
        }))
        assertTrue('Next century',
                (2100..2199).containsAll(century.collect {element -> return 100 + element}))
    }

    void testEach() {
        def numbersResult = ""
        numbers.each {element -> numbersResult = numbersResult + "+" + element}
        assertTrue('Numbers +', Pattern.compile ('(\\+[0-9][0-9])*').matcher(numbersResult).find())

        def staffTelephonesResult = ""
        staffTelephones.each {entry ->
                staffTelephonesResult = staffTelephonesResult + "+" + entry.key
        }

        assertTrue('Names +',
                Pattern.compile ('(\\+[A-Z][a-z]*)*').matcher(staffTelephonesResult).find())

        def centuryResult = ""
        century.each {element -> centuryResult = centuryResult + "+" + element}
        assertTrue('Numbers +', Pattern.compile ('(\\+[0-9][0-9])*').matcher(centuryResult).find())
    }

    void testEvery() {
        assertTrue('Every number 11..14',
                numbers.every {element -> return (element >= 11 && element <= 14)})
        assertTrue('', staffTelephones.every {entry ->
                return [2745, 2746, 2742].contains(entry.value)})
        assertTrue('This century',
                century.every {element -> return (element >= 2000 && element < 2100)})
    }

    void testFind() {
        assertTrue('First is 11', 11 == numbers.find {element -> return element > 10})
        assertTrue('Ken at 2745',
                2745 == (staffTelephones.find {entry -> return (entry.key == 'Ken')}).value)
        assertTrue('Last year', 2099 == century.find {element -> return (element == 2099)})
    }

    void testFindAll() {
        assertTrue('Last two', [13, 14].containsAll (numbers.findAll {element ->
                return (element > 12)}))
        assertTrue('Ken at 2745',
                1 == (staffTelephones.findAll {entry -> return (entry.key == 'Ken')}).size())
```

```
        assertTrue('', 50 == (century.findAll {element -> return (element >= 2050)}).size())
    }

    void testFinIndexOf() {
        assertTrue('Position of 13', 2 == numbers.findIndexOf {element -> return (element > 12)})
        assertTrue('Map indexing',
                        staffTelephones.size() > staffTelephones.findIndexOf {entry -> return
                        (entry.key == 'Ken')})
        assertTrue('', 99 == century.findIndexOf {element -> return (element == 2099)})
    }

    void testInject() {
        assertTrue('Adding numbers',
                50 == numbers.inject(0) {previous, element -> return previous + element})
        assertTrue('All in century',
            century.inject(true) {previous, element ->
                return (previous && (2000 <= element && element <= 2099))
        })
    }

    void testReverseEach() {
        def numbersResult = ""
        numbers.reverseEach {element -> numbersResult = numbersResult + "+" + element}
        assertTrue('Numbers +', Pattern.compile ('(\\+[0-9][0-9])*').matcher(numbersResult).find())

        def centuryResult = ""
        century.reverseEach {element -> centuryResult = centuryResult + "+" + element}
        assertTrue('Numbers +', Pattern.compile ('(\\+[0-9][0-9])*').matcher(centuryResult).find())
    }

// ------properties ----------------

    def numbers
    def staffTelephones
    def century
}
```

MORE ON CLASSES

This appendix considers a number of aspects of classes that we chose to defer when first introducing them in Chapter 12. We consider the visibility of properties and their getter and setter methods and we demonstrate how certain method names are reserved to act as method definitions for the standard operators. We also discuss the support offered by Groovy for navigating through a network of objects.

I.1 PROPERTIES AND VISIBILITY

We have seen how properties can significantly reduce the size of code when defining a class. Groovy seeks to unify the notion of instance fields and methods through the use of properties. Further, we also know that (public) properties in a class give rise to public getters and setters automatically generated for the class. They, in turn, provide the necessary support whereby an instance of a class can be created using named parameters without the need to include a parameterized constructor in the class.

All of these features can be seen when we revisit the Account class first introduced in Chapter 12. It is repeated in Example 01. Here, we create an instance, change its state, and access its state to reveal its values. All this is provided by the auto-generated methods.

```
class Account {
```

EXAMPLE 01
Account class

```
    def credit(amount) {
        balance += amount
    }

    def debit(amount) {          // only if there are sufficient funds
        if(balance >= amount)
            balance -= amount
    }

// -----properties -----------------

    def number               // account number
    def balance              // current balance
}

        // Create an instance
def acc = new Account(number : 'ABC123', balance : 1200)

        // Change state with the automatic setters
acc.number = 'DEF456'
acc.balance = 1500

        // Now use the automatic getters
println "Account: ${acc.number}; balance: ${acc.balance}"
```

Running this script produces the output:

```
Account: DEF456; balance: 1500
```

and demonstrates that the Account object is correctly initialized.

◆

The instance fields of a class can be tagged as public, protected, or private. As its name suggests, a public instance field is accessible to client code. Equally, a private instance field can only be referenced in the class in which it is defined. A protected instance field is accessible to the class in which it is defined and to any subclass; otherwise, it is private to client code.

These *visibility qualifiers* are used to introduce some access control into our code. Making instance fields public exposes them to direct change from client code. When selecting the visibility of the features of a class, we generally aim to conceal the implementation details and only publicize features that support the abstraction represented by the class. Generally, this means that instance fields are given private or protected visibility and operations are public if they characterize objects of the class.

If the instance fields of the Account class were given protected access, so too is the setter method that is automatically generated. This means that the last illustration now no longer executes as previously shown.

EXAMPLE 02
Protected
properties

```
class Account {

    // ...

    def display() {
        println "Account number: ${number} balance: ${balance}"
    }

// ------properties -------------------

    protected number                    // account number
    protected balance                   // current balance
}

        // Create an instance
        // Since the setters are protected then the object instance
        // is not correctly initialized
def acc = new Account(number : 'ABC123', balance : 1200)
acc.display()

        // Change things with the automatic setters
//acc.number = 'DEF456'      // ERROR: Cannot access protected member
//acc.balance = 1500         // ERROR: Cannot access protected member
```

If we execute the code, the output produced is:

```
Account number: null balance: null
```

◆

We have created an Account object, but because the getters and setters for the two properties are protected, the object is not correctly initialized. By default, uninitialized properties are given the null value. Hence, the output produced.

Note how in the listing the instance fields are no longer accessible. If we uncomment the two statements to change the number and balance of the account, the Groovy environment reports the error message Cannot access protected member.

Private or protected instance fields can be supported by providing explicit getter and setter methods. If only a (public) getter is specified, then effectively the property is read-only. If only a setter is defined, the property is said to be write-only. Together, we get the services described by Example 01.

In Example 03, we show two `private` instance fields. The `balance` instance field has been provided with a getter method that can be used to provide read-only access to it. However, as the code shows, the use of the accessor still produces a `null` value. This is not a consequence of the getter but the absence of public setters that work jointly with the default constructor when the object is created. We see this when running the script:

```
Account balance: null
```

EXAMPLE 03
Private properties

```
class Account {

    def getBalance() {
        return balance
    }

    // ...

// ------properties ------------------

    private number                       // account number
    private balance                      // current balance
}

        // Create an instance
        // Since the setters are protected then the object instance
        // is not correctly initialized
def acc = new Account(number : 'ABC123', balance : 1200)

        // However, the balance property is read-only through the public getter
        // But this produces the output:
        // Account balance: null
println "Account balance: ${acc.getBalance()}"
println "Account balance: ${acc.balance}"
```

◆

A resolution can be provided in one of two ways. First, we can include a parameterized constructor for the Account class. This will properly initialize the private instance fields and the accessor will extract the correct value. This solution is shown in Example 04.

EXAMPLE 04
Parameterized
constructor

```
class Account {

        def Account(number, balance) {
            this.number = number
            this.balance = balance
        }

        def getBalance() {
            return balance
        }

        // ...

// ------properties ----------------

        private number                              // account number
        private balance                             // current balance
}
        // Create an instance
def acc = new Account('ABC123', 1200)

        // However, the balance property is read-only through the following
println "Account balance: ${acc.balance}"
```

Now, the output is:

```
Account balance: 1200
```

Example 05 shows an alternative solution. Here, we provide two explicit setters. This program delivers the same output as that in Example 04.

EXAMPLE 05
Public setter
methods

```
class Account {

        def getBalance() {
            return balance
        }

        def setNumber(number) {
            this.number = number
        }

        def setBalance(balance) {
            this.balance = balance
        }
```

```
        // ...

    // ------properties --------------------

        private number              // account number
        private balance             // current balance
}

        // Create an instance
def acc = new Account(number : 'ABC123', balance : 1200)

        // However, the balance property is read-only through the public getter
println "Account balance: ${acc.balance}"
```

◆

I.2   OBJECT NAVIGATION

Unifying properties with instance fields and methods offers an additional feature. Object-oriented applications are characterized by a network of interacting objects. The object instances form relationships, and method execution propagates through the system of objects. The relations established between objects give rise to a graph-like structure. This structure usually has to be traversed to find the required objects and to invoke the required methods.

A graph of objects can be traversed with a syntactic expression similar to XPath (see http://www.w3.org/TR/xpath). The dot-notation is used to express this traversal. As an example, consider a Bank organized as a set of Customers, each having a number of Accounts (as shown in Figure I.1). We might, for example, wish to produce a report on all the Accounts belonging to a particular Customer. Clearly, we need to reference all the Account objects that are associated with the particular Customer that is registered with the Bank. The code to achieve this is:

```
    customers[customerNumber].accounts.each { number, account -> println " ${account}" }
```

A danger of using this form of navigation is that we may experience a NullPointerException when attempting to traverse through a null value. To avoid this, safe navigation is provided by the ?. operator. The preceding may then be written as:

```
    customers[customerNumber]?.accounts.each { number, account -> println " ${account}" }
```

FIGURE I.1   Bank model.

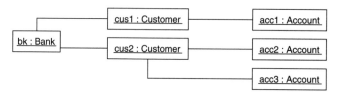

FIGURE I.2   Object diagram.

The customerNumber is used to index the Map of Customer objects and obtain the required Customer. The property accounts for this Customer object references all the Accounts for this Customer. The method each provides iteration across each Account object, and the closure is the action to perform a print of each.

An *object diagram* can prove a useful analysis in advance of developing the class diagram. An object diagram shows the network of objects at some point in the execution of the system. Optionally, it can show possible state information for individual objects. Figure I.2 is one such object diagram. Here, we show one Bank object, two Customer objects, and three Account objects. The diagram also reveals that the first Customer has one Account while the second Customer has opened two Accounts.

Example 06 presents the necessary detail. Notice how object navigation is used in the three display methods.

EXAMPLE 06
Object navigation

```
class Account {

    // ...

    String toString() {
        return "Account: ${number} ${balance}"
    }

    // ------properties ----------------

        defnumber                    // account number
        defbalance                   // current balance
}
```

```
class Customer {

    def openAccount(number, balance) {
        def acc = new Account(number : number, balance : balance)
        accounts[number] = acc
    }

    String toString() {
        return "Customer: ${number} ${name}"
    }

// ------properties -------------------

    def number                                 // account number
    def name                                   // current balance
    def accounts = [ : ]
}

class Bank {
    def registerCustomer(cust) {
        customers[cust.number] = cust
    }

    String toString() {
        return "Bank: ${name}"
    }

// -------properties ----------------

    def name                                   // current balance
    def customers = [ : ]
}

def displayAllAccounts(bank) {
    println "Bank: ${bank.name} (all accounts)"
    println '============================'

    bank?.customers.each { customerNumber, customer ->
        println customer
        customer?.accounts.each { accountNumber, account -> println " ${account}" }
    }
    println()
}

def displayAllAccountsForCustomer(bank, customerNumber) {
    println "Bank: ${bank.name} (customer accounts)"
    println '================================'
```

```
            def customer = bank?.customers[customerNumber]
            println customer
            customer?.accounts.each { number, account -> println " ${account}" }
            println()
    }
    def displayAccountForCustomer(bank, customerNumber, accountNumber) {
            println "Bank: ${bank.name} (customer account)"
            println '================================='

            def customer = bank?.customers[customerNumber]
            def account = customer?.accounts[accountNumber]
            println " ${account}"
            println()
    }

            // create a Bank...
    def bk = new Bank(name : 'Barclay')

            // ...and some customers with accounts
    def cust1 = new Customer(number : 111, name : 'Savage')
    cust1.openAccount(1111, 1200)
    cust1.openAccount(1112, 400)
    cust1.openAccount(1113, 800)

    def cust2 = new Customer(number : 222, name : 'Kennedy')
    cust2.openAccount(2221, 1000)
    cust2.openAccount(2222, 1400)

            // now register customers with bank
    bk.registerCustomer(cust1)
    bk.registerCustomer(cust2)

            // print some reports
    displayAllAccounts(bk)
    displayAllAccountsForCustomer(bk, 111)
    displayAccountForCustomer(bk, 222, 2222)
```

When we execute this example, we get the output:

```
        Bank: Barclay (all accounts)
        ============================
        Customer: 111 Savage
            Account: 1111 1200
            Account: 1112 400
            Account: 1113 800
        Customer: 222 Kennedy
            Account: 2221 1000
            Account: 2222 1400
```

```
Bank: Barclay (customer accounts)
=================================
Customer: 111 Savage
     Account: 1111 1200
     Account: 1112 400
     Account: 1113 800

Bank: Barclay (customer account)
=================================
     Account: 2222 1400
```

◆

I.3   STATIC MEMBERS

Instantiating and initializing an object should be a familiar process. So, too, is the notion of an object's having a set of properties; their values define the object's state. Another possibility is for properties to be class data, and to act as a value shared by all object instances. Such a *class member* is declared as static and is accessed in conjunction with the class name. Example 07 has the (public and final) static member ORIGIN defined in the Point class. The final keyword is used to specify that the value of ORIGIN cannot be changed within the program.

```
class Point {

    def move(deltaX, deltaY) {
        x += deltaX
        y += deltaY
    }

// ------properties ----------------

    def x
    def y

    public final static ORIGIN = new Point(x : 0.0, y : 0.0)
}

def p = new Point(x : 2.0, y : 3.0)
p.move(1.0, 1.0)
println "p: ${p.x}, ${p.y}"

println "Origin: ${Point.ORIGIN.x}, ${Point.ORIGIN.y}"
```

EXAMPLE 07
Static data member

◆

Observe how the ORIGIN member is referenced in the final print statement. It has to be qualified with the name of the class in which it is defined.

The static qualifier can also be associated with class methods. Again, such methods do not belong to a particular object instance. Their behavior is fully described by their input parameters and does not involve state information. An example of this is the mathematical methods, such as sqrt, defined in the JDK Math class:

```
public class Math {

    public static double sqrt(double x) { ... }
    // ... others
}
```

Example 08 illustrates using this method in the definition of the method getLength in class LineSegment. Again, the class name qualifies the name of the method.

EXAMPLE 08
static methods

```
class Point {
    // ...

}

class LineSegment {

    def move(deltaX, deltaY) {
        start.move(deltaX, deltaY)
        end.move(deltaX, deltaY)
    }

    def getLength() {
        def xDiff = start.x - end.x
        def yDiff = start.y - end.y
        return Math.sqrt(xDiff * xDiff + yDiff * yDiff)
    }

    // -------properties ------------------

    def start
    def end
}
def p = new Point(x : 3.0, y : 4.0)
def q = new Point(x : 4.0, y : 5.0)

def line = new LineSegment(start : p, end : q)
println "Line length: ${line.getLength()}"
```

◆

I.4 OPERATOR OVERLOADING

Chapter 2 revealed that everything in Groovy is an object. For example, the integer literal 123 is actually an instance of the class Integer. Further, we saw that when used in an expression such as 123 + 456, this was actually a syntactic sweetener so that we can use conventional algebraic notation. In fact, this expression is a convenience for the method call 123.plus(456). The first operand is the recipient while the second operand is the parameter passed to the method.

Groovy supports *operator overloading* for a predefined set of operators. Each operator is mapped to a particular method name. As has been noted, the + operator is mapped to the method named plus. By implementing these methods in our own classes, we can overload the corresponding operators to act with objects of our classes.

We demonstrate this with the class Vector (see Example 09) used to represent a one-dimensional array of numeric values. Method plus implements vector addition and method multiply implements vector multiplication, as described by:

[a1, a2, a3, ...] + [b1, b2, b3, ...] = [a1 + b1, a2 + b2, a3 + b3, ...]
[a1, a2, a3, ...] * [b1, b2, b3, ...] = a1 * b1 + a2 * b2 + a3 * b3 + ...

where [...] represents a Vector object.

EXAMPLE 09
Operator overloading

```
class Vector {
    def plus(vec) {
        def res = []
        def size = this.values.size()
        def vecSize = vec.values.size()
        if(size == vecSize) {
            for(index in 0..<size) {
                res << (values[index] + vec.values[index])
            }
        }

        return res
    }

    def multiply(vec) {
        def prod = 0.0
        def size = this.values.size()
        def vecSize = vec.values.size()
        if(size == vecSize) {
            for(index in 0..<size) {
                prod += values[index] * vec.values[index]
            }
        }
    }
```

```
                  return prod
        }

    // ------properties ------------------

        def values = []
    }

    def vec1 = new Vector(values : [1.0, 2.0, 3.0, 4.0, 5.0])
    def vec2 = new Vector(values : [6.0, 7.0, 8.0, 9.0, 10.0])

    println "plus: ${vec1 + vec2}"
    println "multiply: ${vec1 * vec2}"
```

◆

Note the use of the arithmetic operators applied to Vector objects in the final print statements. When we run this script, the output is:

```
plus: [7.0, 9.0, 11.0, 13.0, 15.0]
multiply: 130.00
```

The operators that may be overloaded are tabulated in Table I.1.

TABLE I.1   Overloaded Operators

Operator	Method	Description
a + b	a.plus(b)	Addition
a − b	a.minus(b)	Subtraction
a * b	a.multiply(b)	Multiplication
a / b	a.divide(b)	Division
a++ ++a	a.increment(b)	Pre- and post-increment
a−− −−a	a.decrement(b)	Pre- and post-decrement
a === b	a == b	Equality, i.e., same object
a <=> b	a.compareTo(b)	Comparison: −1 if a < b; 0 if a == b; +1 if a >b
a == b	a.equals(b)	Equality
a != b	! a.equals(b)	Inequality
a < b	a.compareTo(b) < 0	Less than
a <= b	a.compareTo(b) <= 0	Less than or equal
a > b	a.compareTo(b) > 0	Greater than
a >= b	a.compareTo(b) >= 0	Greater than or equal
a[b]	a.get(b)	Indexed accessor
a[b] = c	a.put(b, c)	Indexed assignment

I.5   THE INVOKEMETHOD

Appendix B describes how Groovy scripts are implemented as a class. For example, the simple script `println 'hello world'` becomes this class (in the file `Hello.java`):

```
public class Hello extends Script {

    public static void main(String[] args) {
        Hello h = new Hello();
        h.run(args);
    }

    public void run(String[] args) {
        this.println('hello, world');
    }
}
```

In fact, when a method is called as in:

```
this.println('hello, world')
```

the actual invocation is implemented with the method `invokeMethod` inherited from the `Script` class. Hence, we actually have:

```
this.invokeMethod('println', ['hello, world'] as Object[])
```

The method to be called is given as a `String` argument, and the method parameters are provided by an `Object[]`. Example 10 illustrates with an `Account` object which, after initialization, is credited with 200 and debited with 900. This time, the methods `credit` and `debit` are invoked through the inherited `invokeMethod`.

```
class Account {

    // ...

    String toString() {
        return "Account: ${number} with balance: ${balance}"
    }
```

EXAMPLE 10
Method invocation

```
// ------properties ------------------

    def number
    def balance

}

def acc = new Account(number : 'AAA111', balance : 1200)

acc.invokeMethod('credit', [200] as Object[])
acc.invokeMethod('debit', [900] as Object[])

println "acc: ${acc}"
```

◆

If we redefine the invokeMethod in our Account class, we can monitor how methods called on an Account object ultimately execute invokeMethod. In Example 11, we create an instance of the Account class, then invoke pseudomethods credit and debit.

EXAMPLE 11
Redefined
invokeMethod

```
class Account {

    public Object invokeMethod(String name, Object params) {
        println "invokeMethod(${name}, ...)"
        return null
    }

    String toString() {
        return "Account: ${number} with balance: ${balance}"
    }

    // ------properties --------------------

    def number
    def balance

}

def acc = new Account(number : 'AAA111', balance : 1200)

acc.credit(200)
acc.debit(900)

println "acc: ${acc}"
```

When we run this code, the output is:

```
invokeMethod(credit, ...)
invokeMethod(debit, ...)
acc: Account: AAA111 with balance: 1200
```

where we see how the credit and debit method calls are handled.

◆

This scheme can be used as the basis for the *meta-object protocol* (see http://www-128.ibm.com/developerworks/java/library/j-pg09205/ and http://www2.parc.com/csl/groups/sda/projects/mops/default.html). This protocol enables an object to make specific choices that affect its own state or behavior when methods are passed to it at runtime. An illustration of this is shown in the Ant builder section of Appendix K.

I.6   EXERCISES

1. Repeat the seven exercises in Chapter 12 (Section 12.3), this time giving the properties private visibility.

2. Construct a Matrix class to represent a two-dimensional array of numeric values. Include methods plus and multiply to overload the arithmetic operators for objects of this class. The definitions are:

```
[[a00, a01, a02, ...], + [[b00, b01, b02, ...], = [[a00 + b00, a01 + b01, ...],
[a10, a11, a12, ...],      [b10, b11, b12, ...],     [a10 + b10, a11 + b11,...],
...                        ...                       ...
]                          ]                         ]
```

and:

```
[[a00, a01, a02, ...], * [[b00, b01, b02, ...], = [[a00 * b00 + a01 + b10 + ..., a00 * b01 + a01 * b11 + ...],
[a10, a11, a12, ...], [b10, b11, b12, ...], [a10 * b00 + a11 * b10+ ..., a10 * b01 + a10 * b11 + ...],
...                   ...                   ...
]                     ]                     ]
```

ADVANCED CLOSURES

Chapter 9 introduced closures as parametric code blocks that can be referenced and passed as method parameters. An important example of the latter was closures given as parameters to methods that iterated through collections. We saw how methods such as each and findAll can be used to describe some processing to be performed on all the elements of a collection.

In this appendix, we further explore closures by observing that they can also be returned from methods or from other closures. Closures as return values from other closures provide a very powerful framework that can be applied to a variety of problems. For example, we may wish to define the constraints that apply to individual objects, the relationships that must exist between objects or the rules that might apply to certain categories of objects. This is readily achieved with closures.

Consider that an Account has a number, balance, and overdraft limit as properties. We might insist that the overdraft limit be a positive value, for example, an overdraft of 500 pounds. Further, this would determine that the balance could be any value that is greater or equal to the negative value −500 pounds, that is, a balance that is permitted to be a restricted negative value. We will see how closures can be used to express these constraints.

Equally, consider a supermarket that uses special offers to attract new customers and maintain its existing customer base. In one week, there might be a three-for-two offer on breakfast cereals, and in another week, the promotion might be changed to buy-one-get-one-free on cosmetics. In such an ever-changing environment, we need a means of defining these "business rules" and a means to flexibly combine them. We show how closures can provide this flexibility.

The ideas presented here contribute to the multiparadigm approach that is a feature of Groovy. In this appendix, we demonstrate how ideas from functional programming (Thompson, 1999) can be both realized and exploited in Groovy. The functional programming paradigm exploits polymorphism, composition, and computation patterns through higher-order functions. We shall see how we may apply these ideas successfully in Groovy.

J.1   SIMPLE CLOSURES

We have previously described a closure as a code block. The closure can be parameterized to make it more generally useful, it can be referenced, it can be passed as a method parameter, and it can be invoked with the `call` message. Example 01 includes a simple parameterized closure entitled `multiply` that finds the product of two numeric parameters.

```
def multiply = { x, y -> return x * y }

println "multiply(3, 4): ${multiply.call(3, 4)}"        // explicit call
println "multiply(3.4, 5.6): ${multiply(3.4, 5.6)}"     // implicit call
```

EXAMPLE 01
Simple closure

Executing this program demonstrates the execution of the closures and produces the output:

```
        multiply(3, 4): 12
        multiply(3.4, 5.6): 19.04
```

◆

Chapter 9 noted how state may be referenced by closures. In Example 02, we have a `multiplier` variable that is in scope when the `multiply` closure is defined. The closure computes the product of its single parameter and the `multiplier`.

EXAMPLE 02
Scoping and closures

```
def multiplier = 2
def multiply = { x -> return x * multiplier }         // second operand from enclosing scope

println "multiply(3): ${multiply.call(3)}"
println "multiply(5.6): ${multiply(5.6)}"

        // Now do it again but with a different multiplier value
multiplier = 3
```

```
println "multiply(3): ${multiply.call(3)}"
println "multiply(5.6): ${multiply(5.6)}"
```

When we run this code, we get:

```
multiply(3): 6
multiply(5.6): 11.2
multiply(3): 9
multiply(5.6): 16.8
```

This time, we see how variables in scope at the point of definition of a closure can be accessed from within the closure code.

The next illustration demonstrates how a closure can return another closure as its value. In Example 03, the closure arithmetic selects from one of four closures as its return value, based on the String parameter. The program shows how the returned closure can then be invoked as normal.

EXAMPLE 03
Closure return
value

```
          // Various closures
def add = { x, y -> return x + y }
def subtract = { x, y -> return x - y }
def multiply = { x, y -> return x * y }
def divide = { x, y -> return x / y }

          // Select a closure
def arithmetic = { arith ->
    switch(arith) {
        case 'ADD':             return add
        case 'SUBTRACT':        return subtract
        case 'MULTIPLY':        return multiply
        case 'DIVIDE':          return divide
        default:                return add
    }
}

          // Get one...
def addOperation = arithmetic('ADD')
def mulOperation = arithmetic('MULTIPLY')

          // ...and use it
println "addOperation(3, 4): ${addOperation(3, 4)}"
println "mulOperation(3, 4): ${mulOperation(3, 4)}"
```

```
                  // Get one and use it
println "arithmetic('MULTIPLY')(3, 4): ${arithmetic.call('MULTIPLY').call(3, 4)}"
```

The output from this program is given in the following text. It demonstrates that the arithmetic closure returns a closure as its value, which can then be called like any other closure.

```
        addOperation(3, 4): 7
        mulOperation(3, 4): 12
        arithmetic('MULTIPLY')(3, 4): 12
```

◆

J.2   PARTIAL APPLICATION

In Example 02, the multiply closure computes the product of its single parameter and the enclosing variable multiplier. If we now make the multiplier a parameter to a closure that returns the multiply closure pre-prepared to multiply its own parameter with that multiplier, then we have an example of a *partial application* of a closure. This is an example of a general phenomenon, namely, a closure with two parameters (see multiply in Example 04) that can be recast and partially applied to one parameter. This gives a powerful way of forming and, as we shall see later, combining closures. The code is shown as Example 04.

```
        def multiply = { x, y -> return x * y }

                // Now some partial applications...
                // ...both are closures
        def triple = multiply.curry(3)
        def quadruple = multiply.curry(4)

                // Both are partial applications of multiply
        println "triple(4): ${triple(4)}"
        println "quadruple(5): ${quadruple(5)}"
```

EXAMPLE 04
Partial
application

Running the program produces the output:

```
        triple(4): 12
        quadruple(5): 20
```

◆

Observe how the expression `multiply.curry(3)` denotes a closure that multiplies its single parameter by 3. The resulting closure can then be invoked with a single parameter as in `triple(4)`. This partial application of a closure is called *currying*, after the mathematician Haskell Curry. Effectively, the closure `triple` has the definition:

```
def triple = { y -> return 3 * y }
```

with the first parameter removed and all its occurrences replaced with the value 3.

Arithmetic addition and multiplication are described as *commutative* operations. This means that A + B = B + A and A * B = B * A. This is not the case, however, with subtraction and division. We can achieve something similar to the `multiply` closure if we recognize that (in the case of subtraction) we might be setting the value to be subtracted or the value from which to subtract. This is shown in Example 05.

<table>
<tr><td>

EXAMPLE 05

Handling
commutativity

</td><td>

```
def rSubtract = { y, x -> return x - y }
def lSubtract = { x, y -> return x - y }

def subtract10 = rSubtract.curry(10)
def subtractFrom20 = lSubtract.curry(20)

println "subtract10(22): ${subtract10(22)}"
println "subtractFrom20(14): ${subtractFrom20(14)}"
```

</td></tr>
</table>

The output from this program is:

```
subtract10(22): 12
subtractFrom20(14): 6
```

◆

One important observation about currying closures is that the number of actual parameters provided to the curry method must not exceed the actual number of parameters required by the closure. If the closure has, say, three parameters, then the curry method can be called with none, one, two, or three actual parameters.

One of the advantages of partial application of closures will be demonstrated in the next section. Partial application can be considered as a form of simplification whereby a complex task is partitioned into separate subtasks. In the partial application of the `multiply` closure (see Example 04), instead of defining the multiplication of two values, we have separated it so that we can define any number of multiplying closures, such as `triple` or `quadruple`. With these simpler tasks, we can now consider how they might be combined in useful ways.

J.3 COMPOSITION

One way to structure a program is to perform a number of tasks in sequence. Normally, each part is designed and implemented separately. Here, we might consider that a closure represents some simple task to be performed. Combining these using the notion of *composition* can produce complex tasks that are easy to construct. Further, by recombination in different ways, we can readily create new tasks as might be required by the supermarket illustration discussed in the introduction to this appendix.

The `composition` closure is demonstrated in Example 06. Its two parameters f and g represent closures and will apply closure g to x, as in g(x), and then apply the closure f to the result as in f(g(x)).

```
        // Composition closure
def composition = { f, g, x -> return f(g(x)) }

        // Multiply closure and two instances
def multiply = { x, y -> return x * y }

def triple = multiply.curry(3)
def quadruple = multiply.curry(4)

        // Construct a new closure by combining two others
def twelveTimes = composition.curry(triple, quadruple)

println "twelveTimes(12): ${twelveTimes(12)}"
```

EXAMPLE 06
Closure
composition

The output is:

```
twelveTimes(12): 144
```

◆

The closure `triple` is defined as one that takes a single parameter and multiplies it by 3. The closure `quadruple` is defined as one that takes a single parameter and multiplies it by 4. The closure `twelveTimes` is defined as the `composition` of the closure `triple` and the closure `quadruple`. Effectively, this closure `twelveTimes` multiplies its parameter by 4 (quadruples it), and then multiplies the result by 3 (triples it) as defined by the `composition` closure.

This same composition can be used anywhere, including applying it to the elements of a collection. Example 07 shows this in action.

EXAMPLE 07
Compositions and collections

```
          // Composition closure
def composition = {f, g, x -> return f(g(x))}

          // Multiply closure and two instances
def multiply = {x, y -> return x * y}

def triple = multiply.curry(3)
def quadruple = multiply.curry(4)

          // Construct a new closure by combining two others
def twelveTimes = composition.curry(triple, quadruple)

def table = [1, 2, 3, 4].collect {element -> return twelveTimes(element)}

println "table: ${table}"
```

The code applies the twelveTimes closure to each element in the list [1, 2, 3, 4], producing a new list, as shown by the output:

```
table: [12, 24, 36, 48]
```

◆

J.4   PATTERNS OF COMPUTATION

In this section, we explore a mechanism by which we can express closures that embody a *pattern of computation*. One example of this is where we transform every element of a List in some way. Of course, Groovy already has the collect method for Lists and we use this to simplify implementing our pattern. This transformation is usually given the name map. Its behavior is described by Figure J.1. On the left we show some function (closure) f, which, when applied to a single argument (represented by the circle), delivers a value (the square). Now, if we have a List of values of type circle, map f list delivers a List of values of type square produced by applying f to the originals.

In Example 08, we present the map closure. The partial application of map will return a closure that will operate on a single list. Currying the map closure is performed with a closure that is to be applied to each element of a list.

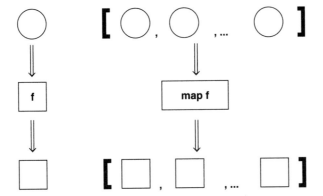

FIGURE J.1   Application of map.

EXAMPLE 08

Mapping

```
           // map closure
def map = {clos, list -> return list.collect(clos)}

           // composition closure
def composition = {f, g, x -> return f(g(x))}

           // Multiply closure and two instances
def multiply = {x, y -> return x * y}

def triple = multiply.curry(3)
def quadruple = multiply.curry(4)

           // closure to triple the elements in a list
def tripleAll = map.curry(triple)

def table = tripleAll([1, 2, 3, 4])

println "table: ${table}"
```

First, observe the map closure. It expects two parameters, namely, the closure and the list of elements to which the closure is to be applied. The closure `tripleAll` is defined to map the `triple` closure to all the elements of a list. This is shown by the program output:

```
table: [3, 6, 9, 12]
```

◆

A useful equivalence involving maps is that if we map one closure (f, say) across a list x and then map the closure g across the result, the overall effect is the same as mapping the composition of g and f to the list. Example 09 demonstrates this equivalence.

EXAMPLE 09
Equivalents

```
            // map closure
def map = { clos, list -> return list.collect(clos) }

            // composition closure
def composition = { f, g, x -> return f(g(x)) }

            // Multiply closure and two instances
def multiply = { x, y -> return x * y }

def triple = multiply.curry(3)
def quadruple = multiply.curry(4)

            // composition of two maps...
def composeMapMap = composition.curry(map.curry(triple), map.curry(quadruple))

def tableComposeMapMap = composeMapMap([1, 2, 3, 4])

println "tableComposeMapMap: ${tableComposeMapMap}"

            // ...equivalent to the map of a composition
def mapCompose = map.curry(composition.curry(triple, quadruple))

def tableMapCompose = mapCompose([1, 2, 3, 4])

println "tableMapCompose: ${tableMapCompose}"
```

The output from this program reveals that our assertion is true:

```
tableComposeMapMap: [12, 24, 36, 48]
tableMapCompose: [12, 24, 36, 48]
```

◆

J.5   BUSINESS RULES

Consider the problem of computing the net price of a specific Book item, taking into account the shop discount and any governmental taxes, such as value added tax (or VAT). VAT is a tax on consumer expenditure. It is collected on business transactions, such as the supply of goods or services. If we were to include this logic as part of the Book class, we are likely to hard-wire our solution. A bookshop may change the value of its discount or apply it to only a selection of its stock. Equally, the government may change the level of the taxation.

The source code for the closure-based approach to solving this problem is presented in Example 10.

```
        // Book class and instance
class Book {

    def name     // properties
    def author
    def price
    def category
}

def bk = new Book(name : 'Groovy', author : 'KenB', price : 25, category : 'CompSci')

        // constants
def discountRate = 0.1
def taxRate = 0.17

        // basic closures
def rMultiply = { y, x -> return x * y }
def lMultiply = { x, y -> return x * y }

def composition = { f, g, x -> return f(g(x)) }

        // book closures
def calcDiscountedPrice = rMultiply.curry(1 -discountRate)

def calcTax = rMultiply.curry(1 + taxRate)

def calcNetPrice = composition.curry(calcTax, calcDiscountedPrice)

        // now calculate net price
def netPrice = calcNetPrice(bk.price)

println "netPrice: ${netPrice}"
```

EXAMPLE 10
Net price

The closure rMultiply is a partial application candidate that adapts the binary multiplication to be a unary closure by using a constant second operand. The two book closures calcDiscountedPrice and calcTax are instances of the rMultiply closure with set values for the multiplier value. The closure calcNetPrice is the algorithm to compute the net price by first calculating the discounted price and then adding the sales tax. Finally, we apply `calcNetPrice` to the price of our book. The output is:

```
netPrice: 26.325
```

Example 11 is concerned with ensuring that the maximum discount our bookshop can give is capped by an upper limit. Therefore, we must compare the discount amount obtained with the capped value and take the minimum of the two in computing the discounted price. This is given in Example 11.

EXAMPLE 11
Capped discount

```
        // Book class and instance
class Book {

    def name              // properties
    def author
    def price
    def category
}

def bk = new Book(name : 'Groovy', author : 'KenB', price : 35, category : 'CompSci')

        // constants
def discountRate = 0.1
def taxRate = 0.17
def maxDiscount = 3

        // basic closures
def rMultiply = { y, x -> return x * y }
def lMultiply = { x, y -> return x * y }

def subtract = { x, y -> return x - y }
def rSubtract = { y, x -> return x - y }
def lSubtract = { x, y -> return x - y }

        // minimum closure
def min = { x, y -> return (x < y) ? x : y }

        // identity closure
def id = { x -> return x }
```

```
         // composition closures
def composition = { f, g, x -> return f(g(x)) }

         // binary composition
def bComposition = { h, f, g, x -> return h(f(x), g(x)) }

         // book closures
def calcDiscount = rMultiply.curry(discountRate)

def calcActualDiscount = bComposition.curry(min, calcDiscount, id)

def calcDiscountedPrice = bComposition.curry(subtract, id, calcActualDiscount)

def calcTax = rMultiply.curry(1 + taxRate)

def calcNetPrice = composition.curry(calcTax, calcDiscountedPrice)

         // now calculate net price
println "bk.price: ${bk.price}"

def netPrice = calcNetPrice(bk.price)
println "netPrice: ${netPrice}"
```

First, observe the identity closure, id. It simply returns with the value of its single parameter. The binary closure min determines the least of its two parameters. The bComposition (binary composition) closure applies a binary closure to the values produced by two unary closures applied to the same value. The partial closure calcDiscount is a unary closure that multiplies the book price with the discount rate. The calcActualDiscount closure compares the discounted price with the capped limit. Finally, the closure calcDiscountedPrice determines the actual discounted price.

Both calcActualDiscount and calcDiscountedPrice are partial applications of the bComposition closure. In the first example, the program finds the minimum and, in the second example, it finds the difference. The bComposition closure is defined as

```
    bComposition = {h, f, g, x -> return h(f(x), g(x))}
```

Here, f and g are the unary closures while h is the binary closure. Note how both f and g are applied to the same parameter x. The actual value for this will be the book price. Here is the program output:

```
    bk.price: 35
    netPrice: 36.855
```

◆

J.6 PACKAGING

These last examples have developed a range of useful closures that can be combined flexibly. It would be sensible, therefore, to package them into a class that can then be imported into an application. A first draft for this class might be:

```
package fp
/**
 * The Functor class contains a series of static closures that
 * support functional programming constructs.
 */

abstract class Functor {

                        // arithmetic (binary, left commute, and right commute)
    public static Closure bAdd      = {x, y -> return x + y}
    public static Closure rAdd      = {y, x -> return x + y}
    public static Closure lAdd      = {x, y -> return x + y}

    public static Closure bSubtract = {x, y -> return x - y}
    public static Closure rSubtract = {y, x -> return x - y}
    public static Closure lSubtract = {x, y -> return x - y}

    public static Closure bMultiply = {x, y -> return x * y}
    public static Closure rMultiply = {y, x -> return x * y}
    public static Closure lMultiply = {x, y -> return x * y}

    public static Closure bDivide= {x, y -> return x / y}
    public static Closure rDivide= {y, x -> return x / y}
    public static Closure lDivide= {x, y -> return x / y}

    public static Closure bModulus  = {x, y -> return x % y}
    public static Closure rModulus  = {y, x -> return x % y}
    public static Closure lModulus  = {x, y -> return x % y}

                        // min/max
    public static Closure bMin      = {x, y -> return (x < y) ? x : y }
    public static Closure bMax      = {x, y -> return (x < y) ? y : x }

                        // identity
    public static Closure id        = {x -> return x}

    public static Closure konst     = {x, y -> return y}

                        // composition
    public static Closure composition = {f, g, x -> return f(g(x))}
```

```
    public static Closure bComposition  = {h, f, g, x -> return h(f(x), g(x))}

                    // lists
    public static Closure head          = {list -> return (list.size() == 0) ? null : list[0]}

    public static Closure tail          = {list ->
                                              return (list.size() ==0) ? [] : list[1..<list.size()]
                                          }
    public static Closure cons          = {item, list ->
                                              def copy = list.clone()
                                              copy.add(0, item)
                                              return copy
                                          }

    public static Closure map           = { action, list -> return list.collect(action) }

    public static Closure apply         = { action, list -> list.each(action) }

    public static Closure filter        = { predicate, list -> return list.findAll(predicate) }

    public static Closure forAll        = { predicate, list ->
                                            if(list.size() == 0)
                                                return true
                                            else if(predicate(list[0]))
                                                return this.call(predicate, list[1..<list. size()])
                                            else
                                                return false
                                          }

    public static Closure thereExists   = { predicate, list ->
                                            if(list.size() == 0)
                                                return false
                                            else if(predicate(list[0]))
                                                return true
                                            else
                                                return this.call(predicate,list[1..<list.size()])
                                          }
        // others ...
}
```

The class includes closures for all the arithmetic, relational, and logical operators. Following our discussion on commutativity, we have provided the normal binary version of the operator together with left and right commutative forms. The closures head, tail, and cons repeat the methods first introduced in Chapter 9. We also have the closures composition, map, filter, and so on. The class is defined asabstract since we have no intention of creating an instance. It simply acts as a package of closures.

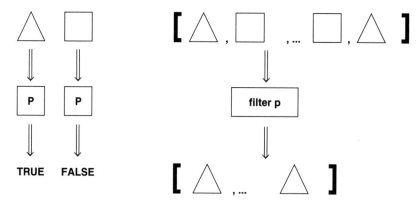

FIGURE J.2   Filter closure.

Figure J.2 describes the filter closure. If p represents some predicate function (closure, returning a Boolean value), then when applied to a triangle, it delivers true and when applied to a square it produces false. Now, filter p list delivers a new List containing only those triangles that satisfy the predicate.

Now, revisiting the previous coding as Example 12, we simplify the application. The first difference to observe is that we are required to reintroduce the call method; otherwise, the Groovy compiler cannot disambiguate the code. Further, the bMin, id, and bSubtract closures must be qualified as members of the Functor class. The program delivers the same output as that of Example 11.

EXAMPLE 12
Using the Functor
class

```
import fp.*

        // Book class and instance
class Book {

    def name          // properties
    def author
    def price
    def category
}

def bk = new Book(name : 'Groovy', author : 'KenB', price : 35, category : 'CompSci')

        // constants
def discountRate = 0.1
def taxRate = 0.17
def maxDiscount = 3
```

```
          // book closures
def calcDiscount = Functor.rMultiply.curry(discountRate)

def calcActualDiscount = Functor.bComposition.curry(Functor.bMin, calcDiscount, Functor.id)

def calcDiscountedPrice = Functor.bComposition.curry(Functor.bSubtract,
                                                Functor.id, calcActualDiscount)

def calcTax = Functor.rMultiply.curry(1 + taxRate)

def calcNetPrice = Functor.composition.curry(calcTax, calcDiscountedPrice)

          // now calculate net price
println "bk.price: ${bk.price}"

def netPrice = calcNetPrice(bk.price)
println "netPrice: ${netPrice}"
```

◆

Class Functor also includes the closures introduced as our patterns of computation. For example, the map closure is used to apply an action (represented by a closure) to a List. Example 13 demonstrates finding the length of each word in a List of words, returning a new List.

EXAMPLE 13
Finding the length of words

```
import fp.*

def size = { text -> return text.length() }

println "map(size, ['Edinburgh', 'Glasgow', 'Perth']): ${Functor.map.call(size,
                                           ['Edinburgh', 'Glasgow', 'Perth'])}"
```

This example produces the output:

```
    map(size, ['Edinburgh', 'Glasgow', 'Perth']): [9, 7, 5]
```

◆

The Functor class also includes the filter closure. This applies a predicate (a Boolean-valued closure) to a List. It returns a List of all the elements satisfying the predicate, in their original order. Example 14 demonstrates finding all words of length 3. The output is:

```
    filter(isSize3, rhyme): [Fee, Fie, Fum]
```

EXAMPLE 14
Filter closure

```
import fp.*

def isSize3 = {text -> return (text.length() == 3)}

def rhyme = ['Fee', 'Fie', 'Fo', 'Fum']

println "filter(isSize3, rhyme): ${Functor.filter.call(isSize3, rhyme)}"
```

◆

Thanks to currying, these closures work together for Lists of Lists. Example 15 shows mapping a filter on to a List of Lists. As in the previous example, we seek words of length 3 in a List of word Lists. We get the result:

```
map(filter(isSize3), rhyme): [[Fee, Fie, Fum], [the]]
```

EXAMPLE 15
Working together

```
import fp.*

def isSize3 = { text -> return (text.length() == 3) }

def rhyme = [['Fee', 'Fie', 'Fo', 'Fum'],
             ['I', 'smell', 'the', 'blood', 'of', 'an', 'Englishman']
             ]
println "map(filter(isSize3), rhyme): ${Functor.map.call(Functor.filter.curry(isSize3), rhyme)}"
```

◆

The closure thereExists (forAll) reports whether some (every) element of a List satisfies some predicate. It can be viewed as a quantifier over Lists. Example 16 demonstrates thereExists and Example 17 shows forAll.

EXAMPLE 16
Using
thereExists

```
import fp.*
def isSize3 = { text -> return (text.length() == 3) }
def rhyme = ['Fee', 'Fie', 'Fo', 'Fum']
println "thereExists(isSize3, rhyme): ${Functor.thereExists.call(isSize3, rhyme)}"
```

The output from this example is given in the following text. Here, we see that there is at least one word of length 3.

```
thereExists(isSize3, rhyme): true
```

◆

EXAMPLE 17
Using forAll

```
import fp.*
def isSize3 = { text -> return (text.length() == 3) }
def rhyme = ['Fee', 'Fie', 'Fo', 'Fum']
println "forAll(isSize3, rhyme): ${Functor.forAll.call(isSize3, rhyme)}"
```

Running this example shows that not all words are of length 3:

```
forAll(isSize3, rhyme): false
```

◆

These quantifiers over lists can be employed to make assertions about the operating of our models. Figure J.3 is a class diagram for an organization. The model shows that employees are given managerial roles over team members. A constraint we might wish to ensure is that every employee has some other employee as his or her manager.

In Example 18, employee JonK has responsibility for KenB and JohnS. However, JonK reports to no one. The forAll closure can be used to identify this inconsistency.

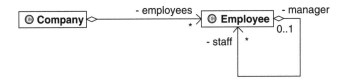

FIGURE J.3   Class diagram.

EXAMPLE 18
Model constraints

```
import java.util.*
import fp.*

class Employee {

    def String toString() {
        return "Employee: ${id} ${name}"
    }
}
```

```
        def addToTeam(employee) {
            staff[employee.id] = employee
            employee.manager = this
        }

// ------properties -------------------

        def id
        def name
        def staff = [ : ]
        def manager = null
}

class Company {

        def hireEmployee(employee) {
            employees[employee.id] = employee
        }

// ------properties -------------------

        def name
        def employees = [ : ]
}

def displayStaff(co) {
    println "Company: ${co.name}"
    println "===================="
    co?.employees.each { entry -> println " ${entry.value}" }
}

def co = new Company(name : 'Napier')

def emp1 = new Employee(id : 123, name : 'KenB')
def emp2 = new Employee(id : 456, name : 'JohnS')
def emp3 = new Employee(id : 789, name : 'JonK')

co.hireEmployee(emp1)
co.hireEmployee(emp2)
co.hireEmployee(emp3)

emp3.addToTeam(emp1)
emp3.addToTeam(emp2)

displayStaff(co)

def hasManager = { employee -> return (employee.manager != null) }

def staff = co.employees.values().toList()
```

```
println "Every employee has a manager?: ${Functor.forAll.call(hasManager, staff)}"

        // Now make JonK a member of own team
emp3.addToTeam(emp3)
println "Every employee has a manager?: ${Functor.forAll.call(hasManager, staff)}"
```

When we execute this program, the output is:

```
Company: Napier
====================
      Employee: 789 JonK
      Employee: 456 JohnS
      Employee: 123 KenB
Every employee has a manager?: false
Every employee has a manager?: true
```

We see from the penultimate line of output that the condition we set is not fulfilled. The predicate closure `hasManager` determines that a given employee has been assigned a manager. The `forAll` closure then determines that this predicate is applicable to all employees.

◆

J.7 LIST REDUCTION

The `Functor` class includes two *list-reducing* closures, `rFold` and `lFold`. These closures are examples of a very general computation pattern. Suppose that we have the list [x1, x2, ..., xn] and we wish to compute x1 + x2 + ... + xn. We can view this equivalently as add(x1, add(x2, ..., add(xn, 0) ...)). The closure `rFold` is described by Figure J.4. At the left, we have `f` as a binary closure, taking a circle value and a square value and delivering a square. Hence, `rFold f e list` delivers a square where the arguments `e` and `list` are, respectively, a square and a `List` of circles. The lower part of Figure J.4 reveals how the function (closure) is folded in from the rightmost element.

```
rFold = { f, e, list ->
    def size = list.size()
    def res = e
    for(index in 0..<size) {
        res = f(list[size -1 -index], res)
    }
    return res
}
```

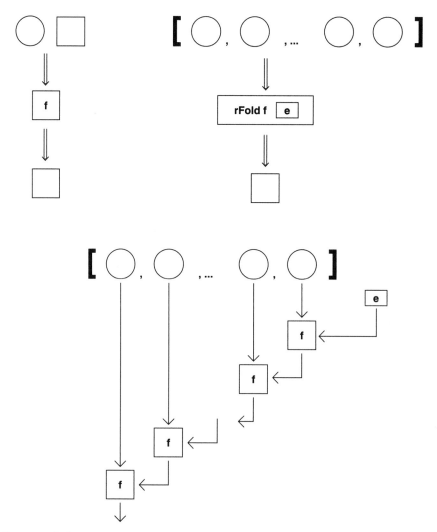

FIGURE J.4   rFold closure.

captures the essence of this reduction in which the parameter f denotes the binary closure, the parameter e is the base value, and the parameter list is the list to process. To compute the sum of a list of integers, we would use bAdd from class Functor as the binary closure and literal 0 (zero) as the base value. Example 19 illustrates.

EXAMPLE 19
List reduction

```
import fp.*

            // Closure sum adds the items in a list
def sum = Functor.rFold.curry(Functor.bAdd, 0)
```

```
println "sum: ${sum([11, 12, 13, 14])}"

def append = { list1, list2 ->
    def result = []
    result.addAll(list1)
    result.addAll(list2)

    return result
}

            // Closure flat flattens a list of lists
def flat = Functor.rFold.curry(append, [])

println "flat: ${flat([[11, 12, 13], [21, 22, 23, 24], [31, 32]])}"
```

◆

Observe how the sum closure is as previously discussed. Using the append closure defined in the program, we can also flatten a list of lists. Here, the base value is the empty list. The output produced is:

```
sum: 50
flat: [11, 12, 13, 21, 22, 23, 24, 31, 32]
```

J.8   EXERCISES

1. Develop a simple closure entitled square to find the product of its single parameter.

2. Develop a simple closure entitled twice to deliver twice the value of its single parameter.

3. Develop a simple closure entitled isEven that determines whether its single integer parameter is even.

4. Using the Functor class developed in this appendix, and the closures dec = Functor.rSubtract.curry(1) and inc = Functor.rAdd.curry(1), predict the value produced by Functor.bMultiply.call(inc(4), dec(4)).

5. Using the closures inc and dec defined in the previous exercise, determine the value of Functor.composition.curry(inc, dec).call(4).

6. Given the closures leftLT = Functor.lLt.curry(3) and rightLT = Functor.rLt.curry(5), determine the value of Functor.bComposition. curry(Functor.bAnd, leftLT, rightLT).call(4).

7. Given the `multiply` closure as defined in Example 04, determine what p, q, and r represent and demonstrate how they can be used.

```
def p = multiply.curry(2)
def q = multiply.curry(3, 4)
def r = multiply.curry()
```

8. Using the `Functor` class described in this appendix, describe the closure defined as `def inc = Functor.1Add.curry(1)`. Now, specify the effect of the closure defined by:

```
Functor.map.curry(Functor.* composition.curry(inc, inc))
```

9. Using the `head` and `tail` closures defined in class `Functor`, predict the effect of calling the following two closures:

```
def hT = Functor.composition.curry(Functor.head.curry(), Functor.tail.curry())
def tT = Functor.composition.curry(Functor.tail.curry(), Functor.tail.curry())
```

10. Use the closures defined in the `Functor` class and redefine as a closure the method upTo declared in Example 02 of Appendix G Now, define the closure `factors` that returns a list of integers that are the factors of its integer parameter:

```
def factors = {n -> ...}
```

Define the closure `isEmpty`, which returns the boolean `true` if its `list` parameter is the empty list:

```
def isEmpty = {list -> ...}
```

Using curried composition, define the closure `prime`, which returns the Boolean `true` if the integer parameter is a prime number (a integer divisible only by 1 and by itself). Now, curry the `filter` closure in class `Functor` with `prime`, then find the prime numbers from 2 to 50 inclusive.

11. The closure `insert` introduces a new item into a sorted list so that the sort order of the elements is maintained:

```
def insert = { x, list ->
    def res = []
```

```
            if(list.size() == 0) {
                res << x
            } else {
                def inserted = false
                for(element in list) {
                    if(inserted == false && x < element) {
                        inserted = true
                        res << x
                    }
                    res << element
                }
                if(inserted == false) {
                    res << x
                }
            }

        return res
    }
```

Now, determine the effect of the closure defined as:

```
Functor.rFold.curry(insert, [])
```

when applied to a list of integers.

12. Given the closure xxx defined by:

```
def xxx = Functor.rFold.curry(Functor.cons)
```

then determine the value produced by:

```
xxx([11, 12], [13, 14])
```

13. Given the closures inc, xComp, and xComposition defined by:

```
def inc = { x -> return 1 + x }

def xComp = { h, f, x, y -> return h(f(x), y) }
def xComposition = xComp.curry(Functor.cons, inc)
```

and the closure xxx defined as:

```
xxx = Functor.rFold.curry(xComposition, [])
```

determine the effect of the expression:

```
xxx([11, 12, 13, 14])
```

and identify which closure from the Functor class is the equivalent of xxx.

14. Using the closures head, tail, and cons defined in the Functor class, develop a closure insert that correctly inserts a new item into a sorted list:

```
def insert = { x, list -> ... }
```

Now, use this closure to implement the closure insertSort that employs the insert sort algorithm to sort a list of values:

```
def insertSort = { list -> ... }
```

MORE ON BUILDERS

Chapters 19 and 20 introduced the notion of Groovy builders. Essentially, Groovy builders allow us to easily represent nested treelike data structures such as XML data. With a builder, specifically a `MarkupBuilder`, we can effortlessly construct XML data. With a `SwingBuilder`, we can effortlessly construct a GUI application comprised of Swing components.

In this appendix, we consider an `AntBuilder` that we can use to construct Ant XML build files (Holzner, 2005) and execute them without having to deal with XML. Also, we briefly demonstrate how we can make our own specialized builders. We assume prior knowledge of Ant.

K.1 ANTBUILDER

Groovy provides the `AntBuilder` class with which we can easily construct and execute Ant XML build files. This is achieved without having to make any direct use of XML. Further, as we have already noted, we can interleave any other Groovy code with the `AntBuilder` code. Example 01 uses an `AntBuilder` to create a directory and to copy its own file to the new directory.

```
import groovy.util.*

def aB = new AntBuilder()

aB.echo(message : 'Start')
aB.mkdir(dir : 'demo')
```

EXAMPLE 01
Create directory
and copy file

```
aB.copy(file : 'example01.groovy', todir : 'demo')
aB.echo(message : 'End')
```

◆

This example is a simple Ant build file that defines an Ant project. The project has one or more targets, each consisting of a number of Ant tasks (see http://ant.apache.org/manual/index.html). The code in Example 01 is effectively the default task and invokes the Ant core tasks echo, copy, and mkdir. The first echoes a message, the second copies a file to a directory, and the last creates a directory.

Example 02 elaborates, this time copying all files with a groovy suffix to the new directory. First, note how the normal Groovy definition for demoDir is intermingled with the builder code. The pseudomethod fileSet specifies the source directory with the dir parameter, while include is used to limit the files to be copied.

EXAMPLE 02
Create directory
and copy all
Groovy files

```
import groovy.util.*

def aB = new AntBuilder()

aB.echo(message : 'Start')

def demoDir = 'demo'

aB.mkdir(dir : demoDir)
aB.copy(todir : demoDir) {
    aB.fileSet(dir : '.') {
        aB.include(name : '*.groovy')
    }
}
aB.echo(message : 'End')
```

◆

In Example 03, we use a scanner (class FileScanner; see GDK) to find all the groovy files in the new directory, and then produce a list of their file names.

EXAMPLE 03
File scanning

```
import groovy.util.*

def aB = new AntBuilder()

aB.echo(message : 'Start')

def demoDir = 'demo'
```

```
def scanner = aB.fileScanner() {
    aB.fileset(dir : demoDir) {
        aB.include(name : '*.groovy')
    }
}

println "${demoDir}"
scanner.each { file ->
    println " ${file}"
}

aB.echo(message : 'End')
```

◆

The following example illustrates how Groovy might be used to construct an Ant build, typical of what might be used by a Groovy developer. Targets are provided to compile Groovy files, execute a script, run unit tests, or clean up. It was used by the authors to develop the larger applications in the later chapters of the book.

The listing defines the Build class. It is designed to operate as a simple Ant build file used to compile files, execute a script, and clean up afterward. The Build class exploits the meta-object protocol (see http://www-128.ibm.com/developerworks/java/library/j-pg12144.html) introduced in Appendix I by redefining invokeMethod. Once we have an instance of this class, we can invoke the pseudomethods compile, clean, and so on, as in:

```
def b = new Build()
b.clean()
```

The invokeMethod redirects the request to an implementation provided by a closure. The sample already given would call the clean closure. We see from its code that it removes temporary files and directories. Similarly, the code:

```
def b = new Build()
b.compile()
```

calls the compile closure. Its code is dependent on the init task, and therefore it first calls the init closure. The init closure creates some temporary working directories and defines new Ant tasks whereby we can call the Groovy compiler at runtime. Thereafter, closure compile executes the Groovy compiler against all *.groovy files in the source directory.

File: *Build.groovy*

```groovy
package build
import groovy.util.*
import java.io.*
import java.util.*
class Build {
    public Object invokeMethod(String name, Object params) {
        def target = targets[name]
        if(target != null)
            target.call(params)
        else
            usage.call(params)
        return null
    }

// -------properties -------------------

    def aB                  = new AntBuilder()

    def ENV_CLASSPATH       = System.getenv('CLASSPATH')
    def ENV_GROOVY_HOME     = System.getenv('GROOVY_HOME')

    def BASEDIR             = '.'
    def SRCDIR              = BASEDIR
    def DESTDIR             = BASEDIR + '/classes'
    def REPDIR              = BASEDIR + '/reports'

    def GROOVLETSDIR        = BASEDIR + '/src'
    def GSPDIR              = BASEDIR + '/src'

    def COMMONDIR           = BASEDIR + '/../common'
    def WEBDIR              = BASEDIR + '/web'
    def BUILDDIR            = BASEDIR + '/build'
    def DEPLOYDIR           = BASEDIR + '/deploy'

    def WEBAPPSDIR          = ENV_CATALINA_HOME + '/webapps'

    def BASIC_CLASSPATH     = 'basic.classpath'
    def basicClasspath      = aB.path(id : BASIC_CLASSPATH) {
        aB.pathelement(path : "${SRCDIR};${DESTDIR}")
        aB.pathelement(location : "${ENV_CLASSPATH}")
    }

    def COMPILE_CLASSPATH   = 'compile.classpath'
    def compileClasspath    = aB.path(id : COMPILE_CLASSPATH) {
        aB.path(refid : BASIC_CLASSPATH)
    }
```

```
def clean = { params ->
    aB.delete() {
        aB.fileset(dir : "${SRCDIR}", includes : '**/*.bak')
        aB.fileset(dir : "${SRCDIR}", includes : '**/*.BAK')
        aB.fileset(dir : "${SRCDIR}", includes : '**/*.txt')
    }
    aB.delete(dir : "${DESTDIR}")
    aB.delete(dir : "${REPDIR}")
    aB.delete(dir : "${BUILDDIR}")
}

def init = { params ->
    aB.taskdef(name : 'groovyc', classname : 'org.codehaus.groovy.ant.Groovyc')
    aB.taskdef(name : 'groovy', classname : 'org.codehaus.groovy.ant.Groovy')

    aB.mkdir(dir : "${DESTDIR}")
    aB.mkdir(dir : "${REPDIR}")
    aB.mkdir(dir : "${BUILDDIR}")
}

def compile = { params ->
    init.call(params)

    aB.groovyc(srcdir : "${SRCDIR}", destdir : "${DESTDIR}", classpath : "${basicClasspath}")
}

def run = { params ->
    compile.call(params)

    aB.groovy(src : params[1]) {
        aB.classpath() {
            aB.pathelement(path : "${SRCDIR};${DESTDIR}")
            aB.pathelement(location : "${ENV_CLASSPATH}")
        }
    }
}

def test = { params ->
    compile.call(params)

    aB.junit(fork : 'yes') {
        aB.classpath() {
            aB.pathelement(path : "${SRCDIR};${DESTDIR}")
            aB.pathelement(location : "${ENV_CLASSPATH}")
        }
```

```
                aB.formatter(type : 'plain')

                aB.batchtest(todir : "${REPDIR}") {
                    aB.fileset(dir : "${DESTDIR}") {
                        aB.include(name : '**/*Test.class')
                    }
                }
            }
        }
    }

    def assemble = { params ->
        init.call(params)

        aB.copy(todir : "${BUILDDIR}") {
            aB.fileset(dir : "${COMMONDIR}")
        }

        aB.copy(todir : "${BUILDDIR}") {
            aB.fileset(dir : "${GROOVLETSDIR}") {
                aB.include(name : "**/*.groovy")
                aB.include(name : "**/*.gsp")
            }
            aB.fileset(dir : "${BASEDIR}") {
                aB.include(name : "**/*.html")
            }
        }
    }

    def deploy = { params ->
        assemble.call(params)

        aB.copy(todir : "${WEBAPPSDIR}/${params[1]}") {
            aB.fileset(dir : "${BUILDDIR}")
        }
    }

    def undeploy = { params ->
        aB.delete(dir : "${WEBAPPSDIR}/${params[1]}")
    }

    def db = { params ->
        aB.delete(dir : "${params[1]}DB")
        aB.sql(url : "jdbc:derby:${params[1]}DB;create=true", userid : '', password : '',
                driver : 'org.apache.derby.jdbc.EmbeddedDriver', src : "${params[1]}.sql")
    }

    def usage = { params ->
        aB.echo(message : '')
```

```
        aB.echo(message : 'Available targets:')
        aB.echo(message : '')
        aB.echo(message : 'clean:        Remove all temporary files/directories')
        aB.echo(message : 'compile:      Compile all source files')
        aB.echo(message : 'deploy:       Deploy the web application as a directory')
        aB.echo(message : 'init:         Prepare working directories')
        aB.echo(message : 'db:           Establish and populate the database')
        aB.echo(message : 'run:          Execute the named script')
        aB.echo(message : 'test:         JUnit tests')
        aB.echo(message : 'usage:        Default target')
        aB.echo(message : '')
    }


    def targets = ['clean': clean,
                   'init'        : init,
                   'compile'     : compile,
                   'run'         : run,
                   'test'        : test,
                   'assemble'    : assemble,
                   'deploy'      : deploy,
                   'undeploy'    : undeploy,
                   'db'          : db,
                   'usage'       : usage
                  ]

}
```

The test closure is used in, for example, Chapter 16, where a sizable amount of unit testing is performed. Equally, the deploy closure is used in Chapter 24 to assemble all the necessary files to deploy to the Tomcat server.

A simple script is used as a driver. The file gbuild.groovy is shown in the following listing.

File: *Build driver*

```
/**
 * Usage:
 * groovy gbuild.groovy clean
 * groovy gbuild.groovy init
 * groovy gbuild.groovy compile
 * groovy gbuild.groovy test
 * groovy gbuild.groovy run script-file-name
 * groovy gbuild.groovy deploy project-name
 * groovy gbuild.groovy undeploy project-name
 * groovy gbuild.groovy db database-name
 * groovy gbuild.groovy usage
 *
```

```
*  groovy gbuild.groovy   default target: usage
*/

def b = new Build()

if(args.size() > 0) {
    def target = args[0]
    b.invokeMethod(target, args)
}else
    b.usage(args)
```

This Groovy script allows us to use the `Build` class as described in the usage comment. For example:

```
groovy gbuild.groovy clean
```

executes the `clean` closure.

Chapter 18 introduced database processing into the library case study. In that example, we established a database with tables representing the borrowers and the publications. The tables are also initialized with representative values. This information is given in the file `library.sql`:

```
create table borrowers(
    membershipNumber            varchar(10) not null,
    name                        varchar(20),

    primary key(membershipNumber)
);

create table publications(
    catalogNumber               varchar(10) not null,
    title                       varchar(40),
    author                      varchar(20),
    editor                      varchar(20),
    type                        varchar(8),

    borrowerID                  varchar(10),

    primary key(catalogNumber),
    foreign key(borrowerID) references borrowers(membershipNumber)
);

insert into borrowers values('1234', 'Jessie');

insert into publications values('111', 'Groovy', 'KenB', '','BOOK', '1234');
insert into publications values('222', 'UML', 'JohnS', '','BOOK', null);
insert into publications values('333', 'OOD', '', 'JonK','JOURNAL', null);
```

The db target accepts this filename as parameter and creates a database named libraryDB, using the file name and the DB suffix. From Chapter 18, we would use:

```
groovy gbuild.groovy db library
```

to create and initially populate the libraryDB database.

K.2 SPECIALIZED BUILDERS

To create a new builder such as the MarkupBuilder or AntBuilder, the programmer must implement a subclass of the groovy.util.BuilderSupport class. The methods to be implemented by the subclass are the following:

```
void     setParent(Object parent, Object child);
Object   createNode(Object name); // a node without parameter and closure
Object   createNode(Object name, Object value);   //a node without parameters, but with closure
Objec    createNode(Object name, Map attributes); // a node without closure but with parameters
Object   createNode(Object name, Map attributes, Object value); //a node without parameters, but
                                                              with closure and parameters
```

For example, method createNode(Object name, Object value) is invoked by the builder when the Groovy code includes:

```
aB.demo() {
...
}
```

The parameter name for method createNode has the name for the pseudo-method demo. The parameter value supplies the closure and its content.

Additionally, the BuilderSupport class has two (hook) methods, which subclasses may choose to redefine to provide specialized behaviors. Method getName is a hook method to allow names to be converted into some other object, such as a qualified name in XML builders. Method nodeCompleted allows nodes to be processed once they have had all of their dependent nodes applied.

```
void     nodeCompleted(Object parent, Object node);
Object   getName(String methodName);
```

Example 04 defines the class MonitorBuilder which subclasses BuilderSupport. Class MonitorBuilder performs no real work. However, it defines these abstract methods to display their name and parameters when invoked. That way, the class monitors where these methods are called when processing builder code.

EXAMPLE 04
MonitorBuilder
class

```groovy
import groovy.util.*

class MonitorBuilder extends BuilderSupport {

    protected void setParent(Object parent, Object child) {
        println "setParent(${parent}, ${child})"
    }

    protected Object createNode(Object name) {
        println "createNode(${name})"
        return name
    }

    protected Object createNode(Object name, Object value) {
        println "createNode(${name}, ${value})"
        return name
    }

    protected Object createNode(Object name, Map attributes, Object value) {
        println "createNode(${name}, ${attributes}, ${value})"
        return name
    }

    protected Object createNode(Object name, Map attributes) {
        return createNode(name, attributes, null)
    }

    protected void nodeCompleted(Object parent, Object node) {
        println "nodeCompleted(${parent}, ${node})"
    }
}

def mB = new MonitorBuilder()

def monitor = mB.database(name : 'library') {
    table(name : 'Book') {
        field(name : 'title', type : 'text')
        field(name : 'isbn', type : 'text')
        field(name : 'price', type : 'integer')
        field(name : 'author', type : 'id')
        field(name : 'publisher', type : 'id')
    }
}
```

When we run this program, the output is:

```
createNode(database, ["name":"library"], null)
createNode(table, ["name":"Book"], null)
setParent(database, table)
createNode(field, ["name":"title", "type":"text"], null)
setParent(table, field)
nodeCompleted(table, field)
createNode(field, ["name":"isbn", "type":"text"], null)
setParent(table, field)
nodeCompleted(table, field)
createNode(field, ["name":"price", "type":"integer"], null)
setParent(table, field)
nodeCompleted(table, field)
createNode(field, ["name":"author", "type":"id"], null)
setParent(table, field)
nodeCompleted(table, field)
createNode(field, ["name":"publisher", "type":"id"], null)
setParent(table, field)
nodeCompleted(table, field)
nodeCompleted(database, table)
nodeCompleted(null, database)
```

The first and final lines show the database pseudomethod created and completed. Between these two events, the other nodes are created and completed. Nested within the database node, there is the table node and, within it, five field nodes are created. The output demonstrates that we can intercept the createNode and nodeCompleted method calls to provide some behavior. For example, the MarkupBuilder issues XML/HTML content.

◆

In Chapter 19, Example 08 reads an XML file describing a relational table and converts it to SQL to create the database table. In Example 05, we do the same with a specialized builder.

EXAMPLE 05
A specialized SQL builder

```
import groovy.util.*
import java.io.*

class SqlBuilder extends BuilderSupport {

    protected void setParent(Object parent, Object child) {
    }
```

```
        protected Object createNode(Object name) {
            println "createNode(${name})"
            return name
        }


        protected Object createNode(Object name, Object value) {
            println "createNode(${name}, ${value})"
            return name
        }
        protected Object createNode(Object name, Map attributes, Object value) {
            this.processStartNode(name, attributes, value)
            return name
        }


        protected Object createNode(Object name, Map attributes) {
            return createNode(name, attributes, null)
        }


        protected void nodeComplement(Object parent, Object node){
            this.processEndNode(parent,node)
        }


        private void processStartNode(Object name, Map atributes, Object value) {
            switch(name) {
                case 'database':
                    out.println "DROP DATABASE IF EXISTS ${attributes.get('name')};"
                    out.println "CREATE DATABASE ${attributes.get('name')};"
                    break
                case 'table'
                    out.println "DROP TABLE IF EXISTS ${attributes.get('name')};"
                    out.println "CREATE TABLE ${attributes.get('name')}("
                    out.print"$.{attributes.get('name')}_ID INTEGER NOT NULL"
                    break
                case 'field':
                    out.println","
                    out.print"${attributes.get('name')}${type To SQL[attributes.get('type')]}
                    break
            }
        }


        private void processEndNode(Object parent, Object node) {
          switch(node) {
            case 'table' :
                out.println()
                out.println ');'
                break
          }
        }
```

```
        // ------properties -------------

    def out
    def typeToSQL = ['text' :         'TEXT NOT NULL',
                     'id' :           'INTEGER NOT NULL',
                     'integer' :      'INTEGER NOT NULL']
}


def sB = new SqlBuilder(out : new File('db.sql').newPrintWriter())

def sql = sB.database(name : 'library') {
    table(name : 'Book') {
        field(name : 'title', type : 'text')
        field(name : 'isbn', type : 'text')
        field(name : 'price', type : 'integer')
        field(name : 'author', type : 'id')
        field(name : 'publisher', type : 'id')
    }
}

sB.out.flush()
sB.out.close()
```

◆

MORE ON
GUI BUILDERS

Chapter 20 introduced basic Swing components using the `SwingBuilder` markup generator. Here, we consider applications that include other components, such as menus, menu items, toolbars, and dialogs, that we might expect to find in a typical graphical application.

L.1 MENUS AND TOOLBARS

A graphical application often includes a menu that provides the user with access to the functions of the program. A menu bar is used to carry a number of menus. In turn, each menu is a drop-down for a number of menu items that represent the services of the application. They are easy to construct with `SwingBuilder` using `menuBars`, `menus`, and `menuItems`. The hierarchy is, as we might expect, with the `menuBar` enclosing the `menus` and each `menu` enclosing the `menuItems`. Each menu has a text label and a shortcut mnemonic. The `menuItems` also have text labels and a shortcut mnemonic in addition to closures that represents the action when the menu item is selected. Example 01 is the Groovy script that produces the GUI as shown in Figure L.1.

EXAMPLE 01
A simple menu

```
import groovy.swing.SwingBuilder
import javax.swing.*

        // Create a builder
def sB = new SwingBuilder()
```

FIGURE L.1   A menu.

```
        // Now the frame
def frame = sB.frame(title : 'Example01', location : [100, 100],
        size : [400, 300], defaultCloseOperation : WindowConstants.EXIT_ON_CLOSE) {
    menuBar {
        menu(text : 'File', mnemonic : 'F') {
            menuItem() {
                action(name : 'New', mnemonic : 'N',   closure : { println 'File + New' })
            }

            menuItem() {
                action(name : 'Open...', mnemonic : 'O',   closure : { println 'File + Open...' })
            }

            separator()
            menuItem() {
                action(name : 'Save', mnemonic : 'S',   closure : { println 'File + Save' })
            }

            menuItem() {
                action(name : 'Save as...', mnemonic : 'A', closure : { println 'File + Save as...' })
            }

            separator()
            menuItem() {
                action(name : 'Exit', mnemonic : 'X',   closure : { System.exit(0) })
            }
        }
```

```
        menu(text : 'Help', mnemonic : 'H') {
            menuItem() {
                action(name : 'About', mnemonic : 'A',    closure : { println 'Help + About' })
            }
        }
    }
}


        // Now show it
frame.pack()
frame.setVisible(true)
```

◆

Establishing the menu is probably better accomplished by using pre-initialized Groovy Lists. Example 02 revisits the previous example but employs a List to construct the menus and the menuItems. In the code, menus represents a List, the items of which are themselves Lists. These enclosed Lists carry the details for an individual menu. They document the name of the menu and its shortcut, then the name, shortcut, and handler for every menu item. The iterator, code, menus.each, processes the List of Lists to assemble the menu bar.

EXAMPLE 02
Menus from lists

```
import groovy.swing.SwingBuilder
import javax.swing.*

            // Menu handlers
def fileNew = {
    println 'File + New'
}

def fileOpen = {
    println 'File + Open...'
}

def fileSave = {
    println 'File + Save'
}

def fileSaveAs = {
    println 'File + Save as...'
}

def fileExit = {
    System.exit(0)
}
```

```
def helpAbout = {
    println 'Help + About'
}


        // Create a builder
def sB = new SwingBuilder()


        // Now the frame
def frame = sB.frame(title : 'Example02', location : [100, 100],
        size : [400, 300], defaultCloseOperation : WindowConstants.EXIT_ON_CLOSE) {
    menuBar {
        def fileMenu = [['File',        'F'],
                        ['New',         'N',    fileNew     ],
                        ['Open...',     'O',    fileOpen    ],
                        null,
                        ['Save',        'S',    fileSave    ],
                        ['Save as...',  'A',    fileSaveAs ],
                        null,
                        ['Exit',        'X',    fileExit    ]
                        ]
        def helpMenu = [['Help',        'H'],
                        ['About',       'A',    helpAbout ]
                         ]


        def menus = [fileMenu, helpMenu]

        menus.each { mnu ->
            def mnuDetails = mnu[0]
            sB.menu(text : mnuDetails[0], mnemonic : mnuDetails[1]) {
                for(k in 1..<mnu.size()) {
                    def mnuItem = mnu[k]
                        if(mnuItem == null)
                            sB.separator()
                        else
                            sB.menuItem() {
                                sB.action(name : mnuItem[0], mnemonic : mnuItem[1], closure : mnuItem[2])
                            }
                    }
                }
            }
        }
    }
}

        // Now show it
frame.pack()
frame.setVisible(true)
```

◆

Most graphical applications support a *toolbar* to accompany the menu bar. It is normally located along the top of the application window immediately below the menu bar. Each toolbar button operates as a shortcut for one of the menu items.

Figure L.2 shows an application with a traditional menu and toolbar. The user has opened the Help menu and reveals the list of menu items. Normally, the user would select one of these items and obtain some functionality from the application. Notice also the toolbar with its New, File, and Save buttons. Our code merely demonstrates the construction of such a menu and toolbar, but does not include any meaningful behavior. Of course, following earlier examples, we could provide appropriate handlers.

Example 03 is the listing for our application. Observe how the menu bar and the toolbar are assembled. Their content is specified in Lists of Lists. This simplifies the construction and possible revisions to the menu and toolbar. Observe how the second iterator menus.each creates and initializes the toolbar buttons with its text and handler. That way, we associate the one handler with the menu item and its corresponding toolbar button.

EXAMPLE 03
Menu and toolbars

```
import groovy.swing.SwingBuilder
import javax.swing.*
import java.awt.*

        // Text area of set size
class FixedTextArea extends JTextArea {

    Dimension getMinimumSize() { return TEXTAREASIZE }
    Dimension getMaximumSize() { return TEXTAREASIZE }
    Dimension getPreferredSize() { return TEXTAREASIZE }
    private static final TEXTAREASIZE = new Dimension(400, 400)
}


        // Menu handlers
def fileNew = {
    println 'File + New'
}

def fileOpen = {
    println 'File + Open...'
}

def fileSave = {
    println 'File + Save'
}
```

FIGURE L.2 Menu bar and tool bar.

```
def fileSaveAs = {
    println 'File + Save as...'
}

def fileExit = {
    System.exit(0)
}

def helpAbout = {
    println 'Help + About'
}
```

```
        // Create a builder
def sB = new SwingBuilder()

        // Now the frame
def frame = sB.frame(title : 'Example03', location : [100, 100],
        size : [400, 300], defaultCloseOperation : WindowConstants.EXIT_ON_CLOSE) {
    def fileMenu = [['File',        'F'],
                    ['New',         'N',     true,    fileNew    ],
                    ['Open...',     'O',     true,    fileOpen   ],
                    null,
                    ['Save',        'S',     true,    fileSave   ],
                    ['Save as...',  'A',     false,   fileSaveAs ],
                    null,
                    ['Exit',        'X',     false,   fileExit   ]
                    ]

    def helpMenu = [['Help',        'H'],
                    ['About',       'A',     false,   helpAbout ]
                    ]

def menus = [fileMenu, helpMenu]

menuBar {
    menus.each { mnu ->
        def mnuDetails = mnu[0]
        sB.menu(text : mnuDetails[0], mnemonic : mnuDetails[1]) {
            for(k in 1..<mnu.size()) {
                def mnuItem = mnu[k]
                if(mnuItem == null)
                    sB.separator()
                else {
                    sB.menuItem() {
                        sB.action(name : mnuItem[0], mnemonic :mnuItem[1], closure : mnuItem[3])
                    }
                }
            }
        }
    }
}

    sB.panel(layout : new BorderLayout()) {
        toolBar(constraints : BorderLayout.NORTH) {
            menus.each { toolMnu ->
                for(k in 1..<toolMnu.size()) {
                    def toolItem = toolMnu[k]
                    if(toolItem != null && toolItem[2] == true) {
                        def toolText = toolItem[0]
```

```
                    def toolAction = toolItem[3]
                    sB.button(text : toolText, actionPerformed : toolAction)
                }
            }
        }
    }

    sB.panel(constraints : BorderLayout.CENTER) {
        widget(new FixedTextArea(enabled : false))
    }
  }
}

    // Now show it
frame.pack()
frame.setVisible(true)
```

◆

L.2   DIALOGS

This final example shows how we might introduce a dialog into an application.
In the listing for Example 04, we subclass the Swing class JDialog to provide our
own specialized dialog. This dialog is populated with two text fields to obtain
the user name and password as might be found in many applications. Execution
of the program appears as in Figure L.3 and the listing in Example 04.

```
import groovy.swing.SwingBuilder
import javax.swing.*
import java.awt.*

        // Text area of set size
class FixedTextArea extends JTextArea {

    Dimension getMinimumSize() { return TEXTAREASIZE }
    Dimension getMaximumSize() { return TEXTAREASIZE }
    Dimension getPreferredSize() { return TEXTAREASIZE }

    private static final TEXTAREASIZE = new Dimension(400, 400)
}

        // Builder
def sB = new SwingBuilder()
```

EXAMPLE 04
An application
with a dialog

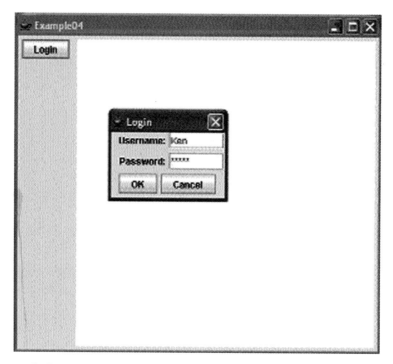

FIGURE L.3   An activated dialog.

```
def loginDialog = null

        // frame handlers
def loginHandler = {
    loginDialog.setVisible(true)
}

        // Now the main panel...
def mainPanel = {
    sB.panel(layout : new BorderLayout()) {
        panel(constraints : BorderLayout.WEST) {
            button(text : 'Login', actionPerformed : loginHandler)
        }
        panel(constraints : BorderLayout.CENTER) {
            widget(new FixedTextArea(enabled : false))
        }
    }
}
```

```
            // ...and finally the frame
def frame = sB.frame(title : 'Example04', location : [100, 100],
        size : [400, 300], defaultCloseOperation : WindowConstants.EXIT_ON_CLOSE) {
    mainPanel()
}


        // dialog handlers
def okHandler = {
    loginDialog.setVisible(false)

    def userName = nameField.getText()
    def userPassword = passwordField.getText()

    nameField.setText(")
    passwordField.setText(")

    if(userName == ")
        println 'NO user name given'
    else if(userPassword == "")
        println 'NO password given'
    else
        println "User: ${userName}"
}

def cancelHandler = {
    loginDialog.setVisible(false)

    userName = "
    userPassword = "

    nameField.setText(")
    passwordField.setText(")
}

def dialogPanel = {
    sB.panel(layout : new BorderLayout()) {
        panel(layout : new GridLayout(2, 2, 5, 5), constraints : BorderLayout.CENTER) {
            label(text : 'Username:', horizontalAlignment : JLabel.RIGHT)
            def nameField = textField(text : "", columns : 20)
            label(text : 'Password:', horizontalAlignment : JLabel.RIGHT)
            def passwordField = passwordField(text : "", columns : 20)
        }
        panel(constraints : BorderLayout.SOUTH) {
            button(text : 'OK', actionPerformed : okHandler)
            button(text : 'Cancel', actionPerformed : cancelHandler)
        }
    }
}
```

```
loginDialog = sB.dialog(owner : frame, title : 'Login', size : [160, 120], modal : true) {
    dialogPanel()
}


        // Now show it
frame.pack()
frame.setVisible(true)
```

◆

BIBLIOGRAPHY

Beaulieu, Alan. *Learning SQL*. O'Reilly, 2005.

Beck, Kent. *Extreme Programming Explained: Embrace Change*. Addison-Wesley, 2004.

Bergsten, Hans. *JavaServer Pages*. O'Reilly, 2003.

Booch, Grady, James Rumbaugh, Ivar Jacobson. *The Unified Modelling Language User Guide*. Addison-Wesley, 2005.

Brittain, Jasonn, Ian Darwin. *Tomcat: The Definitive Guide*. O'Reilly, 2003.

Harvey M. Deitel. *C: How to Program* (International Edition). Prentice Hall, 2003.

Eckel, Bruce. *Thinking in Java*. Prentice Hall, 2003.

Eckstein, Robert, Marc Loy, Dave Woods, James Elliott, Brian Cole. *Java Swing*. O'Reilly, 2002.

Erl, Thomas. *Service-Oriented Architecture: A Field Guide to Integrating XML and Web Services*. Prentice Hall, 2004.

Fisher, Maydene, Jon Ellis, Jonathon Bruce. *JDBC API Tutorial and Reference*. Addison-Wesley, 2003.

Fitzgerald, Michael. *Learning XSLT*. O'Reilly, 2003.

Friedl, Jeffrey. *Mastering Regular Expressions*. O'Reilly, 2002.

Gamma, Erich, Richard Helm, Ralph Johnson, John Vlissides. *Design Patterns.* Addison-Wesley, 1995.

Grand, Mark. *Patterns in Java.* Wiley, 2002.

Holzner, Steve. *Ant: The Definitive Guide.* O'Reilly, 2005.

Johnson, Rod, Juergen Hoeller, Alef Arendsen, Thomas Risberg, Colin Sampaleanu. *Professional Development with the Spring Framework.* Wrox, 2005.

Kernighan, Brian, Dennis Ritchie. *The C Programming Language.* Prentice Hall, 1988.

Link, Johannes. *Unit Testing in Java: How Tests Drive the Code.* Morgan Kaufmann, 2003.

Massol, Vincent. *Junit in Action.* Manning, 2003.

Meyer, Bertrand. *Object-Oriented Software Construction.* Prentice Hall, 1997.

Molinaro, Anthony. *SQL Cookbook.* O'Reilly, 2006.

Ousterhout, John. *Scripting: Higher Level Programming for the 21st Century.* IEEE Computer Magazine, March 1998.

Pedroni, Samuele, Noel Rappin. *Jython Essentials.* O'Reilly, 2002.

van Rossum, Guido, Mark Lutz, Laura Lewin, Frank Willison. *Programming Python.* O'Reilly, 2001.

Tidwell, Doug. *XSLT.* O'Reilly, 2001.

Thomas, Dave, Chad Fowler, Andy Hunt. *Programming Ruby: The Pragmatic Programmer's Guide.* Pragmatic Bookshelf, 2004.

Thompson, Simon. *Haskell: The Craft of Functional Programming.* Addison-Wesley, 1999.

Topley, Kim. *Core Java Foundation Classes.* Prentice Hall, 1998.

Topley, Kim. *Java Web Services in a Nutshell.* O'Reilly, 2003.

Wall, Larry, Tom Christiansen, Jon Orwant. *Programming Perl.* O'Reilly, 2000.

Walls, Craig. *Spring in Action.* Manning, 2004.

INDEX